The Artist's Studio

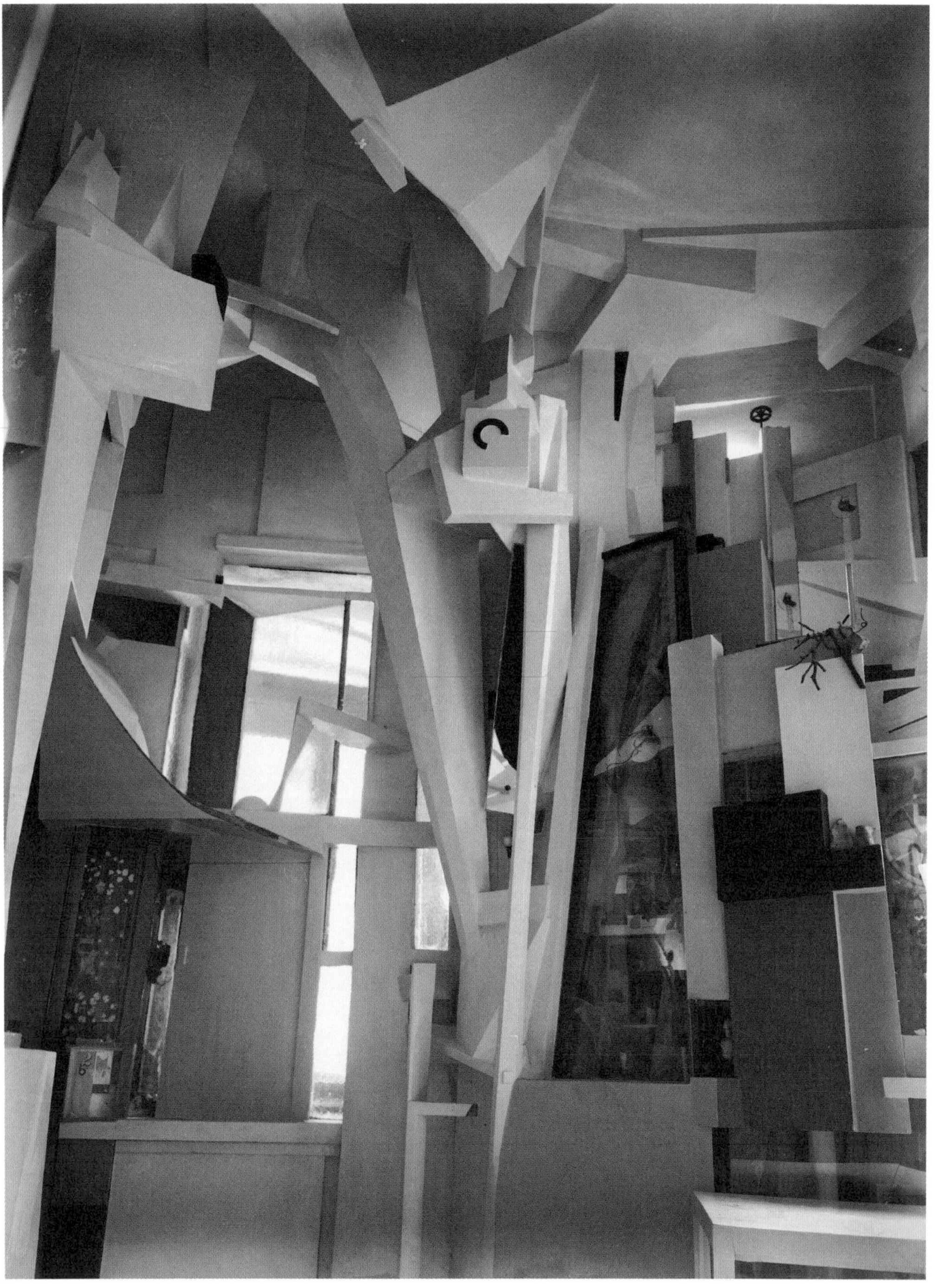

James Hall

The Artist's Studio

A Cultural History

T&H

As usual, I dedicate this book to my family. But also to the neighbours, newts, frogs, snails, butterflies, hover-flies, dragonflies, bees, blackbirds, sparrows, coal tits, crows, woodpeckers, robins, mice, rats, etc. who kept me company during lockdown.

FRONTISPIECE: Wilhelm Redemann, *Kurt Schwitters, Merzbau in Hanover*, 1933, black-and-white print.

First published in the United Kingdom in 2022 by
Thames & Hudson Ltd, 181A High Holborn, London WC1V 7QX

First published in the United States of America in 2022 by
Thames & Hudson Inc., 500 Fifth Avenue, New York, New York 10110

Designed by Anna Perotti

British Library Cataloguing-in-Publication Data
A catalogue record for this book is available from the British Library

Library of Congress Control Number 2022931880

ISBN 978-0-500-02171-2

Printed and bound in China by RR Donnelley

FSC www.fsc.org MIX Paper from responsible sources FSC® C144853

Contents

6 **Introduction**

15 Chapter 1
Luxury and Lameness
The Shield of Achilles

29 Chapter 2
Wisdom's Workshop
Simon the Shoemaker

39 Chapter 3
Struggles in the Scriptorium
Waging War on Dead Skin

48 Chapter 4
Pure Gold
Doing God's (or the Devil's) Work

65 Chapter 5
The Velvet Revolution
Cennini's *Studietto*

81 Chapter 6
Piety and Pretentiousness
Saint Luke Paints the Virgin

88 Chapter 7
'Always Keeping Paper in his Hand'
A School for Art and Scandal

105 Chapter 8
In and Out of the Comfort Zone
Leonardo versus Michelangelo

120 Chapter 9
Creatures of the Night
'Only the Dark Serves to Plant Man'

135 Chapter 10
Making a Spectacle
The Systematic Studio

156 Chapter 11
Mirroring the Process
Velázquez to Reynolds

172 Chapter 12
Women in the Studio
Inspiration, Destitution, Cleaning, Crimes of Passion

199 Chapter 13
Chaste Space
Friedrich to Mondrian

226 Chapter 14
Eliminating Easels
Workshop and Factory

245 Chapter 15
Inside/Outside
Studios for Nomads

270 Notes
280 Select Bibliography
281 Picture Credits
283 Index
288 Acknowledgments

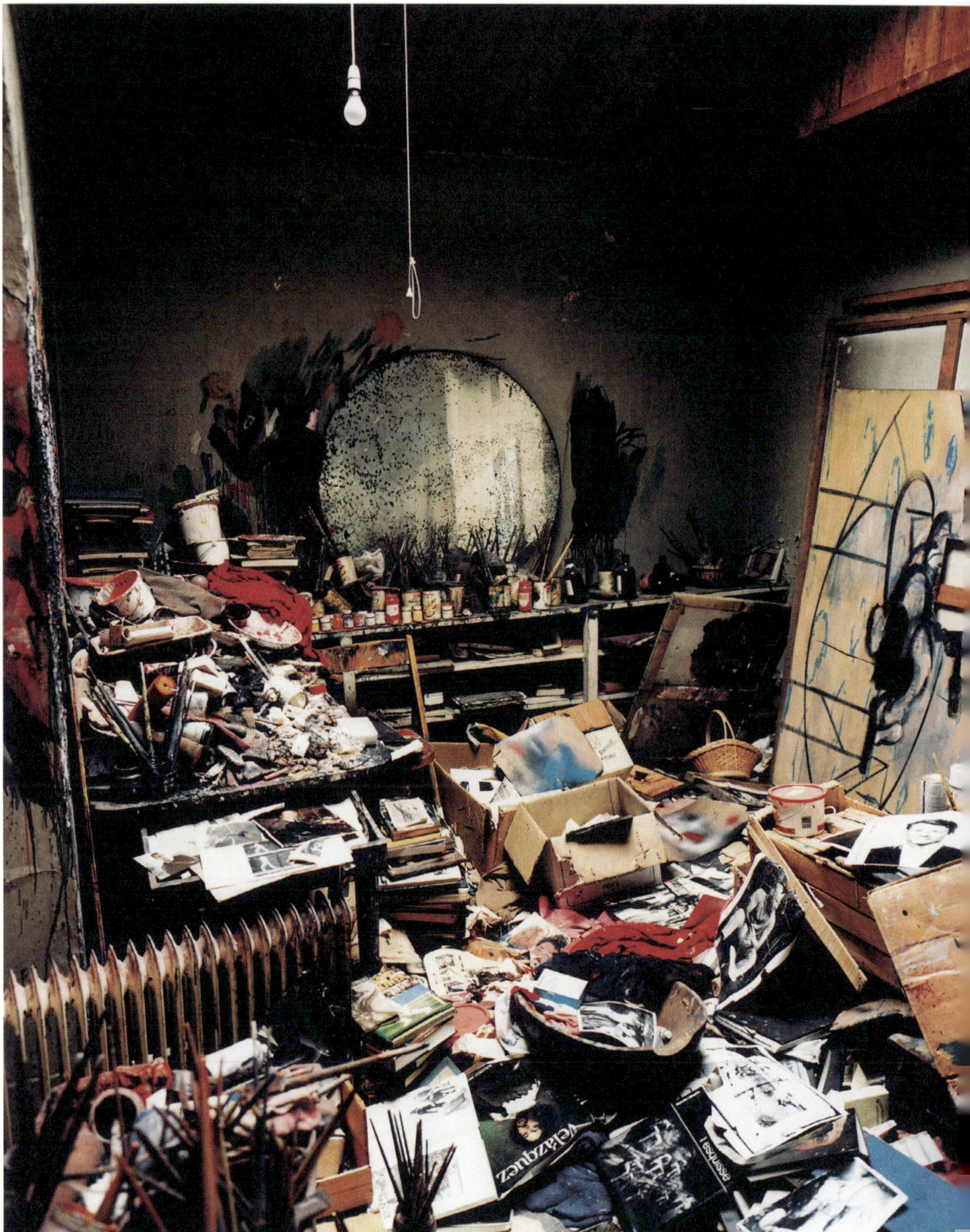

Perry Ogden, *Francis Bacon's Studio at 7 Reece Mews, London*, 1998, black-and-white photograph.

Introduction

'I feel at home here in this chaos because the chaos suggests images to me.'
Francis Bacon

'A little corner of South Kensington moved to Ireland, his birthplace ...
I think it would have made him roar with laughter.'
John Edwards[1]

The conviction that an artist's studio is the crucible of creativity is perfectly exemplified by the removal of Francis Bacon's London studio, some years after his death, to a museum in Dublin, the city where he was born. Over a period of three years, from 1998 to 2001, the delirious dereliction of Bacon's workspace was reconstructed with mind-boggling archaeological precision. It was a humongous 3-D jigsaw comprising more than 7,000 bits and pieces, all catalogued on a database.[2]

At 4 by 8 metres (13 by 26 feet), it is a modern counterpart to the Holy House of Loreto, a room of 4 by 6 metres (13 by 20 feet) comprising rough brick walls and fresco fragments. Reputed to have been the Virgin Mary's humble abode in Nazareth, the Holy House was airlifted by angels to a basilica in Central Italy on 19 December 1294 (things moved faster back then). Both rooms are sites of pilgrimage in predominantly Catholic countries: the Bacon room is a destination for lovers of art, the Virgin room for believers in miracles.

The preservation and homecoming of Bacon's studio are part of a much larger phenomenon. The big selling point – and queuing point – of a Modigliani exhibition in 2017–18 was a virtual reality headset tour of a simulated version of the artist's shabby Paris studio as it looked in 1919. It featured sardine cans, cigarette packets, empty bottles and a few paintings, but no hashish or humans. The conservation of famous artworks such as Rembrandt's *Night Watch* is increasingly enacted *in situ* and on camera; the museum or church is thereby turned into a studio, the restorers into stars of Warhol-style live-streams that can last for years. During Covid lockdowns, online studio 'visits' provided a vital window.

This book traces a history of popular interest in the artist's workplace that extends far beyond romantic and Renaissance cults of the artist. Making sense of it all has required a certain amount of sleuthing and lateral thinking. Historic interiors are poorly and sporadically documented until well into

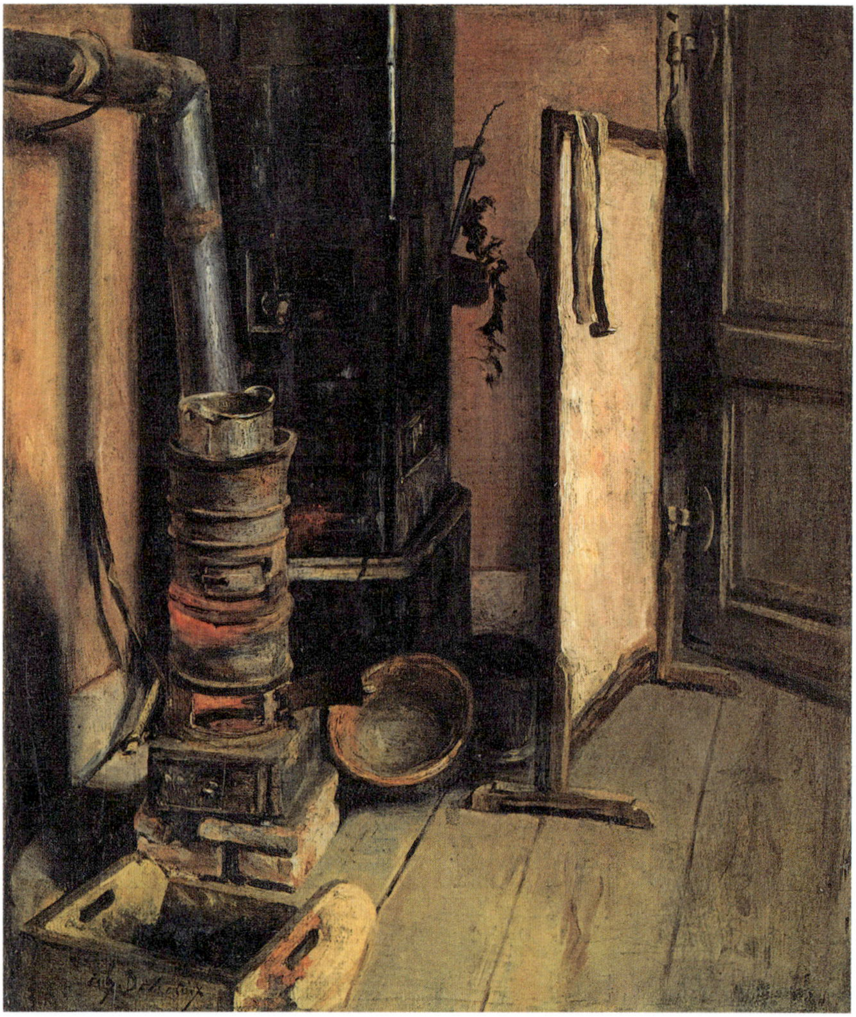

Eugène Delacroix, *Corner of the Studio*, c. 1830, oil on canvas.

the age of photography – and the camera often lies, and bores.[3] A further frustration is that so many portraits of artists emphasize social status rather than labour and mess. But despite the patchy documentary record, it is still possible to construct a compelling narrative that identifies key examples, actors, trends and turning points.

In the chapters that follow, I explore not only the internal architecture and contents of the studio but the activities and encounters, personal as well as professional, that take place there. The studio is not just a stage that offers a spectacle. It is a space that distils the magic and mystery of human creation, of body and mind working in harmony, often collectively. This is why so many poets and philosophers, starting with Homer and Socrates, have been drawn to studios.

In some respects the bare architectural bones of the studio are its least interesting aspect, since artists' needs are relatively consistent and straightforward, with variations for different media and genres. A goldsmith may need less space than a metalworker, a still-life painter than a history painter; the sculptor, weaver, printmaker and potter may need their studios to be on the ground floor. Most practitioners want sufficient dry and draught-free space, stable flooring, security, easy access, quiet neighbours, an even, diffused light and a consistent, tolerable temperature; the fires of inspiration will not burn brightly with a cold stove and oven. When Bernini carved the bust of King Louis XIV in a room in the Palais du Louvre on an ill-fated visit to France, he caught a chill because of broken windows, whereupon Cardinal Barberini advised him to wear a bearskin coat and cotton-wool wadding. Later on, the room became stiflingly hot when packed with visiting courtiers, adding to the sculptor's frustration and exhaustion. However, the most irksome studio visitors are insects and vermin; Bernini was dismayed to find mouse droppings staining his marble.[4] More recently, Bruce Nauman's seven-screen film projection *Mapping the Studio* (2001) showed a nocturnal mouse infestation to which his cat was blithely indifferent.[5]

***

Many invaluable case studies of artists' studios have been published in recent years, and a couple of excellent brief general histories. But the overwhelming tendency is to focus on painters, with a few sculptors thrown in. While there is admittedly far more evidence available about painters' studios – often in the form of paintings of them at work – this bias gives a distorted historical picture by leaving out other makers. As far as possible I have tried to correct the imbalance, taking my cue from Diderot, who in the mid-18th century recognized artisans as essential workers deserving of more respect and better pay.

The Italian term *studio* – initially *studietto* and *studium* – was first coined in 15th-century Padua. It was the artistic equivalent of a scholar's study, or *studiolo*: a private room where the artist worked on a small scale, made drawings, modelled in wax and clay, kept study collections of drawings and plaster casts, and did some reading, writing and thinking. More prosaically, it could be the place where they did admin.

In England prior to 1600, the term *workshop* was used for makers of all kinds; then painters started using the imported term *cabinet* as well as *closet* and *painting room*. *Studio* entered the English language in the mid-18th century as a word for a sketch and then, around 1800, in the modern sense, as a term for the artist's premises. It was first applied to painters and sculptors, then photographers and even dentists, those hit-and-miss sculptors of human teeth.[6] In France, *atelier* has been used indiscriminately since the Middle Ages for the workplaces of artisans and artists.[7]

Although the term *studio* was appropriated by anglophone painters and some sculptors in the 19th century, in the 20th any claim to exclusive ownership was strongly resisted. The world's most influential art journal in the years around 1900 eschewed distinctions between the fine and the more functional arts. *The Studio: An Illustrated Magazine of Fine and Applied Art* (founded 1893) promoted the Arts and Crafts Movement. The term *studio pottery* was coined. There was a belief that studio-like processes – drawing, thinking, designing, model-making and so on – were essential to all forms of visual production if they were to be creative, and that craft knowledge and collaboration were vital for the fine artist. Over the last century, design studios (a term whose first recorded use was in 1894[8]) have proliferated in all sorts of contexts, from fashion to the car industry. Hairdressing salons are a fascinating case that I will discuss in relation to the most famous studio of all, Warhol's Factory. By the same token, many modern painters have rejected the notional ivory-tower exclusivity of the studio. Like Warhol, they have chosen to live and work in former industrial buildings; or, like Bacon, they have created carefully choreographed squalor, albeit with champagne flute in hand.

This semantic instability and imprecision reflects the fact that the artist's workplace is a porous, ever-changing entity that exists in a symbiotic relationship with artisans' workshops, monks' cells, scholars' studies and other indoor and outdoor spaces. Indeed, many artworks are made on site, from prehistoric cave painting to photography and street art. The perpetual yin and yang of opposing and complementary tendencies makes this a very rich topic.

***

There are distinct geographical limits to this history, because it is only very recently that fascination with the artist's studio has gone global. Depictions of the artist or artisan at work first appeared in countries bordering the Mediterranean Sea: in ancient Egypt, Greece and, to a lesser extent, Rome. There was a resurgence of interest in Christian Europe during the late Middle Ages, with at least four saints being practising artisans. This interest never waned. American artists joined the studio party while working in late 18th-century London.[9] In Asia, by contrast, depictions of artists and artisans at work are extremely rare.

One explanation for this geographical concentration is that the creation myths of Mediterranean societies involve fabricator gods. God is most frequently an architect or sculptor, moulding humankind out of clay, as in the biblical creation story. In Egyptian myth, he is a potter. Some early Greek writers made him a painter, though this idea only really took off during the Renaissance, when God painted the whole world into existence.[10]

The absence of imagery of artists at work does not denote a lack of sophisticated interest in the arts, whether theoretical or practical. Calligraphy and painting were popular and prestigious pastimes for the educated elite in medieval Japan and China. Painting competitions were held, in which each side presented paintings in pairs for judgment. The most famous example of an *eawase* (picture contest) occurs in the seventeenth chapter of Murasaki Shikibu's *The Tale of Genji* (c. 1000 CE), sometimes considered the first novel (overleaf). Genji, illegitimate son of the former Japanese emperor, is an accomplished painter and calligrapher, as is the current emperor. In the grand finale of the competition Genji submits his own autobiographical paintings, which have been made with spontaneity and emotion. They reduce male and female courtiers to tears.[11]

But while there are some Japanese and Chinese depictions of men and occasionally women looking at pictures, there are very few of pictures being painted, or of Genji at work.[12] This must be because, while the elite painters were supremely accomplished, they were not professional artists selling their work into a market, and there was little desire to draw attention to potentially undignified manual labour. Calligraphy is more frequently depicted, albeit

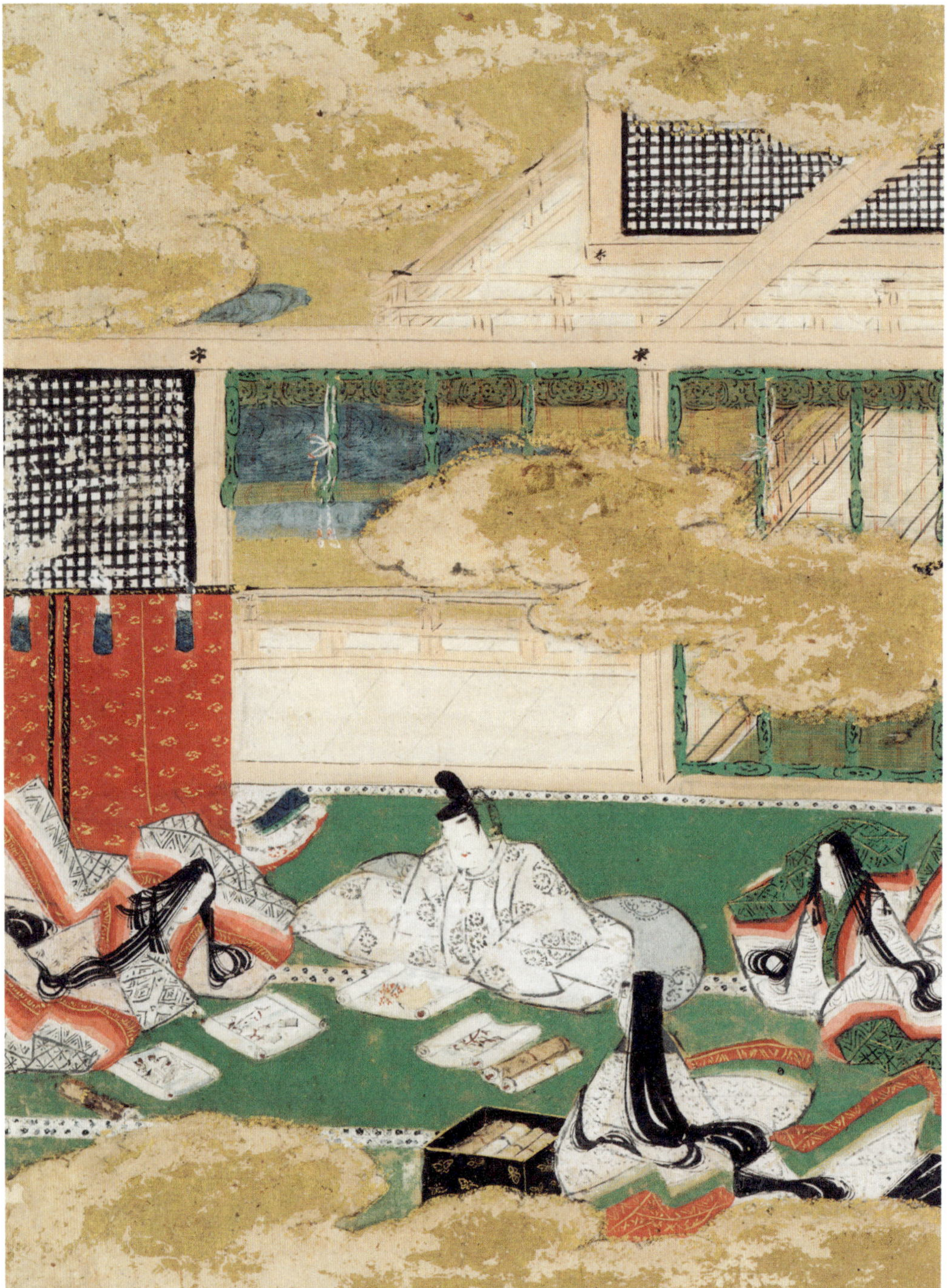

Tosa Mitsunobu, *The Picture Contest* from *The Tale of Genji*,
1509–10, ink, colour, and gold on paper.

at the still, pensive moment of *luo bi*, 'lowering the brush', before the first stroke is made. It is largely in the low-status genre of portraiture that we find a few depictions of men and also women at work.[13]

What we do have in abundance are exquisite porcelain paintbrushes, brush boats, brush rests in the shape of mountain ranges, ink-stones with fitted boxes. These were handed down and treasured through the centuries. The brush, ink, ink-stone and paper were considered to be *wenfang sibao* – 'the four treasures of a scholar's studio'. The earliest surviving European painter's palette seems to be William Hogarth's from the mid-18th century, at the dawn of the romantic cult of genius.[14]

***

The Artist's Studio: A Cultural History charts the evolution of the artist's workplace from ancient Greece – where the basic principles of the artist's studio were established – to the present day. The chapters are broadly chronological, comparing realities with myths. Mythical and divine makers, and some amateurs, are included; so too are craftspeople such as shoemakers and textile workers.

We begin with Homer's riveting account in the *Iliad* of Thetis' visit to the palatial workshop built by the lame smith-god Hephaestus. She orders a new suit of armour for her son, Achilles. Thetis is the first in a long line of glamorous studio visitors, but Homer doesn't allow her any art chat. Socrates is revealed as the originator of the artist interview, conducting seminars in workshops in Athens. Ancient Rome's main contribution is the story of Pygmalion, where the studio becomes a private domain of erotic encounters between male artist and female statue or model.

In the Middle Ages I focus on the scriptoria or writing-rooms, where illuminated manuscripts were made, and on goldsmiths' workshops. The latter had to be open to the street, with 'secret spaces' banned to prevent the adulteration of materials. Cennino Cennini's private *studietto* in Padua, by contrast, was a very secret space; in an astonishing treatise, he idealized small-scale art made by well-toned, unhurried men in fine clothes. 'Slow' art starts here. Cennini stressed the importance of drawing, and momentous Renaissance innovations would follow: drawing from sculpture and the live model, and nocturnal drawing. Painting at night begins much later, above all with Picasso.

I reassess Leonardo's infamous contrast between the painter's luxurious studio and the sculptor's filthy workshop. Michelangelo would heroize precisely those aspects of the sculptor's profession that Leonardo derided, and was overtly anti-studio. This is reflected in a previously unrecognized drawing showing the young sculptor hard at work, performing Herculean labours.

As prints, drawings and plaster casts became more widely available, artists were able to form more comprehensive study collections – what I call the 'systematic studio'. This coincided with the emergence of academies of art and their varied curricula. A key figure was Rubens, in Antwerp, who constructed bespoke studios and display areas with top-lighting. His magnificent home studio and garden became a tourist attraction, with visitors allowed to watch the great man and his assistants at work.

Watching the artist at work and learning how to draw or paint became popular pastimes in the 17th century, among women as well as men. Elisabetta Sirani in Bologna, a city noted for female artists, was one of the most adept operators. Women became important tastemakers. In Paris, Bernini was surprised to be visited by so many female courtiers; he also criticized the lavish decor in Louis XIV's bedroom for being too feminine in character, which his chaperone blamed on the king's mother. Vermeer's *The Art of Painting* seems to wallow in similarly 'feminine' taste.

Portrait painters such as Velázquez added to the studio spectacle by placing mirrors behind them while they worked, so that sitters could see themselves alongside the emerging image. This fashion coincided with the increasing availability of large mirrors and the rise of experimental science. The home studio of architect John Soane, stuffed with mirrors and a huge study collection, was a notable example of a new phenomenon: the artist's house as public museum, where genius presents itself to posterity.

During the 19th century there was a reaction against 'feminine' studio space full of casts, knick-knacks, textiles, upholstered furniture and trophies of empire. Inspired by monks' cells and artisans' workshops, the studios of avant-garde artists were barely furnished and gave no indication of the artist's education. The ideal garret had no furniture at all. In France many artists such as David, Courbet and Matisse occupied former religious buildings. The 20th century saw the arrival of the 'white cube' and factory studio.

Finally, we explore the modern rejection of the static, solitary artist's studio in favour of more open and mobile alternatives. Portable painting boxes allowed 19th-century artists to go anywhere, as did Roger Fenton's 'photographic van' and Monet's boat studio. 'Rooms with a view' were rented. More recently, artists have set up temporary studios in shops, offices, galleries – anywhere, really. As Marina Abramović says: 'Good art is never made in studio. Good art I make in life.'[15]

Chapter 1

Luxury and Lameness

The Shield of Achilles

We start at the very top, near the summit of Mount Olympus, in the gleaming headquarters of the Greek gods.

The earliest description and dramatization of an artist's workplace comes near the climax of Homer's *Iliad* (c. 700 BCE), when the sea-nymph Thetis visits Hephaestus to commission state-of-the-art armour for her son, Achilles.[1] Hephaestus is the fire god, patron deity of craftsmen who depended on his transformative heat (the Roman equivalent was Vulcan, as in volcano).[2] Although in many ways fantastical and unique in ancient literature, Homer's account of his workshop includes elements that recur in the history of the artist's studio.

The episode was illustrated on Greek pottery, our main source for scenes of everyday life during this period (overleaf). There are about fifty images of craftsmen and -women on surviving pots, all dating from c. 540–460 BCE. Metalworkers are the most frequently depicted, followed by potters.[3] These two crafts were closely related, as both needed fire for kilns and foundries. In Athens the workshops of metalworkers and potters clustered round the Temple of Hephaestus, near the marketplace.[4]

Hephaestus' versatility and productivity puts Leonardo to shame.[5] He is far more than an arms manufacturer. Ambidextrous and wise, he has made virtually everything on Mount Olympus. He is also a cunning magus, fabricator of intelligent automata including Pandora, the first woman, with her fateful box containing many evils and a single good. Most gods wear something made by Hephaestus, and Homer calls the gods 'shining' and 'gold-gleaming';[6] Thetis, who is ushered in by Hephaestus' wife, Charis, wears silver footwear. The house, which the lame god built for himself, stands out; it is 'imperishable,

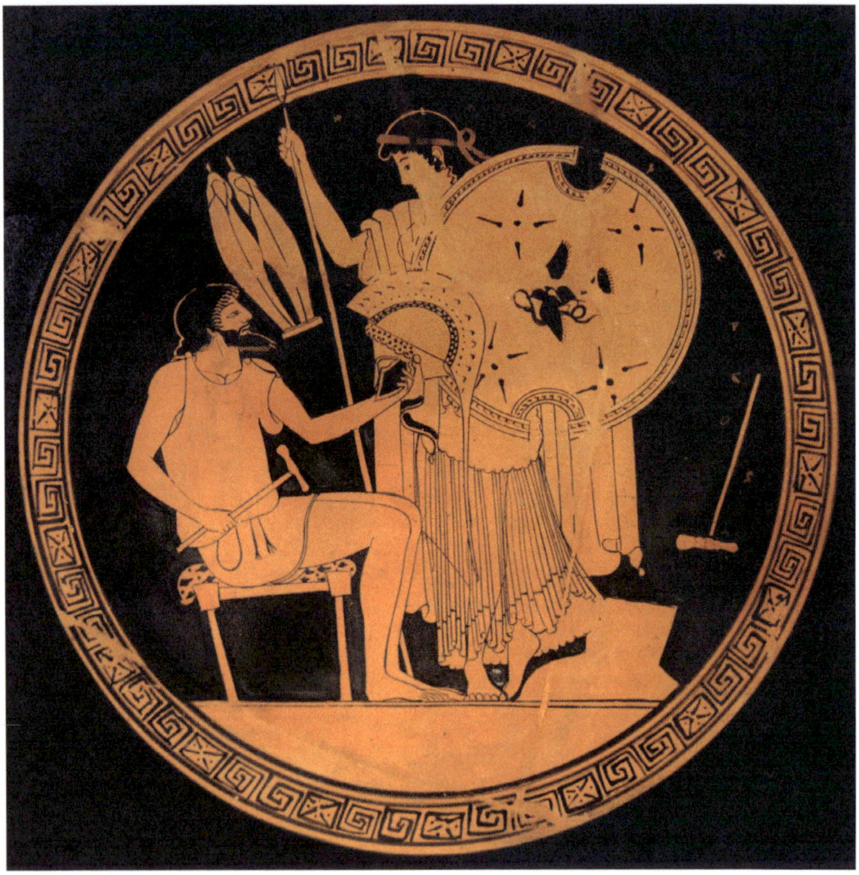

Foundry Painter, *Hephaestus and Thetis*, c. 510 BCE, interior of a terracotta kylix (drinking cup).

starry' and made from bronze: 'She found him bustling about, sweating, and busying himself with his bellows, for he was forging tripods, twenty in all, that were to stand around the wall of his well-built hall; under the base of each one he had fixed wheels of gold, so that of their own accord they could enter the gods' assembly and then return again to his house – a wonder to look upon' (18.369–82).[7]

The cult of the artist's studio is often predicated, as here, on ownership or long-term occupation of rented property. If an artist has not constructed or designed their own workplace, it is defined through decor and the presence of artefacts and tools. Here the starriness[8] evokes not only the cosmic splendour of Hephaestus' work, but the sparks emitted by wood and coal fires and by hammering, chiselling, filing. The building is a multi-function open-plan hall, similar to Mycenaean palaces and the cellae of Greek temples, with their central hearths. The visit from a glamorous patron would later become a standard trope – the most famous being those by Alexander the Great to his court painter Apelles, and the Virgin Mary and Christ Child to their painter, Saint Luke. Hephaestus lays on unspecified entertainment for his visitor, presumably musical.

The reality for most human artisans was rather different. In the ancient world they were often slaves, with sons learning from fathers, daughters learning from mothers. Women specialized in making and cleaning textiles – they are shown in one vase painting weighing wool, spinning yarn, weaving, and folding finished fabric in a proto-factory system (overleaf). Their elegant uniform is improbable, even if Penelope, wife of Odysseus, was celebrated for weaving in the central hall of her palace. Backgrounds are not depicted by Greek pot-painters (as in Egyptian wall painting, which has some images of craftsmen). Walls are alluded to by having tools and artefacts hanging in mid-air. They would have been regularly whitewashed to increase light, but work was also done outdoors in a yard.

Slaves did most of the manual work and comprised about a third of the population in late 5th-century Athens, as in the American South before the Civil War. One hundred and twenty slaves were employed in the shield workshop of Polemarchos, a free resident alien who paid taxes but was not allowed to own land. At Sparta there were seven times as many slaves as citizens (who were always male), and no citizen was allowed to do manual work.[9] Some Greek cities banned citizens associated with manual labour from holding government positions.[10] Artisans rarely owned property or land, an essential qualification for citizenship.[11] Using Socrates as a mouthpiece, the landowner, soldier and historian Xenophon claimed in a dialogue on estate management (*c.* 380 BCE) that artisans – unlike farmers, who owned land and property – would not fight an invader; rather, they would sit down and do nothing.[12] Xenophon was obsessed by the idea that artisans were unhealthily sedentary.

Artisans were praised for their technical skills but, unlike poets and musicians, they had no special muse to inspire them. To this end, the Athenian statesman Solon (*c.* 638–*c.* 558 BCE) claimed: 'The sculptor works with his hands, but it is the poet who is established as the benchmark of much desired wisdom.'[13] There was no special word for artist and so no easily expressed distinction between, say, painters and tanners. Nonetheless, versatile artisans such as Phidias (*c.* 500–430 BCE), who made colossal cult statues and oversaw

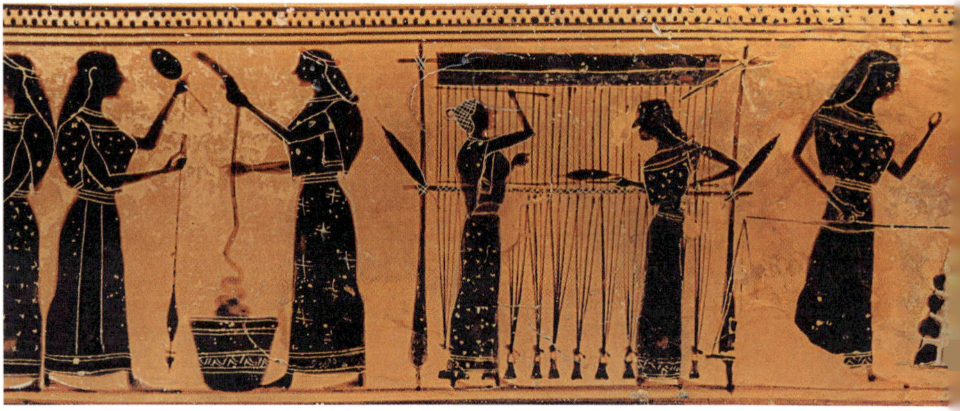

Pericles' sculpture programme on the Parthenon,[14] and statue and portrait makers including Praxiteles and Lysippos (court sculptor to Alexander the Great) do seem to have become prosperous.[15] Apelles reputedly sold a golden portrait of Alexander for twenty talents.[16] Polygnotos – the first to paint women in transparent drapery, and to depict open mouths and teeth – was given free food and lodging by Delphi city council: an unremarkable perk by late medieval and Renaissance standards, but worth noting in the ancient world.[17]

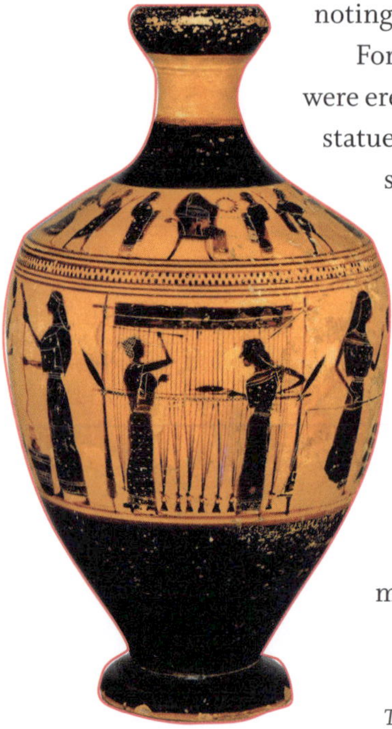

For large sculpture commissions, temporary facilities were erected. Open-air furnaces and casting pits for bronze statues have been found; forges were located in open-sided roofed structures or lean-tos. When Phidias was commissioned to make a colossal enthroned statue of Zeus at Olympia (*c.* 430s BCE) funded by the spoils of war, a workshop was built near the temple with the main room measuring roughly 18 by 12 metres (59 by 39 feet), and over 13 metres (43 feet) high – very similar to Monet's large studio at Giverny. It later became a Christian basilica.

Because Phidias' statue was made from precious materials including gold, ivory and coloured glass

Above and left Attributed to the Amasis Painter, *Textile Workers*, *c.* 550–530 BCE, terracotta lekythos (oil flask).

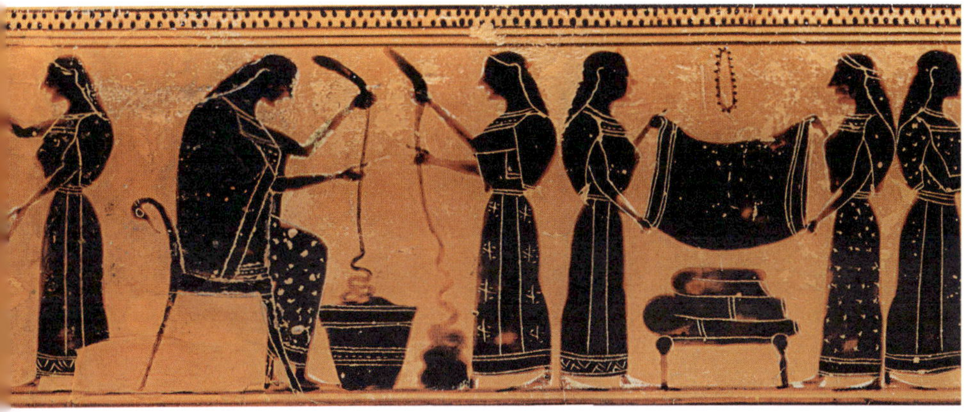

mounted on a wooden frame, the workshop was built of limestone blocks 1 metre (3 feet) thick and had heavy wooden doors.[18] Thefts of materials were a perennial problem (and still are: in 2016, thieves cut through wire cages in Anselm Kiefer's vast studio in a former warehouse near Paris to steal a 10-tonne lead sculpture and 12 tonnes of raw marble). Phidias was accused of stealing gold for his colossal statue of Athena in the Parthenon. This charge may have been politically motivated owing to his friendship with Pericles; likewise the claim that he 'procured free-born women who visited the building site' for the statesman.[19] But filching and pimping may have been a way to boost earnings.[20]

Homer's account of Hephaestus is not entirely divorced from artisanal reality; human artisans could have sympathized with the fire god's lameness and sweatiness. The son of Zeus and Hera, he was born lame, whereupon his disappointed mother hurled him off Mount Olympus (*Iliad* 18.395ff.).[21] He fell to earth and survived only because Thetis nurtured him secretly in her cave, which became his workplace (mining and metallurgy were often carried out in caves, the first workshops). For nine years 'he forged much cunning handiwork, brooches, and spiral arm-bands, and rosettes and necklaces'. He was taught by semi-human creatures including Cyclopes and Telchines.

The other gods laugh 'unquenchably' at Hephaestus' lameness when they see him huffing and puffing through the palace of Zeus (1.600).[22] But by virtue of being rejected, disabled and bullied, this god feels all too human. His lameness (and perhaps asthma) almost certainly symbolizes the physically hazardous nature of metalwork, as would be spelled out in Bernardino Ramazzini's treatise *Diseases of Workers* (1700/13), the first systematic medical study. In terms of health and safety, little had changed since Homer's day. Metalworkers typically became short-winded, splenetic, lethargic and eventually consumptive; mercury, used in gilding, caused vertigo, asthma, pallor, paralysis and palsy. Gazing into furnaces dried and damaged the eyes, while dangerous levels of dehydration increased the temptation to drink unsanitary water. Sulphurous fumes from red-hot iron and coals attacked the eyes 'like very sharp thorns', causing ophthalmia; too much standing brought on varicose veins and ulcers; fine work could lead to blindness, hammering to deafness.[23] Metalwork was nonetheless far preferable to working in a mine: women in mining communities could expect to have anything up to seven husbands.[24] Recent studies of bones from a workmen's cemetery in ancient Egypt found numerous compression fractures of the spine, caused by carrying heavy loads.[25]

Ramazzini does not mention accidental injuries and illnesses. The scanty surviving ancient sources are silent except for details of serious injuries sustained by apprentices at the hands of their master, or Emperor Hadrian's summary execution of the architect Apollodorus for criticizing his plans.[26] But there is evidence from later periods. Being crushed was and is a constant hazard for sculptors. In 1726 François Dumont, celebrated for his marble *Titan Struck by Lightning*, died from injuries sustained when a lead curtain for a tomb fell on him. Benvenuto Cellini, while casting *Perseus and Medusa* (1545–54), set fire to his workshop; the stress brought on a fever, and he kept shouting 'I'm dying!' On another occasion, a steel splinter flew into Cellini's eye while he was sharpening chisels. His sight was 'miraculously' saved by a surgeon, who bathed the injury in blood taken from veins on the wings of two live pigeons.[27] Safety visors and goggles as we know them today were not invented until the 20th century, but Cellini wisely recommended leaving the fire-gilding of statues to specialists, who all died young because of mercury fumes. (In the 1980s, Andy Warhol never went to his screen-printer's unventilated studio for fear of solvent fumes.[28])

For some elite Greeks, such insalubriousness was morally repugnant. Xenophon claimed that all manual work was held in disdain in Greek cities because artisans had to sit indoors, 'and in some cases spend the day by the fire. Softening of the body leads to softening of the mind.'[29] Not only the metal melts. Similar complaints were made by other Greek and Roman writers.[30] On the face of it, there is little more incentive for anyone to visit an artisan's workplace than a salt mine, and there should have been no demand for depictions, however idealized and deep-cleaned. But these attacks on manual workers should be treated with caution: the writers protest too much and their derision is often a reflex rhetorical cliché contradicted by other things they say. At the root of it is a political need to keep the lower classes in their place, thereby maintaining order and a reliable supply of those splendid artefacts on which the elite were so dependent. Xenophon, a professional soldier, required the best armour that the human counterparts of Hephaestus could make. As we shall see, he visited workshops with Socrates. His complaint about softened minds may in fact be an expert criticism of the 'softer', more naturalistic styles of contemporary sculpture.

Patronage-seeking authors may have been envious of the vast sums private and public patrons spent on crafted objects: excess and luxury were frequently condemned.[31] The Greek word *poet* means 'maker', and visual artists were rival makers – competing alarmingly well in the representation of reality, and especially of the gods.[32] Solon, who confined wisdom to poets, was himself a poet. By 500 BCE, bronze was the leading material for life-size sculpture: it could depict fingernails and eyelashes, and gods could be made to look scarily alive, with outstretched arms and legs that seemed to move like Hephaestus' automata.[33] As Homer thrillingly attests, what could be more fun than visiting an artisan's workplace to witness the magic in action? After Dante in the *Inferno* compared the boiling pitch used in Venice's massive Arsenal to that found in hell, it became even more of a tourist attraction.[34] And what are we to make of those well-born women visiting Phidias' building site on the Acropolis?

***

It is often assumed that Homer's depiction of Hephaestus shows he shared the Greek elite's contempt for artisans.[35] But Homer takes a nuanced approach, in which the prevailing note is awestruck fascination and admiration. Hephaestus has the finest palace and a devoted wife, 'lovely Charis [grace, charisma] of the glistening veil' – which also underscores the fact that workshops tend to be family businesses. In Homer's *Odyssey* Hephaestus is married to Aphrodite, goddess of love, who cuckolds him with Ares, god of war. But he has the last laugh, trapping them *in flagrante* in a metal net finer than a spider's web: 'slow though he is, he has outstripped Ares' (8.266–342).

Homer was evidently thrilled by workshops, even if he got some of the technical aspects wrong.[36] Hephaestus' disabilities, appearance and 'orphaned' state are marks of distinction and attraction rather than objects of shame. Catalyst for heroic levels of invention, his lameness is comparable to the blindness that was supposed to give bards – including Homer – access to higher truths. The supreme warrior Achilles had a fatal weakness in his heel; Socrates' famously ugly body housed the most beautiful mind. Greeks loved polarities and paradoxes, and Pythagorean philosophers compiled a table of opposites.[37] In that context, Hephaestus is in fact exemplary.[38] His marvellous workshop and its contents more than make up for any physical limitations of their maker: 'He shifted the bellows away from the fire, and collected all the tools with which he worked into a silver chest; with a sponge he wiped his face on both sides, and both his hands, and also his powerful neck and hairy chest, and put on a tunic, and took up a stout staff, and came to the door, limping. Women servants moved nimbly to support their lord; these were made of gold, and resembled living young women' (18.412–22).

These primordial Alexas function as prosthetic limbs, surrogate mothers, wives and, of course, slaves. They are precursors to Pygmalion's statue of his ideal woman, brought to life by his prayers to Venus, goddess of love. Uncannily lifelike sculptures and mannequins resembling automata would be standard components of artists' studios from the late Middle Ages onwards. In this, their first outing, they have been invented to remedy a lack in their maker. Homer clearly sees Hephaestus' lameness not as a failing but as an unalloyed boon that brings about a golden age of manufacture and of marvelling at what's made. Creating splendid tools, machines, workspaces, etc. transcends humankind's intrinsic core disabilities – just as armour does. The disabled Hephaestus in his starry workshop is an inspiration and model for all humans.

This compensatory conception of cultural and technological development echoes evolutionary theories that see them as necessary evils brought about by the ending of the first Golden Age. We find it in Hesiod's didactic poem *Works and Days* (c. 700 BCE) and in the Book of Genesis, probably written down in the next century. When Adam and Eve are expelled from the Garden of Eden, they experience cold, hunger, illness, ageing and homelessness for the first time. So *Homo faber* – man the maker, who works by the sweat of his brow – is born (Genesis 4). After the Fall, Adam and Eve's offspring make – in the marvellous words of the blind poet John Milton – 'tents of various hue' and instruments with 'melodious chime'. Then:

> The liquid ore he drained
> Into fit moulds prepared; from which he formed
> First his own tools; then, what might else be wrought
> Fusile or graven in metal. (*Paradise Lost*, 1674, XI.570–3)

Ever since Homer, the artist's workplace has played a crucial role in expressing the Graeco-Christian concept of culture as remedial. One of the clearest and most moving illustrations, with canvases of various hue, is a studio scene painted by the Rome-based French artist Pierre Subleyras (1699–1749) shortly before his death.[39] Subleyras, who specialized in religious paintings and portraits, had for several years been ill with stress, exhaustion and eventually tuberculosis.

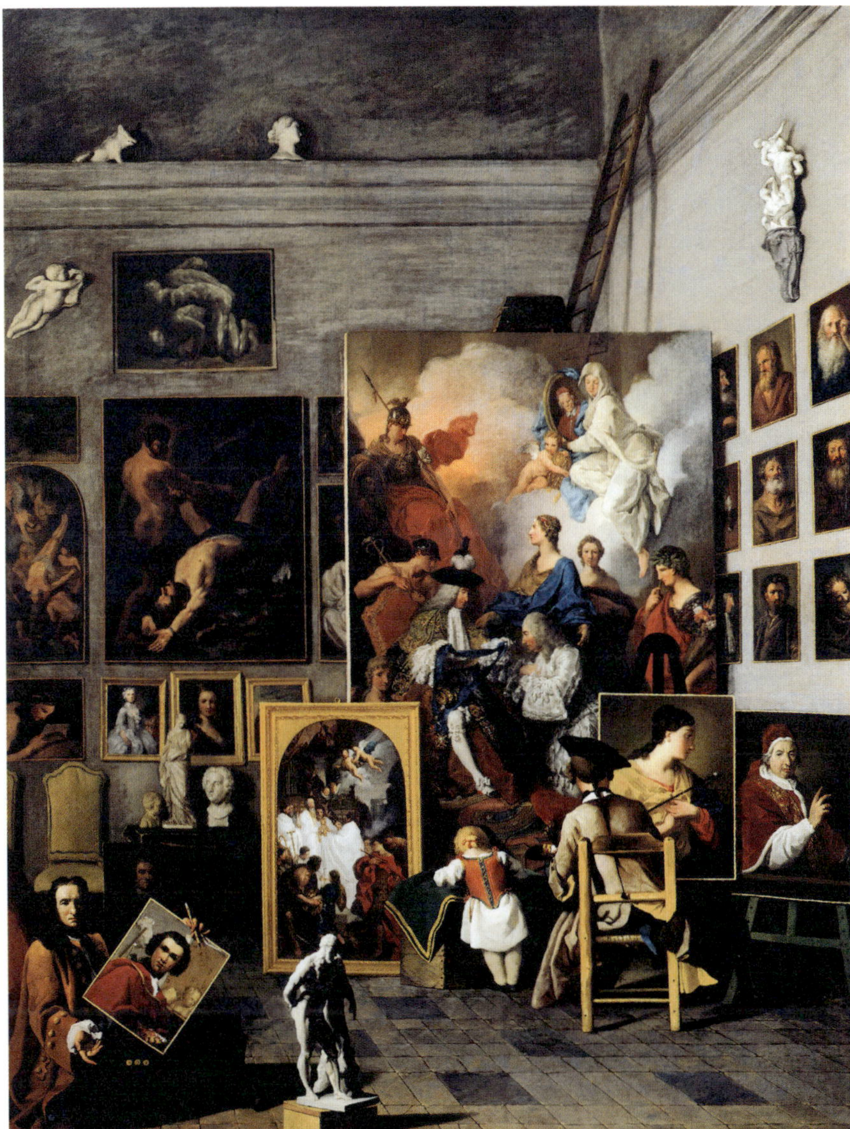

Pierre Subleyras, *The Artist's Studio*, 1746, oil on canvas.

We see him slumped on a low stool at bottom left, gaunt and with lifeless legs. But this 'lame' and breathless man has learned the lesson of Hephaestus.

The artist is accompanied by an ideal survey of his paintings and, in the foreground, a plaster cast of the heavily restored Farnese *Hercules*, resting between labours. Wholeness has been regained through art, and to this end Subleyras holds up a self-portrait of himself in his prime. Another, more recent one stands on the floor behind. Two childhood versions of himself intently paint and draw (toddlers wore unisex clothing, bodices promoting good posture).[40] He painted another vigorous self-portrait on the back of the canvas with a crayon holder clenched between his teeth. He is carried along, as it were, by memories of his younger, healthier selves. In all, Subleyras multiplies himself by five. The hall-like room, without visible ceiling, is sky-high, as are the ladder and the cornice with casts. This stretched logic demonstrates how, in his Rome studio, Subleyras has transcended his stricken self and achieved the sublime. Unfortunately, he left his miniature-painter wife and four children nothing 'except his fame and his example'.[41]

***

Homer revels in man-made as well as divine artefacts (Hephaestus had anyway learned his skills on earth).[42] Penelope's weaving of a funeral shroud for her son Laertes is central to the *Odyssey*: for four years she tells her suitors that she will give them an answer when she finishes, but she secretly unravels each day's work at night. The all-too-human Odysseus is revealed at the climax of the *Odyssey* as the proud maker of a roofed marital bedroom and bed: 'It was my work and mine alone' (23.190). They are united in crafty craftsmanship, and their palace is simultaneously their workshop.

The importance of human craftsmanship is underscored in Homer's 125-line description of the shield of Achilles, the most magnificent of prostheses.[43] Hephaestus orders his bellows to start up: 'and the bellows, twenty in all, began to blow on his crucibles, giving out well-moderated blasts from all directions, to help Hephaestus as he hurried to this place and to that .... Into the fire he threw bronze that does not wear away, and tin and precious gold, and silver; then he positioned a great anvil on its anvil-block, and in one hand took up a powerful hammer, and in the other took up some tongs' (18.470–7).

The shield is a microcosm, with five circles. There are depictions of planets and stars; a city at peace, with marriages and court cases in progress; a besieged city; farmers at work; the grape harvest; livestock and herdsmen;

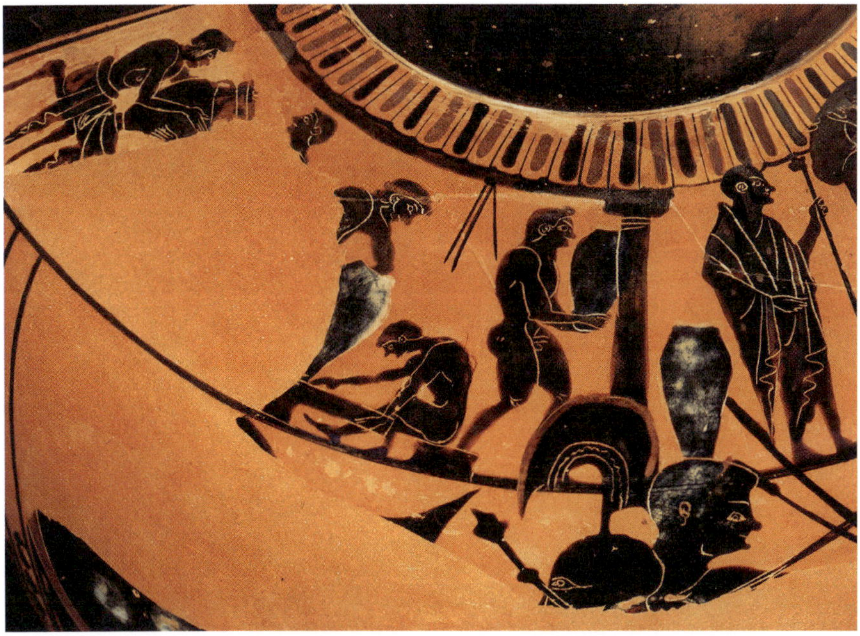

Attributed to a painter of the Leagros Group, *A Pottery Workshop* (detail), 520–510 BCE, shoulder of a hydria vase.

a lion hunt; and finally an inlaid dance floor where young men and girls 'worth many cattle' dance beautifully. The shield's rim depicts the ocean.

Homer climaxes with astonishing craft similes that plunge us right back into an artisan's workplace. The dance floor is compared to one made at Knossos by Daedalus,[44] mythical first human craftsman and maker of automata. The dancers go round 'lightly with skilful steps, like the motion a potter gives his wheel when testing it out to see how it will run'. Homer's allusion to a potter's wheel echoes the placement of the ocean on the circular shield's rim, for the water with which the potter lubricates the clay flows over the edge of the wheel-head. A surviving fragment of a hydria vase depicts a potter's workshop, with a clothed master overseeing his naked workmen, probably slaves; a seated boy pushes the wheel-head round as an adult male potter makes a tall jar. The boy uses eyes and fingers to check the wheel remains level – exactly the skill that Homer mentions.[45] The potter at his wheel is like a brilliant dance master, just as Hephaestus conducts his choir of bellows. Workshops express a supreme harmony, the synchronized dance of mind, body and machine.

***

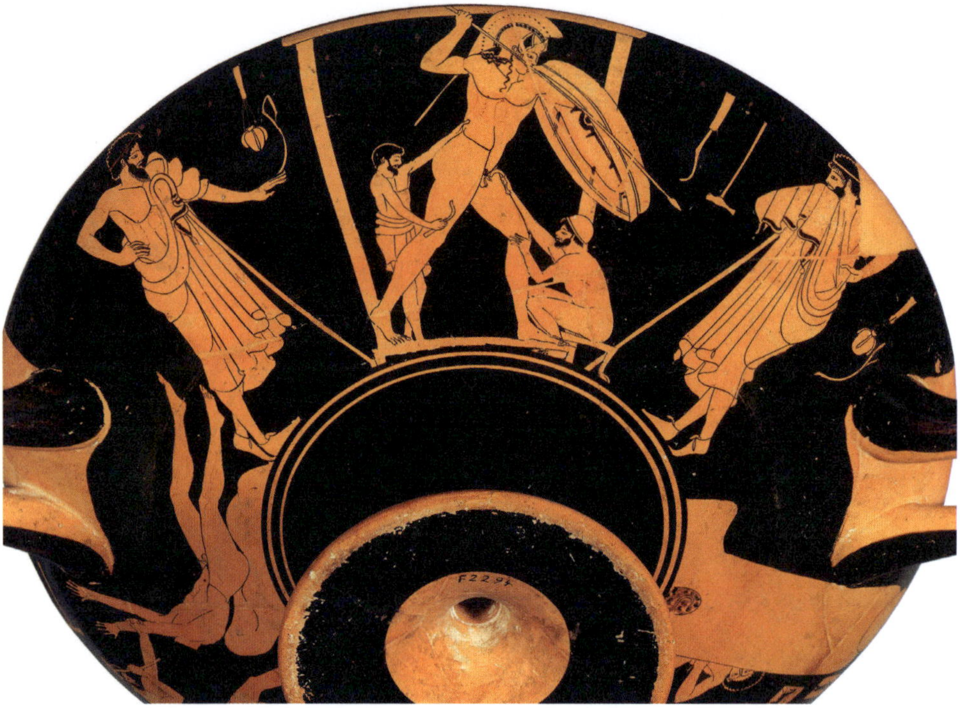

Above and opposite Foundry Painter, *A Bronze Workshop*, *c.* 510 BCE, exterior of a painted clay kylix (drinking cup).

The finest depiction of a human workshop is on a drinking cup by the so-called Foundry Painter (*c.* 490 BCE), likely made in Athens (see page 16). It is in the latest fashion, with red figures against a black ground.[46] The Foundry Painter is known for a blokeish wit well suited to drinking cups used at banquets (i.e. a sex scene where the woman leans on a bloated wineskin resembling female breasts; a urinating sex worker; etc.). In the centre we see, framed within a patterned roundel, Hephaestus seated on a cushioned stool. The well-to-do sat on cushions until the development of upholstery in the 18th century. He is putting the finishing touches to Achilles' helmet with an iron hammer. Thetis looms large over him, too close for comfort, a customer in a hurry. Behind her is an anvil wedged into a mound of earth; a second identical hammer and a pair of greaves hang from the undefined back wall. The painter hasn't depicted Hephaestus' lameness or attempted to follow Homer's impossibly detailed description of the shield. There is instead an eagle carrying a snake – portent of the impending Trojan defeat (*Iliad*, 12.200–10) – surrounded by four stars.

On the outside of the cup is a continuous painted frieze depicting a bronze foundry in unmatched detail. Two diminutive men (probably slaves) smooth down the surface of a colossal striding warrior; they use curved strigil rasps made from iron (bronze strigils were used by athletes to scrape oil and dirt off their skin). They have applied oil to the sculpture's surface taken from the small jars hanging on the back wall. The statue stands on a scaffold used for lifting and securing sections of sculpture. The warrior is naked, clothed only in shield and helmet; a rasp is castratingly close to his genitals (more blokeish wit). Two large-scale overseers look on, clothed and shoed; the one towards whom the spear points seems to shrink back gingerly, as if the statue were alive.

The other side shows two naked men stoking a rather phallic furnace. One sits on a cushioned stool, genitals comically dangling, and stokes the fire with a hooked rod; the other operates the bellows with vim. A man with heroic physique looks on, leaning on a mallet with annoying insouciance. They would normally wear protective clothing, probably leather aprons. Further along, a man wearing a loincloth assembles a headless statue propped on a large pile of earth. It is in a less stiff, softer style than the striding warrior.

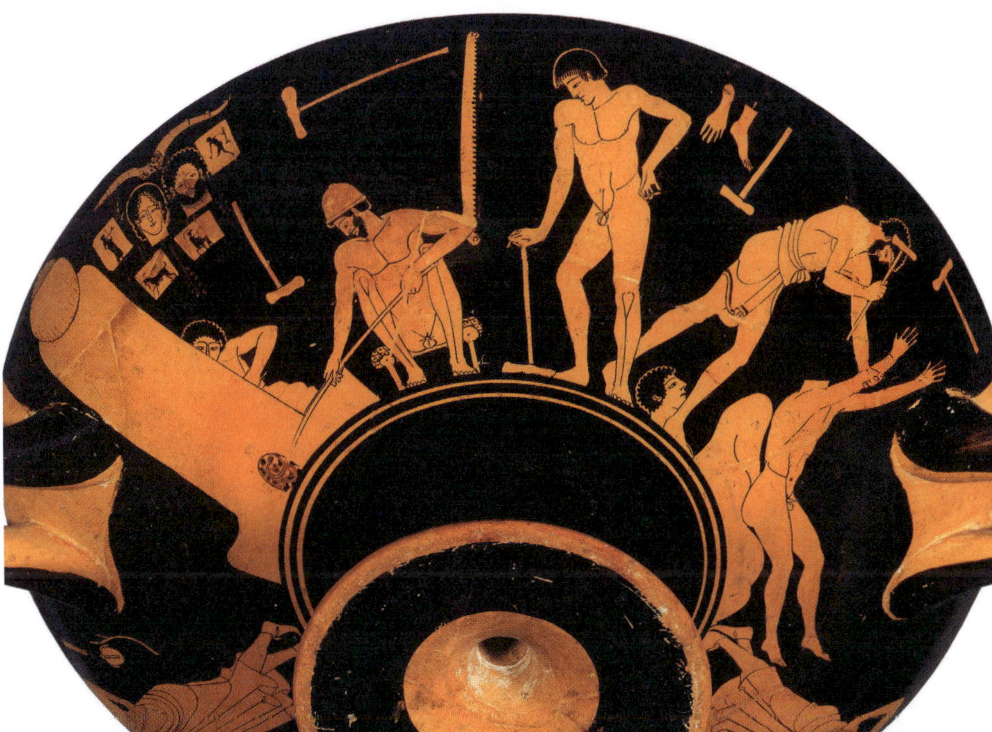

He attaches the right hand by hammering the join, which will be soldered. The head, still waiting to be fixed in place, gazes up lugubriously from the floor. Large bronze statues were usually made in large and small sections. The penis, scrotum, middle toes, beard, locks of hair, nipples, lips, eyelashes, eyes and teeth were often cast separately, the last two made from silver.[47] Strangely, there are no tongs.

The purpose of this statue is much debated. While the outstretched arms resemble contemporary figures of athletes, the outstretched feet mean he would stand on tiptoe – a practical impossibility for a heavy bronze statue. This is partly a visual gag – which will be endlessly recycled – about the violence that sculptors mete out to their 'live' statues, cutting, burning, scraping, hitting: the arms are outstretched in supplication. On the back wall is a fearsome dogtooth saw. But as it adorns a drinking pot, this could be an imaginary statue of a fallen drunkard, a follower of the wine god Dionysus.

A beguiling feature of the scene is the pictures on the wall, surmounted by two curving horns from a sacrificial bull. They are apotropaic votive panel paintings and reliefs: presents for the gods, intended to safeguard high-risk castings. Like the bronze statues, they are stylistically diverse and varied in content. There is a draped figure with staff; a hieratic male and female head; a naked, wobbly man with a hammer (Hephaestus?); a jumping goat (sacrificial?); and a seated, draped female figure (a goddess?). The head of the bearded man, juxtaposed with the man with a hammer, could be (self-) portraits of the workers rather than gods. The female head is similar to that of Thetis. Votive panel pictures, often hung in temples, were called *pinakes* – 'wooden boards' – from which the Italian and German terms for picture gallery ultimately derive (*pinacoteca*, *pinakothek*). Here we see the beginnings of the idea of the workplace as art gallery, and as shrine to human ingenuity and versatility. Some votive pictures were probably done by pot painters for their sculptor neighbours; here they act like *cartes-de-visite*, evidence of artistic community.

Chapter 2

Wisdom's Workshop

Simon the Shoemaker

In the previous chapter we heard how Solon made a hard and fast hierarchical distinction between the wisdom of a poet, inspired by a muse, and the technical know-how of artisans. In fact, Athenian workshops became a mixture of seminar room and visitor attraction in which artisans played an active role. The activities in the workshop were 'good to think with', to borrow the famous phrase of anthropologist Claude Lévi-Strauss.

That some poets did take a close interest in artisanal activities is borne out by one of the so-called Homeric *Hymns*, composed in Homeric style sometime between *c.* 525 and 350 BCE. 'Homer' visits a potter's studio and shows a detailed knowledge of their craft. He has been commissioned to write a song to ward off evil spirits that might jeopardize their firings.[1] As we have seen, apotropaic images performed the same function. A mask of a bearded chthonic deity, a god of the underworld, often presided over the mouth of the kiln like a gargoyle on a medieval cathedral.

However, in the Homeric hymn, 'Homer' pulls a fast one and threatens dire consequences if the potters don't pay him properly: 'If you will pay me for my song, O potters,/Then come, Athena, and hold your hand above the kiln!/May the cups and vases all turn a good black,/May they be well fired, and fetch the price asked .... /But if you turn shameless and deceitful,/Then will I summon the ravagers of kilns,/Both Smasher and Crasher and/Unquenchable and Shaker and/Unbakeable, who cause much trouble for this craft./Stamp on stoking tunnels and chambers, and may the whole/kiln be thrown into confusion, while the potters loudly wail .... /And if anyone bends over to look into the spy hole, may his/whole face be scorched, so that all may learn to deal justly.'[2]

That Homer, or a modern equivalent, could be imagined visiting a potter's workplace, exchanging expert banter, suggests not just that Homer's potter's wheel reference was well known, but that writers did visit and talk to artisans. The most compelling evidence comes, ironically, from Xenophon, hitherto wheeled in from stage left as archetypal villainous Artisan-Basher. Xenophon was a devoted disciple of Socrates (469–399 BCE), who had to commit suicide for holding sceptical views about the delinquent Greek gods. In his *Memorabilia* (after 371 BCE), Xenophon turned his recollections of Socrates into a series of exculpatory dialogues, in which visits to workshops are central. The critiques of craftsmen spouted by Socrates in Xenophon's treatise on agriculture are largely forgotten.[3]

The famously short, ugly and unkempt Socrates was brought up as a mason/sculptor and claimed descent from Daedalus, mythical first human craftsman, and the maker of automata and of the first self-portrait (erected in the Temple of Hephaestus at Memphis).[4] Socrates considered Daedalus a martyr: 'Have you not heard how Daedalus was seized by Minos [king of Knossos in Crete] because of his wisdom and forced to be his slave?'[5] Socrates embraced poverty, chastity and the life of the mind, but continued to visit workshops for intellectual and practical reasons.[6] Young men were not allowed to enter the marketplace in Athens, so Socrates and his followers frequented the surrounding workshops, using them as informal classrooms.[7] When the statesman Critias tried to ban Socrates from talking to anyone under 30, he quipped: 'Socrates, you will have to avoid your favourite topics: cobblers, builders and metalworkers; for I think you have already worn them threadbare.'[8]

Socrates believed that virtue was gained only through sweat and work.[9] In a dialogue by his disciple Plato, the *Apology*, he praises craftsmen for having 'knowledge of things that I did not have knowledge of, and in this way they were wiser' (22d).[10] Although Plato (*c.* 429–347 BCE) is best known for dismissing painting as a pale imitation of 'absolute existence' or ideas, he too visited workshops. He frequently discusses painting in his philosophical works using a precise technical vocabulary, and was reputed to have studied painting in his youth.[11] So the much-maligned artisan's workplace actually played a vital role in the development of new ideas. In a lawsuit against an Athenian artisan in *c.* 400 BCE, the plaintiff alleged that the defendant's workplace was the headquarters of a gang of thuggish young slackers; the artisan replied that all Athenians frequented workshops.[12]

One of Socrates' hosts was Simon the Shoemaker, who reputedly wrote down thirty-three of their conversations, thereby making the first Socratic dialogues.[13] In 1953, the ruins of a one-storey, irregularly shaped workshop were discovered at the south-western perimeter of the Agora; the floor was covered in hobnails and a pot fragment was found inscribed with the name Simon. It has been claimed that this was the site of Simon the Shoemaker's house. If so, it can be considered *the* seminal studio-academy, insofar as it was a mecca for making, meeting, talking and thinking.[14] It consisted of two rooms and a courtyard with a well. Simon was later idealized by Cynic philosophers for his asceticism, self-sufficiency and independence from the worlds of money and power. He turned down a request from Pericles to come and live in his household. In one apocryphal Cynic epistle he contrasts the moral probity of his own profession with the wealthy: 'I hear that you ridicule our wisdom in the presence of [the tyrant] Dionysus. I admit that I am a shoemaker and that I do work of that nature, and in like manner I would, if it were necessary, cut strips of leather once more for the purpose of admonishing foolish men who think that they are living according to the teachings of Socrates when they are living in great luxury.'[15]

Plato – with his anti-art hat on – complained in *The Republic* that poets and painters produce likenesses of a shoemaker without knowing anything about how the shoe is made (10.601). He must have known this was untrue, both because of the popularity of workshop visits, and from the visual record.[16] An Athenian black-figure jar (*c*. 500–490 BCE) asserts the dignity of labour and demonstrates a profound appreciation of shoemaking. A shoemaker cuts a sandal sole to size for a girl standing on his work table (overleaf). The painter has adjusted her body size to fit the available space, like a statuette on a pedestal. She raises her dress to expose her foot and gestures towards the shoemaker, who gestures back. Behind her, an assistant holds a sandal and an older man looks on, gesturing. It is unclear if he is the girl's husband or father, or the shop-owner. A bowl of water (for softening leather) and a finished sandal are placed on the floor, with tools and equipment hanging on the back wall. Everything is immaculate and tautly chic. The *diphros* (straight-legged stool) and table are particularly elegant, with white lead paint denoting inlaid ivory embellishment. No one is distracted or bored; there is supreme synergy, total absorption in the task at hand.

None of Simon the Shoemaker's dialogues survive, and some scholars doubt they ever existed, but Xenophon gives us a vivid flavour of Socrates' encounters with a painter, a sculptor and a breastplate maker. Socrates does most of the talking, but it is not all one-way traffic, and he often summarizes what the artisans already do and say. Xenophon says of Socrates, 'I was

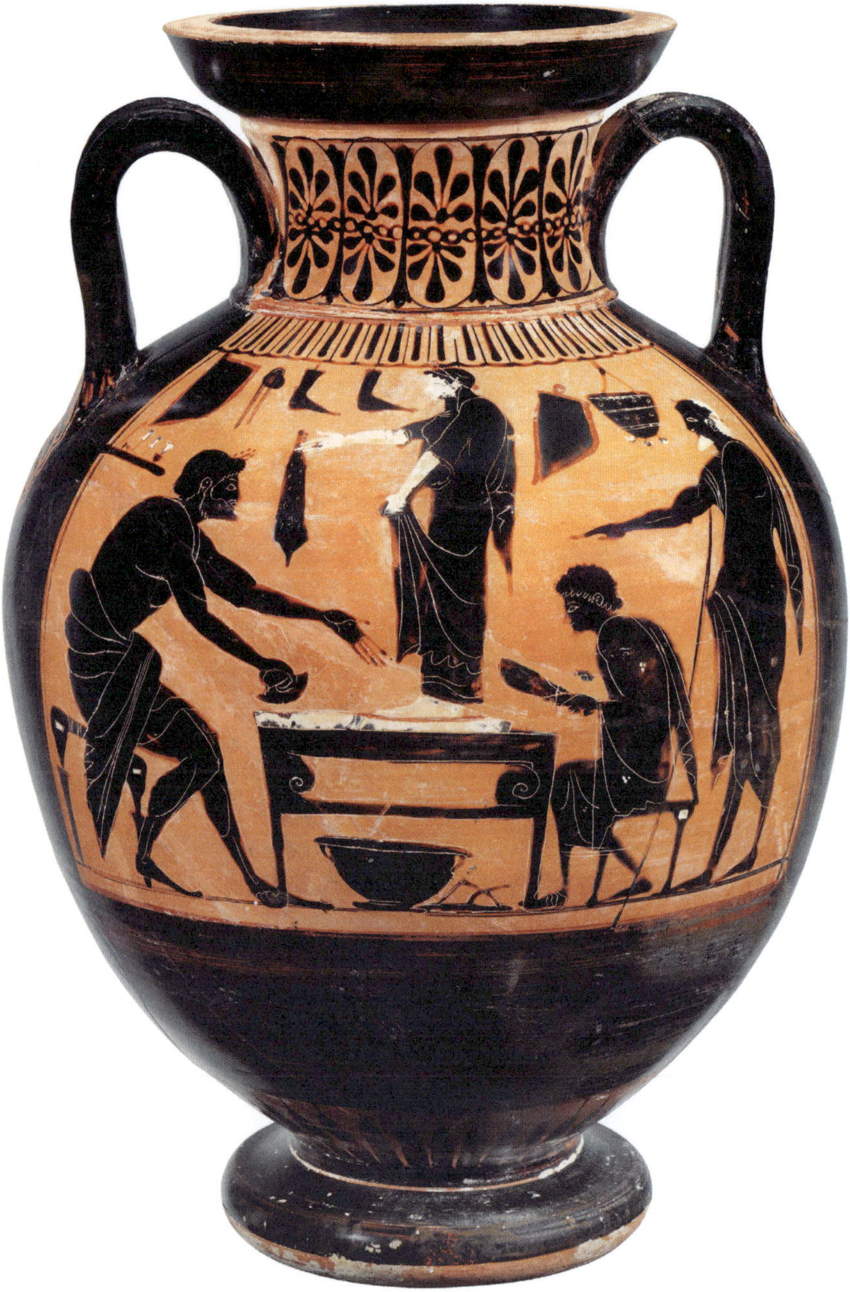

Plousios Painter, *A Shoemaker's Workshop*, *c.* 500–490 BCE, exterior of an amphora.

never acquainted with anyone who took greater care to find out what each of his companions knew' (*Memorabilia* 4.7.1). Socrates makes a vital point that is all too often forgotten by writers: 'We test sculptors not by making a judgment on the basis of their speeches, but on whether they have made beautiful sculptures' (2.6.6.).[17]

With the painter Parrhasius – reputed to have signed his work 'One who lived in luxury' – Socrates discusses how the artist imbues 'likeness' into a figure and visualizes the passions of the soul; we are also introduced for the first time to the idea of the artist's model, or rather models: 'As it isn't easy to come across one single model who is beyond criticism in every detail, you combine the best features of every one of a number of models and so convey the appearance of entirely beautiful bodies.' Parrhasius confirms that this is how he operates. Here, momentously, we have a vision of the studio crowded with models, or potential models – an eclectic mode surely made possible by the presence of 'gangs' of Athenian youths. This modus operandi, and Parrhasius' expertise at depicting the passions, underlie his masterpiece, a personification of the *demos*, the People of Athens. This *demos* expresses more than a dozen contradictory qualities – the boastful and humble, the unjust and compassionate – in one figure at the same time.[18]

With the sculptor Cleiton, Socrates is fascinated by the way his statues appear to move while remaining beautiful: 'That the runners, wrestlers, boxers, and gymnasts that you make, Cleiton, are beautiful I both see and know' (3.10.6). Socrates appears to be surveying actual sculptures and clay models in the workshop rather than remembering what he has seen *in situ* around Athens; the workplace is a showroom that offers a unique mini-retrospective of Cleiton's work.

The most brilliantly interactive visit is to Pistias, maker of the finest breastplates. The level of analysis and connoisseurship here suggests that Xenophon may have had some input to this section (Pistias may have been his own armourer). Pistias is far from being a fire-softened artisan. He is the first example of an artist who gives pithy, epigrammatic replies to questions from visitors; these will become a trademark of Italian Renaissance artists including Donatello and Michelangelo.

The discussion centres on proportion. Socrates asks: 'Why do you sell your breastplates for more, although you do not make them stronger or [from] costlier [materials] than others?' 'Because, Socrates,' Pistias says, 'I make them better proportioned' (3.10.9 10). Socrates then asks if Pistias judges this by size or by weight, and whether a well-proportioned breastplate can fit an ill-proportioned body. Pistias replies that 'what fits is well proportioned'. Socrates adds admiringly that those breastplates that fit 'seem almost not like a thing carried but like an appendage'. He is thinking of breastplates sculpted to imitate the musculature of the torso. Here we sense Socrates and Xenophon examining Pistias' merchandise with expert eye and hand.

Pistias and Socrates would have known the *Canon*, a mid-5th-century treatise on sculpture by Polykleitos (active 460–415 BCE) that established geometrical principles for the making of perfectly proportioned statues of the male nude. Polykleitos orchestrated the most remarkable, and perhaps the first, private view in antiquity. He made two statues simultaneously: one according to his detailed system of mathematical proportions, in which even finger joints were measured, and the other in the most popular current style. He then invited people to visit his workshop and comment on the second statue: 'In accordance with the opinion of each person who came into his workshop, he altered something and changed its form, submitting to the advice of each person. Then he put both statues on display. The one was marvelled at by everyone, and the other was laughed at. Thereupon Polykleitos said, "But the one that you find fault with, you made yourselves; while the one that you marvel at, I made."'[19]

We have already seen the juxtaposition of statues and pictures in different styles on the Foundry Painter's drinking cup; now the workplace has become a schoolroom where patrons and public are educated about art, science and beauty – and about their own stupidity.

***

Every Greek treatise on the visual arts is lost, including one by Apelles. Only one Roman treatise survives: that of Vitruvius on architecture. For information about artists, we are reliant on volumes 33 to 37 of the *Natural History* by Pliny the Elder (23–79 CE). Most of Pliny's knowledge came from lost Greek sources, especially Duris of Samos, who wrote a collection of biographical anecdotes. Pliny shoehorned enthusiastic pen-portraits of artists into his section on minerals, because sculptors used stone and painters' pigments were made from ground stone and plants.

Pliny used the Greek old masters, such as Phidias, Polykleitos and Apelles, as sticks with which to beat his own era. Imperial Roman art was decadent because it was made from costly materials plundered from the earth. Vainglorious portraits and frivolous wall paintings proliferated. He mocked

Emperor Nero's gilding of Lysippos' marble statue of Alexander the Great, which so diminished its value that the gold was later removed (34.63).

While Pliny is attentive to artists' technical innovations, he never mentions visiting a studio and has little conception of them being places worth visiting, except by other artists. Alexander the Great is the exception to prove the rule. When he visits Apelles' studio, he is politely advised to stop talking about painting because the boys grinding pigments are laughing at his ignorance (35.36.85–6). By the same token, Pliny describes a competition between Apelles and Protogenes in the former's studio over who could draw the thinnest line. For Pliny, studios are principally the preserve of experts competing in the same sector, not melting pots for the mingling of different classes, as in Socrates' and Polykleitos' Athens.[20]

Pliny anyway thinks there is nothing worth seeing in the studios of great painters apart from works in progress.[21] This emerges in a rather condensed discussion of fame. Fame, he insists, has only been bestowed on painters of portable panel pictures (tabulae),

> for they did not decorate walls, merely for owners of property, or houses, which would remain in one place and which could not be rescued from a fire. Protogenes was content with a cottage in his little garden; Apelles had no wall frescoes in his house: it was not yet the fashion to colour the whole of the walls. With all these artists their art was for the benefit of cities, and a painter was the common property of the world. (35.37.118)

The best painters are too focused on producing panel pictures for an international clientele to concern themselves with costly makeovers or with material possessions, which would only be a distraction. Pliny's Cynic-style idealization of the unadorned home-studio cottage, and his critiques of luxury, would fuel later debates surrounding studios.

Undoubtedly the Romans' most original contribution to this history is the eroticization and feminization of the studio. The Greeks had introduced the idea of an erotic relationship between the artist and a female model, but the Romans ran with it. Pliny praises the fact that when Apelles fell in love with Alexander the Great's favourite mistress, Campaspe, while painting her nude, Alexander gave her to him (35.36.86–7). Pliny also gives a positive account of Praxiteles' depiction of his mistress Phryne as Aphrodite. But he lambasts the

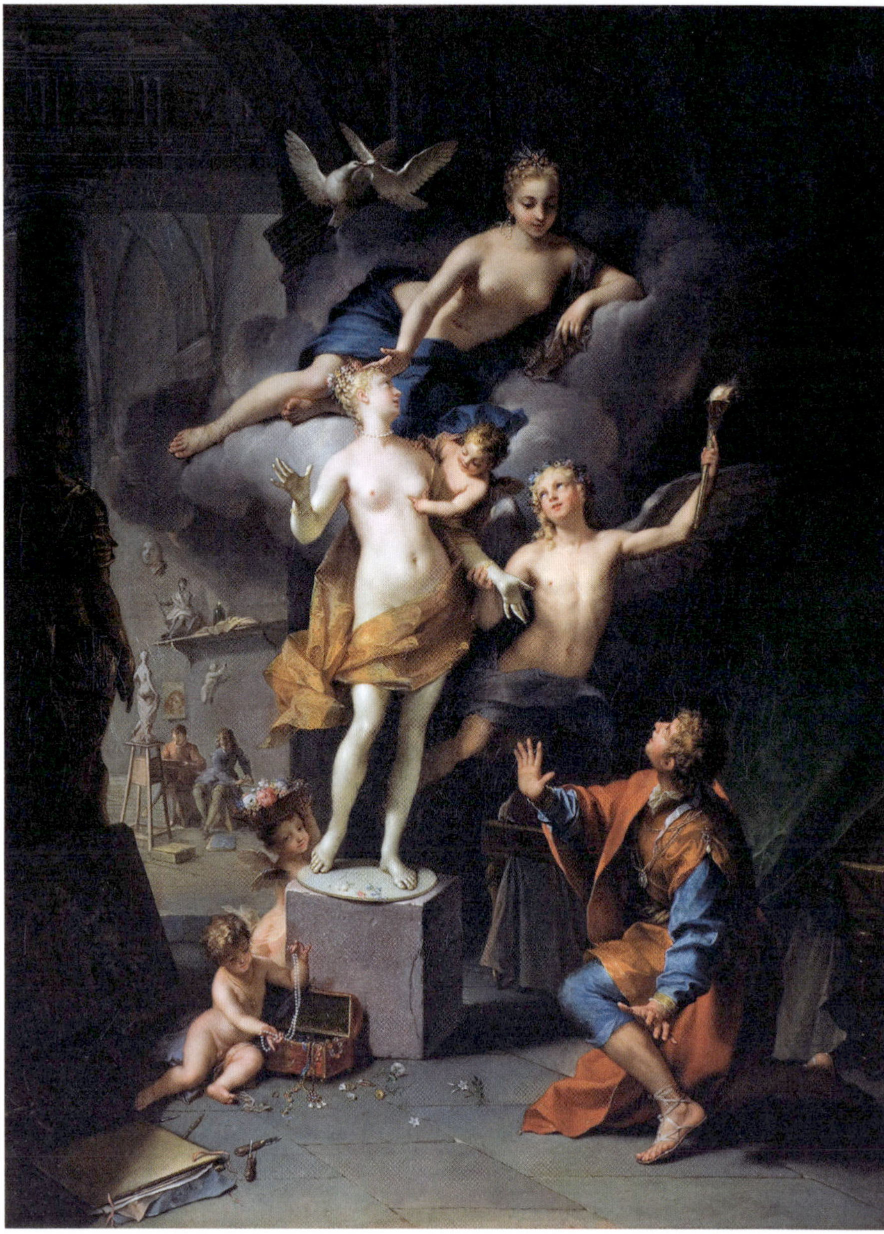

Jean Raoux, *Pygmalion and Galatea*, 1717, oil on canvas.

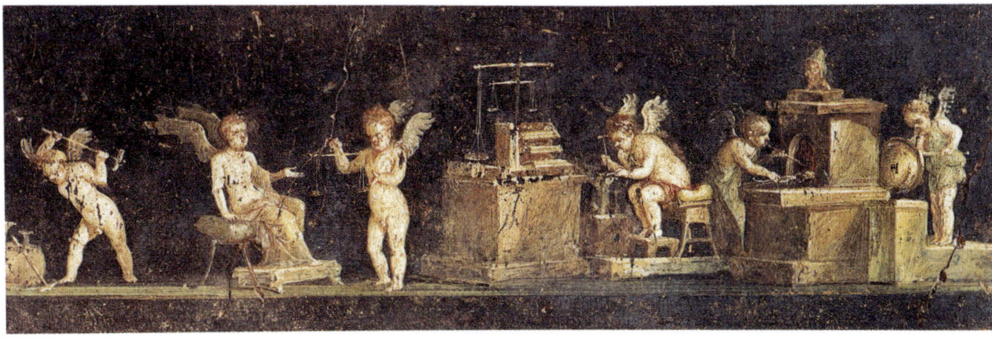

Anonymous, *The Cupid Frieze: Goldsmiths' Workshop*, before 79 CE, wall painting from the triclinium (dining room), House of the Vettii, Pompeii.

Roman painter Arellius for prostituting his art in an outrageous way, 'by always paying court to any woman he happened to fall in love with, and consequently painting goddesses but in the likenesses of his mistresses; and so his pictures included a number of portraits of harlots' (35.37.120). For Pliny, it would seem that erotic excitement in the studio was ideally monogamous – and heterosexual.

In this respect, he was similar to Ovid (43 BCE–17/18 CE), who took these anecdotes into the realm of insanity. Ovid's story of the sculptor Pygmalion is the most popular studio story of all time (*Metamorphoses*, 10.238–97). There are no surviving depictions of the scene from antiquity, but we do have Jean Raoux's exquisitely detailed 18th-century version, created at a time when the story was especially popular because of debates concerning naturalism and the beginnings of consciousness. Pygmalion, disgusted by the ways of the local women, created a beautiful ivory statue of his ideal woman, which he kissed, embraced, dressed, undressed and took to bed. He eventually prayed to Venus to make a live version, but instead Venus made the statue itself come alive, creating a flesh and blood version of Hephaestus' compliant female automata.

Ovid envisages love and desire for perfect beauty as the main drivers for the creation of art, rather than money or religion. The statue is not for sale, though it obviously provides many benefits in kind when it comes to life. Pygmalion's studio is an intensely private space where personal fantasies are gratified (Raoux tries to normalize it by showing students at work in the background). The belief that great art is made with love was first put forward in Plato's *Symposium*, a dialogue in which the guests at a banquet offer their definitions of love. Agathon says that love is king of the gods, the most beautiful and best;

anyone touched by love (i.e. the love of beauty) can become a good poet or artisan (195–7). Some decorative wall paintings in Pompeii give this notion a charming visualization (preceding page). Little winged erotes (Cupids and Psyches) are shown busily working away in the dining room of the House of the Vettii at Pompeii (before 79 CE). This house was owned by two wealthy freedmen, and was being decorated when Vesuvius erupted.[22] Pliny would not have regretted the loss of such frivolous wall paintings.

Erotes, and Cupid's girlfriend Psyche, are shown making textiles, perfumes, wine, bread, garlands and jewelry – some of which the Vettii family probably traded. Six goldsmith erotes strive mightily at forge and furnace, carefully weighing and delicately hammering. Jewelry is itself the prime love token. A chest with three tiers contains precious materials. The idea that craftsmen work for love increases their status by suggesting they are themselves lovable, and more than mere tradespeople; at the same time, they are infantilized so that they appear to pose no serious threat. Erotes work uncomplainingly, never striking or rioting. The Vettii and their friends can eat and drink in peace. They died happy.

Chapter 3

Struggles in the Scriptorium

Waging War on Dead Skin

With the rise of Christianity, a new, more aggressive approach to making emerges in relation to the manuscripts produced in the scriptorium (writing room). This was usually located in or near the library in a monastery or cathedral, though a variety of spaces were used including, in warmer windless weather, cloisters (overleaf).[1] Books were needed for daily prayer and reading, and some were decorated and illustrated.

Saint Isidore of Seville (c. 560–636 CE), archbishop and author of an etymological encyclopedia that remained a standard work for nearly a thousand years, composed militaristic verse admonitions to be placed over the door of his cathedral's scriptorium: 'He who knows how to struggle with dead skin with his pen, let him come here if he wishes, and wage his wars here.'[2] Isidore was adapting the ideas of his fellow Spaniard Prudentius, whose allegorical poem *Psychomachia* (early 5th century) portrayed existence as a conflict between the virtues and the vices for the Christian soul. Isidore's martial metaphor, whereby the workshop is an attritional battle zone, was unknown in antiquity, and variations on it would have a long afterlife in art myth and theory. It catapults scribal work from a position of low-status manual work, as performed by slaves during the Roman Empire, into elite single combat.

Isidore's metaphor alludes to several aspects of the manufacturing process (as well as to Christ becoming 'dead skin' on the cross). Parchment is made from animal skin stretched while wet, then scraped.[3] Hundreds of animals would be killed to make a large codex. To rule lines, holes would be pricked to mark the line ends and a pointed stylus dragged across the page. Scribes' engagement was also potentially violent because they wrote with a sharpened reed or quill pen held at right angles to the page.[4] In the other hand the scribe

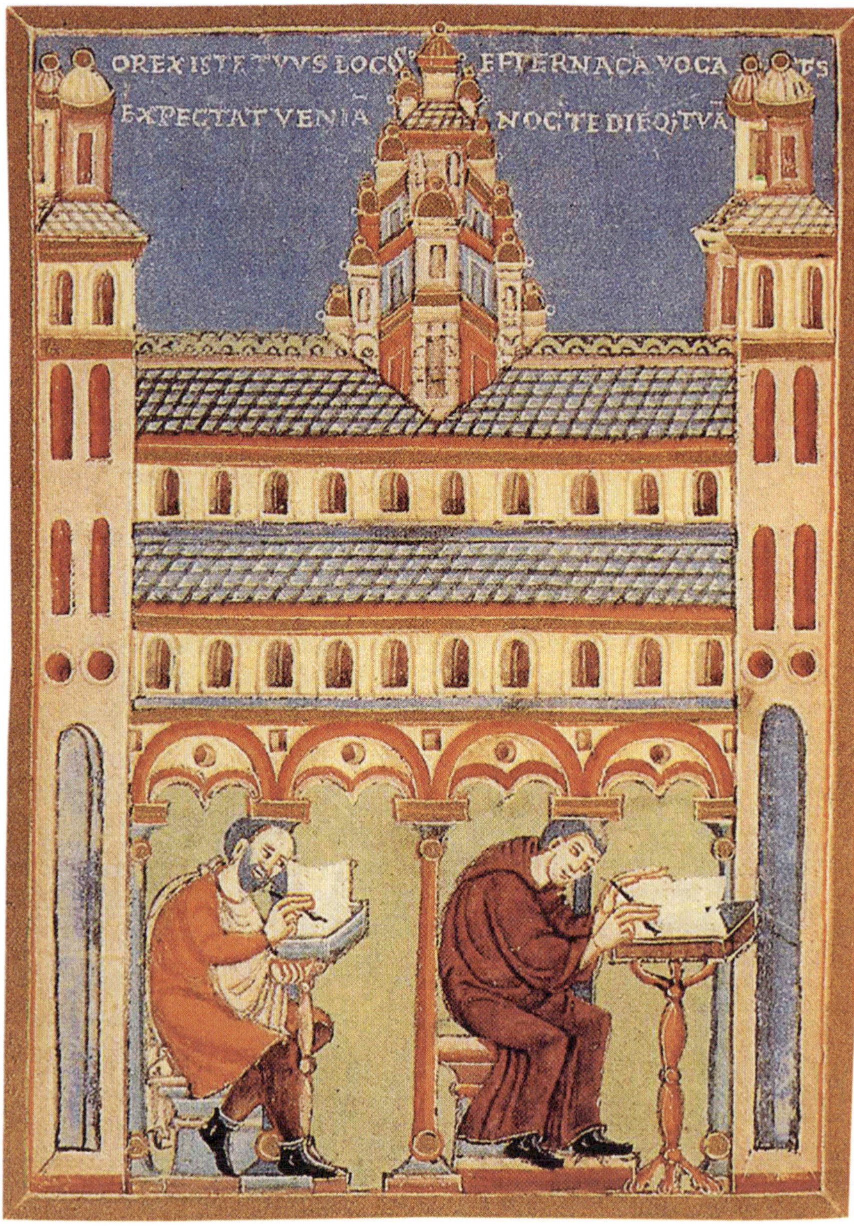

Scribe and Illuminator at Echternach Abbey, Pericope Book, mid-11th century, ink on parchment.

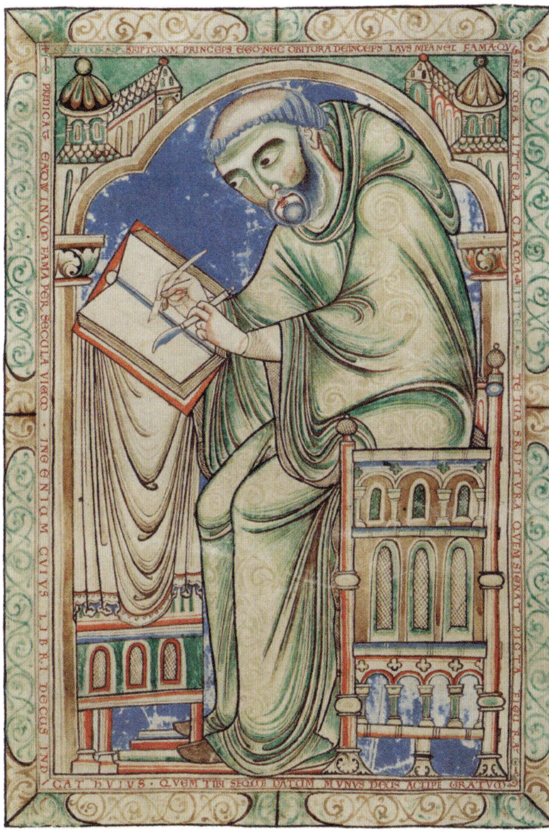

Eadwine at Work, psalter, Christ Church, Canterbury, *c.* 1140, ink on parchment. The inscription reads: 'I am the prince of scribes; neither my fame nor my praise will die quickly.'

held a penknife, for sharpening the quill (which needed to be done perhaps sixty times a day) and keeping the parchment in place.[5]

Scribes as depicted during this period often resemble surgeons, and occasionally even assassins.[6] They worked on one unbound page at a time, but are generally shown working on entire books so that we appreciate the scale of the task. Illuminations were usually added after the writing, with gaps left at the relevant points for initials and the like. Sometimes pre-painted parchment patches were glued in, or whole pages inserted.[7] Similar collaborative procedures can be seen in a rare Mughal colophon portrait showing the court painter Mohammed Daulat and the scribe Abd al-Rahim

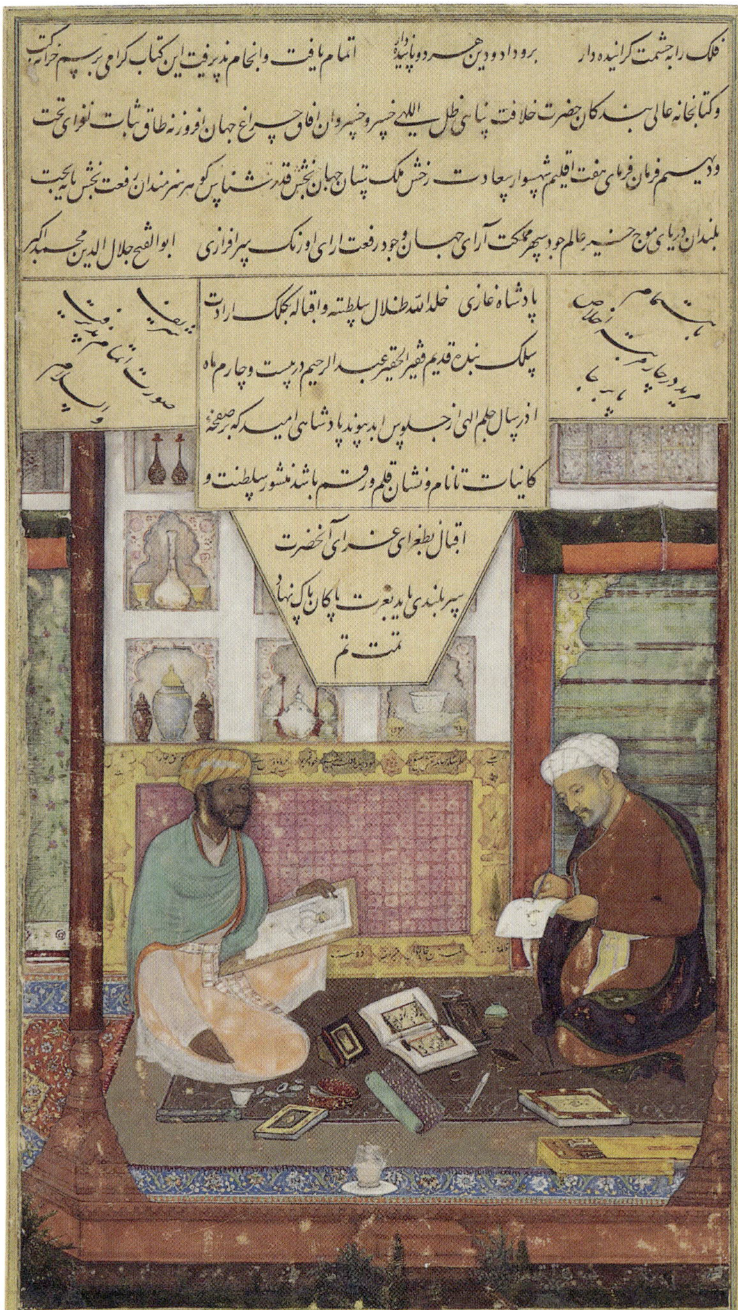

Mohammed Daulat, colophon portrait from the 1595–6
Khamsa of Nizami, ink on parchment.

('Amber-pen') working on a book while sitting on a verandah. It is an idealized idyll, however, with painting materials not easily to hand and the scribe's paper unsupported.

In antiquity, scribes – usually slaves – sat on stools, balancing papyrus scrolls or tablets on boards on their laps. Papyrus sheets were rarely larger than 33 by 23 cm (13 by 9 inches). From around Isidore's time, however, with the advent of deluxe codexes twice that size and the higher social status of monks (many of whom were younger sons of aristocrats), a scribe would typically sit at a sloping stand or desk. This upright position made their work appear even more physical, like fighting on horseback.[8] The scribe's entire arm was involved in moving the hand across the page, prompting a scribal exclamation: 'Three fingers write but the whole body labours.'[9]

Making manuscripts, again like waging war, was better not done in winter. It was a war against frozen fingers as much as against recalcitrant materials. Eye-strain was a perpetual problem for scribes everywhere. In around 1400, a report from the head of the Timurid royal bookmaking workshop noted that Mawlana Ali's eyes had been sore for several days after designing a double-page frontispiece for a *Shahnama*.[10] A later royal calligrapher, Mawlana Sultan-Ali, recommended practising small script during the day and large script in the evening.[11]

Isidore's other verse admonitions prescribed silence, and double whippings on the bare back for lateness. So the scribe's scraping, piercing and scratching of the 'dead skin' was a warning as well as a call to arms: thus will the whips write on your back![12] The main monkish vices would be itemized in the preface to Theophilus' *On Diverse Arts*, an 11th-century treatise produced in a monastic context: 'empty chatter and scurrility, inquisitiveness, drinking, orgies, brawls, fighting, murder, fornication, theft, sacrilege, perjury and other things'.[13]

The most blatantly militant medieval image of a scribe-illuminator is by a lay artist, Hildebert, who trained in or near Cologne, a major centre of art production in Northern Europe (overleaf).[14] It is a marginal illustration at the end of Book 15 of Saint Augustine's *City of God*. Hildebertus sits on a monumental cushioned seat before a lectern-desk held up by the front paws of a lion standing on its hind legs. This can only symbolize the leonine courage and strength required to transcribe Augustine's massive treatise, with its twenty-two books. A codex rests on the lectern next to two inkhorns and extra quills, but Hildebertus, armed with a huge penknife, is otherwise engaged. He is currently doing battle not with 'dead skin', but with live fur. He turns

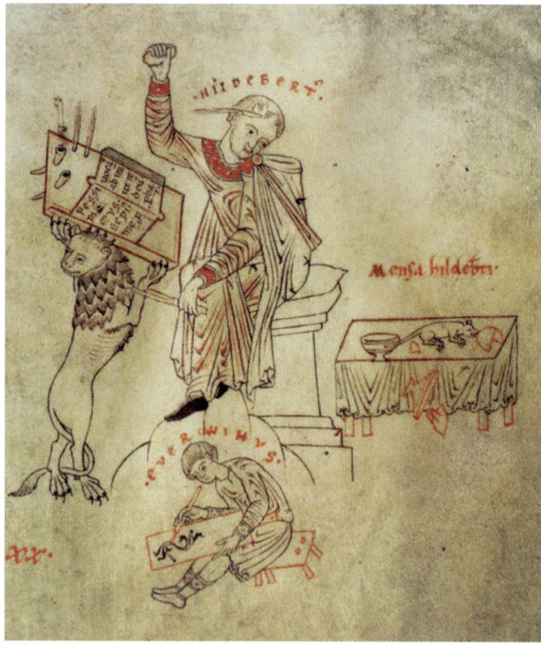

Hildebertus and Everwinus, marginal illustration in Saint Augustine, *City of God*, *c.* 1150, ink on parchment.

left, like Christ on Judgment Day, to throw a sponge at a mouse scampering across his dining table, pretentiously covered with a white cloth. The Latin text in the codex explains: 'Damn you, wretched mouse exasperating me so often!' Mice *were* mortal enemies. They could eat books as well as bread and cheese. The boy apprentice Everwinus, seated like a Roman slave on a very low stool at his master's feet with a board on his lap, does not look up: he is practising a flourish to decorate one of the less prominent initials, perhaps glued in. Everwinus is no mouse, and never wants to be flogged. He appears in another marginal illustration bowing down before Hildebertus as he proffers paint pots. One doubts the indispensable Everwinus was quite so servile.

From the 11th century, with economies improving and populations increasing after the Viking era, paid secular craftsmen from the towns increasingly worked alongside monks and were given board and lodging (though some abbots insisted they be segregated). In *c.* 1135 Master Hugo, a metalworker and illuminator celebrated for making part of the Bury Bible, stayed at St Albans monastery, probably working in the chapter house, which housed the library and scriptorium.[15] A mid-11th-century image shows us a lay illuminator working alongside a monk scribe, as Master Hugo would have done (page 40). The front wall of the monastery opens up like a doll's house. A plan of an ideal monastery, the oldest surviving European architectural drawing, sites the scriptorium above the library; a first-floor location meant better lighting. Seven windows are set between evenly spaced columns, with space for two scribes to sit opposite each other at a desk table. The scriptorium adjoins the apse of the abbey church, with the abbot's house adjacent.

The scriptorium was one of the only places apart from the church buildings that is likely to have had glazed windows, a great luxury. The expense of wax candles and oil lamps made a window seat – ideally facing north or east[16] – absolutely vital. *Game of Thrones* lighting schemes, with forests of flame and clouds of smoke (soot, known as lampblack, was used as pigment for black paint), were unknown – too costly, dirty and dangerous. Mirrors

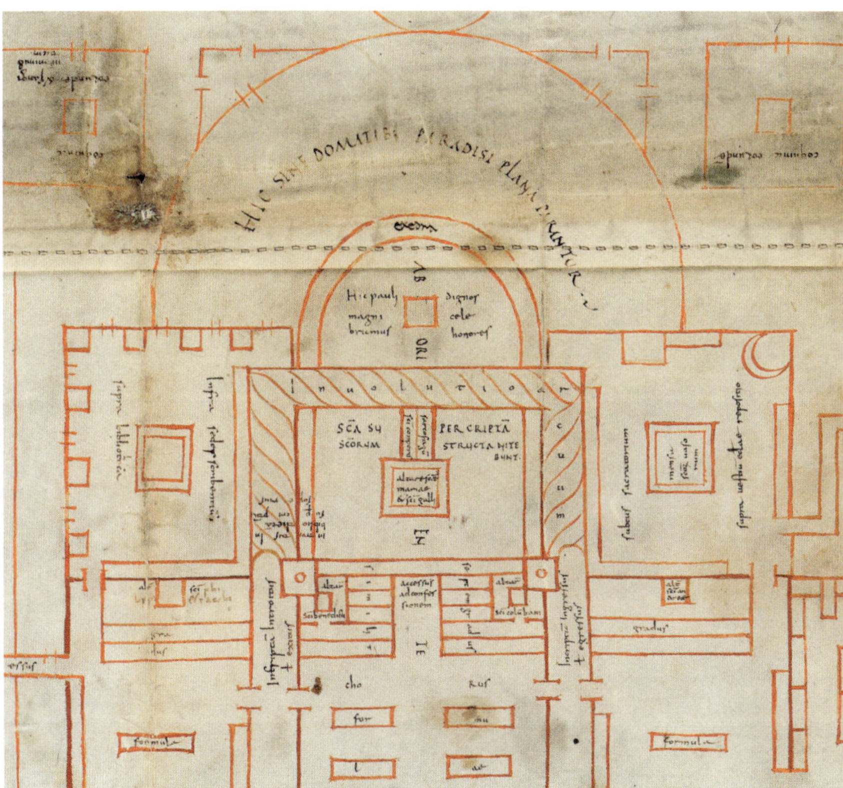

Plan of an Ideal Monastery with 52 Buildings (detail), c. 819 or 827/830, ink on parchment. The scriptorium is located on the upper left, adjoining the apse.

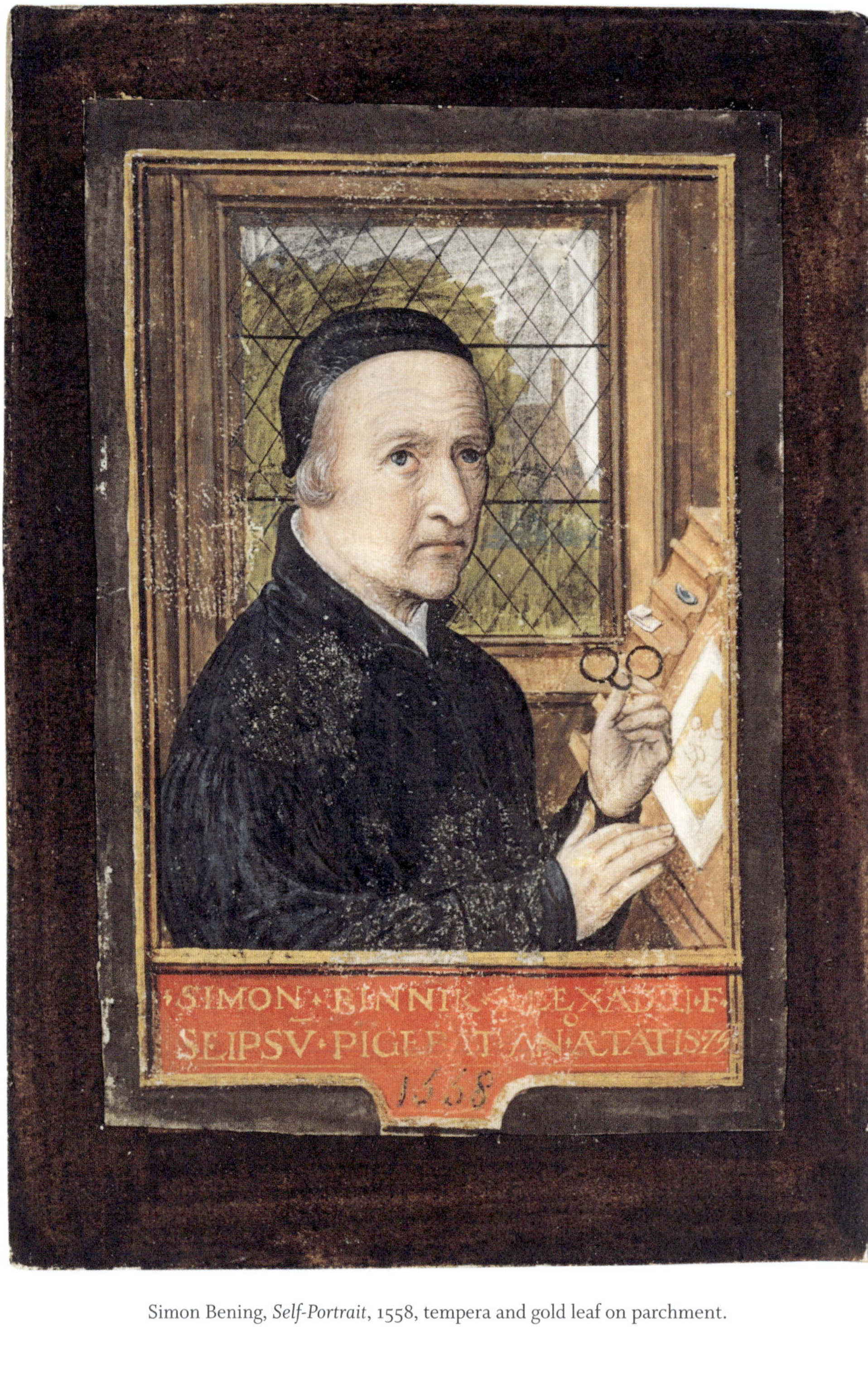

Simon Bening, *Self-Portrait*, 1558, tempera and gold leaf on parchment.

made from polished metal and glass could be used to direct and increase light, and convex mirrors for magnification. Whitewashed walls and polished floors could also help. Scribes and illuminators rarely worked at night. The prevailing wisdom was spelled out in the Gospel of Saint John (9: 4): 'I must work the works of him that sent me, while it is day: the night cometh, when no man can work.'

The great monastic past is evoked in a post-Reformation self-portrait by Simon Bening in Bruges, one of the most successful lay illuminators of his time. He sits at a desk in his well-appointed, wood-panelled studio with a leaded window looking out over a garden. An illumination of the Virgin and Christ Child is in progress, the vellum presumably pinned in place. To his left is a wooden shelving unit, with a shell for pigment and what may be an eraser. The Latin inscription highlights his great age and ancestry: 'Simon Bening, son of Alexander, painted himself in 1558 at the age of 75.' He wears a black jerkin and cap (to stop hair and dandruff falling onto wet paint) and a thoughtfully furrowed brow. His tired – or visionary – eyes now need the assistance of spectacles, an Italian invention of *c.* 1290. Despite the view through the glazed window to an enclosed garden, this is one of the more claustrophobic self-portraits. Hemmed in by the frontal frame/parapet and by his desk, this faithful automaton will paint until his dying day. There is no slacking or Protestant heresy here.

Chapter 4

Pure Gold

Doing God's (or the Devil's) Work

The earliest detailed description of a workshop occurs in a marvellous yet mysterious medieval treatise, Theophilus' *On Diverse Arts* (*c.* 1125). The author claims to be a 'humble priest ... unworthy of the name and profession of monk'; he has written not for personal fame or money, but so that artefacts can be made to 'increase the honour and glory' of God.[1] Grovelling self-deprecation was standard practice for medieval courtiers and authors,[2] but Theophilus – undoubtedly a pseudonym – eats humble pie in all three prefaces to the treatise's sections on painting, glass-making and metalwork. These protestations are understandable, as he is doing something very new in Christian Europe: he is catering for the growing interest in, and respect for, the activities of the artisan.

Throughout the treatise no artisan is named. Theophilus does, however, say that God chose masters by name to build a tabernacle: a reference to Bezalel and his assistant Aholiab, credited in the Old Testament as makers for Moses of the Tabernacle and Ark of the Covenant, as well as of the tent enclosure and priests' equipment and vestments.[3] God filled Bezalel with wisdom, understanding and knowledge (overleaf). It is the only ringing endorsement of an artisan in the Bible (Exodus 31: 1–5).

Theophilus sees himself as heir to this wise, multimedia creating chosen one. His name, usually translated as 'lover of God', is likely to be the less modest 'loved by God'.[4] Bezalel ('protected by God') may have taught apprentices, but Theophilus selflessly shares his knowledge and moral code with everyone via his treatise. Hard manual work, he claims, wards off the sins of sloth. The Rule of Saint Benedict (516 CE) advocated manual work, but few Benedictines now followed this commandment; their lives were devoted to prayer and study. Manual work was subcontracted to lay servants and specialist outsiders.[5] Theophilus is reasserting the value of monk artisans, or of monkish virtues, in a sector increasingly dominated by itinerant goldsmiths from towns. But he acknowledges their world when he gives instructions for making decorated saddles for ladies, polished horns for huntsmen, coloured glass rings and bracelets, embellished furniture and knives, and vessels decorated with animals, birds and flowers.[6] In the second panel of an image from c. 1400 (overleaf), Bezalel and Aholiab are shown at the counter of their shop: they too are now townies.

Some scholars think Theophilus is Roger of Helmarshausen, an outstanding goldsmith and manuscript painter connected to several Benedictine monasteries in the Rhine–Meuse region of north-western Germany, clustering around Cologne, the leading centre for art production – along with Paris – in Western Europe.[7] During the period *c.* 900–1200, benefactions made monasteries the most richly endowed European institutions and major centres for art production. But because of the prefaces' sophistication, written in loosely rhyming verse, it has also been proposed that Theophilus may have been a bishop or abbot who was a practising artisan.[8]

The most extensive art treatise to survive from the Middle Ages, *On Diverse Arts* was the first text in Europe to give reliable detail about a wide range of technical processes. Theophilus explains working methods and how to make materials, tools, mills, kilns and furnaces. He makes the earliest reference in Western Europe to paper (made from linen rags) and describes how to make a church bell, an organ and oil paint. There are a few concessions to folklore: temper tools using the urine of a goat that has been starved for three days, then fed on ferns; or use the urine of a small red-headed boy (3.21). More straightforwardly, use your own earwax, spittle and urine ('This is mixed with lightly sprinkled urine'; 3.33). Excrement is another component. We not only see Theophilus' workshop in our mind's eye, we smell it in our mind's nose.

At the start of the third book, on metalwork, which occupies two-thirds of the text, Theophilus describes how to construct a goldsmiths' workshop. His exclusive concern with this type is both personally motivated and a tribute to the prestige of goldsmiths' work. The medieval church – with a few ascetic exceptions such as Cistercian foundations – was no less enchanted by gold, silver and precious stones than Nero and Imperial Rome. The rarity, expense, purity and lustre of gold and silver were believed to connect these metals to the divine. Psalm 12 epitomizes this value system:

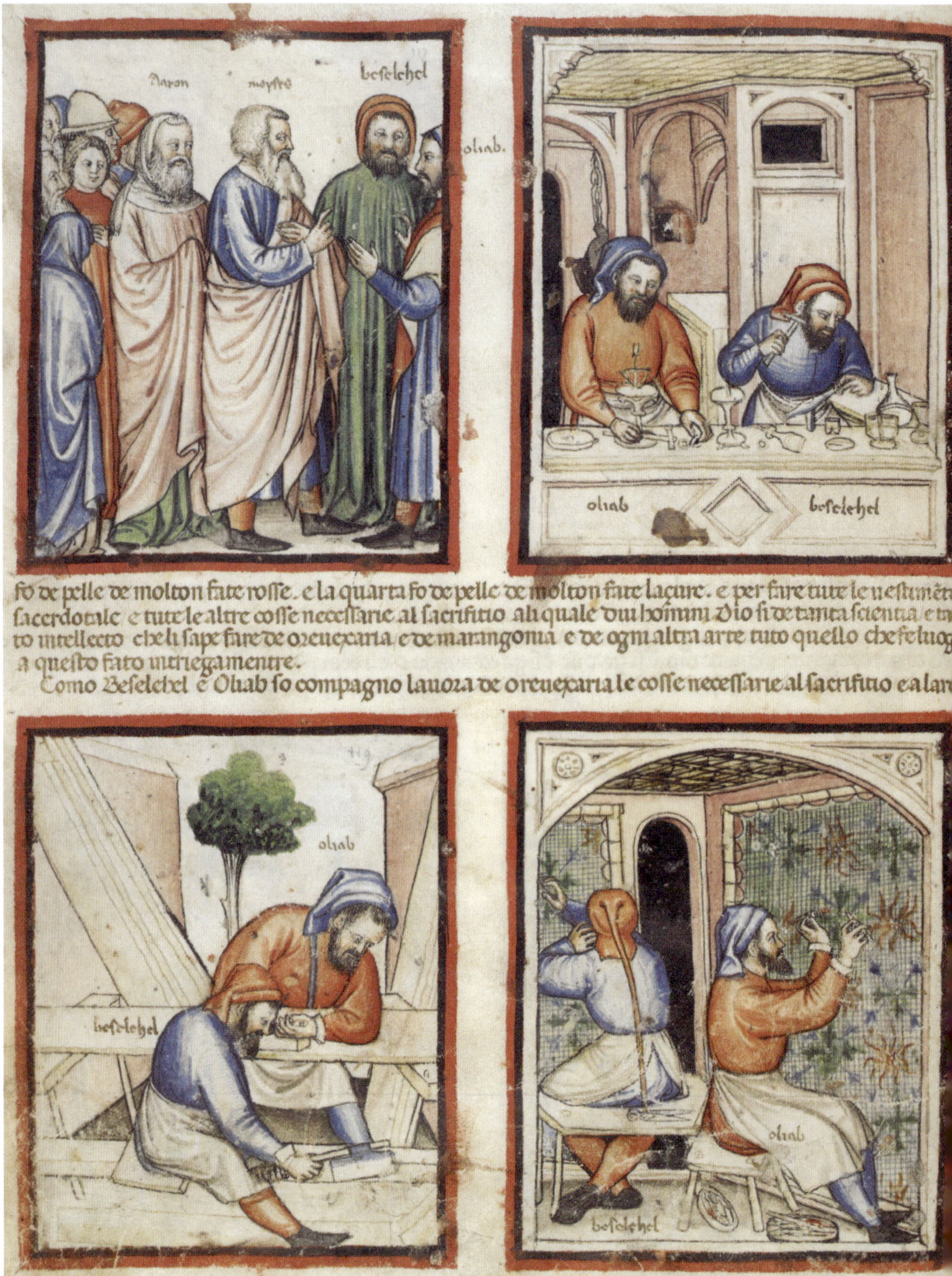

Above and opposite Bezalel and Aholiab in the Paduan Bible Picture Book, *c.* 1400, ink with colour washes on parchment.

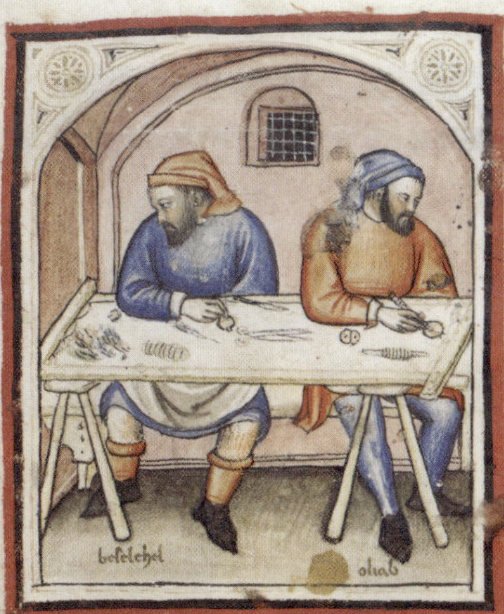

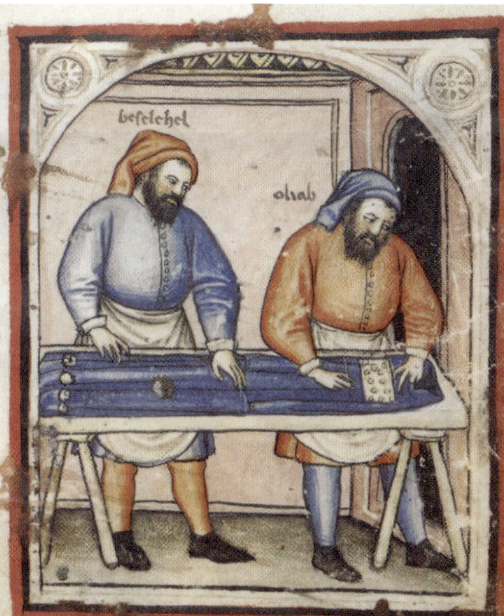

Como Beselehel e Oliab so compagnò lavora el Candeliero de oro.
Como Beselehel e Oliab so compagno lavora le colone del tabernaculo.

123

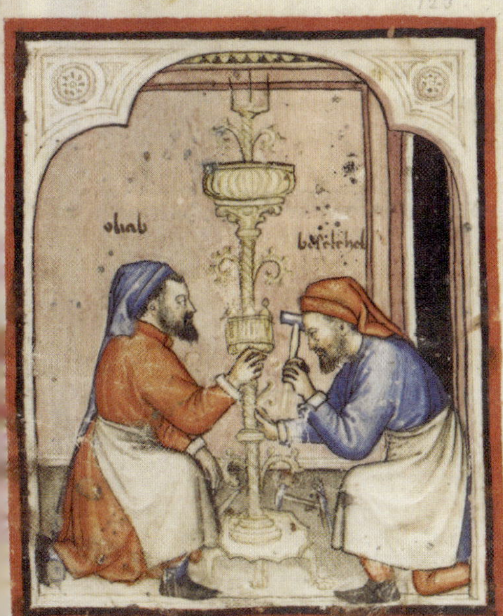

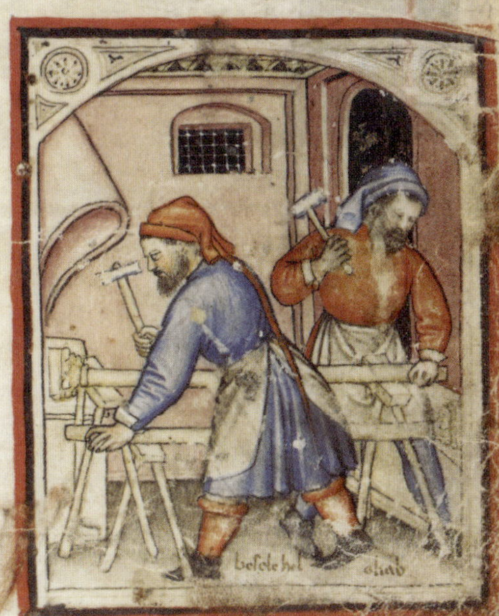

The words of the Lord are unalloyed:
silver refined in a crucible,
gold purified seven times over.[9]

The first patron saints for artisans who were themselves practising artisans were both goldsmiths: the French bishop Saint Eligius (588–660) and the English Benedictine archbishop Saint Dunstan (909–988). A folk song records the occasion when Dunstan 'pull'd the devil by the nose/With red-hot tongs, which made him roar,/That he was heard three miles or more.' The devil stalked goldsmiths in the hope of destroying the economic system. They made dies for coins,[10] tested their purity, lent money, sold jewels and, like Benvenuto Cellini, became Masters of the Mint. 'False coining' was a capital crime.

***

Only the wealthiest monasteries needed or wanted to have deluxe metalwork made on site, so when Theophilus describes the workshop, he is proselytizing for his own calling: 'I. THE CONSTRUCTION OF THE WORKSHOP: Build for yourself a spacious and lofty building, extending in length towards the east. In its southern wall make as many windows as you want and can accommodate, setting them five feet apart. With a wall reaching to the top, separate off a half of the building for the work of making castings and for working copper, tin and lead. Again divide the remaining half in two with a wall – one part for working gold and the other for silver (avoiding adulteration was crucial). The windows should not start higher than one foot from the ground, and should be three feet high and two feet in width.'[11]

Theophilus is nothing if not ambitious. But the few measurements are oddly prescriptive, and there is insufficient detail for a prospective builder. The space is orientated like the nave of a church: the altar was usually at the east end. 'Spacious and lofty' makes it sound even more like a church, though workshops, like kitchens, needed high ceilings to draw up smoke and heat. Although Theophilus does not specify its length, subdividing the space by halving suggests it is modelled on Romanesque church architecture, where proportions were based on the module of a square: for instance, the ground plan of Cologne Cathedral (*c.* 870) is a series of repeated and interlocking squares.[12] The south-facing windows should have shutters; they were at best 'glazed' with parchment or fabric soaked in linseed oil and mounted on wooden stretchers, which gave a reduced, diffused light.

Theophilus gives no information about construction materials or location. The workshop exists in splendid isolation. The Saint Gall plan is more informative. Goldsmiths are in a workshop block at the southern perimeter of the site, flanked by a mill, bakery, brewery and granary.[13] The workshop block houses saddlers, shoemakers, curriers, turners, sword-grinders and shield-makers (abbeys had to provide weapons and manpower for the secular ruler's army). The goldsmiths are in a separate annex with blacksmiths and fullers (who cleaned woollen cloth), possibly because of the fire hazard, toxicity and the smell. The premises in the annex are identical, around 25 feet square, but with separate sleeping accommodation taking up nearly a third of the total space; each unit could accommodate about four workmen comfortably.[14] Poorer artisans generally lived in or over the workshop.

Theophilus' designs for windows and worktables are baffling. It is a mystery why his spacious workshop should have such low windows, one foot above the ground and extending no more than four feet high. It would be a security risk, as well as impractical on cold and windy days: the slightest draught would wreak havoc with gold particles and leaf, which could be about one-thousandth the thickness of a hair. Windows in medieval workshops are usually placed much higher up, with much of the work done while standing. Leon Battista Alberti, in his treatise on architecture (1443–52), recommends placing windows sufficiently high to protect from winds and unhealthy breezes, and to give good illumination: 'light is seen by the face, not by the feet'.[15]

A partial explanation for this oddity is given in the next section, where we learn that the worktables are to be sunk into the ground: 'II. SEATING FOR THE WORKMEN: Then dig a trench in front of a window, a foot and a half from the wall containing the window and at right angles to it, and having a length of three feet and a width of two. This you line round with boards. Let two of these boards project half a foot above the trench, in the centre, opposite the window. On them you fix a table, two feet wide and three long, crosswise over the trench to cover the knees of those sitting in the trench, and so smooth that particles of gold or silver, which fall upon it, can be carefully swept up.'[16] The window is exactly the same size as the tabletop and the trench, in keeping with the love of repeating modules. Theophilus envisaged two people working at each table: in a later description of the chasing of a cruet, we are told that the master has to give his hammer to a boy assistant, 'who should be sitting opposite you' (3.59).

The elaborately constructed table is of Theophilus' design; no artisans are known to have used a sunken table, which would necessitate sitting on the floor, thereby inhibiting movement around the workshop. In pictures, artisans invariably sit on stools, benches or chairs, their feet often resting on a cushioned footstool, podium or mat to protect them from the cold ground – or they stand. A cold posterior was to be avoided at all costs: a popular late medieval subject was Christ on the Cold Stone, in which his tormentors have left him to sit naked on a rock.[17]

Theophilus has adapted elements of pit-houses, a universal archaic building type that was still in use for workshops. *Grubenhäuser*, as they were known in German, were partially sunk into the ground, and the sides of the hole lined with wood.[18] They kept the warmth in and draughts out. Cellar workshops – usually with poor lighting from a small street-level window – were a related, more long-lived type still being used by the goldsmiths who worked in a long row of houses in Cheapside, London (1500s).[19] Leonardo da Vinci drew a design for the 'most useful, lightest and warmest' cellar window.[20] But there is no evidence that tables, as opposed to entire rooms, were ever sunk into the ground. The pit was often covered with a raised wooden floor and the underpart used for storage – but not for dangling legs.

Theophilus' scheme is remarkably similar to the traditional Japanese *horigotatsu* (literally 'ditch – fire – foot-warmer'), a dining table recessed into a hole in the ground with a brazier inserted to keep legs and feet warm. Yet one might doubt sunken tables were ever common in European workshops, and Theophilus says nothing about keeping artisans warm. While the anchored legs of a submerged table could have given extra stability, a sunken table seems very impractical. They are complex to build, restrict movement, are prone to damp and make it difficult to retrieve particles of gold and silver that fall into the trench.[21] The depiction opposite of a goldsmiths' workshop is much later, but it shows the need for mobility; so too does the fresco in the House of the Vettii shown in Chapter 2.

Theophilus' designs for windows and worktables seem to have been guided by religious symbolism. The low sitting position exemplifies the artisan's humility and hard labour, both essential for a monk's penance; it reminds them that a grave awaits, and the pits of either purgatory or hell. The digging of the trench also echoes the back-breaking processes involved in mining for raw materials, which Theophilus mentions later in the same book (3.63); north-western Germany was an important mining region.[22] In the first preface, Theophilus had justified the use of expensive materials: 'Foolish is the merchant who suddenly finds a treasure in a hole in the ground and fails to pick it up and keep it.'[23]

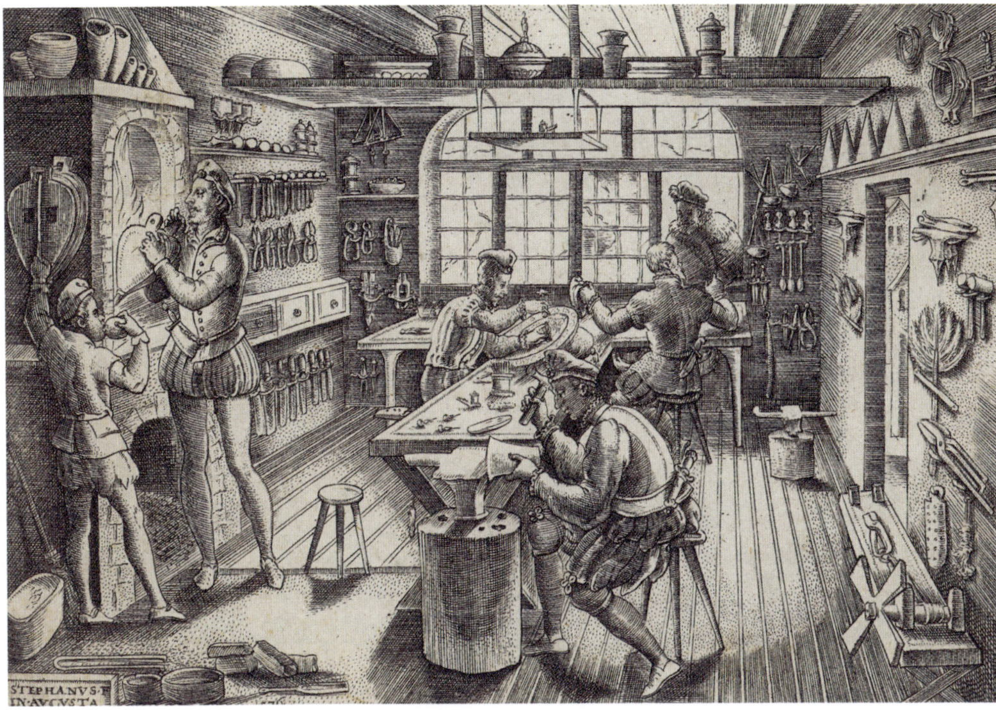

Étienne Delaune, *Goldsmiths' Workshop*, 1576, engraving.

Goldsmiths' shops, and the activities that took place within them, had become key religious symbols. Just as the gleam of the finished product was associated with paradise and the divine, so the manufacturing processes were increasingly associated with purgatory – the zone between heaven and hell where venial sinners (the moderately bad) were purged. Whereas hell-fires destroyed (with the devils being compared to malign blacksmiths, bashing and pincering the mortal sinners as they would dull, rust-prone iron), purgatorial fires, like those of the honest goldsmith, refined.[24] Prayers from the living could speed the sinner's passage through purgatorial fire. So Theophilus asks his readers to reward his 'labour of instruction' by praying for him every time they profit from a book in which pyrotechnics are all-pervasive. He gives instructions on how to build four types of glass kiln and two types of metalworking furnace; there are sixteen references to fire in the first book on painting alone.

***

On Diverse Arts is not your average instruction manual, and there is still debate over its intended readership.[25] The detail can be selective, with some important stages in the making process, and measurements, missing; unlike in a herbal, there are no illustrations.[26] The earliest surviving manuscript copies tended to be bound together in a single volume with theoretical treatises – on architecture (Vitruvius), agriculture, medicine, herbals, lapidaries – and sometimes with moralizing texts, rather than with other art recipe books.[27] The demand for such a sophisticated text is, however, in keeping with a contemporary reappraisal of the so-called mechanical or manual arts, and more inclusive approaches to education.

Hugh of Saint Victor (d. 1141), a German theologian who lived in Paris at the Augustinian abbey of Saint Victor, is a significant figure. The abbey was founded in 1108 on the outskirts of Paris, and its residents were secular clergy, 'canons' who taught and fraternized with the laity. Intellectual breadth was encouraged, and a rational understanding of the natural and man-made world. Paid professional scribes worked in its busy scriptorium; its library was open to the public.[28] Although Hugh regarded the mechanical arts – textiles, carpentry, agriculture, commerce, medicine, and so forth – as inferior to the speculative arts such as geometry, maths and logic, he believed that they helped humankind overcome physical defects and deprivations experienced after the Fall. They should therefore be studied and admired. From want, 'the infinite varieties of painting, weaving, carving, and founding have arisen, so that we look with wonder not at nature alone but at the artificer as well'.[29] In his visionary text *On the Mystical Ark of Noah*, Hugh explains how to construct an ark, which for him becomes a symbol of the christian church, piloted by Christ. Hugh gives precise measurements, colours and materials and envisages a plan being drawn with compass and ruler, then painted. An allegorical image of Contemplation surmounts the ark, portrayed in the likeness of a goldsmith smelting fragments of a broken vessel. The molten gold runs through a pipe into a coin die impressed with the likeness of God.[30] The realism of Theophilus' workshop is leavened by mystical ark-style components.

Richard of Saint Victor (d. 1173), a Scottish emigré follower of Hugh, would use even more dazzling goldsmith metaphors in his own *Mystical Ark*, a guide to various modes of contemplation. Richard compared his own labours writing the text to Bazelel's labours making the Ark of the Covenant from gilded wood: Bazelel learned and practised 'one contemplation after another by much work and practice'. Wise people are not ashamed 'to labour in the gilding of our ark'. Those who mix gold with dross are not welcome in the workshop: 'You have no gold; nor do you know the art of goldsmithing.'[31] Richard then uses a visceral metalwork metaphor to describe the continual formation and reformation of the soul. It is 'beaten work': 'Oh how often it is necessary to place one's gold in the fire and draw it out again … and hammer it with frequent blows on all sides before one forges the angelic form [of the soul] …. What skill and care are needed.'[32]

Saint Isidore had invented the idea of scribal work as a struggle involving destruction as well as creation; now the doctrine of purgatory had made the goldsmith's workshop central to ideas of self-improvement and realization. Centuries later, Michelangelo, who was otherwise as dismissive as Pliny of gold as an art material, would still be adapting such metaphors to secular love poetry. Goldsmiths use fire to refine gold and 'bring it to the highest quality', in the same way that a phoenix comes back to life after being burned: 'If I die by burning, I hope to rise again to a purer life.'[33]

Hugh's and Richard's technical knowledge would have owed much to visits to goldsmiths' workshops in Paris. Goldsmiths congregated on the Grand Pont (Great Bridge), which connected the Grand Châtelet, a fortress with law courts and prison on the north bank of the Seine, to the royal palace on the Ile de la Cité (overleaf). It was the site of one of Saint Eligius' miracles, where he cured a blind man. The abbey of Saint Victor was nearby, on the Left Bank. Jean de Garlande in his *Dictionarius* (1220s) said that 'goldsmiths sit before their furnaces and tables on the Grand Pont and make drinking bowls of gold and silver and brooches and bracelets and pins and buttons, and choose garnets and jasper, sapphires and emeralds for rings'.[34] The bustling Grand Pont, the royal palace and the Petit Pont on the southern side are the setting for an illustrated *Life of Saint Denis*. Here, a goldsmith makes goblets (implausibly using a heavy anvil hammer); his neighbour is a moneylender, offering useful synergies; a huntsman with a falcon passes by; on the Petit Pont, a porter takes a sack of produce into the palace and a woman sells a pair of scissors.

The bridge location ensured plenty of quality footfall, better security and easier control of fires. (For similar reasons, goldsmiths still congregate on the Rialto in Venice and the Ponte Vecchio in Florence.) It did not, alas, afford protection from water: in 1280, flooding destroyed the bridge and it had to be rebuilt.

In 1292 the city authorities undertook a census for King Philip IV to raise taxes for wars.[35] There were eight goldsmiths on the bridge, each recorded as paying tax of between 2 and 12 sous (there were 20 sous to the libre, or pound), with Denisot of Tours the highest earner. A German and an English goldsmith each paid 3 sous, the same amount as their neighbours, an independent

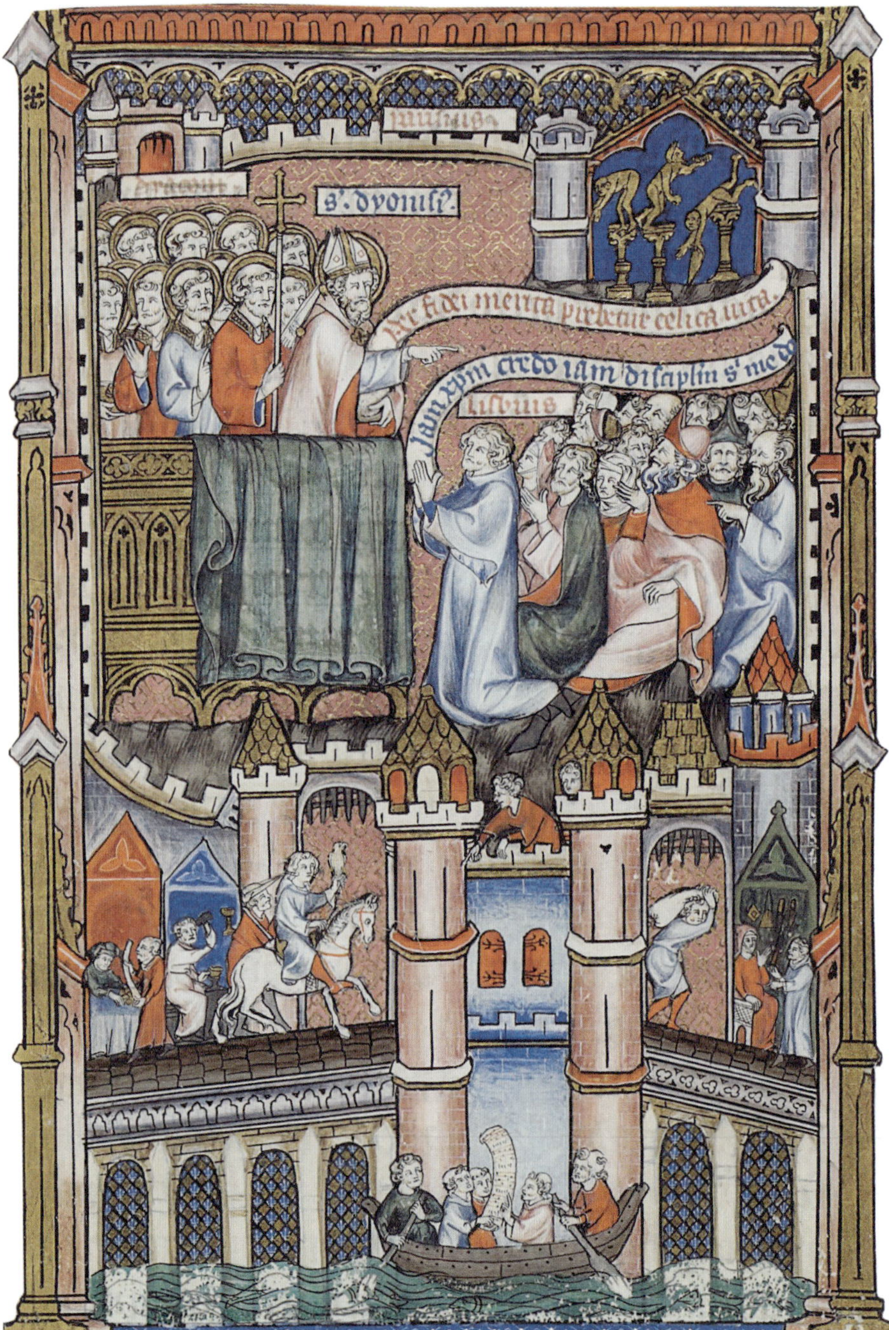

Above *The Conversion of Lisbius* from a *Life of Saint Denis*, 1317, ink and gold leaf on parchment. **Opposite** Detail, workshops on the Grand Pont.

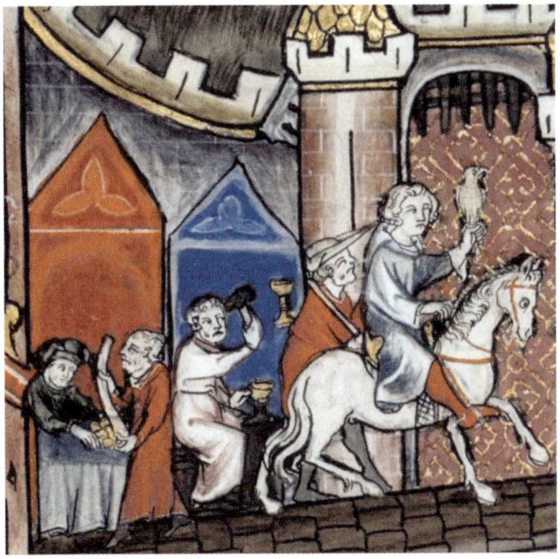

scholar and a gardener. The average for the goldsmiths on the Grand Pont, 5 sous, is on the low side, perhaps because of higher rents or competition. The average for all 116 goldsmiths in the census is around 9 sous. The highest, at 60 sous, is 'la fame Pierre Bouvart' – a widow who had inherited her husband's workshop. The overall figure increases further if we include six goldbeaters making gold and silver wire and gold leaf, usually in books of 300 leaves.[36] They average 19 sous, with a spread of 2 sous to 58 sous. The Grand Pont average would increase enormously in the late 1290s when the king's goldsmith, Guillaume Julien, rented two premises there: a workshop and a boutique showroom, which his sons would inherit.[37]

The Grand Pont set-up has been emulated by modern artists with idealism and irony. In December 1961, Claes Oldenburg opened The Store at his studio in a former shop in New York, retailing his own Pop sculptures. In 1993, Tracey Emin and Sarah Lucas rented a shop in East London for six months, living there and making and selling merchandise on site. Lucas explained: 'The thing is, we're open and whatever we're doing is open. That's the main thing about having a shop, that we're open, which is not the case if you've got a studio .... It's not discriminating about who comes in.'[38] They planned to call it 'Golden Years', but opted for 'The Shop'. Lucas, who had just graduated from Goldsmiths College, might have added that their set-up circumvented dealers.

***

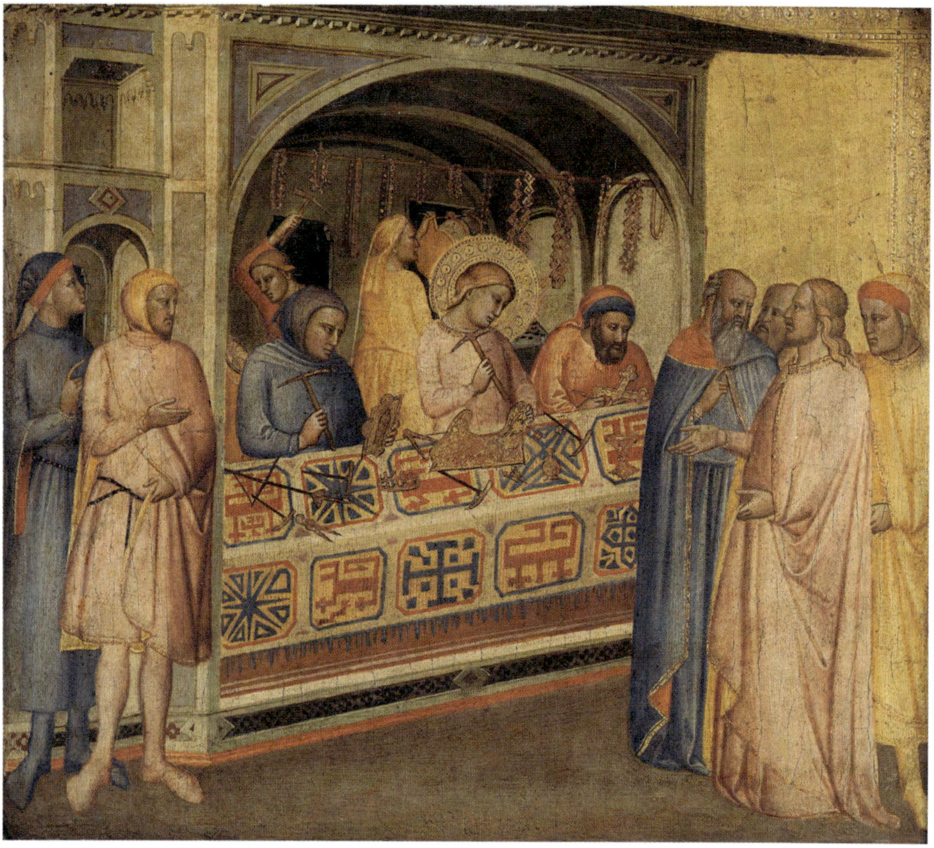

Master of the Madonna della Misericordia, *Saint Eligius in His Goldsmith's Workshop*, c. 1370, tempera and gold leaf on panel.

The most spectacular depiction of a goldsmiths' workshop is a Florentine painting of *c.* 1370 in a monumental style influenced by Giotto.[39] It is one of several narrative scenes adorning the predella (base) of a lost altarpiece dedicated to Saint Eligius, patron saint of the confraternities of goldsmiths and blacksmiths. Confraternities were lay brotherhoods with a religious and charitable purpose. The absence of tongs (symbol of blacksmiths) suggests that the work was most likely commissioned by the goldsmiths; they met at the church of Sant'Eligio, which had been incorporated into the hospital of Santa Maria Nuova.[40] An inventory of 1376 records a new arrival at the church: 'Item, one silver tabernacle of glass with the relics of St Egidio and other relics'. The goldsmith Francesco di Vanni had received the considerable sum of 43 gold florins to make it, though much of that would have paid for materials.[41]

Shops and workshops in towns were usually located on the ground floors of residential buildings and palaces, providing rental income for the owner. There was little zoning.[42] Botticelli had to move out after a cloth-weaver moved in next door, his looms making the building shake. The problem was resolved – according to Vasari – only when Botticelli balanced a rock on the top of his house; any vibrations would have sent it crashing through the weaver's roof.

Nonetheless, some trades clustered together. The prestigious Via Vaccareccia in Florence, connecting the Piazza della Signoria with the New Market, was full of goldsmiths and silk-weavers. A tax list of 1378 suggests goldsmiths were then at their numerical and economic peak.[43] They were among the best paid of skilled artisans in Florence, with many owning land and property. They were allowed to make more products than their counterparts in other Italian cities and use a wider variety of materials, including base metals such as bronze.[44] By the same token, painters often did their own gilding and punchwork decoration, like that on Eligius' halo.[45]

The corner site of Eligius' workshop maximizes light – very necessary because of the overhanging roof. It fits Alberti's description of an ideal shop: 'If at a junction, it should occupy the corner position ... almost the sole concern should be to entice customers to buy the goods on display.' The unrealistic lack of shutters means it is not 'reinforced against the assault of both man and weather'.[46] Many artisans lived on site, usually out of economic necessity rather than choice.[47]

The three goldsmiths working out front, and the variety of products, may reflect the consolidation of production into partnerships that took place in this period.[48] By working in full view the goldsmith advertises his wares, maximizes light and shows customers he is not adulterating or using yellow tin. Florentine goldsmiths were forbidden to work in 'secret places' within the shop, especially at night, to prevent such activity.[49] By the same token, butchers, grocers and oil vendors were prohibited from keeping weights and measures out of sight.[50] Eligius is a youthful golden boy, and his large halo with punchwork decoration makes him a perfect trade sign. The workshop contributes massively to street theatre.

The lack of religious artefacts is striking, but goldsmiths' mainstay was small-scale jewelry.[51] Jean de Garlande's list of goldsmiths' work on the Grand Pont is entirely secular. In Petrus Christus' pin-sharp *A Goldsmith in his Shop* (1449), a single religious artefact (a cylindrical crystal reliquary) is vastly outnumbered by secular products; there are gold coins from Germany, England

and Burgundy on the table. The goldsmith may be Willem van Vleuten of Bruges, who worked for Philip the Good, duke of Burgundy.[52] He weighs a finger ring to price it up, with weights and measures in full view. He looks at his customers with wide, baby eyes. There's no shiftiness, nothing shady, barely a cast shadow. The large convex mirror would have been used for directing light and for magnification.[53] As in the depiction of the Grand Pont, there is a man with a falcon, this time reflected in the mirror. Perfect vision is emphasized, in man and in nature. The goldsmith has an aquiline nose.

In the Eligius panel, religious items (the cross, and a rectangular pax with the standing image of a saint) are far outnumbered by the crown, saddle, flask, goblet and (hanging on the rail) a dazzling array of twelve necklaces, circlets and girdles. This was an accurate reflection of the market.[54] There are no clergy among the six expensively dressed male customers and onlookers. Less plausible are the fine clothes worn by the workers, and their hammering away on a soft Arabic carpet. Moneylenders draped textiles on the counter to show they were open for business, and here it would enhance the display of finished goods rather than cover the worktop.[55]

Eligius hammers nails into a carved wooden saddle overlaid with gold leaf and decorated in the fashionable Arabic style. It was commissioned by King Clothar of the Franks. Eligius made two saddles instead of one from the materials provided, impressing the king with his honesty because he could have filched the surplus gold. He would become a trusted adviser to Clothar and his successor. In the background, gold is being beaten on a rounded 'knob' anvil mounted on a block; hanging bellows are being operated, sending red streaks of flame from the black vents of the furnace; merchandise hangs on a long overhead rail fixed to the walls.

Three types of tool are shown: pump drill, compass and hammer. They are carefully chosen. There are no big hitters – no tongs, punches, chisels or pliers – and all seven hammers are of the same delicate type, a bronze horn-shaped instrument with small circular and pointed ends.[56] More robust hammers can be seen in other images.[57] Jean de Garlande also flags up this type of hammer: 'The skill of the goldsmiths hammers out gold and silver sheets with slender hammers on iron anvils.'[58] Refinement is emphasized: a heavy hammer with a wide, convex end would in fact be needed to make gold sheet. One thinks back to the exquisite hammers used by the erotes in the House of the Vettii. The goldsmiths wield these slender hammers with excessive upswing, doubtless to telegraph gestures and suggest commitment. The handles are twice the usual length of approximately 20 centimetres

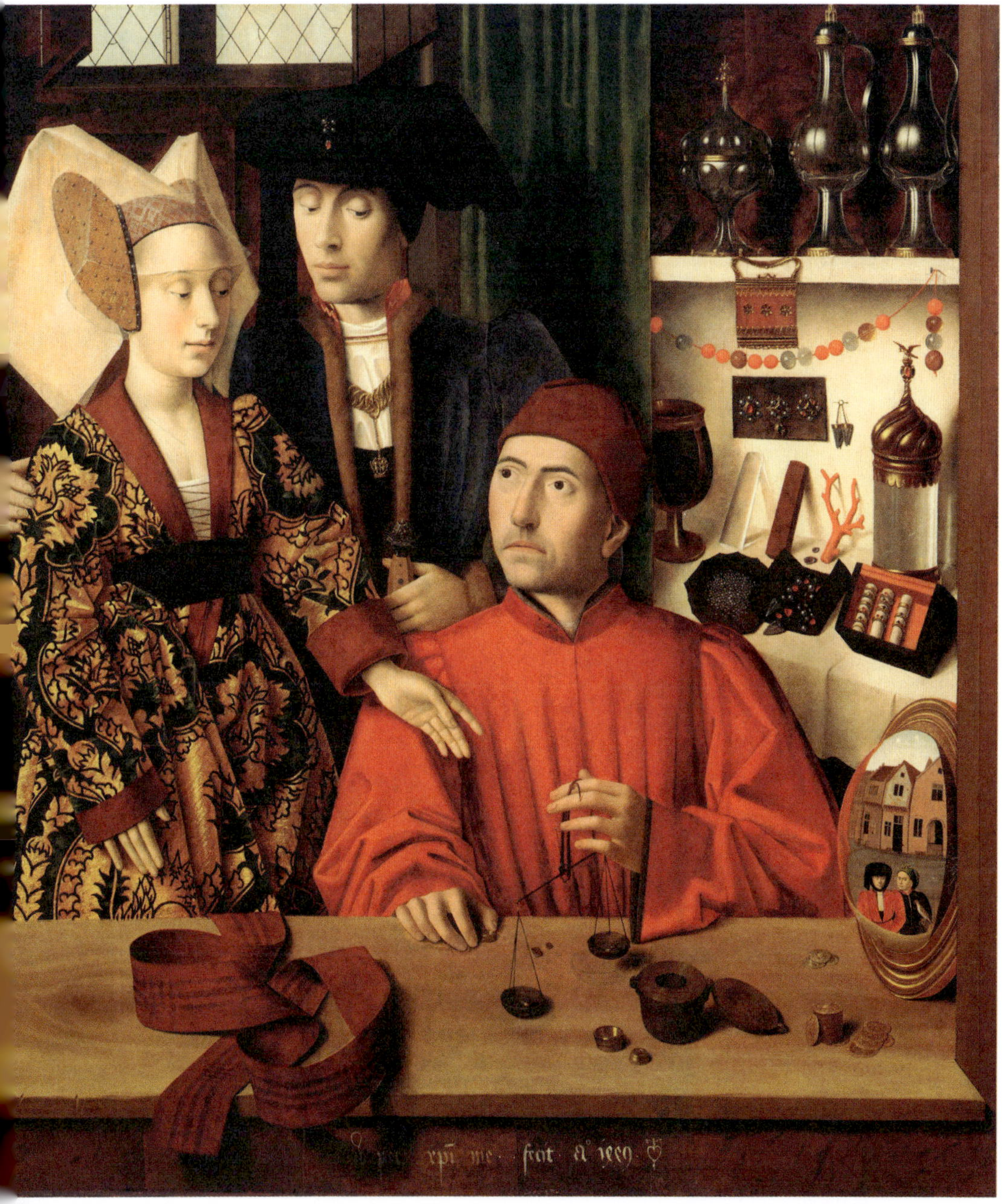

Petrus Christus, *A Goldsmith in his Shop*, 1449, oil on panel.

(8 inches). Pythagoras developed his theories of musical harmony after hearing the sound of hammers pounding in a forge, and we sense a higher musicality here.[59]

Harmonious refinement is further emphasized by the way the tools are arranged on the counter, ready for a right-hander to pick them up, and by their wire-like thinness. This alludes to an aspect of art that was being increasingly emphasized: drawing and measurement. Theophilus only mentions these in passing. More recently, Boccaccio, in the *Decameron* (1348–53), had said that Giotto depicted nature 'with stylus [a metal drawing implement, made by a goldsmith], pen and brush', while his contemporary Petrarch said that all the arts spring from drawing.[60] Cennino Cennini's *Book of Art* (c. 1400) was the first treatise to give drawing star billing: the intellect of aspiring artists, it states, 'will take delight in drawing', and apprentices should be 'drawing all the time, never leaving off, either on holidays or on workdays'.[61] It also instructs the reader how to draw and measure up for a wall painting, using compass, plumb line, and string pulled taut to 'snap' lines into the picture surface.[62]

Here compasses are prominently placed at the front of the counter, and a second set is by the saddle. The top of the pump drill forms an isosceles triangle, and the heads of the swinging hammers could be the arcs of a circle (they echo the circle of Eligius' halo and the building's arch). If the goldsmith's workshop and furnace were a model for the refining processes of purgatory, here their actual tools have been refined and gilded in order to make perfect art possible. The stylus-like slenderness of all the tools simultaneously turns them into lines and into makers of lines. The cult of the drawn line would soon underpin the transformation of the artisan's workshop into the artist's studio. That shift is prophesied here.

Chapter 5

The Velvet Revolution

Cennini's *Studietto*

We left Saint Eligius and co. busily banging away in their open-plan corner shop in broad daylight; they and their merchandise were in full view of passers-by on the crowded street. This was in line with guild regulations that forbade working in 'secret places', especially at night.

The Renaissance concept of the studio involved a literal and symbolic turning away from the street. It required a notional rejection of the strict time management of commerce, of manual labour and religious life. At its most basic level, it meant supplementing the workshop with 'secret places' and creating a mystique around them. This would ultimately give rise to the myth that artists, like alchemists, used secret recipes and methods – the so-called 'secrets' of the old masters.

The Florentine painter Cennino Cennini (*c.* 1360–before 1427) pioneered this development. *The Book of Art* (*c.* 1400) marks the shift from medieval humility (art as a consequence of the Fall; art rooted in reverential copying of a master) to a Renaissance emphasis on the imagination (*fantasia*), social climbing and drawing from nature.[1] In fact, not just *drawing* from nature: Cennini concludes with a stunning account of how to make plaster casts from live heads and bodies (including the artisan's own) using breathing tubes. He judiciously advises mixing the plaster with tepid rosewater if the model is a lord, king, pope or emperor (§238).

Cennini wrote his treatise in Padua, a great university city to the west of Venice on the river Brenta. He married a wealthy local woman, Donna Ricca ('Rich') di Cittadella; they lived with his trumpeter brother in the north-west of the city. Both men were paid *familiares*, retainers at the cultured court of Francesco Novello da Carrara, ruler of the territory. The Paduan Bible Picture

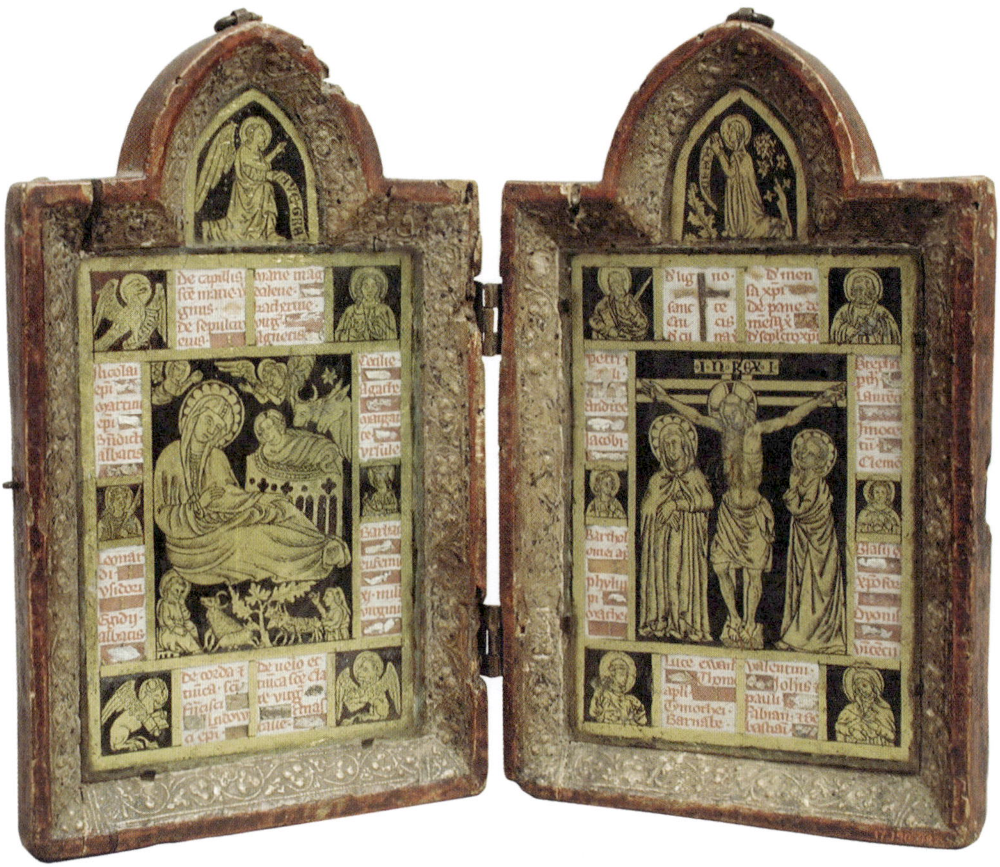

Reliquary diptych with the Nativity and Crucifixion, late 14th century,
Umbria or the Marches, gilded glass, wood and parchment.

Book, with its seven images of Bezalel and Aholiab at work (see pages 50–1), was probably made for Francesco, and suggests an active interest at court in how things were made. Just as with Theophilus' treatise, there is debate about Cennini's target audience because of the sophistication of some passages. There are parallels with a humanist educational treatise written for Francesco Novello's son *c.* 1402–3.[2]

Like Theophilus, Cennini devotes much of his treatise to recipes, tools and methods, mostly relating to drawing and painting. He concludes with brief sections on mosaics, stained glass, decorated cloth, casting in bronze and gesso. He also, surprisingly, explains how to apply paint to female and male faces. Painters, he says, sell make-up to women directly from their workshops, especially in Tuscany. He would rather women just washed in fresh water because cosmetics ruin skin and blacken teeth, making old women hideous (§234). He praises Paduan women for avoiding make-up.

Cennini shows more concern for wellbeing and odours than Theophilus, in keeping with his social aspirations. Don't mix red lake with urine to make a paste, 'because it stinks straight away' (§44); eat and drink moderately and well; don't damage your hands by throwing stones or using crowbars; and don't spend too much time with women, as your hands 'will flutter and flap much more than a leaf does in the wind' (§29). Total dedication is required, so Cennini recommends an apprenticeship of twelve years. Other sources show that training was usually shorter, starting at 12 years old, and could take place in several workshops.[3]

There is a subtle but seismic innovation when, towards the end, Cennini explains how and where to gild and engrave a clear glass panel (§200). The technique known as *verre églomisé*, whereby you scratch and scrape away the gold leaf to create the image and then paint the scraped area, was popular in Padua.[4] The glass panel was the centrepiece of a reliquary, with tiny relics (*relicta* is Latin for 'remains') set into compartments in the frame or, as opposite, fixed to pieces of inscribed parchment. Padua had some of the best Christian relics. The basilica of Saint Anthony had ten reliquaries with the bones, skin, viscera and clothes of the charismatic Franciscan preacher Saint Anthony of Padua.[5] They included his jaw, tongue and finger: perfect emblems for a disputatious university city.

Cennini considers the making of reliquaries the most holy branch of art, necessitating 'great piety' – and great drawing.[6] After a few days, when the glue fixing the gold leaf to the glass has dried, the artisan should take 'a completely flat tablet, lined either with black linen canvas or sendal [a cheap silk]; and get yourself a little study [*studietto*] where no one will bother you at all, and which has just one window covered with [oiled] cloth; and you will put your desk, like a writing desk, at this window in such a position that the window shines above your head as you stand facing it' (§200).

We find something similar in the image of Bezalel and Aholiab, who appear to have stretched parchment tight across their tabletop to create a smooth surface. They are engraving the names of the twelve tribes of Israel onto two onyx stones that will be sewn to the shoulders of a sleeveless garment worn by Jewish priests. Coloured threads and round bells (to be sewn along the bottom) are on the left, and a roll of gold wire on the right. The single high window is covered by a security grille.

By taking the gold leaf into a secret room, Cennini is challenging the spirit, if not the letter, of the rules governing goldsmiths. As a *familiaris*, he is unlikely to have been subject to guild regulations anyway. But to reassure doubters, he emphasizes the holiness of the task and object. Cennini even recommends a neck and chest massage on the previous day, 'to get it all unburdened and soothed of blood and fatigue' (§201).

This is no ordinary job, and the *studietto* no ordinary place. Cennini envisages a room similar to a scholar's study, or *studiolo*, in keeping with his belief that artisans should act as if they were studying theology, philosophy or other liberal arts (§29). *Studioli* were in the vanguard of a vogue for specialized domestic spaces furnished with new types of bespoke furniture.[7] They could be separate rooms at the top of the house, or 'en suite' wooden cubicles inserted into the corner of a large existing room, often a bedchamber. Built-in furniture was raised off the cold floor on a wooden platform. They rarely had a fireplace, which is why depictions of scholars show them well wrapped. No fireplace did at least mean it was less draughty.[8] Cennini's sounds like a small room near the main workshop.

Cennini's father, a notary who drafted deeds and contracts,[9] probably had a *studietto*. The notary Lapo Mazzei (1350–1412) from Prato fondly mentions his 'humble study' in his letters, the only place he could be 'free and alone'. He would go there at night: 'I remain alone at home, in bed and in my study, as happy as the good hermits are on a mountain, and I feel no winds either from left or right.'[10] This means it is mercifully free from draughts and distractions. A luxurious approximation of Cennini's idea of the *studietto* appears in a manuscript copy of Boccaccio's biographical book *On Famous Women* (overleaf). Eirene, one of the few female painters mentioned by Pliny, is alone, with no one to prepare paints. She sits at a canopied desk holding

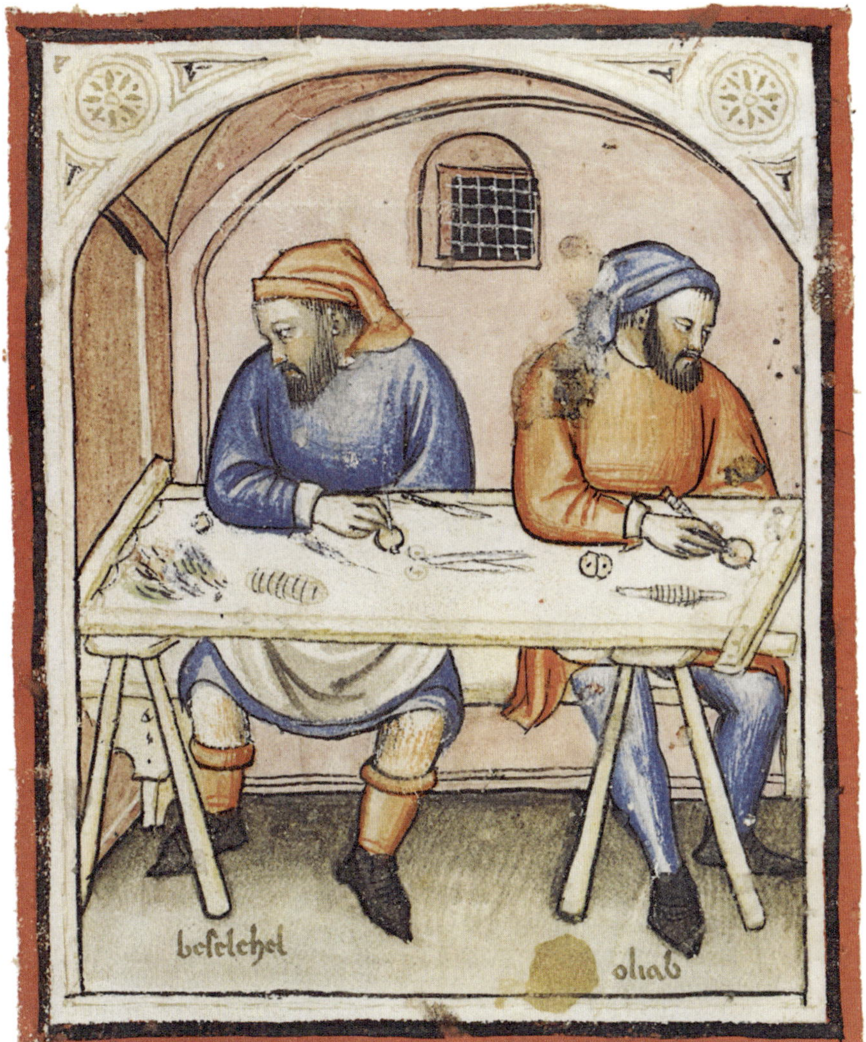

Bezalel and Aholiab in the Paduan Bible Picture Book (detail, fifth scene).

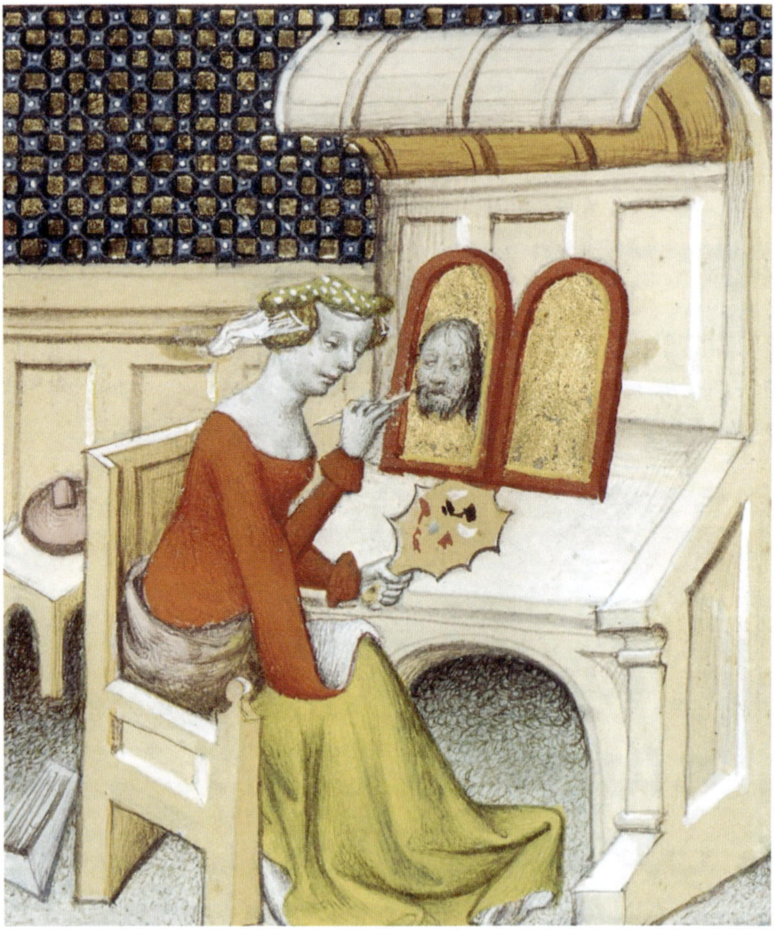

Eirene in her Studietto, *c.* 1400, illumination from Boccaccio's *On Famous Women.*

a palette – the earliest depiction. With princessly piety, she paints a private devotional diptych with the face of Christ on a gilded background.

Padua was home to a great humanist university – or *studio*, as they were called. Although Cennini wrote his treatise in the vernacular rather than in Latin, the preferred language of humanism (which, as the son of a notary, he would have known), the vernacular had been made respectable by the great achievements of Dante, Petrarch and Boccaccio. The last two stressed the importance of solitude and solitary study, and criticized Dante for worldliness and womanizing.[11] At the end of his life (1367–74), Petrarch had lived in Padua and in a nearby country villa at Arquà, thanks to the patronage of

Francesco Novello's father. He had written biographies of famous Christians and pagans who sought solitude (1346); he insisted that scholars, like hermits and monks, require solitude and a secret room for contemplation.[12] When Petrarch mentions monks, he is probably thinking of Cistercians, who lived alone in self-contained, detached cells furnished with bed, chair, table, bookcase and stove, with an attached prayer room, walled garden and a workshop or storage area.[13] Petrarch did not consider himself solitary in his built-in study, however: 'I exert all my mental powers to flee contemporaries and seek out the men of the past,' he wrote. 'I am happier with the dead than the living.'[14]

Cennini alludes to Petrarch when he insists that the visual arts, which require imagination as well as manual dexterity, deserve to be 'enthroned next to theory and crowned with poetry' (§1). Petrarch claimed to have been crowned with laurel leaves on the Capitoline Hill in Rome on 8 April 1341: a distinction accorded to poets and emperors in antiquity, and a practice revived for the Paduan humanist Albertino Mussato by the communal government in Padua in 1315. Petrarch had tried, unsuccessfully, to grow laurel trees in his gardens.

Unlike the low apertures in Theophilus' workshop, the light in Cennini's *studietto* comes from a high window. In the treatise he pays great attention to the fall of light in churches and when drawing, as well as to the depiction of light (§8, 9). Here the high window shuts out the street and draughts as he works with 'great piety' on the reliquary glass. Alberti, in his treatise on architecture, says that 'the window openings of a temple should have modest dimensions and should be placed high up, where they have a view of nothing but the sky, which will not divert the minds of celebrant or supplicant from divine matters'.[15] Cennini appears to want to approximate the atmosphere of the reliquary's probable destination – a private chapel, church treasury or sacristy.

***

Something astonishing happens when Cennini takes us into the *studietto* to engrave or draw on glass. The glass is laid on the cloth-covered tablet and, while 'invoking God's name', the artisan takes a very fine engraving needle: 'Begin drawing the figure that you want to do lightly with this needle. And make sure that the first drawing does not show very much because you can never rub it out. And so do it lightly until you have firmed up your drawing. Then start working as if you were using a quill pen ... and the work should not be done in a hurry but rather with great enjoyment and pleasure' (§201).

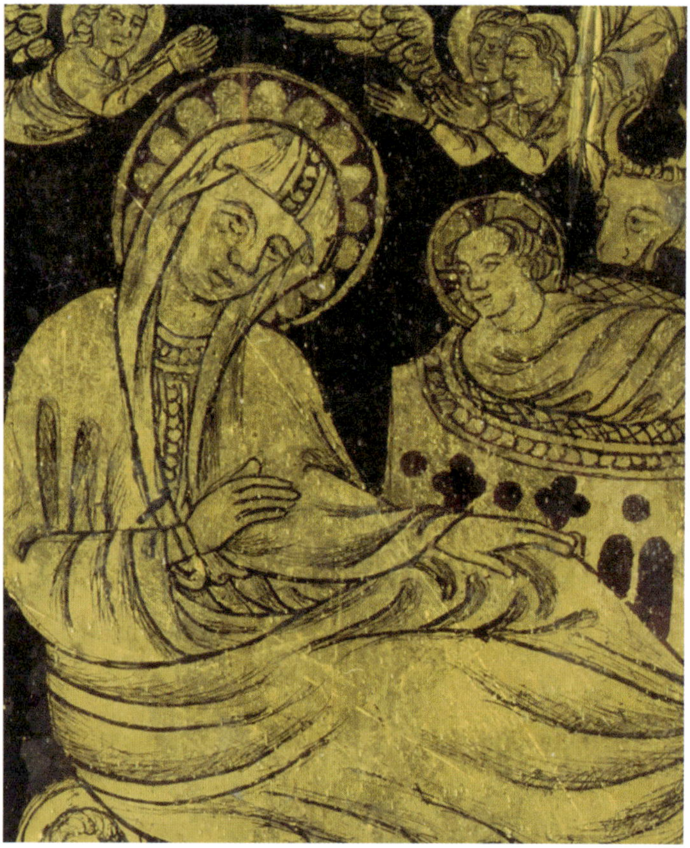

Reliquary diptych with the Nativity and Crucifixion (detail).

Cennini appears to be joyfully improvising and working freehand rather than copying a prepared template. In some respects, this contrasts with his earlier advice. He had taken great pains to insist that apprentices should learn by copying the work of famous masters in local churches, carrying their paper in a folio-sized pouch made of pasteboard or thin wood (§29). He explains how to make tracing paper and how to 'copy a head, or a figure, or a half figure, as you find it attractive, by the hand of the great masters' (§23).[16] The 'great masters' meant Giotto and his school, to which Cennini belonged. He had been taught by Agnolo Gaddi, who was taught by his own father, Taddeo Gaddi, a pupil of Giotto. This 'family' connection gave Cennini great kudos in Padua, where Giotto had painted three major fresco cycles.[17] Like Petrarch, Cennini appears happier communing with the dead than the living.

In the secluded *studietto*, however, Cennini makes his design from scratch by scratching, and takes pleasure in the unhurried process of perfecting it. He doesn't wage war on dead skin, ruthlessly going in for the kill; instead, like a masseur, he lightly caresses living glass as if probing it until he finds the sweet spots. We can see this in action in a detail of the glass reliquary opposite, where there is a revision to the Virgin's right hand. The fingers and thumb have been shortened in relation to the lightly etched preliminary 'sketch', and the thumb moved. This might be construed as an error caused by excessive womanizing. But the artisan, as in other glass reliquary diptychs,[18] seems to exploit and appreciate the vibrancy generated by 'sketchy' mark-making and shading. The artisan's hand is permitted to 'flutter far more than leaves do in the wind', as is appropriate only in the presence of the Virgin Mary.

The creative freedom Cennini experiences in his *studietto* is in keeping with other things he says. At various points he opens the door to imagination, contemplation and relaxation. Having insisted the apprentice study the great masters, he adds that with imagination (*fantasia*) this will be the springboard for developing his own style (§27); *fantasia* and manual dexterity will allow him to 'find invisible things hiding in the shadow of ones in nature', and enable him to 'compose a figure standing upright, sitting, half-man, half-horse as he pleases' (§1). This last passage is adapted from Horace's *Art of Poetry* – where it is a scathing criticism of the unfettered imagination. Cennini's blatant contradiction of Horace is in line with the teaching of the humanist Gasparino Barzizza, who opened a school in Padua in 1407. He believed that imitation of antique sources should not take the form of direct copying but should involve addition, subtraction and inversion.[19] Cennini's *studietto* is an inversion of the workshop – almost to the point of perversion.

***

Cennini's radicalism is most glaring in his attitude to time, which marks a turning point in the history of art. He is the first writer on art to treat timekeeping and duration as a central issue, as well as the first to talk about trial and error.[20]

In traditional recipe books, the standard way of referring to time is as follows (and I quote from Cennini): let paper soaked in glue dry 'for two or three days and it will be good tracing paper'. But no one had mentioned the following, which I paraphrase:

HISTORIC TIME: I was trained for twelve years by Agnolo Gaddi; Gaddi's father, Taddeo, was Giotto's follower for twenty-four years.

STAGES OF TRAINING: Apprentices, after spending a year using a stylus, should start using a pen.

MEALTIME: Eat 'at least twice a day ... digestible and wholesome dishes and light wines'.

OPEN-ENDED TIME: Grind this black pigment 'for the space of half an hour, or an hour, or as long as you like ... if you were to work it up for a year it would be so much blacker and a better colour'.

PERSONALIZED TIME: Consider 'in your own mind how much [fresco] work you can do in a day'.

CALENDAR TIME: Practise wall painting for six years while 'drawing all the time, never leaving off, either on holy days or on workdays'.

ME TIME: Have a massage the day before doing important work.

LEISURE TIME: No messing with women or throwing stones.

Cennini may have been looking at Pliny, who gives some dates, but his intensified feeling for time and timekeeping stemmed from more recent developments. During the 14th century, public work bells were introduced in towns, competing with church bells (Cennini says work/draw on holy days!). Technological developments led to the installation of mechanical clocks in clock towers.[21] The corollary was an increase in regulation, and in disputes over working hours and meal breaks (Cennini proposes at least two meal breaks).[22] In 1344, Ubertino da Carrara installed a clock with a dial in the tower of his palace in Padua. Made by Jacopo Dondi dall'Orologio ('of the Clock'),[23] it struck the hours from one to twenty-four and showed the days, months and phases of the moon. Jacopo's son Giovanni Dondi dall'Orologio became the most celebrated medieval clockmaker. He designed and built the Astrarium (1348–64), an astronomical clock that showed the hours and years and the planets. It also had dials for the religious, legal and civil calendars.

No one was more obsessively and creatively time-conscious than Petrarch, who marvelled at the Astrarium.[24] He provided more precise information about his own life, including dates and hours, than anyone previously. He subdivided his life into four-year periods and dated his letters: 'Padua, on the thirteenth of January, from the bed of my pains, in the eleventh hour of the night' (he would have just heard the bell-tower clock striking twenty-three times; it was 1368).[25] In later life, Petrarch arranged all 366 – a leap year's worth – of his love poems addressed to Laura in chronological order, carefully noting the years wasted in unhappy longing ('the eleventh year ...'). He devised a punishing schedule: six hours' sleep, two hours for necessities, sixteen for work. Emulating Emperor Augustus, he would read or write, or dictate to a scribe, or be read to, while being shaved or having his hair cut; he even did some of these things while eating and horse-riding.[26]

In his workshop and *studietto*, Cennini both embraces and resists measured time – and therein lies his claim to be a liberal artist 'enthroned next to theory and crowned with poetry'. His insouciant manipulation of time emerges during a discussion of how to inscribe a panel with charcoal and ink to make an underdrawing (§122). The charcoal should be 'tied to a little cane or stick so that you stand back from the figure, which is very helpful to you during composition'; those lines that 'do not turn out well' should be erased with the plume of a feather. When the drawing is finished, 'leave it be for a few days, going back to it now and then to have another look and remedy the parts that still need it'; this is recommended 'if it is on a very prestigious panel painting, which you expect to bring you profit and admiration'. If all else fails, 'you may copy and examine things done by other good masters'. Cennini's stop-start, trial-and-error working method slows down the production process, removing it from a rigidly commercial or monastic time frame. The work 'should not be done in a hurry but rather with great enjoyment and pleasure' (§2).

The medieval ideal was to plan everything in advance. Geoffrey of Vinsauf compared the poet to an architect whose 'impetuous hand does not leap into action .... Let the inner compasses of the mind lay out the entire range of the material.'[27] Cennini's approach is more like that of the Roman orator Quintilian, who recommended putting a speech aside until the ardour of creation had subsided; then you could read it again dispassionately, like a stranger – and revise it.[28] But Quintilian only appears to envisage one revision. Murasaki Shikibu's *The Tale of Genji* (c. 1000 CE) offers an interesting parallel. The Japanese emperor loves painting above all else, and is attracted

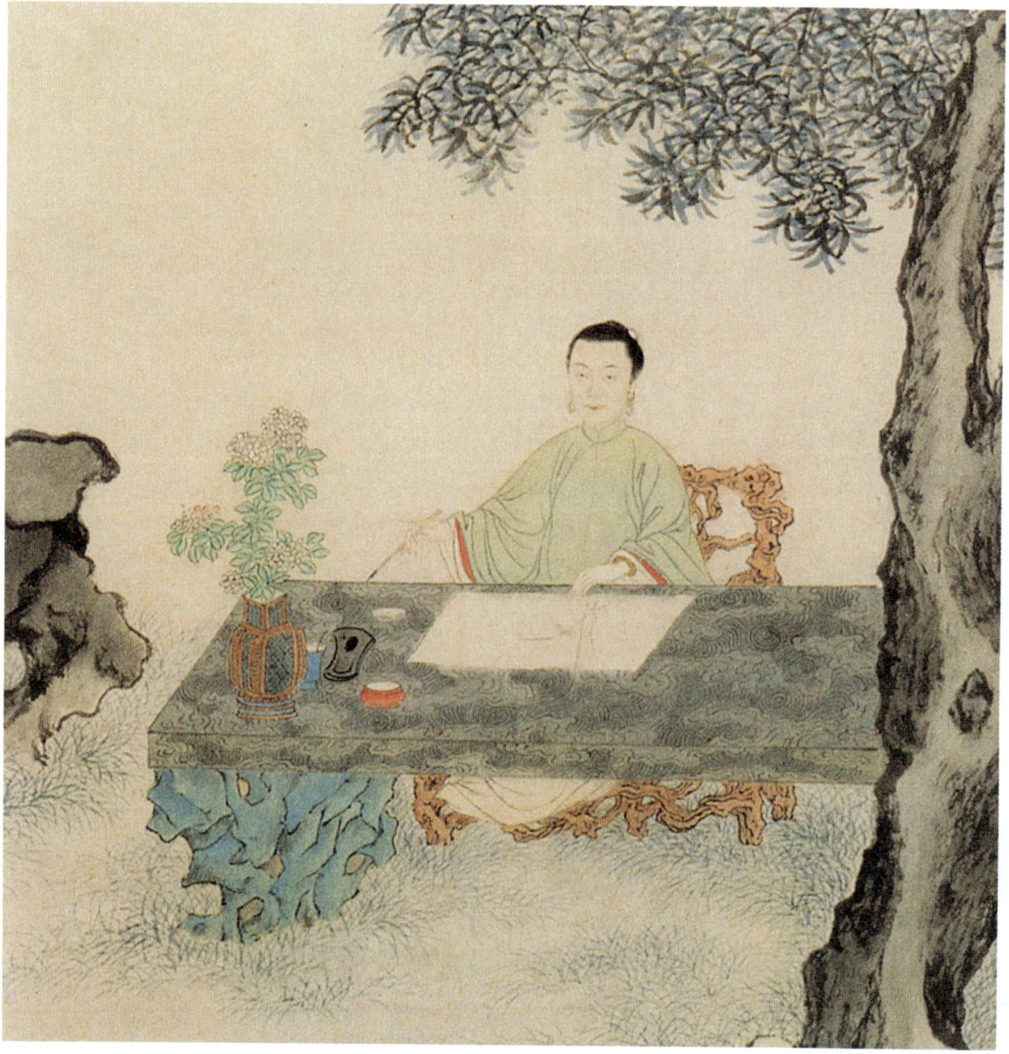

Pan Gongshou, *Wang Yuyan Sketching Orchids* (detail), 1790, ink and watercolour on paper.

to women who paint; one 'lovely lady ... reclining sweetly beside him, would pause gravely to consider the next stroke of her brush'.[29] The thoughtful pause of an elite lady artist is best represented in Pan Gongshou's *Wang Yuyan Sketching Orchids*,[30] commissioned by Wang's scholar husband after her death. She is fancifully shown, as so often in Chinese art, out of doors; but it is unclear whether this is thinking time, or time taken to recharge the brush with ink. By the same token, in Chinese ink painting no second thoughts are possible.

Cennini is the European founding father of slow art. His most open-ended timing – best grind the black pigment for a year – seems both provocatively casual and extreme, as if it were the Laura of colours, to be perpetually obsessed over. It is striking that Bezalel and Aholiab in the Paduan Picture Book both look away as they do their engraving, as if they have just read Cennini's treatise and are daydreaming. Or maybe Bezalel *is* Cennini.

The cult of slow art would be perfected by Leonardo in ducal Milan in the 1490s, working intensively on the *Last Supper* for a day, then spending three or four days 'without touching the work, yet each day he would spend several hours examining it and criticising the figures to himself'.[31] The *Mona Lisa*, started in 1503, may have been completed only in 1517. Such erratic behaviour put the artist in a similar bracket to the gentleman aristocrat who does not work for a living. Relevant too is the Emperor Augustus' motto *Festina lente* ('Make haste slowly'), and his favourite saying: 'That which has been done well has been done quickly enough.'[32] But taking time is always a luxury.

Various stop-start stratagems have been developed by later oil painters, almost of necessity. Oil paint – unlike the traditional tempera, where pigment was mixed with egg yolk – takes a long time to dry, sometimes weeks and months, and is built up in layers. Theophilus considered oils excessively time-consuming and tedious, suitable only for portable artefacts that could be dried in the sun. Dürer preferred the speed of engraving. The use of oils was perfected and popularized in the Netherlands in the 15th century, and then spread to Venice and the rest of Italy. With Titian, drying time became a beneficial cooling-off time. In old age he supposedly 'turned the picture to the wall and left it for months without looking at it, until he returned ... and stared critically at it, as if it were a mortal enemy .... If he found something which displeased him he went to work like a surgeon .... Thus, by repeated revisions he brought his pictures to a high state of perfection and while one was drying he worked on another.'[33] The French landscape painter Camille Corot called this, portentously, the 'incubation period'.[34]

Marcel Duchamp became a Leonardesque master of procrastination. His wife, Teeny, explained how he went about crafting his final multimedia masterpiece, *Etant donnés* (1946–66): 'He worked on it all the time, but never like a workman. He would work for fifteen or twenty minutes and then he'd smoke a cigar or study chess problems or do something else.'[35] Another variant on this same theme is modern portrait painters demanding endless sittings – Cézanne (115 sittings for his dealer Ambroise Vollard), Whistler (over 70 for Cicely Alexander), Giacometti (weeks and months) and Freud (6 to 9 months). 'Uncommercial' slow portraits, during which the artist gets to know the sitter rather well, often sell for stratospheric prices. Slowness has become a brand.[36]

***

Cennini's *studietto* affects his concept not only of time, but also of space. The room is small, the word *studietto* a diminutive. The work done there is small: each glass panel of the reliquary is 11 by 8 centimetres (4⅜ by 3⅛ inches). And yet the reliquary's importance and status are in inverse proportion to its size, as are Bezalel's onyx discs. The miniaturizing tendency brings Cennini closer to the scholar, working with books, and it puts a high value on drawing, which is close to writing and is small-scale. Drawing would be taught – perhaps by Cennini – at Barzizza's school in Padua. Alberti studied there around 1416–18, and it can hardly be coincidental that drawing became the foundation stone of his treatise on painting.[37]

This 'small is beautiful' ethos drove Cennini to prefer panel painting to fresco, despite fresco being the medium to which most of his treatise is dedicated: 'And know that working on panel is really for a gentleman, since you may do anything you want to with velvets on your back ... and during this [process] you have time to be able to get up from your work and rest for a while, and think over this work that you have in hand; work on panels wants to be done with great enjoyment' (§157).

Instead of a soothing massage and that pious reverential feeling, the mood music is now created by the pleasurable feel of fur-lined or wool-lined velvet. The most luxurious of fabrics, velvet was usually made in plain colours and imported from Venice.[38] Sumptuary laws and records of fines show that successful artisans dressed their wives in fur-lined velvet.[39] Many later artists – including Dürer and Velázquez – portrayed themselves wearing velvet.[40] As a *familiaris*, Cennini would have worn velvet livery at court. But it beggars

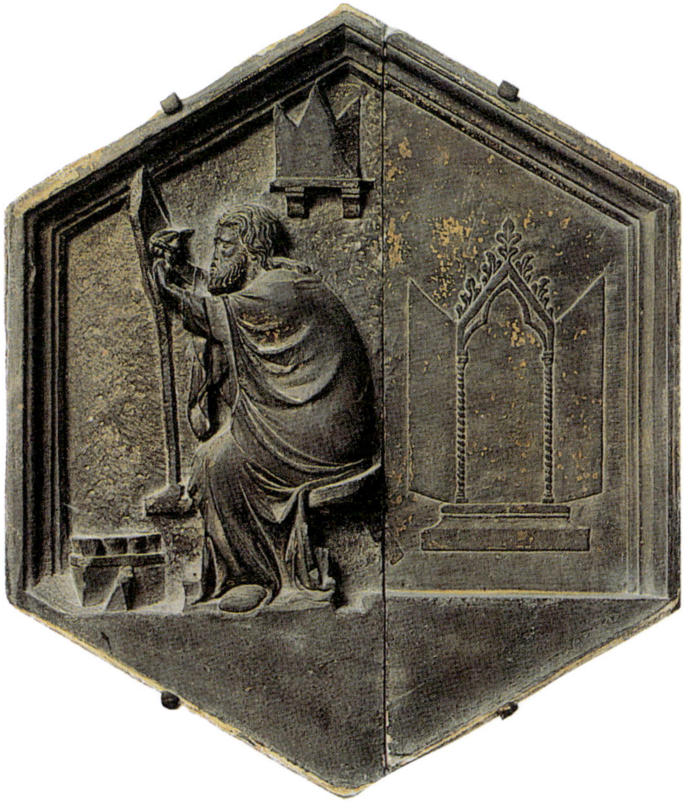

Attributed to Andrea Pisano, *Painting*, c. 1337, marble.

belief that he would have risked wearing velvet while painting, even under an apron – and even if he was married to a Donna Ricca.

Cennini claims panel painting is less time-consuming, leaving more opportunity for relaxation and thought. He may have been thinking of the Roman painter Famulus, who Pliny says only worked for a few hours each day but 'took his work very seriously, as he always wore a toga, even when in the midst of his easels [*machinis*]' (35.37.118–20). The plural 'easels' is telling, however. It sounds like Famulus has a big workshop operation, which he oversees, with pictures at different stages. Surviving 15th-century inventories show numerous unfinished works in the workshop; a supply of semi-finished Virgin and Child images could be kept at the ready, with attendant saints and details quickly worked up according to a client's specifications.[41] The master's involvement could be limited to giving a drawing to his assistants (think of all those *Salvator Mundis*).

The painter portrayed at the base of the cathedral bell-tower in Florence, designed by Giotto, is the first depiction of an artist to hint at this kind of complex workshop system (preceding page). It is one of a series of reliefs, in two horizontal bands, attributed to Andrea Pisano (begun 1330s). The lowest band features scenes from Genesis, including the labours of Adam and Eve after the Fall, and depictions of practitioners of the mechanical arts and sciences. For the first time, painting, sculpture and architecture were included, with each represented by a bearded worthy wearing long robes.

The painter sits before his easel, intently working on a diamond-shaped panel. Two small triptychs are on the back wall. The various levels of detail and abstraction suggest different stages of completion; the one on the shelf looks as though it has been turned to face the wall, protecting the surface. But by virtue of being displayed on the cathedral bell-tower, he – and his invisible workshop assistants – must be working to the bell.

The earlier description of Titian was largely mythical, put about by Palma il Giovane, one of his assistants: 'repeated revisions' were rare in his sophisticated workshop. His own painting room was on the first floor of his detached palazzo in Venice, with a larger workshop on the ground floor where assistants churned out copies. Titian would make occasional revisions to gestures and other details.[42] On 29 February 1568, the art dealer Niccolò Stoppio wrote: 'Everyone says [Titian] no longer sees what he is doing, and his hand trembles so much that he cannot bring anything to completion, but leaves this to his pupils. He has a German in his house, Emanuel ... who is excellent and does many things for him which he then finishes with two strokes of his brush and sells as his own work.'[43]

Illness and old age also make the hand flutter, and that was why an efficient workshop was vital.

Chapter 6

Piety and Pretentiousness

Saint Luke Paints the Virgin

The similarity of Cennini's *studietto* to a scholar's study and a private chapel was further underpinned by the dedication of his treatise to Saint Luke the Evangelist, the 'first Christian painter'. Luke was believed to have painted panel portraits of the Virgin and Child and of the adult Christ. The rise in importance of Saint Luke as a painter during this period was a crucial factor underscoring Cennini's shift in emphasis from commercial workshop to high-minded studio.[1] It was Luke's rebirth as an artist that would ultimately lead to the decline in status of Saint Eligius and of goldsmiths, and the rise in prestige of painting. Few nowadays have heard of Eligius. Luke would become a model for the literate easel painter with luxurious studio who paints from live models, working for love rather than money (overleaf).

The cult of Saint Luke the painter began in Constantinople in around the 8th century.[2] It was a useful myth to justify the church's use of images, especially during the iconoclastic controversies. Luke was credited with painting five different types of half-length images of the Virgin and Child. Many icons were claimed to have been painted by him, becoming cult images. There was a logic underpinning Luke's makeover; Saint Paul says Luke was a doctor by training. Apothecaries sold pigments as well as medications, and recipes for painters and doctors were bound together in the same books. Greek writers used the term *pharmak[ei]a* for pigments.[3] Luke's paintings were drugs insofar as they effected miraculous medical cures and protected cities.[4] As a doctor, he could be regarded as rich – certainly rich enough not to have to sell his pictures. (In 1520, the painter Lucas Cranach was granted a licence to open an apothecary by his patron, the Elector of Saxony; he became the second-richest citizen in Wittenberg.)

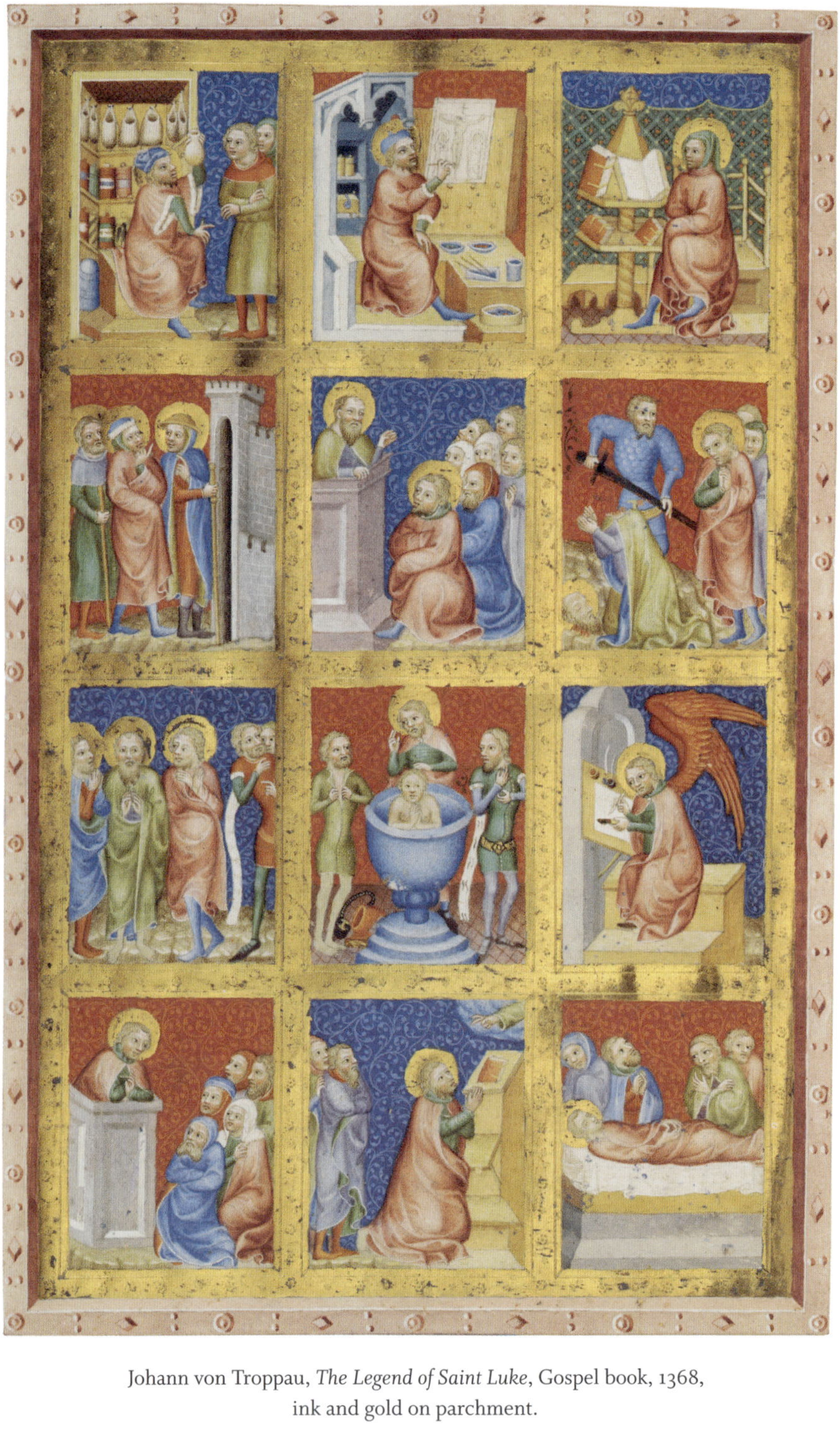

Johann von Troppau, *The Legend of Saint Luke*, Gospel book, 1368, ink and gold on parchment.

Padua was the city of Saint Luke, even if Rome had the most venerated icons. In 1177 the remains of Saint Luke were miraculously discovered below the church of Santa Giustina after an earthquake; Luke's remains had supposedly been smuggled out of Constantinople to Padua in 337, along with one of his portraits of the Virgin and Child.[5] A chapel to house his relics was built around 1316. Luke was the first great Christian writer and historian – perfect for a university city. He says more about the childhood of Jesus than any other gospel writer, and is the only one to describe his conception and the Annunciation. According to tradition, he also wrote the Acts of the Apostles, making him responsible for over a quarter of the New Testament. He wrote in a 'charming and decorous' style.[6]

The first images of Luke painting the Virgin and Child, usually outside, appear in 11th-century Byzantine manuscripts. In Western Europe it was only during the 14th century, when he became the patron of painters' guilds, that his activities as a painter, rather than his products, became of interest. This may be because previous generations had been unwilling to draw attention to the manual aspects of Luke's practice and workshop, or because it was regarded as more important to show him writing. The earliest surviving miniature, by the Bohemian scribe and painter Johann von Troppau, appears in a sumptuous Gospel book of 1368. Before each of the four Gospels, a dazzling full-page miniature is paired with an illuminated initial on the opposite page. The life of each Evangelist is illustrated in twelve framed scenes.

Luke's first three scenes form a triptych showing him performing different occupations. On the left, he talks to customers at his apothecary; jars are arrayed on the shelves behind, no doubt clearly labelled and some brightly coloured (apothecaries spent more on packaging and purpose-built shelving than any other traders).[7] On the right, he sits alone in his richly decorated study, reading a book on a raised book wheel.

The painter's workshop is placed in the middle of the triptych, the most enclosed and 'secret' place. The enveloping architectural furniture is a product of the painter's *fantasia*. There is no indication that Luke gave all his riches away to follow Christ; far from it. The back of his chair incorporates shelf compartments, the lower supporting a golden chest that may contain gold leaf, money and expensive materials such as lapis lazuli, the finest blue, which came from Afghanistan via Venice and which is lavishly used here. The painter's containers are even more deluxe than those in the apothecary. His tools and paints are laid out before him in five containers, like instruments

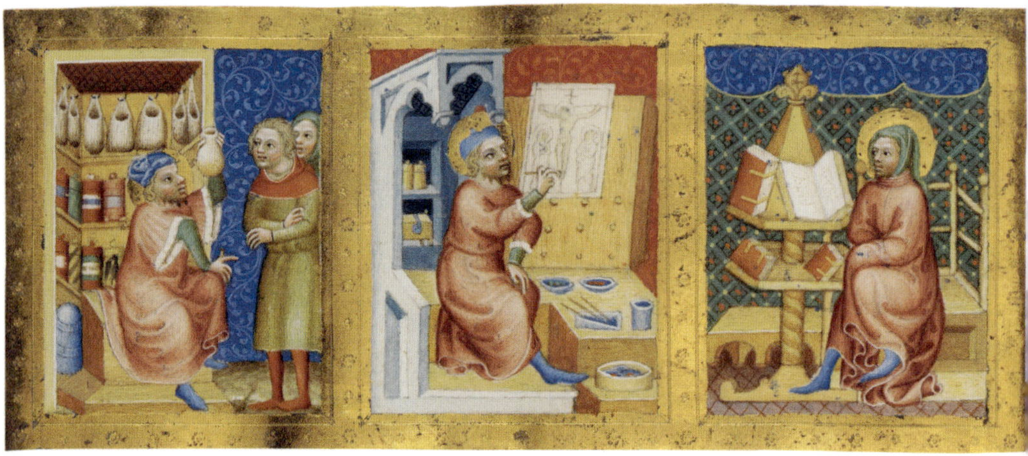

John of Troppau, *The Legend of Saint Luke* (detail).

of the Passion: two dishes or shells with red and green paint, a jar of water or oil, and a brush holder. The 'dog bowl' on a lower step contains pigment submerged in water to keep it fresh.

Luke is painting Christ on the cross, flanked by the Virgin and John the Evangelist. The panel surmounts the top of the peg-board easel, so Luke has to look up, like Mary and John in the picture. He is working from memory, imagining himself once again gazing up at the cross. His paintbrush 'kisses' Christ's feet. He has sketched in the underdrawing in charcoal and ink, and underpainted the flesh tones in green earth. This method, which 'cooled' the superimposed reds and pinks, was still being used by later artists including Leonardo and Vermeer. The size of the easel invites the question of why Luke is painting such a small picture – it could be much taller and wider. But it underscores his historical role: to make easel paintings that could be exported to Western Europe and carried in procession. He exemplifies Pliny's contention that only painters of portable panels become internationally famous, because their works can travel and be saved from fire.

In 1314, painters in Florence joined the Guild of Doctors and Apothecaries, whose patron saint was Luke. Then, in 1339, the Florentine painters formed their own confraternity of Saint Luke, which met at the church of Sant'Egidio until 1450 (the church was rededicated to the Virgin in 1419, a symptom of Eligius' impending decline). The Florentine painters commissioned the earliest documented altarpiece showing Saint Luke painting, but this is lost.

The earliest surviving Saint Luke altarpiece, and the finest, was made by Rogier van der Weyden (1399/1400–1464) soon after he was appointed town painter of Brussels in 1436 (overleaf). Together with his contemporary Jan van Eyck, Rogier was the most celebrated painter in Europe during the 15th century, and even more influential. *Saint Luke Drawing the Virgin* (c. 1435–40) was probably the altarpiece for the chapel of the Brussels painters' guild. It is one of the earliest depictions to show the Virgin before Saint Luke as if sitting for a portrait, and the first to show him drawing rather than painting.[8] Saint Luke, dressed in fur-lined velvet, may be a self-portrait. Indeed, whenever artists depict themselves painting a Virgin and Child (see Chapter 3), they implicitly identify themselves with Luke.

It is odd that Saint Luke was never credited with having painted the Annunciation, since he was the only Evangelist to describe it. Rogier gets round this by having Luke act out an Annunciation, half kneeling, half hovering angelically before the breastfeeding Virgin and the blissfully gurgling Christ Child. This is a picture type – the *Madonna lactans* – that Luke devised. The setting has further similarities with Annunciations, as the Virgin is often located in her home in Nazareth, with a garden glimpsed through a narrow doorway, symbolizing her virginity and fecundity. But here the enclosed garden is an uncultivated yard.

Rogier has made the most exalted of sitters come to the painter's studio (conversely, the angel of the Annunciation visited Mary). The narrow doorway in his luxuriously appointed workshop-studio leads into a cosy *studiolo* with glazed windows. Saint Luke's Gospel is open on the desk, guarded by his house-trained symbolic ox. The open rear part of the main 'workshop' is an architectural *fantasia* that would be both windswept and cold. It suggests a cloister, with the Romanesque columns evoking early Christian architecture; it also evokes a standard workshop, with a central opening onto the street flanked by counters for merchandise.[9] The man and the woman looking out over the city below might be customers waiting their turn; but it seems unlikely they are paying customers. Their relaxed, leisurely, affectionate demeanour simply underscores that this is a trade-free zone where no one is in a rush.

Rogier's picture is always compared with Van Eyck's similarly structured Rolin *Madonna* (c. 1435), and he was almost certainly influenced by it. But the background of that picture bursts with economic activity: ships, bell-towers, bustling crowds. This mercantile utopia was a compliment to Rolin, chancellor of the Duchy of Burgundy, whom Van Eyck initially depicted with a bag of money. Rogier's river and town are eerily empty, the land unfarmed.

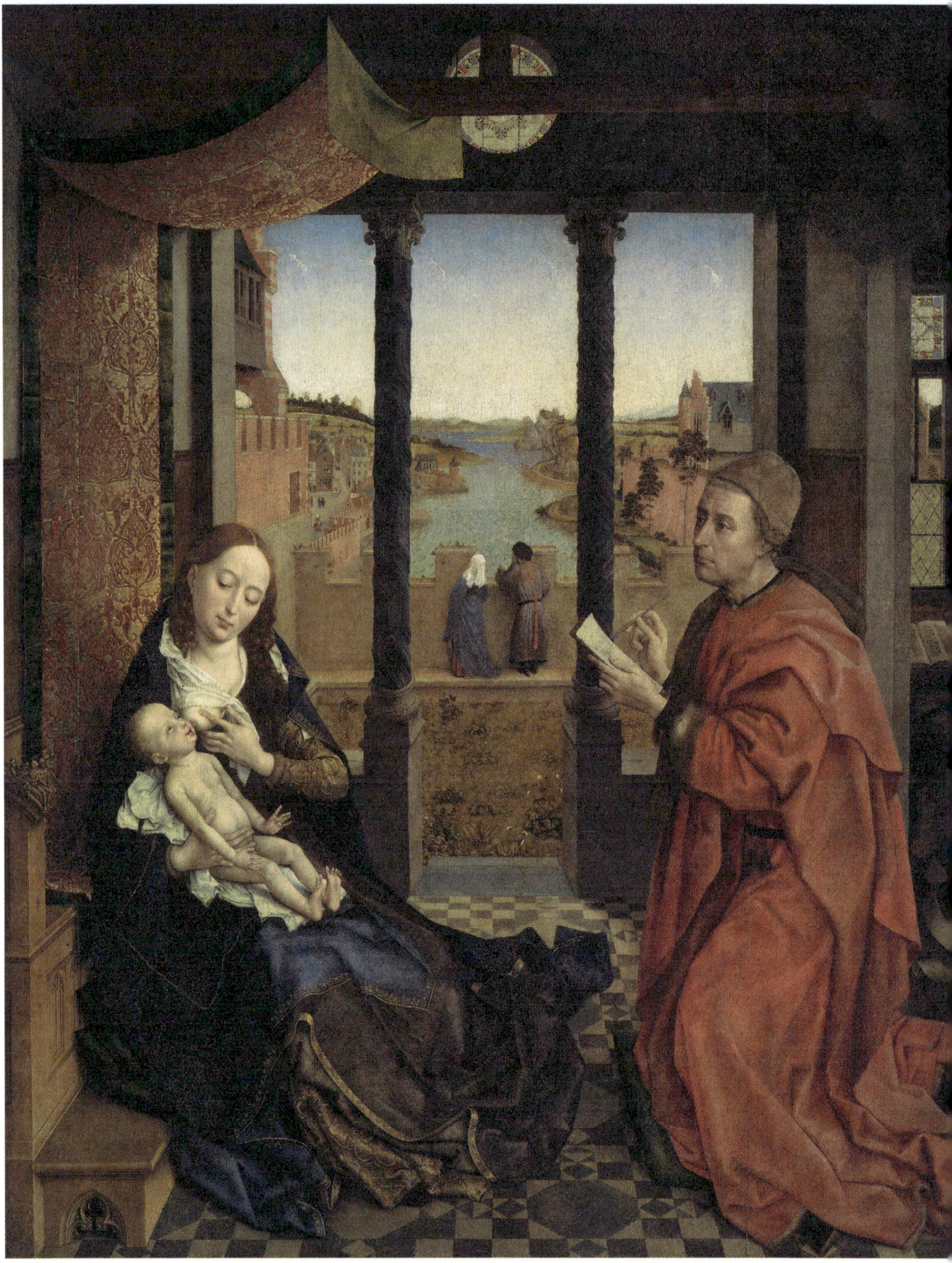

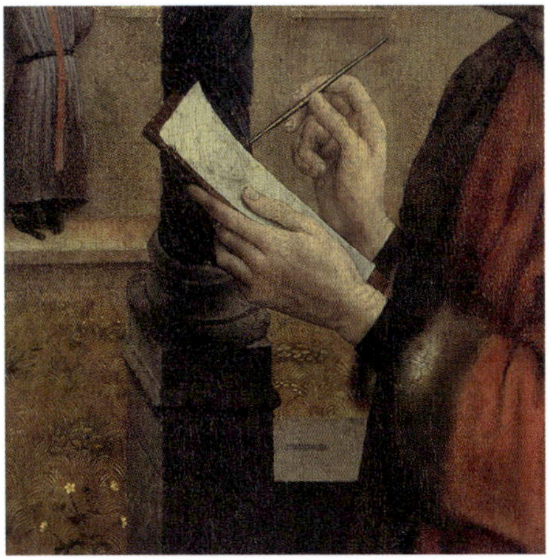

Opposite Rogier van der Weyden,
Saint Luke Drawing the Virgin, c. 1435–40,
oil and tempera on panel. **Above** Detail.

Rogier's Saint Luke is a tour de force of suspended animation. Time has stopped. His hands float up elegantly before him, holding his tool with the delicacy of an angel holding a lily or sceptre. Even the paper curls up off the wooden tablet, like gold leaf. His right hand ever so lightly touches, with tips of forefinger and thumb, his metal drawing implement. He is using a technique known as metalpoint, whereby a metal stylus would react chemically with a piece of paper coated with powdered bone or lead white, leaving a dark line. It was difficult to use because mistakes could not be corrected and the resulting image was faint, but you could draw without interruption, unlike with ink, where the pen needed recharging.[10] The paper could always be recoated and reused. The stylus's leather container hangs at Luke's waist.

Leonardo found metalpoint most convenient for quick-fire sketching: 'Be sure to take with you a little book with pages prepared with bonemeal, and with a silverpoint [stylus] briefly note the gestures of the bystanders and how they are grouped. This will teach you how to compose narrative paintings.'[11] Rogier's hovering artist is a dynamic recording angel, spontaneously note-taking. He is making a head study of the Virgin, but the sitter has changed position. The fluency of Saint Luke is stopped in its tracks by an unexpected movement from his live models, and by his pursuit of artistic perfection.

Chapter 7

'Always Keeping Paper in his Hand'

A School for Art and Scandal

On 30 October 1467, the 70-year-old Paduan painter Francesco Squarcione contracted to give a four-month training course, priced at two ducats.[1] For around forty years, Squarcione had been running – not without controversy – the first documented private art school. His new pupil, Francesco Guzon, was the son of a local painter. He was almost certainly Squarcione's last pupil, 137th in a distinguished line that included Marco Zoppo, Carlo Crivelli and his star alumnus, Andrea Mantegna.

Francesco's father either lacked the necessary skills or felt his son needed some top-up tuition. Guzon would live in Squarcione's house, near the basilica of Saint Anthony. He could expect to be taught 'the principle of a plane with lines drawn according to my method, and how to put figures on the said plane, one here and one there, in various places on the said plane, and place objects, namely a chair, bench or house ... and teach him to understand a man's head in foreshortening ... and teach him the system of a naked body, measured from the front and behind, and to put eyes, nose, mouth and ears in a man's head at the right measured places'.[2]

Guzon senior was paying for the newfangled 'sciences' of art that had been developed in Florence and Tuscany: linear perspective, foreshortening and proportion. These high-status methods had been brought to Padua by recent Florentine arrivals such as the painters Filippo Lippi (in Padua 1430s) and Paolo Uccello (1444–5), and especially the sculptor Donatello (1443–53). Alberti, pioneering explicator of perspective in his 1435 treatise on painting, had studied in Padua. The pedantry with which Squarcione spells it all out – 'one here and one there' – shows how novel these ideas were. His claim to be teaching 'my method' gives his course the allure of secret knowledge.

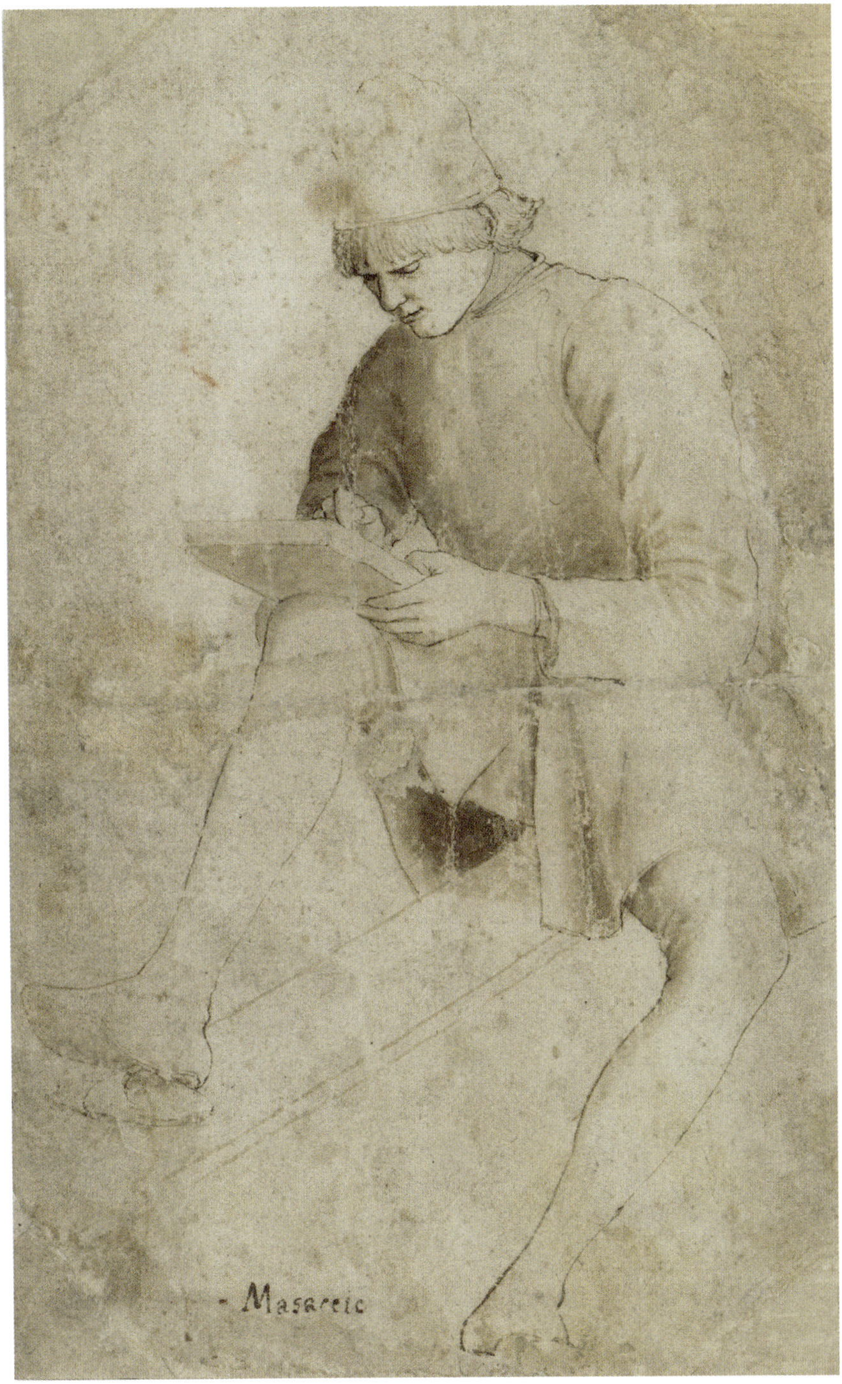

Workshop of Maso Finiguerra, *Youth Drawing*, 1450s, pen and ink with wash on paper.

But the USP of Squarcione's school was his collection of drawings by Italian masters, casts and originals of antique and modern Italian sculpture, and antique coins and medals. Some of this study collection had been accumulated on his travels round the Eastern Mediterranean and Italy. The contract flags up this precious treasure trove: 'Always keeping him with paper in his hand, [I will] provide him with a succession of models, one after another, with various figures in lead white [for highlights], and correct these models for him, and correct his mistakes so far as I can and he is capable … if he should damage any drawing of mine the said Guzon is required to pay me its full price.'[3]

To promise paper on demand was astonishing. Paper made from pulped rags remained a pricey commodity, even though production had increased with growing demand from book publishers. Gutenberg's famous Bible, printed with movable type, had been published at Mainz *c.* 1455. A print run of 300 copies was cheaper and faster to produce than a single handwritten copy on parchment. But in the mid-15th century, the price of a sheet of the smoothest paper was still equivalent to a week's wages for an agricultural labourer.[4] I suspect Squarcione would have provided paper only after a design had been worked out with stylus on a reusable wooden tablet.[5]

Guzon would have looked very like the young apprentice in a drawing from the workshop of the Florentine goldsmith and designer Maso Finiguerra (preceding page).[6] Several similar drawings survive of Finiguerra's apprentices at work. It was a standard workshop exercise that would have honed skills in life drawing, shading and foreshortening, as well as fostering cooperation and rivalry. The drawings advertise the credo of advanced workshops: that drawing is the foundation of the visual arts. One drawing has an aspirational mantra inscribed in an unsophisticated hand: 'I want to be a good draughtsman and to become a good architect.' Mastery in drawing meant mastery in all the visual arts. Finiguerra bequeathed fourteen albums of drawings to whichever family member took over his workshop.

The drawing in ink and brown wash has almost no corrections. It has been carefully worked out in advance, probably with a wooden tablet like the one used by the boy being portrayed. With our schoolmaster Squarcione hat on, we would say that the light and shade are crude and inconsistent, the foreshortening exaggerated. Its maker hasn't quite learned how to 'place objects'. Eyes, nose and mouth are in the 'right measured places', but the ear is exiled to the end of the plank-like jaw. The boy is a descendant of Hildebertus' assistant, Everwinus (see page 44) – but a distant one. He is powerfully monumentalized, feet pushing against the edge of the page. His pose and focus recall the famous antique bronze of a boy pulling a thorn from his foot. Last but not least, there is no Hildebertus to upstage or bully him.

Squarcione's promise to provide 'a succession of models, one after another' is a landmark moment. This artistic speed-dating is a far cry from Cennini's more monotheistic emphasis on the Giotto tradition. The insistence on compensation for damaged drawings shows there was now a market for such studio properties. The will of the Paduan humanist Felice Feliciano, in 1466, refers to 'drawings and pictures on paper by many excellent masters of design'.[7] The windows of Squarcione's packed study rooms would have been secured with iron window grilles.[8] But grilles could not prevent pupils stealing. In 1474, Squarcione's son took retrospective legal action to reclaim 'a cartoon with certain nudes' by the Florentine artist Antonio del Pollaiuolo, and eighteen other drawings. They had been taken by a departing pupil, Giorgio Schiavone.

***

Like Cennini, Squarcione was the son of a notary, and he initially worked as a tailor and embroiderer. Judging by his two or three surviving paintings, he was a plodding journeyman striving for a modern Tuscan look, a canny follower of artistic fashion rather than a pioneer. He seems to have opened the school as a way to make money and gain status in a city of learning. His commissions, and output of paintings, were correspondingly meagre. The inspiration seems to have been Gasparino Barzizza, whose private school in Padua (1407–21) was the first in which teachers and pupils lived in the house of their master; Cennini's ambitious proselytizing may have influenced him too. Demand for education in Padua had increased since its conquest by Venice in 1404, and in 1434 a law made it compulsory for Venetians attending university to go there. Squarcione's school prophesies the transition from the world of workshops, where apprentices learned from a single master and his work, to that of art academies, where a wider range of models – sculptural, pictorial and human – were studied.

There was a shadier side to the operation. A key part of Squarcione's business model was to adopt the best pupil as his son. This was standard practice, as family members were exempted from guild membership fees and caps on numbers of assistants.[9] Squarcione profited handsomely from sales of pupils' work, just as Raphael, Titian, Rubens and Rembrandt would do. But several of his pupils and assistants complained he took the credit for their own endeavours. He was involved in sixteen legal disputes, and has been called 'sly and dubious'.[10] On the other hand, his large number of pupils suggests he got most things right. In 1452, Squarcione met Emperor Frederick III during his visit to Padua.

Squarcione's success enabled him to acquire the neighbouring house, a common solution to space shortages: in the 1460s an illuminator in central Paris acquired three adjoining houses, which gave him a prized corner block on the main route to the cathedral.[11] Squarcione's upsizing was conceptual as well as material. He initially referred to his premises as a *bottega* (workshop), but soon upgraded it to a *studium*. An inventory taken on 24 May 1455 tells us that the main house contained a large *studium* 'with reliefs, drawings, and other things within it', and a second, small *studium* 'in the house called the house of reliefs'. Alberti believed that even copying a bad sculpture was better than copying a good painting, because it helped you learn about light and shade. Now a painter's workshop had become a sculpture museum.

No inventory of Squarcione's collection survives, let alone views of the *studium*; but the reliefs were probably narrative scenes from Roman sarcophagi and profile portraits, as well as statuettes and fragments of statues. Padua was the leading centre in Northern Italy for the study and collecting of antiquities. The larger items would have been propped against and fixed to the walls, with smaller items kept on shelves. The shelving and grouping of sculptures may have influenced the house style of the workshop. Squarcione and his pupils often place objects on shelves and stand figures on pedestals, making them seem simultaneously tangible and collectable.

Marco Zoppo's *Virgin and Child with Angels* (opposite) is a delightful case in point. Zoppo (1432/3–1478) is best known for an album of blatantly homoerotic drawings, with frolicsome boys just like his angels. The picture was painted in 1455, the year Zoppo was adopted – though the adoption was annulled the same year because Squarcione married and became a father, meaning Zoppo would lose any inheritance. The eight boy angels and the Madonna and Child show that Squarcione had casts of Donatello's Paduan reliefs and bronze statuettes. The angels' pale skin advertises their plastery origins; Zoppo had part-paid for his tuition with plaster brought from his home town, Bologna. Plaster was also crucial for drapery studies, which were made using linen soaked in plaster and draped over a jointed wooden mannequin.[12]

Zoppo flaunts 'the system of a naked body', not only 'measured from the front and behind', but duplicated in mirror image; he uses rudimentary perspective, and foreshortens still-life objects that show awareness of

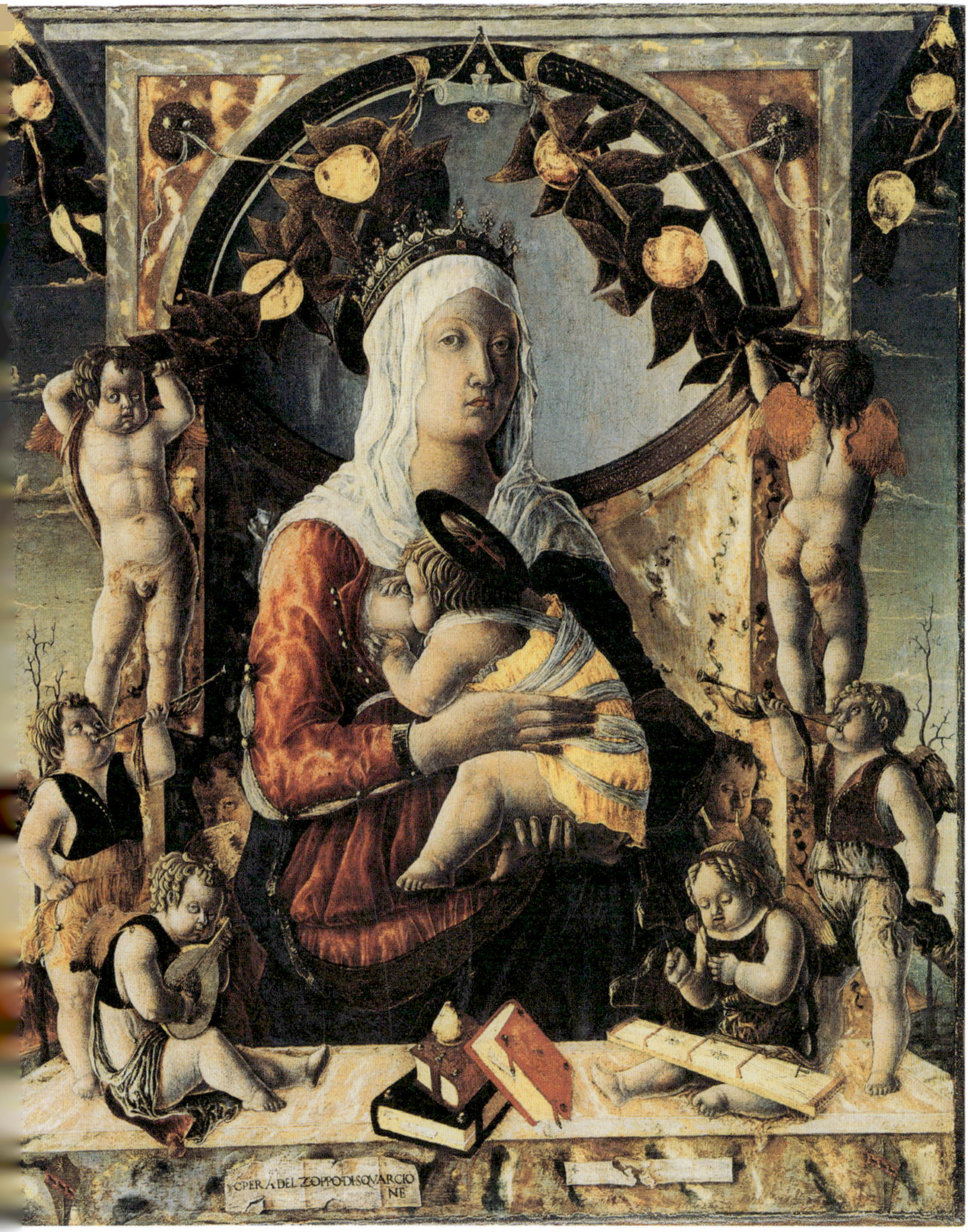

Marco Zoppo, *Virgin and Child with Angels*, 1455, oil on canvas.

Netherlandish art; he deploys light and shade. This is the staged and self-conscious synthesis of antiquity and modernity, art and nature, for which Squarcione's students paid. The Virgin's *sangfroid* in the face of gratuitous 'art for art's sake' visual pyrotechnics is impressive. The marble parapet at the front probably echoes the shelves on which smaller items in Squarcione's collection were displayed.

The Virgin normally has a single book. The three books shown here, in picturesque disorder, advertise the fact that Zoppo paints in the university city of Petrarch. There is a surfeit of paper in the picture: not just book pages but the two torn pieces affixed to the front of the shelf, an influential innovation that became a trademark of Squarcione's studio.[13] One of these *cartellini* bears the artist's signature – 'Opera del Zoppo di Squarcione' – which signals his adoption. The relics stored in the gilded glass diptych discussed in the previous chapter were identified by parchment *cartellini*, and the shelves in the *studium* may have had similar *cartellini* identifying sculptures.[14] They underscore the literary credentials of Squarcione's workshop, and the new centrality of paper: he wrote an autobiography, which has been lost.[15]

***

In 1465, Squarcione boasted to a prospective pupil: 'It was I who made a man of Andrea Mantegna, who worked for me, and I will do the same for you.' Mantegna was a master of perspective and foreshortening. But the student later sued, complaining that Squarcione, despite his promises, had been incapable of teaching him 'the true rule of perspective'.[16] This is taken as proof that Squarcione was a charlatan, and that Mantegna taught himself the more sophisticated stuff. Squarcione's expertise may have been more on a par with that of Zoppo.

But we shouldn't be too quick to condemn. Everyone struggled with perspective, or had doubts about it.[17] In 1506 Dürer, who was living and working in Venice, had to go all the way to Bologna to perfect his understanding of perspective and geometry. He wrote to a friend back home in Nuremberg: 'I will ride to Bologna where someone is willing to teach me the secrets of the art of perspective. Then in roughly eight or ten days I'll set off to ride back to return to Venice.'[18] Dürer's perspective would be criticized by the learned French cleric Jean Pélerin in *De artificiali perspectiva* (Toul, 1509). Pélerin 'corrected' the columns and coffered ceiling in Dürer's woodcut *Presentation in the Temple*, illustrating his own version.[19]

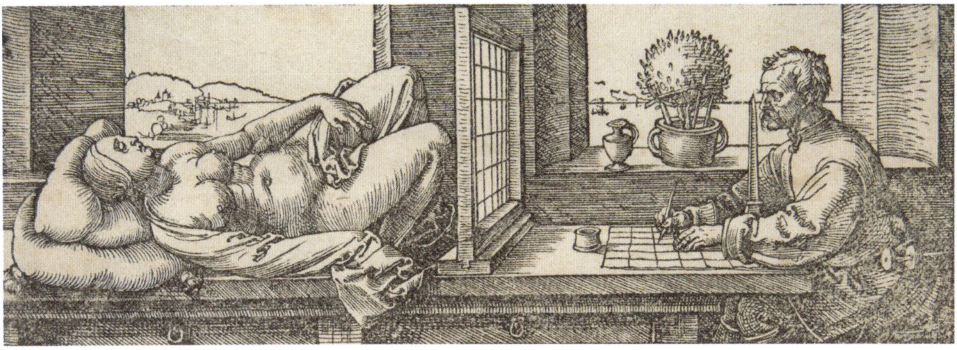

Albrecht Dürer, *Draughtsman Making a Perspective Drawing of a Reclining Woman*, 1525 (this print c. 1600), woodcut.

Dürer later devised his own perspectival machines, which he illustrated in his treatise *Instruction in Measurement with Compass and Ruler* ... (1525). Four woodcut prints show a po-faced, venerable artist using a variety of methods to draw objects in perspective. One machine is portable, enabling him to draw a male portrait in a bedchamber. In the studio, perspective machines are placed on a long oak table, enabling the artist to draw a lute, a jar, and a female nude located at the far end. The table on which the woman reclines in Venetian style is placed before two large window embrasures (with wonky perspective) opening onto a very Venetian lagoon. The use of a grid for perspectival drawing had been recommended by Alberti.

To the clothed artist, the woman is in near crotch shot. He strives to rival the Italian mastery of foreshortening exemplified by Mantegna and Michelangelo. He plots her position on the framed net, then transfers the grid references to the squared-up drawing paper. The net, table and sighting mechanism double as barriers to keep the artist well away from temptation, like a Catholic confessor's grille. Dürer's perspective machines treat static figures and objects indiscriminately, and these prints pre-empt Caravaggio's quip that painting still life requires as much artistry as figures.

Squarcione's student may have had an unhealthy interest in perspective. Leonardo kept revising his views on perspective and was aware of its distortions, not least the limitations of monocular vision from a single viewpoint.[20] He drew the earliest surviving depiction of an artist drawing with a perspective machine (*c.* 1478–82), but seems to have considered it purely an aid for drawing complex still-life objects (overleaf).[21] His only image of an artist at work, it is the most plausible self-portrait. It sends a very mixed message. The

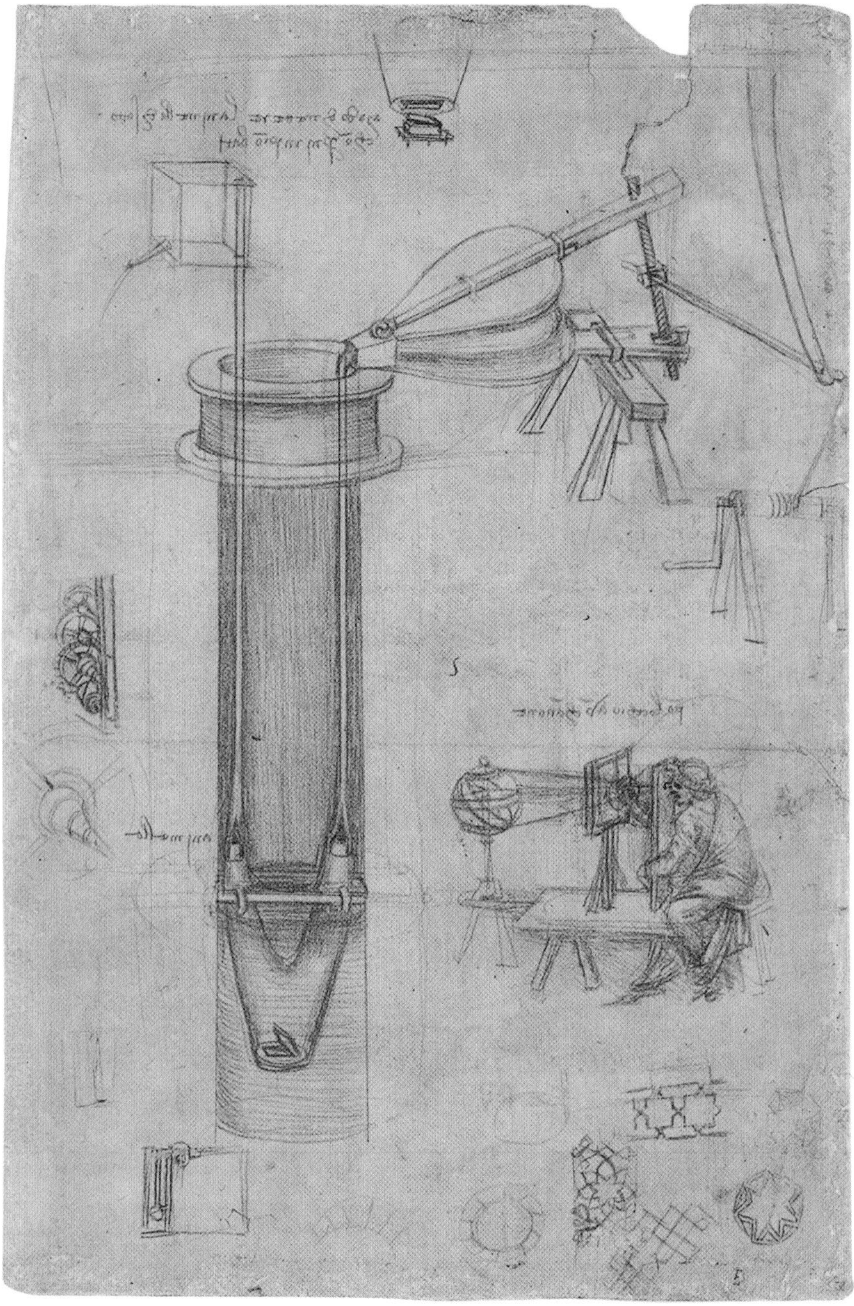

Leonardo da Vinci, *Design for a Hydraulic Pump and a Draftsman Drawing an Armillary Sphere with a Perspectograph*, c. 1478–82, ink on paper.

artist's absorption in the task is total, and surprisingly physical. He is drawing an armillary sphere onto a framed transparent veil by peering with one eye through a hole in a wooden panel.[22] The artist is seated in a kind of riding position, like an illuminator at the lectern, and his embrace of the viewing panel and trestle table with arms and legs, together with the explosion of visual rays from his eyes, is both manic and erotic.[23] Arms and back are as curved as the armillary rings. It is unclear how he can keep his extended and bent drawing arm steady. Leonardo's contemporaneous sketches of a squirming Christ Child grasping a struggling cat come to mind.

***

There is no specific mention in Guzon's contract about painting or drawing from live models. However, his course occupied the winter months, as did Dürer's course (late October to early November). Painting, like modelling, was a warm-weather activity because of faster drying times, nimble fingers and unfrozen feet. Masons also operated on a seasonal basis, with construction work stopping between All Saints (1 November) and the feast of the Purification of the Virgin (2 February). Master masons might spend the winter working on designs in a wooden tracing house, often erected on site, while masons only cut stone.[24] Dürer lamented the arrival of winter because 'the days grow so short one cannot do much'.[25] Paints took longer to dry anyway in perpetually damp Venice.[26]

Here Leonardo explains how drawings of the male nude made in summer could be used in winter: 'The long winter evenings should be utilised by young students in studying the things prepared during the summer … it would be useful to bring together all the drawings from the nude which you did in the summer, and select from among them the best limbs and bodies, and practise them and commit them to memory.'[27]

This procedure goes back to Parrhasius' practice of selecting the best male body parts (see page 33). Leonardo would also have performed anatomical dissections in winter. With no preservatives, the corpses – usually those of criminals – putrefied more slowly in cold weather. So ideally you studied live models in summer, drawings and corpses in winter. That said, in 1508–9 Leonardo wrote an intriguing reminder: 'Go to the baths *every* Saturday to see nude men' (my italics).[28]

Cuzon would have copied drawings of male nudes, mostly by Florentine artists – though the star exhibit by Pollaiuolo may already have been stolen.

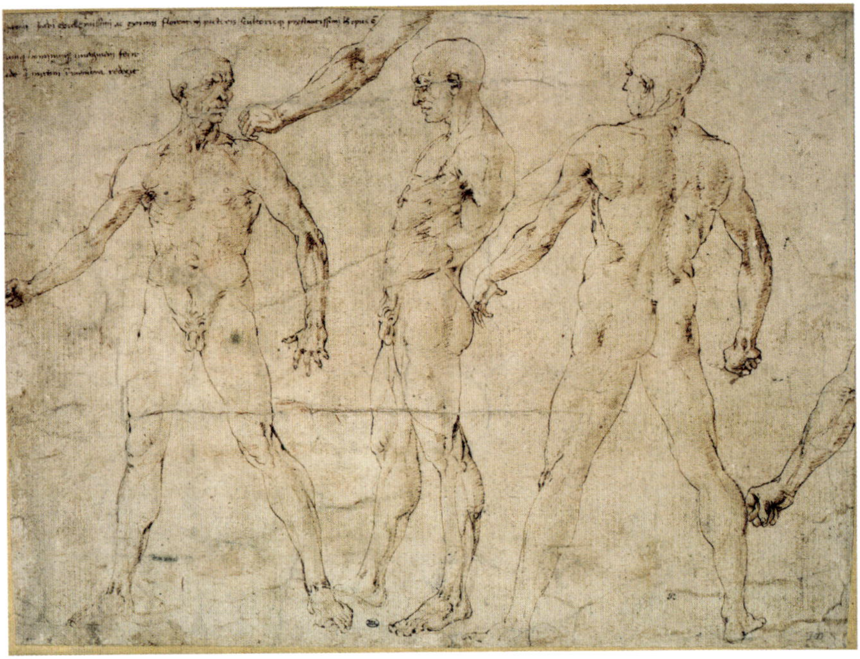

Antonio Pollaiuolo, *Male Nude Seen from Front, Side and Back*, early 1470s, pen and brown ink on paper.

Cennini had recommended making life casts of bodies in around 1400, but drawing the male nude first became fashionable in Florence in around 1450.[29] Pollaiuolo, a sometime associate of Finiguerra, was celebrated for his male nudes in vigorous action, and for bronze statuettes designed to be viewed from all sides; his nudes were still being used as workshop models by Dürer and Cellini. His large signed print *Battle of Naked Men* (1470s) made him famous round Europe. Prints would eventually supersede model books as visual sources.

This drawing – conceivably the stolen one – shows a mature, bald athletic man in a belligerent pose from the front, back and side, with separately drawn left and right arms.[30] The pose was inspired by fighting figures on the sides of Roman sarcophagi. The model's outstretched arms would have been supported by a pole or suspended rope. The anatomy looks pretty convincing and the head is distinctive, but Pollaiuolo simplifies by picking out selected muscles and tendons with clean contours. Shadow is minimized. A Latin inscription underscores the antique association: 'This is the work of the excellent and famous Florentine painter and sculptor Antonio di Jacopo. When he depicts man, look how marvellously he renders the limbs.' Could this have been written by Squarcione?

Leonardo ends his advice on life drawing by turning to the choice of model: 'Select someone who is finely built from the waist up and who has not been brought up wearing [tight-fitting] doublets and whose body consequently has not lost its natural bearing, and make him perform light and graceful movements.' Leonardo here touches on the difficulty of finding 'natural' Golden Age bodies in sophisticated urban societies. The inadequacy of European models would become a common refrain. Only one of Michelangelo's models was identified in his authorized biography: he dissected the corpse of a 'most beautiful' Moor, whose cause of death and status are not mentioned. Bernini disliked the male models at the Académie Royale in Paris and urged the king to buy Middle Eastern slaves, who had the best bodies; he had acquired some Levantines from Italian slave ports and 'found them very satisfactory'.[31] In London in around 1810, artists were in raptures about a black sailor from Boston, Massachusetts called Wilson, whose body rivalled the finest antique statues. He nearly suffocated when a whole-body cast, up to his chin, was being made.[32]

By the 18th century, increasingly efficient stoves would make nude modelling in winter viable at the larger art academies. The Rome branch of the Parisian Académie Royale in Palazzo Mancini had a summer and winter life room; the male model would be positioned by the stove.[33] But for individual artists, heating remained an issue. In 1861–2, Gustave Courbet had to abandon work on a statue of a fisher boy 'because my studio does not allow me to have anyone pose in the nude in winter'.[34]

***

Cennini considered it a waste of time to draw women, as 'none of them have perfect proportions', and this view was supported by antiquity. There was no Vitruvian woman. Pygmalion creates a sculpture of his ideal woman because he can't find a suitable living version. Zeuxis was forced to select the best parts from five different women when painting a picture of Helen of Troy. Far simpler to use lithe, androgynous youths, antique Venuses and jointed mannequins.[35]

The less prudish and less classical North Europeans pioneered the use of female models. Women could be seen nude in public bath houses, which doubled as brothels, and both Van Eyck and Van der Weyden made famously louche paintings of bathers.[36] In the 1490s Dürer made images of male and female bathers, systematically showing a variety of ages and body types. He eschewed a single Vitruvian ideal in his weirdly pluralist illustrated treatise on proportion (1528), offering instead eleven types and BMIs for both sexes. The reclining nude model in the woodcut shown on page 95 is characteristically female. Italian artists, especially in Venice, with its closer links to Northern Europe, would increasingly use female models, though the first documented payments are recorded by Lorenzo Lotto in 1541. Lotto does not specify who his models were, but they may have been sex workers.

Benvenuto Cellini raises the ever-present issue of the motivation for using female models – art or exploitation. In Rome in 1528, Cellini relates that 'I had taken a charming and very beautiful young girl as my maidservant; I used her as a model and also used to enjoy her in bed to satisfy my youthful desires .... I kept the young girl in a tiny ramshackle bedroom next to mine.' In Paris in the 1540s, matters were more complicated with his servant Caterina, daughter of a sex worker. Cellini claimed that he kept her 'chiefly to assist me in my art'. He kicked her out when he caught her *in flagrante* with his assistant Pagolo. After she unsuccessfully sued Cellini for mounting her 'in the Italian way' (i.e. sodomy, punishable by burning at the stake), he forced Pagolo at swordpoint to marry her. Unable to find a suitable replacement, Cellini got Caterina back to model for thirty *soldi* per day, which wasn't cheap. He made her pose 'in great discomfort for hours at a stretch. And in her discomfort, she was as much annoyed as I was delighted, since she was very beautifully made and won me great honour.'[37] Cellini's sadistic sessions with Caterina were punctuated with more sex, and vicious beatings whenever she annoyed him. The slick stylization of his female nudes makes one wonder if a female model was ever really necessary.

Live modelling was a momentous innovation that would transform the concept of art and artist – albeit more in theory than in practice: it is hard to tell how much derives from a single live model, and how much from other artworks or memorized types. Formulaic as many of the poses and viewpoints became, they still encouraged a wider range and faster documentation of possible poses. Never before had models been shown in triplicate with back views, which became a Renaissance trademark.[38] By the same token, with summer-to-winter work cycles, perfecting the figure could take far longer.

Studying nude models and their anatomy also underpins a shift from artists working in public to private, for practical and moral reasons. It seems unlikely that nude modelling, even with a loincloth, would have taken place in an unglazed ground-floor workshop open to the street or in a window, as with Dürer's reclining figure. Admittedly, the first formal declaration about live male modelling known to me that concerns decency dates to 1705, in the statutes of the Royal Academy of Saint Luke in Paris. Members and their sons, apprentices and associates were permitted to study the live model 'behind closed doors and with every appropriate decency'.[39]

The development of a sometimes risqué culture of secrecy around the studio was central to the rise of the Renaissance artist. Dürer searches for the 'secrets' of perspective, and perspective itself – with its plunging depths, foreshortening and vanishing points – is predicated on establishing distances, some of them unfathomable. Vasari said that Michelangelo was 'constantly flaying dead bodies, in order to study the secrets of anatomy'.[40] Hidden depths are also created by light and shade, and by having humans with their backs turned towards the viewer, suggesting privacy, interiority, secrecy. Alberti recommended having a figure looking out of the picture, their 'forbidding glance' telling the viewer not to approach, 'as if he wished their business to be secret'. When Squarcione boasts of having 'my method', he claims exclusivity.[41]

***

Many of the social and cultural markers mapped out by Cennini, Squarcione and Alberti were attained by Mantegna (*c.* 1431–1506). While Squarcione inaugurated a shift from *bottega* to *studium*, his greatest pupil went from *studium* to *palazzo*. His palatial house in Mantua, fifty miles west of Padua, is one of the first self-designed artist's houses (overleaf), and would inspire later artists such as Giulio Romano and Rubens.[42] As so often in the Renaissance, a master of drawing and design had become an architect.[43]

Mantegna was a prodigy, adopted by Squarcione as a child. He had the adoption annulled in 1448, complaining that Squarcione had earned over 400 ducats from his teenage work. In 1458 he was appointed court painter to the mercenary soldier Ludovico II Gonzaga, marquis of Mantua. His salary was 'the least of his rewards'. The appointment continued under his successors, despite Mantegna's extreme slowness (due to perfectionism) and difficult character. Construction of his house started in 1476 on land donated by Ludovico, showing that Mantegna, the most revered Italian artist, was a prized courtier. He was knighted in 1484. The plot eventually encompassed 1 ha (2½ acres), with extensive orchards. The size of the house, thefts of building materials, and the Gonzagas' frequent cash flow problems meant it took about twenty years to complete. It faced onto a piazza that fronted the

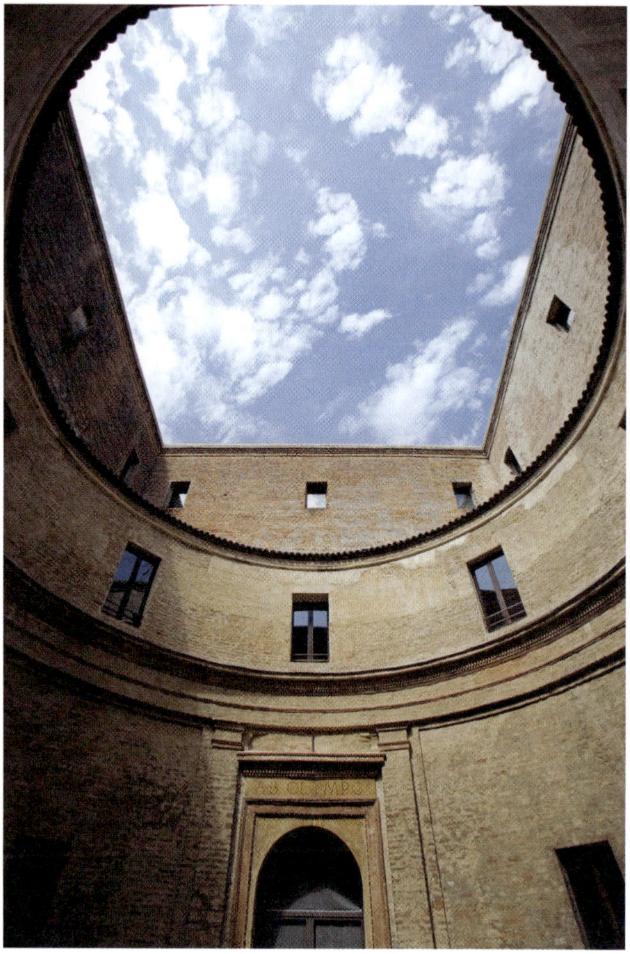

Casa del Mantegna (Mantegna's House), Mantua.

centrally planned church of San Sebastiano, designed by Alberti. In 1496 Mantegna's house was the starting point for a civic procession when his great altarpiece, *Santa Maria della Vittoria*, was carried across the piazza to the church. It celebrated Duke Francesco II Gonzaga's victory over the French in the Battle of Fornovo (1495).

First and foremost, the house asserted Mantegna's status as a property-owning citizen: a cornerstone bore a Roman-style inscription celebrating the bestowal of the land, with measurements of the plot's length and breadth, and the date construction started. Built of local brick, terracotta and wood, the house is a cubic structure with three storeys and fifteen rooms. Unlike in many other Italian cities, including Florence, the best houses in Mantua did not have shops at ground level because of strict zoning and snobbery about commercial activity – though rental income would have helped Mantegna's finances.[44]

The focal point, an open-roofed atrium, was not at the front of the house but hermetically concealed in the middle. It was a spectacular circular courtyard, open to the sky like an amphitheatre, a circle within an encompassing square. Its symmetry and proportions evoke antique examples, and Alberti's church, but the insertion of a circular courtyard at the heart of a house was novel. It was almost certainly decorated with some of Mantegna's celebrated collection of antique sculpture. In 1483, Lorenzo de' Medici had visited, as Francesco Gonzaga reported to his father, Federigo: 'His Magnificence took himself off to the house of Andrea Mantegna, where he saw with great pleasure various paintings ... and certain sculpted heads and many other antique pieces, by which it seems he was much delighted.'[45]

AB OLYMPO ('From Olympus') is inscribed above each of the four monumental doorways in the courtyard. This was one of many Gonzaga family devices, but its appropriateness here is multiple. It pays homage to Gonzaga patronage; it alludes to Hephaestus' starry, palatial workshop on Olympus;[46] it refers to Prometheus' theft of fire from Olympus, which made the human arts possible. A fiery sun motif decorates the paved floor. The stoking of Mantegna's fires was, in fact, done by the Gonzagas: firewood was included in the contract. Prometheus would be central to the frescoes in the even larger house built in Mantua in the 1540s by the Gonzaga court artist and architect Giulio Romano.

Painted decoration covered the external and internal walls, but little survives. It has been conjectured that the large painting workshop was on the ground floor down the left-hand side, its windows facing south-west. There was a door directly into the courtyard. A slightly smaller room at the garden end of the house probably housed a *studiolo* containing paintings, prints, drawings and antiquities. The most ambitious work done here was a series of nine monumental mural paintings, *The Triumphs of Caesar* (1484–92), a military procession into Rome with booty that showcases Mantegna's considerable antiquarian expertise.

Mantegna would have planned his works using a range of artistic and human resources. His reliance on antique sculpture had been noted early on. Squarcione had criticized Mantegna's frescoes of the life of Saint James in the Ovetari Chapel, Padua (1450s), for having the hardness of antique marbles and lacking the softness of living flesh. Mantegna responded by painting more naturalistic figures in the fresco cycle of Saint Christopher on the opposite wall. He also included eight portraits of contemporaries as costumed bystanders.[47]

To achieve a happy medium between ancient and modern, stone and flesh, Mantegna seems to have taken to dressing up in antique costume. Life modelling had increased the self-consciousness and theatricality of the workshop, and no one was more into fancy dressing – and fancy undressing – than Mantegna. In September 1464 he and some friends, including the drawing collector Felice Feliciano, dressed up as Romans, complete with laurel wreaths, for a boating expedition on Lake Garda. They visited paradisal gardens 'sacred to the muses', a shrine to Diana and her nymphs, and a 'temple' to the Virgin Mary; they looked at antiquities, including Roman inscriptions.[48] They were heirs to Petrarch, who lived and breathed classical antiquity.[49]

Mantegna's immersion in antiquity was immortalized in a swashbuckling bronze portrait bust, most probably first displayed on the left wall of the house's entrance hall. After his death it was transferred to his impressive funerary chapel in Sant'Andrea, Mantua, also designed by Alberti.[50] With its severe expression and naked torso, it evokes the heroic nudity of Roman portrait busts. This masterpiece of fancy undress asserts the centrality of antiquity, the male nude and live modelling.[51]

In the summer months, portrait sittings and modelling could have taken place in Mantegna's courtyard. In the early 1490s, Leonardo proposed: 'If you should have a courtyard that you can with ease cover with a linen awning that will provide a good light. Or when you want to take a portrait do it in dull weather, or as evening falls, making the sitter stand with his back to one of the walls.'[52]

In 1502 Duke Francesco, who had married Isabella d'Este in 1490, evicted Mantegna, already in financial difficulties, from his dream home. He wanted to incorporate it into the palace he was building alongside. Francesco offered Mantegna part of the medieval *Domus Mercati* (house of the market) in Piazza Purgo (a name derived from *purga della lana* – 'cleaning of wool'). This was an important commercial district, so at ground level there were shops beneath an arcade. It must have been humiliating for the venerable Prince of Painters to end up in Piazza Cleaning; Mantegna never lived there.[53] Eventually, in 1505, he bought a house, paying for it in stages, so as not to 'go here and there like a vagabond'. He died the following year. His bronze bust was erected on the side wall of the funerary chapel, from where he still glowers and glints at visitors, the ideal male model.

Chapter 8

In and Out of the Comfort Zone

Leonardo versus Michelangelo

In the 1490s, when Leonardo was employed by the duke of Milan, he made some wittily incendiary comparisons between painting, poetry, music and sculpture. They belonged to a literary genre known as the *paragone* ('comparison'), designed for courtly entertainment and debate. In contrast to classical antiquity, with its emphasis on competition *within* professions,[1] the *paragone* promotes competition *between* professions. Leonardo's most brutal face-off was between painting and sculpture, because he described the artists' respective workplaces and conditions of work. Coinciding with the completion of Mantegna's house in Mantua, it underscored the importance of the studio for the projection of artistic identity.

For Leonardo, painting invariably comes out on top as the universal art form. Guided by science and nature, it instantaneously satisfies the supreme sense: sight. Painting is also the most civilized art form to practise, with the studio pictured as an effort-free earthly paradise: 'The painter sits before his work at the greatest of ease, well dressed and applying delicate colours with his light brush, and he may dress himself in whatever clothes he pleases. His residence is clean and adorned with delightful pictures, and he often enjoys the accompaniment of music or the company of the authors of various fine works that can be heard with great pleasure [when read or recited aloud].'[2]

The velvet revolution of Cennini and Saint Luke is camped up here. Sight and hearing – pre-eminent among the five senses in classical and Christian cultures – are amply rewarded. Leonardo conveniently forgets that the most prized studio properties were sculptures; many painters, including Leonardo himself, acted as consultants for collectors of antiquities.[3]

Even if Leonardo is being economical with the truth about decor, he is correct in suggesting that painters would have had finished work on view: typically, workshop models and merchandise that demonstrated the product range to patrons. The timing of the patron's visit was important, however. Ramazzini, in *Diseases of Workers*, warned that the 'odors of varnish and oils make [painters'] workrooms smell like a communal latrine'.[4]

An account of a visit to Leonardo's living quarters shows they did indeed contain finished paintings and albums of drawings. In 1516, he emigrated to Amboise in the Loire Valley to be court artist and magus to King Francis I, who considered him a great philosopher and loved listening to him.[5] He lived well, on a high salary, in the Manoir du Cloux, connected to the nearby royal residence by an underground tunnel to facilitate visits. Since 1490 Amboise had been the king's preferred country residence, with good hunting.

After lunch on 10 October 1517, Leonardo was visited by the cultivated Cardinal Luigi d'Aragona. His secretary, Antonio de Beatis, wrote in his diary that the 'old man' showed Aragona three 'most perfect' paintings, a portrait of 'a certain Florentine woman done from life ... another of a young John the Baptist, and a Madonna and child seated on the lap of St Anne'.[6] The portrait was most likely *Mona Lisa*. All three paintings, with the possible exception of the Baptist, had been started years earlier in Florence and Rome. With the left-handed artist's right hand now paralysed, Beatis reported that he only taught and drew; he let his Milanese assistant, Francesco Melzi, who worked 'quite well', do the painting. A rather fanciful re-creation, with velvet hangings, has been devised in the château for modern visitors (overleaf).

The three pictures are now considered autograph, so workshop products may have been confined to a separate studio used by Melzi. Leonardo was then designing an equestrian monument to be cast in bronze, so this may have been worked on elsewhere too.[7] He also shows his visitors an 'infinity of volumes all in the vernacular' devoted to anatomy – 'he has dissected more than thirty bodies of men and women of all ages' – water, hydraulics, mechanics and 'many other things'. Beatis believes they should be published, as nothing comparable has ever 'been accomplished by a human being'.[8] The Amboise studio was a shrine to Leonardo the painter and polymathic maker of illustrated treatises. There is a premature sense of permanence and completion about it, more like that of a museum. No mention is made of unfinished works, or parting gifts, or acquisitions of even a sketch.

Leonardo's ideal studio has musical and literary entertainment laid on. Vasari later claimed that this had indeed been the case. During the sittings for the portrait of Lisa del Giocondo, begun in Florence in 1503, Leonardo employed entertainers: 'While Leonardo was painting Mona Lisa's portrait, he engaged people to play and sing, and jesters to keep her cheerful and remove that melancholy which painting usually gives to portraits.'[9] Vasari never met Leonardo or saw the portrait and was likely reporting local legend: the unusual smile was in fact an attribute or owner's mark, indicating her married name (Giocondo means 'cheerful', 'smiling'). But there may have been a grain of truth in what he said; bored sitters were a common problem.[10] Court artists often devised entertainments.[11] Leonardo, a fine musician, was famous for his jokes, brain-teasers, caricatures and automata – and for illusionistic paintings with telescopic foreshortened arms, prodding fingers and weird smiles.

Too much amusement had its drawbacks, however. Nicholas Hilliard, miniature painter to Queen Elizabeth I of England, warned in a treatise that even a small movement 'is the greatest cause of losing a likeness in a picture'. Only bland entertainment is desirable: 'Discrete talk or readings, quiet mirth or music offendeth not, but shortens the times and quickens the spirit both in the drawer and he which is drawn.'[12]

Spending quality time with an important sitter in a pleasant studio sounds good in theory – beneficial for status and for getting a good likeness – but speed was usually paramount. It was standard practice to make a drawing of the head, which could be done at a time and place of the sitter's convenience. Rogier van der Weyden's Saint Luke wisely draws, rather than paints, the distracted Virgin and wriggling Child. Jan van Eyck made colour notes on his drawing of the busy Cardinal Albergati (*c.* 1435) when he visited Bruges: 'the iris of the eye, near the pupil ... brownish yellowish, bluish at the contour near the white ... the white also yellowish, the nose a sanguine-brownish colour ... the lips very whitish-purple, the stubble of the beard quite greyish, the chin reddish ...'.[13] Leonardo made a profile drawing of Isabella d'Este, who was easily bored, difficult to please and bad at posing. With the artist seated at her side rather than in front, she could more easily be entertained. The painting could be done later (or not, in the case of Isabella's portrait) without the sitter present. Clothes, collars, armour and jewelry might be lent, and placed on a compliant mannequin or model. Queen Elizabeth I's clothes might be worn by a lady-in-waiting.[14]

Leonardo next turns his attention to sculpture. Among many defects, it has limited subject matter (no landscape backgrounds) and lacks colour and

Overleaf Conjectural recreation of Leonardo da Vinci's studio, Château Clos Lucé (formerly the Manoir du Cloux), Amboise.

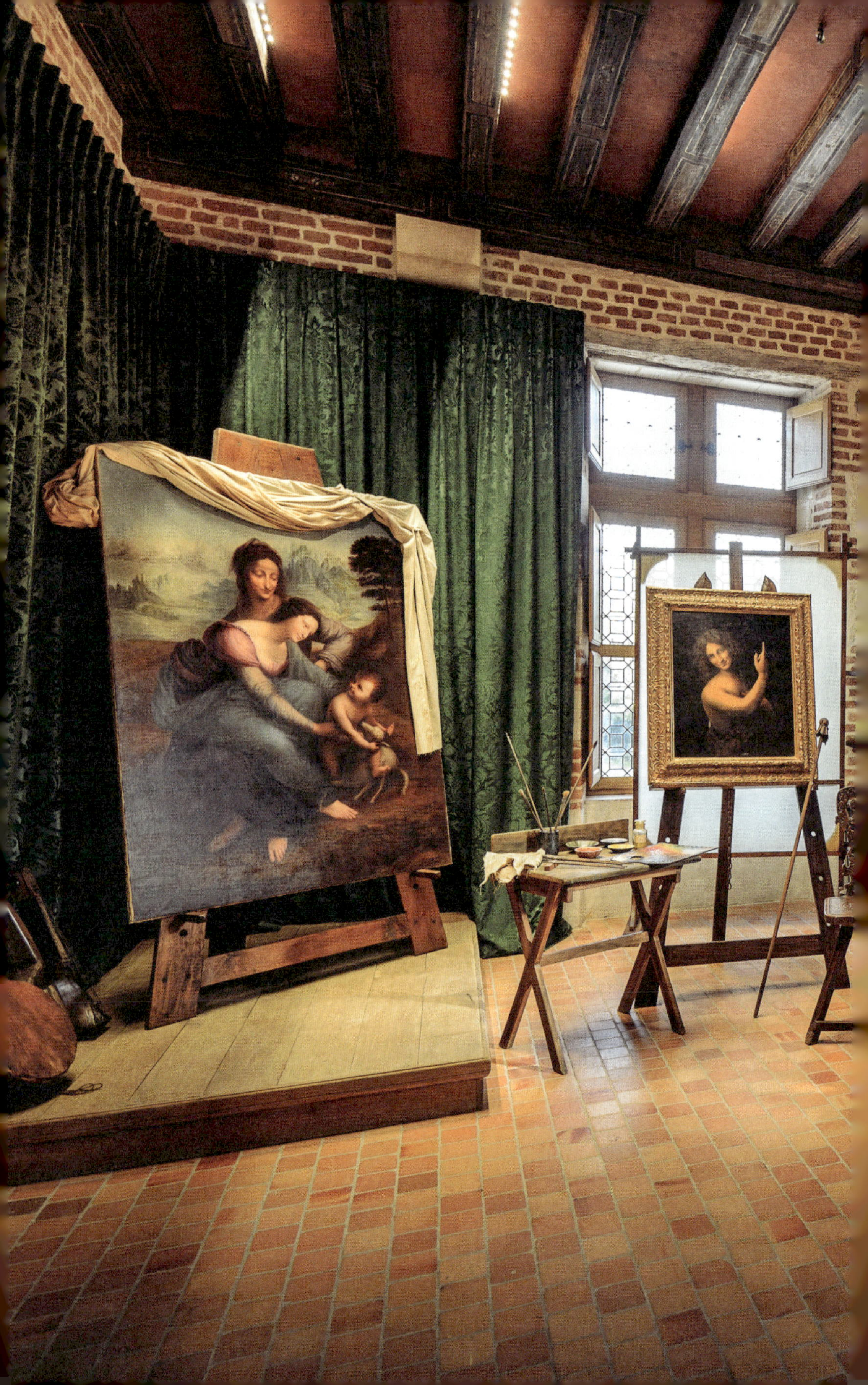

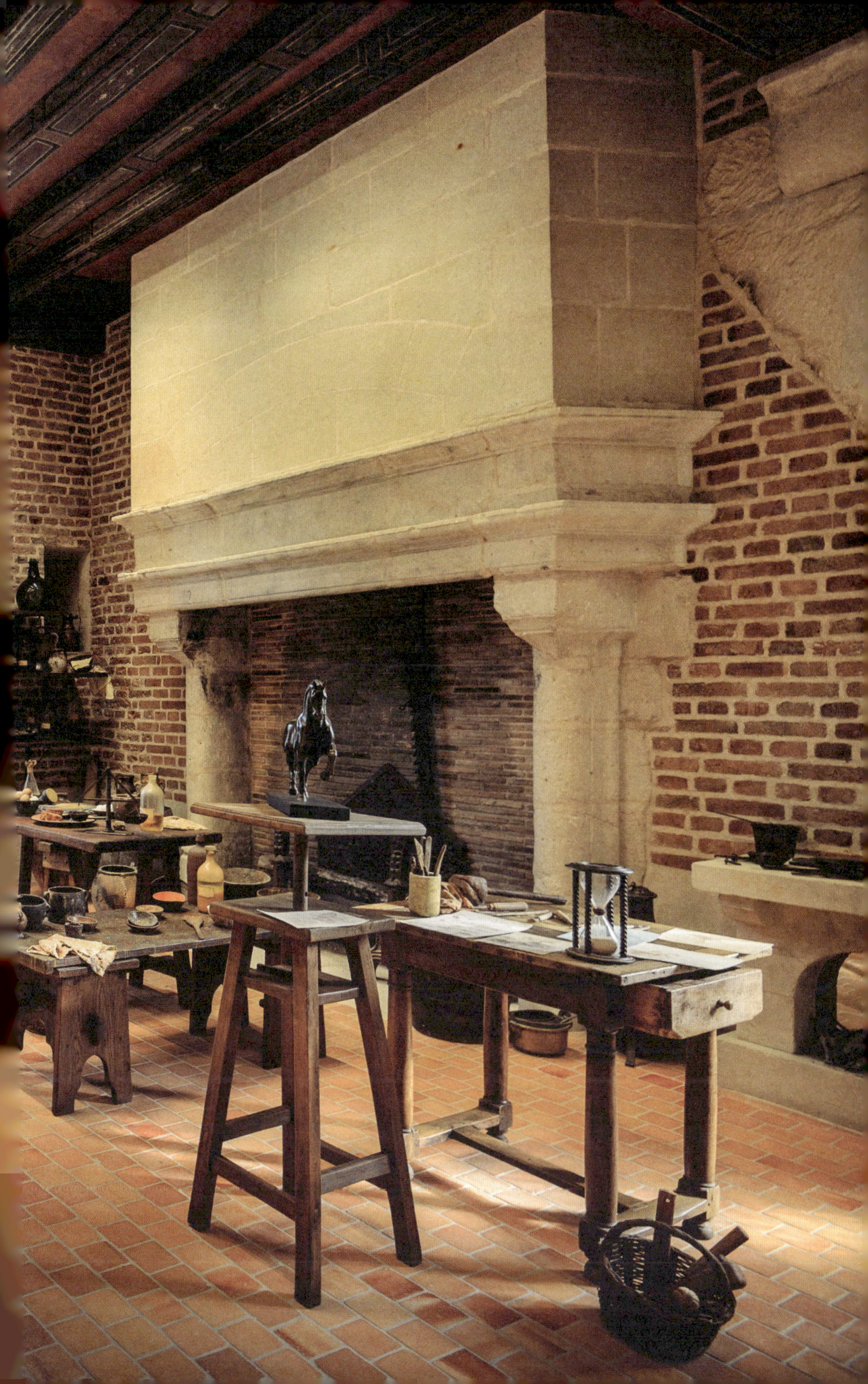

atmosphere. He draws a savage caricatural portrait of sculptors and their workplaces: 'The sculptor undertakes his work with greater bodily exertion than the painter, and the painter undertakes his work with greater mental exertion .... [Hammering] is an extremely mechanical operation, generally accompanied by great sweat which mingles with dust and becomes converted into mud. His face becomes plastered and powdered all over with marble dust, which makes him look like a baker .... His house is in a mess and covered in chips and dust from the stone.'[15]

On the face of it, Leonardo's case is a persuasive one: sculptors' workshops can be insalubrious places. John Ruskin observed in 1860 that the Pre-Raphaelite sculptor Alexander Munro, 'like all sculptors, lives in a nasty wood house full of clay and water-tubs, so I can't go without catching cold'.[16] Brancusi complained that 'marble dust penetrates all. I've tried everything, even masks, but still it penetrates into you through the pores.'[17] Leonardo knew what he was talking about. In the 1490s, he designed an equestrian monument in bronze of his patron's father. Some of the numerous wax and clay models would have been clogging up his studio. The French invasion of Milan in 1500 brought it to an ignominious end: the life-size clay model was used for shooting practice.

***

Closer inspection reveals major flaws in Leonardo's defence of painting. Sedentary art-making requires a drastic reduction in picture size, even if Leonardo did sketch out a pulley mechanism that moved larger paintings up and down the wall so the painter could work while seated.[18] Effortless ease – as Cennini implied with his preference for panel painting over fresco – can occur only with small easel pictures, miniatures and drawings. 'Light brushes' were used for fine detail. The finest were made of squirrel or ermine hair, fox tails or mouse whiskers, pushed into the split end of a quill.[19] Pictures painted exclusively with light brushes would end up in a *studiolo*; so no large altarpieces or frescoes like the *Last Supper* (1495–8).

Leonardo's strategic shrinking of the parameters of painting and studio risked taking male artists into the 'petite' realm traditionally allotted to women painters such as Eirene (Chapter 5). Lavinia Fontana (1552–1614), taught by her Bolognese painter father and married to his assistant, was one of the first professional women artists, as well as having eleven children. She was unusual in securing commissions for altarpieces, but portraits remained her

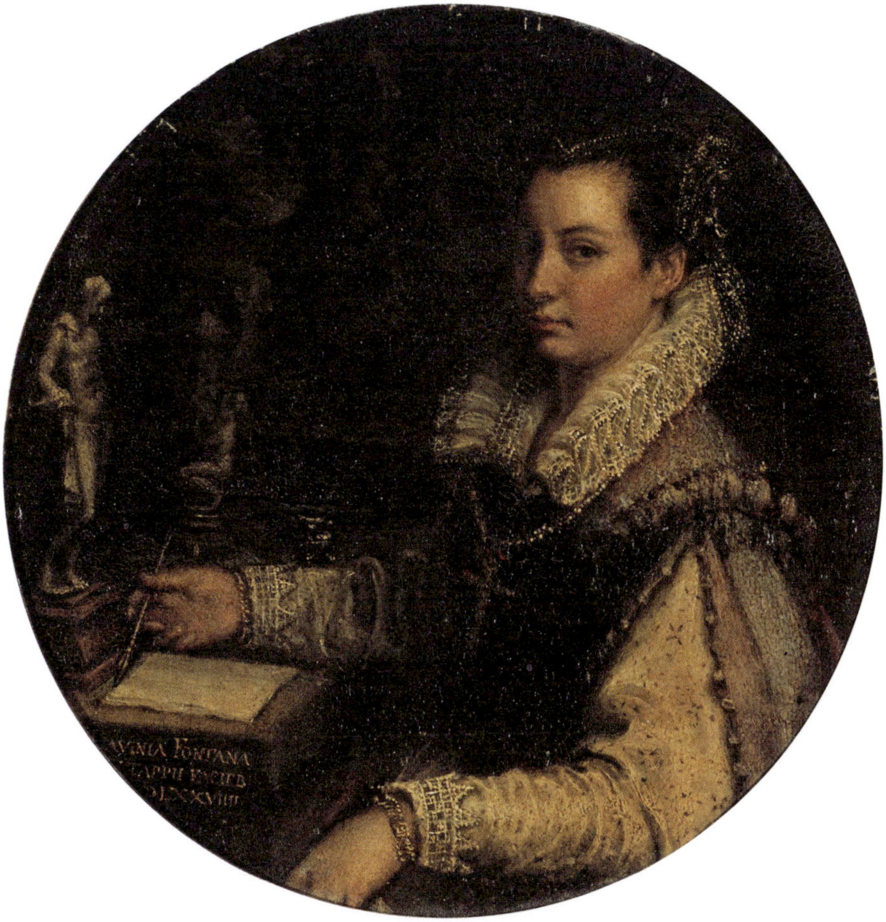

Lavinia Fontana, *Self-Portrait*, 1579, oil on copper.

staple. A miniature self-portrait on smooth copper was painted for a collector of portraits of famous men and women. Seated in a tiny, packed *studiolo*, Fontana exudes polished determination. Her small plaster casts are neatly arranged in box shelves. She still respects female decorum (huge crucifix, constricting clothes) and permits herself only a tiny piece of blank paper. She holds a *porte-crayon* – a metal casing holding a piece of charcoal or chalk. But her hand lies limp, giving no promise of muscular exertion. This is the refined world of super-light implements, with no indication that Fontana could make large oil paintings on stretched canvas, its rough weave and give requiring stiff hog-hair brushes.

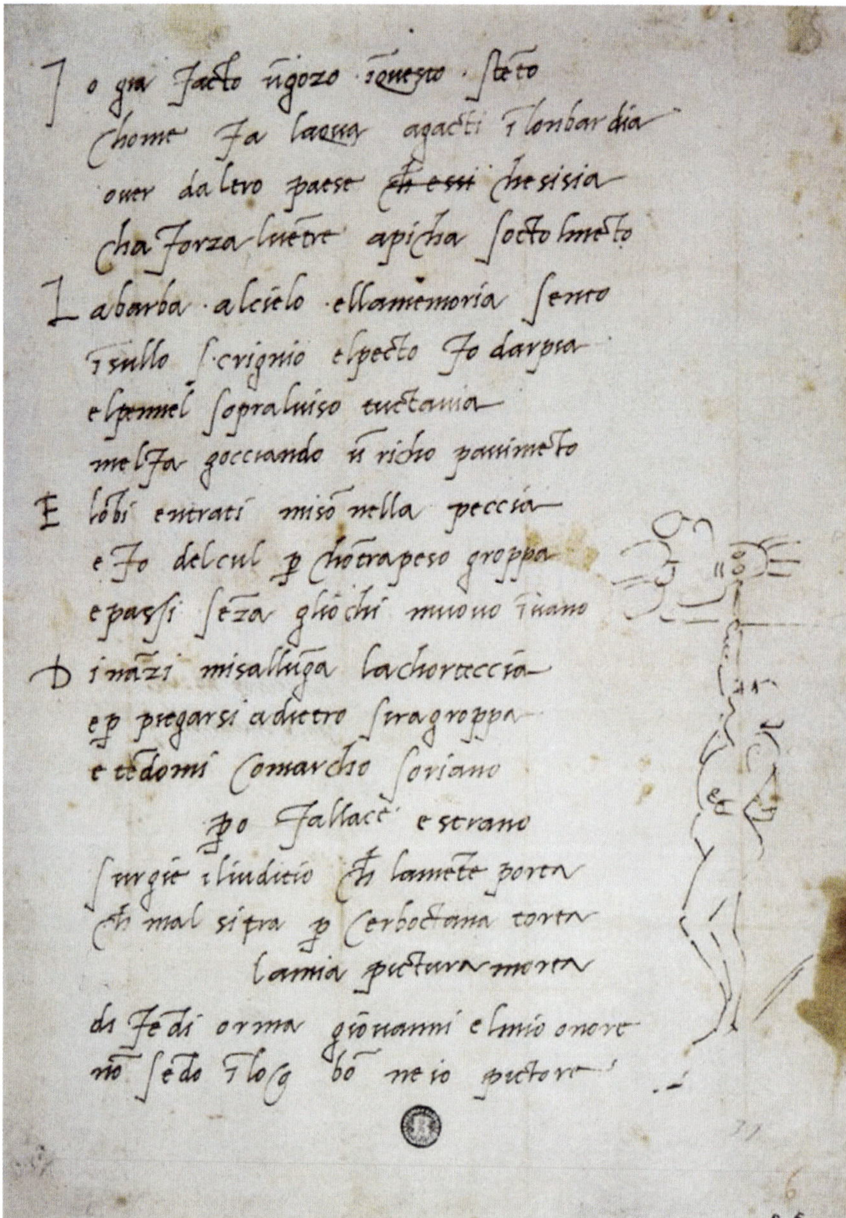

Michelangelo, *Sonnet with Self-Portrait*, 1511–12, pen and ink on paper.

Three centuries later, the full implications of the triumph of easel painting were spelled out in a diary entry by the French painter Eugène Delacroix (1798–1863). He was then painting a pair of murals and a ceiling for a chapel in the Parisian church of Saint-Sulpice. He was sceptical about easel painting per se, despite or because of his brilliance at it. His whipping boy was the Neoclassical easel painter Nicolas Poussin (1594–1665), symptom of the withering of art's ambitions and parameters: 'One stands confounded at the force, the fecundity, and the universality of those men of the sixteenth century. Our miserable little pictures painted for our miserable dwellings, the disappearance of those Maecenases whose palaces were, for generations, the refuge of works of art .... Less than a hundred years later, Poussin already does no more than paint small pictures (1 Jan 1857).'[20] Delacroix would have known Poussin's self-portrait in the Louvre, in which small framed pictures are stacked up behind him ready to go.

Delacroix's greatest 'universal' artist was Michelangelo (1475–1564), famed for his awesome *terribilità*. It was indeed Michelangelo who posed the biggest challenge to Leonardo's ideal, and who became a patron deity for modern 'anti-studio' and 'post-studio' artists. When planning the *Last Judgment*, aged 60, he derided Sebastiano del Piombo's proposal to execute it in oils rather than as a fresco: 'Painting in oil is an art of women and of people who are lazy and wealthy, like Sebastiano.'[21] He fell off the *Last Judgment* scaffold, injuring himself. The historian Paolo Giovio, in the first biographical sketch (*c.* 1527), claims Michelangelo lived in 'incredible filth'; Vasari says he wore the same calf-length boots for months, and when he removed them his skin came away.[22] Small wonder that Francis Bacon, modern master of the squalid studio, adored him, especially his depictions of the male nude.

Michelangelo's refusal to idealize the studio is epitomized by his quip when a sculptor took great trouble arranging the lights of his studio windows to show his work to best effect: only in 'the light of the piazza' is a work properly judged.[23] Michelangelo not only spent years in the quarries at Carrara, searching out the finest marble: he told his official biographer Ascanio Condivi about his youthful ambition to carve a vast sculpture on the side of the mountain. The only self-portrait of him at work wallows in being stretched to breaking point, sixty feet off the ground. The sketch illustrates a burlesque poem in which he lists the privations of painting the Sistine Chapel ceiling (1508–12) standing on a bridge-like scaffold fixed to the chapel walls. His chin 'points to heaven', and 'I feel the nape of my neck on my hump.' His paint-spattered face becomes 'a richly decorated floor .... I cannot see where to put my feet.' He bends like a semicircular Syrian bow, and completely loses it: 'The thoughts that arise in my mind are false and strange, for one shoots badly through a crooked barrel.'[24] Serious painting is as demanding and dirty as sculpture – or warfare.

Michelangelo framed himself in relation to Hercules, who performed ten heroic labours (including cleaning the Augean stables), and to the visionary poet Dante, who journeyed through the ultimate shithouse, hell. His first recorded statue (now lost) was of Hercules, and this mythical hero offered an alternative to Leonardo's view of labour. The 'choice of Hercules', or 'Hercules at the crossroads', was an episode first related in Xenophon's *Memorabilia*, his biography of Socrates: the youthful Hercules is approached by two women signifying Virtue and Vice. Virtue is austerely attired and offers to take him along a high path that is desolate and mountainous. Vice is a beguiling sex kitten who offers the easy, low, horizontal road of soft, sedentary pleasures. Hercules follows Virtue and performs the ten great labours. In the Renaissance, this story was known in numerous variants; in one, an architect builds a ten-storey school surmounted by a statue of Virtue.[25]

For Michelangelo, art-making was not labour-intensive in the sense of menial drudgery, but Labour-intensive: a process of heroic conquest.[26] This attitude was evident when he carved the *David* (1501–4), the first colossal nude since antiquity. The block had been botched and abandoned in a yard in the cathedral workshops forty years before. Proposing to make it without adding new pieces, he presented a wax model to the commissioners. Vasari says that only Michelangelo 'had courage enough' to make it without additions; Michelangelo envisaged his feat in even more heroic terms. The only surviving sketch – for the right arm and chest – is accompanied by a three-line ditty: 'David with the sling and I with the bow. Michelangelo'. Just as the boy David triumphed over the giant Goliath, so the young Michelangelo will triumph over the giant block. The 'bow' (*arco*) probably refers to the *seste ad arco*, the compass used to scale up small models.[27]

Vasari says Michelangelo built 'a walled enclosure surrounding his worktables and the marble block, and he worked continuously without anyone seeing'; a Herculean hermit in a cave.[28] Models, drawings, tools and abrasives for the final smoothing and polishing would be placed on trestle tables. Countless chisels were required, sharpened and repaired by specialists. A wooden scaffold would be built round the block, set back slightly for better visibility and access.

A heroic depiction of a Michelangelesque sculptor appears unexpectedly in the margin of the first Florentine printed edition of Dante's *Divine Comedy* (1481).[29] The drawing illustrates *Inferno* 2.37–9, when the poet has a 'crossroads' crisis moment. Having called on the muses for help, Dante confesses his doubts: 'I am not Aeneas, nor St Paul.' The commentary says that Dante

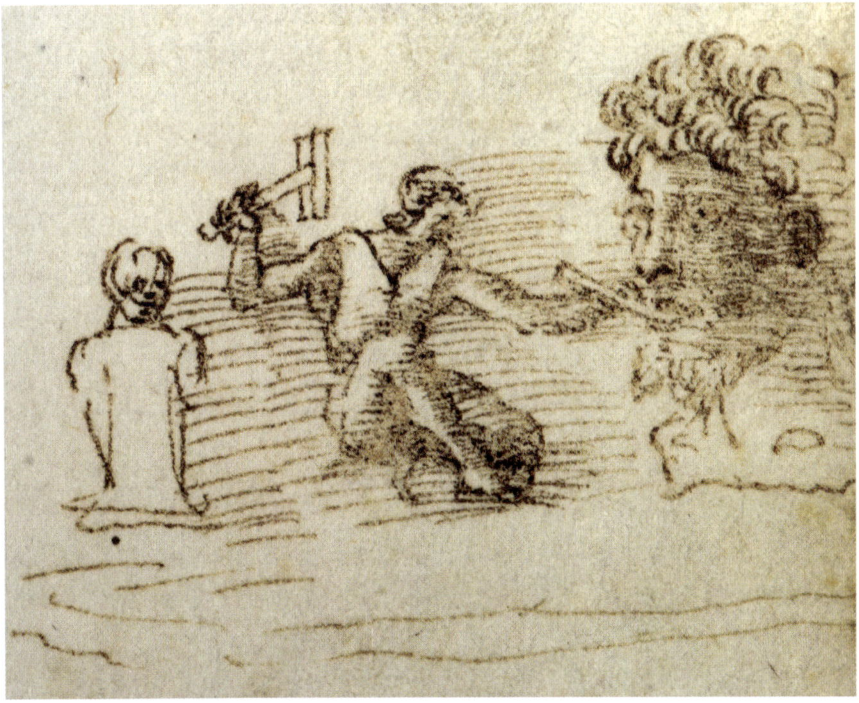

Unknown Florentine artist, *A Sculptor at Work*, c. 1503–10, ink on paper; marginal illustration in Cristoforo Landino's edition of Dante's *Divine Comedy*, Florence 1481.

'cowers before the size and difficulty of the task and is dismayed by the mental effort'. Having been assured of divine approval, he bravely takes the 'high and wooded path' through hell.

The sculptor, hitherto unrecognized, can only be Michelangelo during or after his triumphant achievement carving the *David*. Michelangelo may have chosen the passage and supplied a drawing which the unknown draughtsman, always considered a Florentine, adapted. He was not only an Aeneas among sculptors, but an expert in Dante: 'Oh that I were he!', he wrote in the 1540s.[30] The unevenness of the lightly sketched ground suggests he is in a dusty courtyard (in his youth, he had worked in Lorenzo de' Medici's sculpture garden, an arcaded courtyard full of antique sculpture). He has been working on an antique-style statuette that resembles the mischievous young faun that clings to the leg of Michelangelo's drunken *Bacchus* (1496–7). It lacks arms, suggesting the sculptor may have botched it or smashed it (he wields his mallet perilously close).

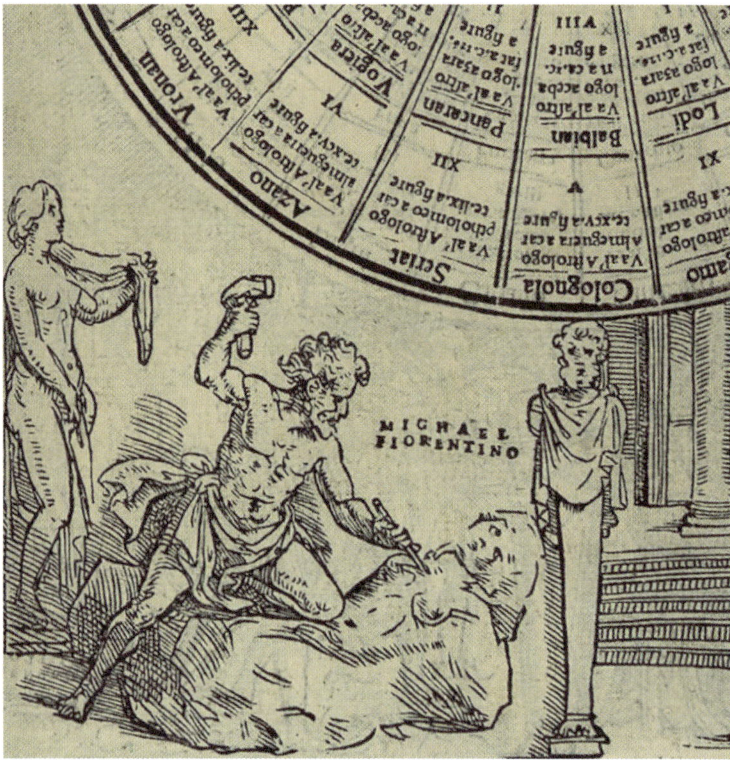

Sphera de Ariete (detail), illustration from Sigismondo Fanti's *Triompho di Fortuna*, Venice 1526.

The sculptor has now moved on to bigger challenges: a colossal head similar to antique heads of Aeneas and to those of Michelangelo's statues of saints Paul and Peter (1501–4), made for an altar in Siena Cathedral.[31] The intensity of the stare recalls *David*. The sculptor twists like the seated *ignudi* on the Sistine ceiling.[32] He is dressed for vigorous, sweaty action in a labourer's singlet, limbs bare, arms fully extended. That only the sculpture's head is shown is surely due to space limitations. But it could be inspired by Michelangelo sitting on a high platform to carve the head of *David*.

The first published image of Michelangelo at work in his workshop is the most vehement image of an artist to date. It appears in a 1526 edition of Sigismondo Fanti's astrological lottery book, *Triompho di Fortuna* (Venice). The page is that of Aries, sign of Fire and of Mars.[33] 'MICHAEL FIORENTINO' is a demonic Pygmalion, clad only in loincloth. He carves the Medici Chapel *Dawn*, shown in reverse and still unfinished. He embodies artistic *furor* – inspired fury. Michelangelo plants one knee on *Dawn*'s groin and smashes his mallet with full force onto a punch chisel planted over her heart. She turns towards us with a pained expression, as though he were both destroying and creating her. The implied violence of the Fanti woodcut partly reflects the importance of anatomical dissection. Michelangelo had first participated in a dissection in around 1494 in the hospital of Santo Spirito, Florence. He was indicted for grave-robbing in Florence in the early 1500s.[34] *Dawn*'s liveliness suggests we may be witnessing a vivisection. This is the first depiction of a sculptor at work surrounded by antique-style statues. They too are uncannily alive, stony automata.

The vigour with which Michelangelo attacked the marble block was no myth. Paolo Giovio wrote in his mini-biography that 'none after the ancients has carved marble with such skill and rapidity'.[35] This remained the case even in his old age, as we learn from a French eyewitness, Blaise de Vignère: 'I have seen Michelangelo, although more than sixty years old and no longer among the most robust, knock off more chips of a very hard marble in a quarter of an hour than three young stone carvers could have done in three or four, an almost incredible thing to one who has not seen it; and I thought the whole work would fall to pieces because he moved with such impetuosity and fury, knocking to the floor large chunks three or four fingers thick with a single blow so precisely aimed that even had he gone even fractionally further than necessary, he risked losing it all.'[36] That calculated risk-taking is exactly what we see in the *Triompho di Fortuna*.

***

Michelangelo's poem doesn't entirely exaggerate the horrors of painting the ceiling. Condivi says the artist's eyesight was temporarily damaged, and he had to hold letters above his head to read them. But the fresco belies the poem's larger claims. Far from becoming 'crooked', the quality improves. There were no motor control issues, either, when he wrote the poem. He used his finest humanist cursive script, reserved for the most important recipients, slanted towards the right and with calligraphic flourishes.[37] Its controlled elegance contrasts with the contents, and suggests this was a literary exercise as much as a *cri de coeur*. He probably wrote the poem seated at a desk in a relatively comfortable *studiolo* like that included in his later plan for a palazzo in Rome.[38] When necessary, he dressed like a courtier, and he appears in patrician velvet in late portraits.

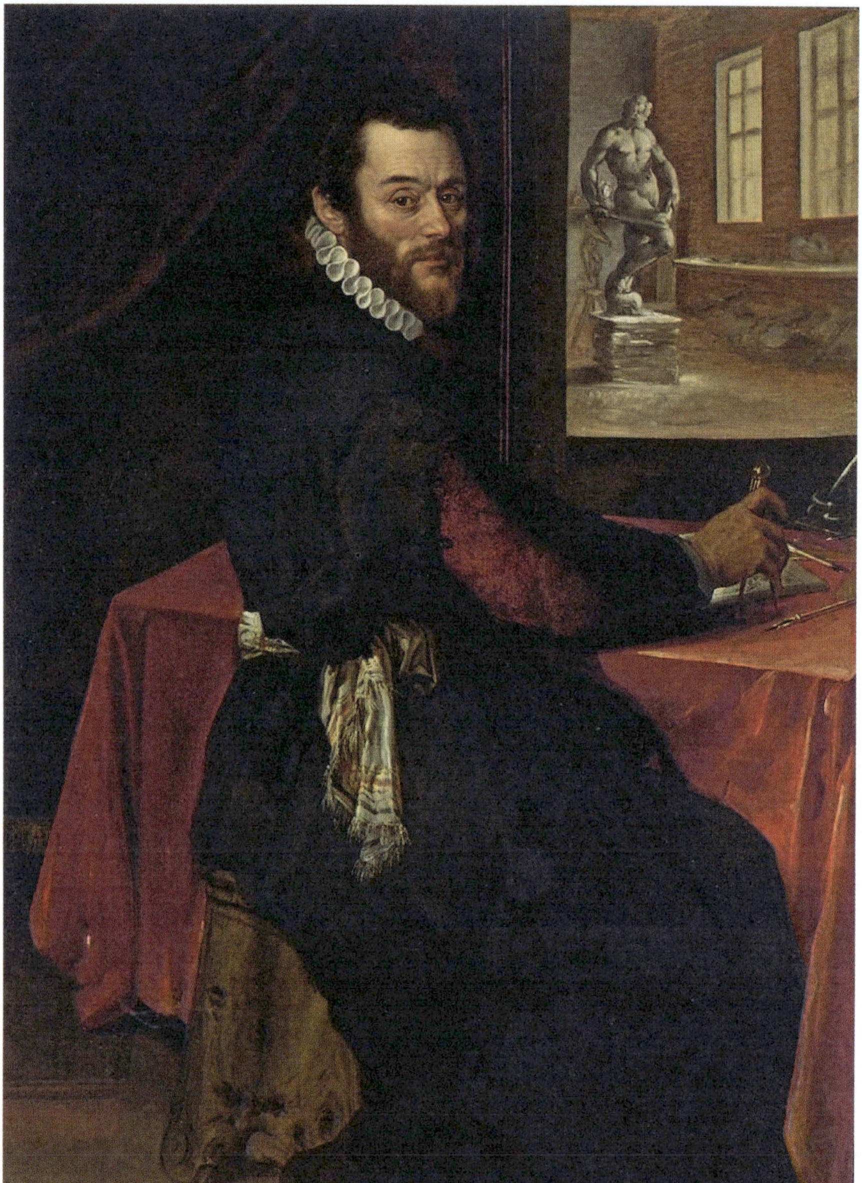

Flemish School, *Portrait of Giambologna*, 1570s, oil on canvas.

Michelangelo's basic set-up may have been a more insalubrious and spartan variant of what we see in a portrait of the Flemish-born sculptor Giambologna (1529–1608). The new Michelangelo, Giambologna dominated sculpture in Florence during the late 16th century and was so highly valued by the Medici that he was forbidden to leave the city. We know from an inventory drawn up after his death that on the ground floor of his house he had a *scrittoio* next door to a *studio*, and a much larger sculpture workshop.[39]

The *scrittoio* contained three landscape paintings, eleven portraits and four of Giambologna's architectural models. A wall bracket displayed sculptural models. The room name suggests it was where he did his paperwork, and perhaps some drawing. The walls of the *studio* were decorated with eleven landscape paintings and nine portraits, genres in which the Flemish excelled. There were sixteen wall brackets for stucco models and two shelves of wax models. Landscapes offered pleasant escapism – from studio, court and city, and from figure sculpture. The *studio* also contained a small table about 1.2 metres (4 feet) square with a stone top, on which sat an ebony ink holder and table clock. This seems to be where the sculptor is calmly sitting in the portrait, the table now covered by a velvet cloth, but with nothing so time-serving as a clock. Finely dressed in velvet, silk and lace, he is armed with dividers and *porte-crayon*.

The contents of Giambologna's workshop were not listed in the inventory because his sculptures belonged to the Medici. The workshop would not have opened directly onto the *studio*, as it does in the picture, because of dust, draughts and noise. Here we see Giambologna's colossal statue of Neptune (3.4 metres or 11 feet high), destined for the Fountain of the Ocean (1570–5) in the Boboli Gardens. He is a classic dynamic automaton, ready to burst through the oiled paper windows, run to the gardens and jump onto the fountain bowl. A measured-up ink drawing survives for the fountain, and this may be what Giambologna is now working on. None of his many assistants is allowed to intrude on his creative solitude.[40]

Giambologna discreetly acknowledges Michelangelo even as he upstages him. A plaster arm fragment, evoking Michelangelo's *Dawn* and *Night* in the Medici Chapel at San Lorenzo, lies abjectly on the long, crescent-shaped worktop below the windows. Casts after the Medici Chapel sculptures were standard studio props, and the chapel had become a study room for artists: Vasari called it a 'school of the arts'. Messy reality intrudes with the tarpaulins, wood and tools below the worktop and the marble chippings round *Neptune*. But all this is easily overlooked background detail, and we are more likely to dwell on the suave courtier, perched on his richly carved walnut stool.

Chapter 9

Creatures of the Night

'Only the Dark Serves to Plant Man'

Drawing at night by artificial light became a crucial component of artistic practice during the Renaissance, further increasing the mystique of the studio. The flame from candles and oil lamps was Promethean fire, propelling artists to new creative heights and depths.

Nocturnal drawing was decisively put on the cultural map by the Florentine sculptor and draughtsman Baccio Bandinelli (1493–1560). Prior to Bandinelli, only Dürer could claim to be a more inventive or prolific self-portraitist – though Dürer never made a print self-portrait, or any image showing himself at work.[1] Bandinelli was also the first self-portraitist to make sculptural props central to his self-image, and the first to accord himself demiurgic powers. His self-absorption and abrasive personality inspired loathing and mockery of many contemporaries, including Michelangelo; he was recently dubbed Michelangelo's 'evil twin'.

Agostino Veneziano's widely disseminated print after a Bandinelli drawing is the first known depiction of an academy of art. The inscription on the table says 'Academy of Bacchio Brandin in Rome in the place called Belvedere 1531'. Brandini was his birth name; Bandinelli a noble name adopted to qualify for knighthood. The Belvedere ('beautiful view') was the pope's summer villa, on a hill by the Vatican Palace. From 1503 until 1513,

Opposite above Agostino Veneziano after Baccio Bandinelli, *The Academy of Baccio Bandinelli*, 1531, engraving. **Opposite below** Ambrogio Brambilla, *Aerial View of the Vatican Belvedere*, 1579, engraving. It shows the courtyard of the Belvedere, with St Peter's under construction at top left and the Belvedere villa itself, with statue court, at far right.

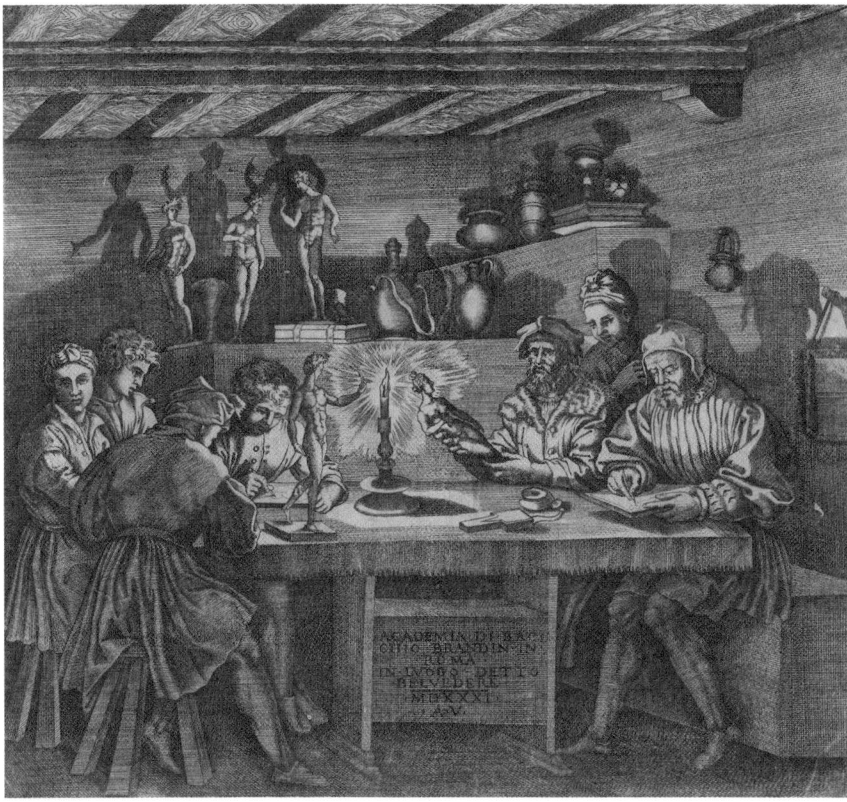
ACADEMIA DI BAC
CIO BRANDIN IN
ROMA
IN LVOGO DETTO
BELVEDERE
MDXXXI
A.V.

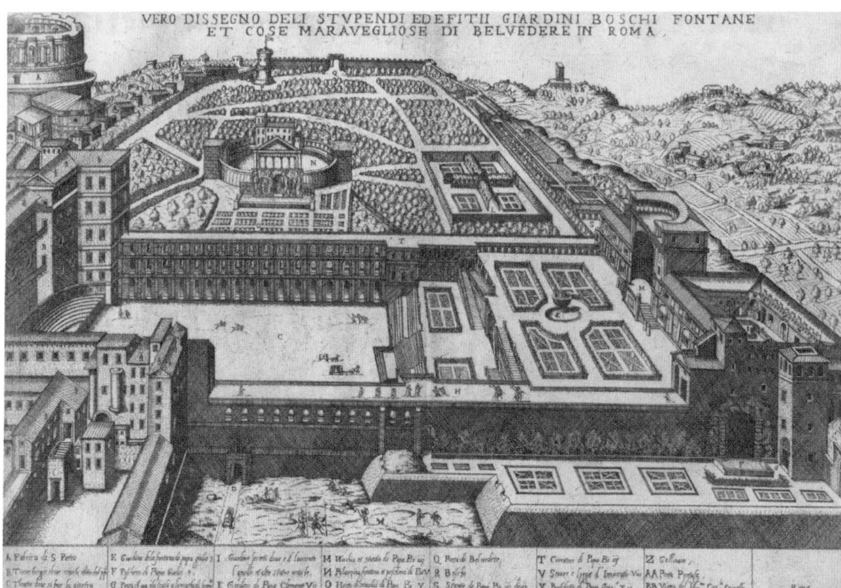
VERO DISSEGNO DELI STVPENDI EDEFITII GIARDINI BOSCHI FONTANE
ET COSE MARAVEGLIOSE DI BELVEDERE IN ROMA
A Fabrica di S. Pietro
Q Porta di Belvedere
R Boschi
Z Gallinaro
Roma

the architect Bramante built a sculpture court in the villa's garden for the pope's finest antique statues, including the *Apollo Belvedere* and *Laocoön*. He linked the villa to the Vatican by a series of open stairways and terraces and a long arcaded corridor. Leonardo, much admired by Bandinelli, lived there in refurbished rooms with a kitchen from 1513 until 1516, before moving to France. A counter for grinding pigments was provided; two windows were rebuilt. It is never referred to as a *bottega* (workshop) in documents,[2] and Leonardo himself always used the term *studio* or *studiolo*.

Bandinelli may well have occupied Leonardo's rooms, with a separate sculpture workshop. His use of the term 'academy' is natural insofar as Plato's philosophical academy took place in a grove near Athens, and Renaissance revivals had pastoral villa settings. The first modern use of the term was by the humanist Poggio Bracciolini in 1427, in relation to his villa near Florence filled with antique busts. Leonardo had an 'Academia Leonardi Vinci' in Milan – probably an informal discussion group – but nothing is known about it.[3] Despite its garden setting, Bandinelli's academy is defiantly windowless and nocturnal. The beautiful views are inside, not outside.

Bandinelli had been in Rome in the early 1520s to make a life-size copy of the *Laocoön*, reimagining missing parts; he also made a new arm for the original sculpture. A powerful sense of wholeness, and indeed security, is given by the cubic beamed space, and by numerous intact sculptures and objets d'art. The students draw antique-style statuettes similar to those made by Bandinelli. A portable inkwell and attached pen-case lie on the table. Bandinelli, swathed in the warm, fur-lined coat of a scholar, carefully holds a standing Venus, communing with antiquity in feminine form. It is a secular Holy of Holies, with perpetually burning sanctuary lamp.

One could justifiably complain that even if Bandinelli's subject matter is novel, little here would have surprised Squarcione or Mantegna. It visualizes the early Renaissance ideal of the artist 'at home' in a comfortable *studiolo*, surrounded by small-scale sculptures that here court each other with dancers' gestures. Its cosiness is reinforced by the vases, jugs and goblets, suggestive of prosperous domesticity and a reminder that Bandinelli's father was a goldsmith.[4] The brass candlestick is a fashionable Islamic type that had been introduced into Europe through Venice. Bandinelli takes us into a commercial world of portable and reproducible commodities to be enjoyed intimately – like the print itself. The exclusive focus on drawing from statuettes does not exactly make it prophetic of future art academies, with their more varied curricula.

A devil's advocate might also point out that it was hardly unusual to work at night, providing you could afford oil, wax or fat for tapers. Nocturnal study had been fashionable at least since the translation into Latin of an Arabic health handbook in the 13th century. It recommended nocturnal study to prevent oversleeping, which dehydrated the body.[5] Less glamorously, night work was legalized in Paris early in the 14th century, with the 'overtime' a response to falling wages.[6] Similar pressures may underlie the legendary story told by Vasari of the diabolical subterfuges devised by the artist Buffalmacco (active c. 1315–36) to stop night work by his Florentine mosaicist master and a noisy neighbour, a female wool-spinner, so he could get more sleep.[7]

Drawing, especially of sculptures, could be undertaken at night because both are monochrome media, making colour distortion by artificial light irrelevant. 'At night all cats be grey,' went the proverb.[8] Leonardo recommended drawing during winter evenings, and even found it useful 'when in bed in the dark to run the imagination over the surface delineations of forms previously studied'.[9] Dürer, on a lucrative tour of the Netherlands in 1520–1, drew up to three portraits a night.[10]

Artificial light remained a luxury, so regular nocturnal drawing was a status symbol that in theory put the artist into the same bracket as the elite. During the 15th century the upper classes in Italy began to go to bed and eat supper later, and by 1500 Northern Europe had followed suit.[11] The apogee of refined nocturnal activity was Castiglione's *The Courtier* (1528), an idealized evocation of four consecutive nights of cultivated after-dinner conversations at the court of Urbino, presided over by the duchess.[12] When Pietro Bembo's concluding speech is finished, the participants throw open the shutters and are astonished to find it is dawn: 'They go to their rooms without torches, for the daylight was sufficient.' The book was written in Rome in the early 1520s when Bandinelli was resident there, and he would later claim that Bembo and Castiglione had visited his studio.[13]

Working by candlelight in Bandinelli's windowless and draught-free interior is clearly more than just a status symbol, however. It transforms the idea of art and artist. The candle casts dramatic, show-stealing shadows onto the walls of statuettes, students, jars and vases. The shadow cast by the man seated at far right transforms him, with ear flaps splayed demonically. At first sight, this would seem to be a reference to Pliny's delightful anecdote about Butades tracing her departing lover's shadow cast on the wall by lamplight.[14] But here shadows are larger than the source object, hinting at colossal possibilities and at the magnifying, multiplying play of male artists' imaginations.

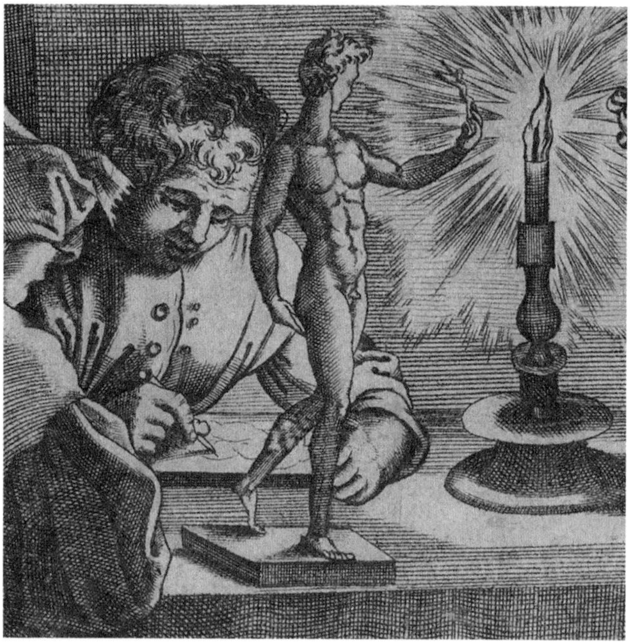

Agostino Veneziano after Baccio Bandinelli, *The Academy of Baccio Bandinelli* (detail).

Michelangelo believed night was the prime creative time because it was when babies were made: 'Only the dark serves to plant man.'[15] Night is in fact the prime growth period for plants, children and young animals.

What makes Bandinelli's academy both radical and prophetic is the awesome nature of its lighting. Night work here is inspirational privilege rather than punishment. The hyperbolic lighting – a single candle would never produce so much light, and such a large flame would produce clouds of black smoke – takes the scene far beyond the realm of reason and science. The key to it all is the male statuette on the table. His left hand, reaching towards the flame, holds a tiny standing figure with arms outstretched. This usually overlooked detail means he is Prometheus holding the first man, created with the aid of fire stolen from the gods.[16] The first man has just woken and is now running away from the fire's heat. Florentine humanists considered Prometheus a sage rather than a thief who stole the fire of superior wisdom from God and infused man with it. They interpreted his agony when punished – his liver pecked by an eagle – as the suffering experienced by thinkers and creative types.[17]

So despite the exertion, cost and eye-strain, nocturnal drawing and study connect art and artists directly with the divine. On a practical note, the pope had probably paid for Bandinelli's candles, which could be stored in the box-like basket hanging on the wall. Candles (like firewood) were often part of a courtier's salary, with candle stubs a perquisite. Churches, with their vast chandeliers, were the biggest consumers of wax candles, the vast expense justified by claiming that bees, like the mother of Jesus, were virgins. Not surprisingly, lights were outlawed in Protestant churches.[18]

***

The visionary aspects of Bandinelli's academy are held in check by the delicacy with which the artist holds the female statuette, and by the elegance of the artefacts. Such decorousness is left far behind in his second depiction of a nocturnal gathering, made in Florence (1545–50). One of the most thrilling depictions of an artist's studio, it foregrounds the sublime rather than the beautiful, the masculine rather than the feminine, turbulence rather than tranquillity. Brutally mutilated fragments, rather than intact sculptures, are showcased.

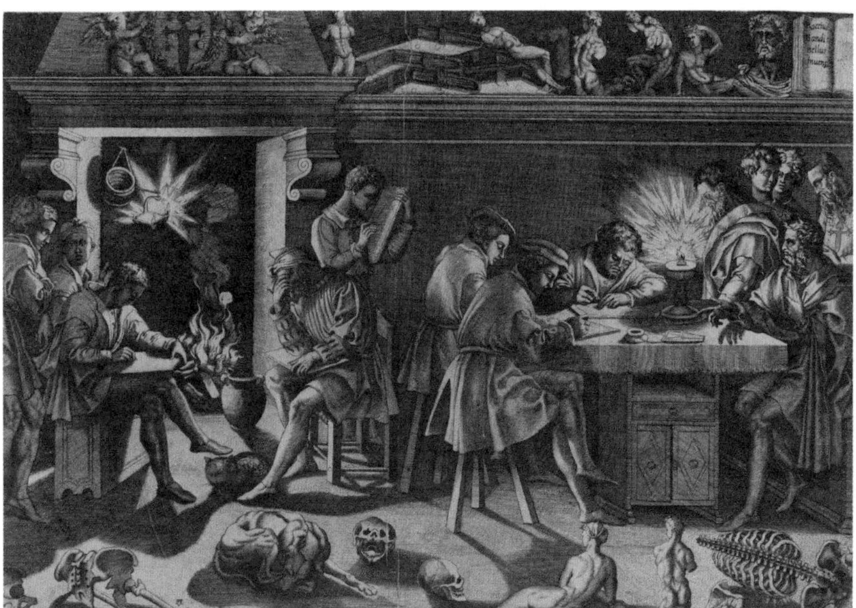

Enea Vico after Baccio Bandinelli, *Bandinelli's Night Class*, 1545–50, engraving.

The trestle table with students sitting on stools is reprised (without inscription). All else has changed. We could be eavesdropping on a wizards' coven or alchemist's lair. No one looks out at us or is orientated towards us. Bandinelli is the long-bearded man on the far right, but we are not privy to what he and his two students are looking at. He wears the Cross of the Order of Santiago, having been knighted by Emperor Charles V in 1529. We now have more of the components of the academic curriculum of the future – skeletons, casts and weighty books – but they are laid out in an unsystematic, fragmentary manner, as though a bomb has gone off. Bandinelli doesn't inscribe the print with the civilizing term 'Academia'. There is suffering, death and darkness.

This is the first depiction of an artist's studio to explicitly showcase anatomical study, and it is done in a casually brutal way. The skulls and bones strewn on the floor are a knowing nod towards Andreas Vesalius' illustrated bible of human anatomy, *De humani corporis fabrica* (1543), dedicated to Charles V (Vesalius performed vivisection on dogs, so the mastiff had better watch out). Vesalius' frontispiece illustration showed him touching the entrails of a dissected female corpse in a crowded anatomy theatre in Padua. Bandinelli has here tried to upstage him. He probably owned some bones and a skull, but not necessarily a complete skeleton. He would have worked, like Michelangelo, from 'flayed' anatomical figures in wax, as well as from drawings and, of course, from Vesalius. Vasari tells us that 'Baccio devoted himself with great study and solicitude to examining and reproducing the most minute details of anatomy, persevering in this for many months and years.'[19]

The mysteriously myopic student standing beneath the corbel of the fireplace is drawing from memory a version of Vesalius' expressively posed illustration of the muscles of a flayed man. Vesalius' 'ruin' of a man stands before architectural ruins, and Bandinelli creates a ruinscape of objects in the horizontal bands at top and bottom of the print. The ruinscape of studio properties would become a standard symbol of the artist's studio. It showed that the artist's understanding was more than skin deep, and that he could redeem the broken world with his art – just as Bandinelli had done when he restored the *Laocoön*.[20]

Diligent, round-the-clock study is the bedrock of artistic education and practice. But this is useless without the fire and lightning flash of inspiration, which takes hold of the artist's mind and body. We now have three spectacularly starry light sources reshaping the palatial interior. A triple oil lamp is suspended on an articulated rod over a log fire in the grandiose fireplace – the main source of artificial light in larger rooms. Bandinelli's alter ego stares

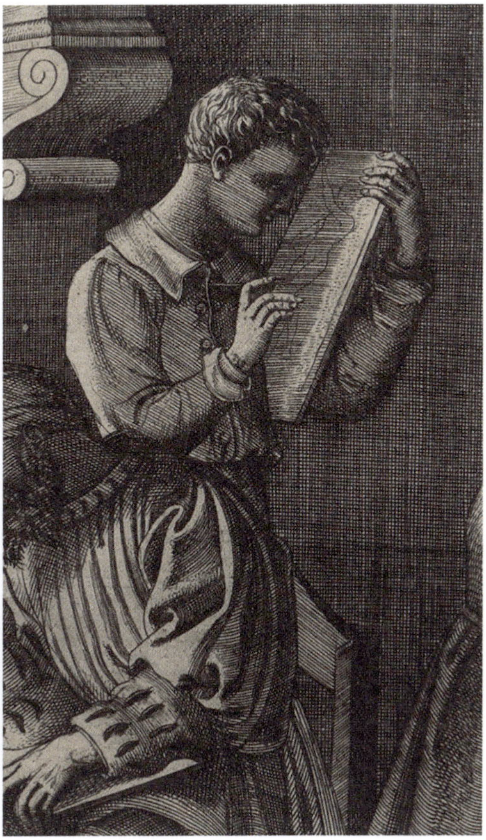

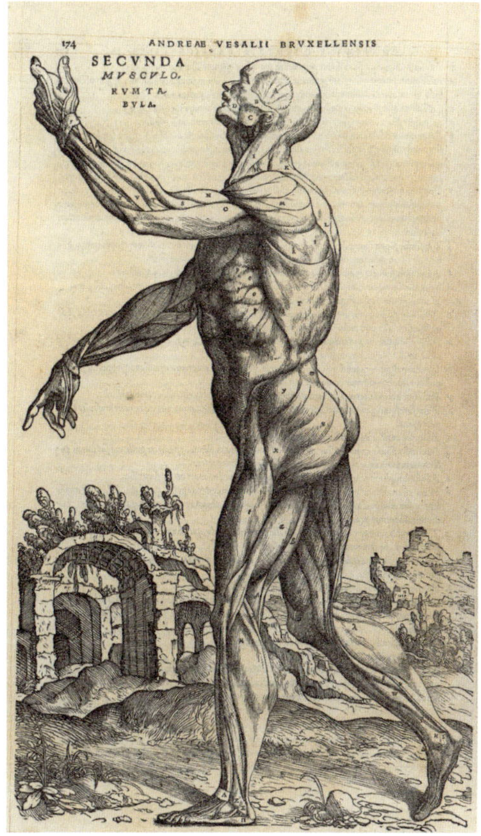

Above left Enea Vico after Baccio Bandinelli, *Bandinelli's Night Class* (detail). **Above right** *Secunda musculorum tabula*, from Andreas Vesalius, *De humani corporis fabrica*, Basel 1543.

entranced into an oil lamp, bathing his face and chest in its splintered rays, like Saint Francis receiving the stigmata. It recalls scrying, a form of divining performed at that time by boys staring into a reflective surface of some kind, often a cup filled with oil. It damaged their sight.[21] Intense bodily engagement with Promethean fire would be taken even further by the teenage Bernini. When planning a sculpture of his name saint, Lawrence, being burned on a gridiron (*c.* 1615), he burned his thigh on a brazier while standing before a mirror studying the 'painful contortions' of his face.[22]

The super-stretchy shadows here dramatically increase perspectival depth and hallucinatory intensity. Bandinelli's shadow-play in his prints would influence the North Italian artist Carlo Urbino, author of an illustrated treatise partly inspired by Leonardo's theories. In an illustration of perspective and

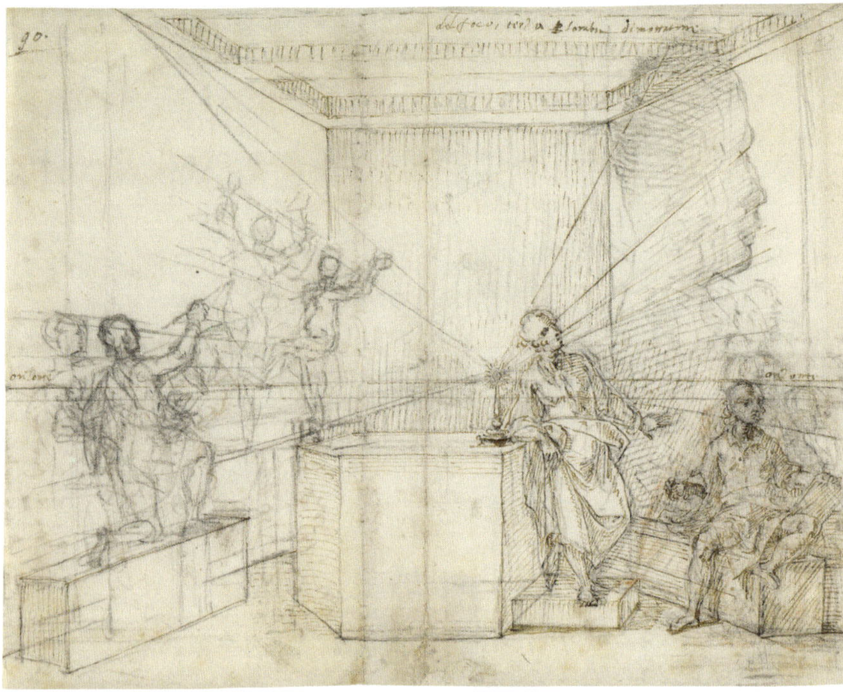

Carlo Urbino, *Of Fire. Third Demonstration of Shadow*, c. 1560–70, black chalk, pen and brown ink, red chalk, lines inscribed with stylus on laid paper.

cast shadow, artists make and draw the shadows of male figures cast on the wall by the light of a single candle. Benvenuto Cellini, in a treatise on drawing (1560s), recommended a similar method of posing a male model between a whitewashed studio wall and a light, and then drawing round the shadow. But he insisted the lamp be placed in such a way as to minimize distortion.[23] Urbino, like Bandinelli, abandons all restraint.

No one in Bandinelli's second print draws from a model set before them; they draw from within – from a mixture of memory and imagination. Most are thinking rather than doing. Only two pens are depicted for the five 'draughtsmen' (quills and a pen holder are clearly shown in the earlier print). The seated figure to the right of the hearth with his head in his hands is thinking, dreaming, planning blind, in a pose of melancholy introspection – the epitome of the suffering artist. Whereas the previous print was entirely sedentary, here seven of the thirteen figures stand, adding to the sense of restless deliberation.

***

Vasari's biography of Bandinelli is largely a hatchet job on an 'envious and malicious' man. But Bandinelli had been Vasari's teacher, and if he had learned anything, it was the importance of night work. Vasari would become its greatest proselytizer in print, paint and art education.

Vasari tells us in the *Lives* that, while in Rome to study (1532), he copied at night the drawings made by his friend Francesco Salviati during the day, and vice versa.[24] This commitment is in line with a nice anecdote he relates about Luca della Robbia (1400–1482): Luca drew by night, putting his feet into a basket of wood shavings to stop them freezing. In only one instance in the *Lives* does night drawing pose a danger to health. This is because the offending artist, Paolo Uccello (1397–1475), is a monomaniac obsessed by linear perspective, which had rather gone out of fashion in Vasari's day (Michelangelo foreshortens figures but eschews plunging perspectival backgrounds). Vasari relates that Uccello spent the whole night in his study (*scrittoio*), becoming solitary, melancholy and very poor; he left his heirs not money but chests full of drawings. On being called to bed by his wife, he merely sighed: 'Oh, what a sweet thing is this perspective!'[25] Uccello is the first in a long line of artists for whom nocturnal artistic endeavour was sweeter than sleep or sex.[26]

This admonitory anecdote is the exception to prove the rule, and Vasari tells the strangest of stories to get Michelangelo on board the night train. In old age, he rose to carve at night (doubtless one of the unfinished Pietàs). He made 'a cap from thick paper, and over the centre of his head he kept a lighted candle'.[27] Vasari says he saw him using this hands-free head torch several times. The candles were not beeswax, but tallow made from clarified goat's fat, 'which are excellent'. He sent Michelangelo four bundles of tallow candles weighing forty pounds – a very generous gift that was initially rejected.

The story is a modern foundation myth for nocturnal artists, as well as an excuse for Vasari to boast of the friendship. The paper hat would have been a fire hazard and, every time Michelangelo moved his head, molten tallow – which has a lower melting point than beeswax and was more commonly used in cooler climes – would have dripped and splashed. The pages of many Renaissance books are defaced by oily stains and burns from accidental spillages.[28] Despite what Vasari says about the excellence of goat tallow, the burnt wick of tallow candles needs trimming ('snuffing') eight to ten times an hour to prevent guttering and to keep a consistently clear flame. Left unattended, they lose two-thirds of their brilliance within around ten minutes.[29] As the candle burned, the angle of the light would also have changed. Vasari would have known it was goat's tallow because of the overpowering smell:

> Base and unlustrous as the smoky light
> That's fed with stinking tallow
> (Shakespeare, *Cymbeline*, I.iv.733–4)

In the end, the story rather backfires and comes to symbolize the squalor in which Michelangelo lived as much as his nocturnal drive.

***

Vasari frescoed his houses in Arezzo and Florence with a staggering number of fire and night scenes, many depicting famous art stories from antiquity. In Arezzo, several *grisaille* panels also resemble night scenes ('At night all cats be grey'). Pliny says very little about night work – there is Butades; one painting of a boy blowing coals; and Apelles painting thunder and lightning.[30] So Vasari was faking a nocturnal art past.

Decoration of his house in Florence – given to him by his patron, Duke Cosimo I de' Medici – began in 1561. Vasari frescoed the reception room with inspiring art stories loosely based on Pliny.[31] He placed his own self-portrait bust above the fireplace, making himself appear suitably Promethean, and beside it painted the origin of painting. Whereas Pliny said that a man had first drawn round a shadow cast by sunlight, Vasari showed a young man drawing

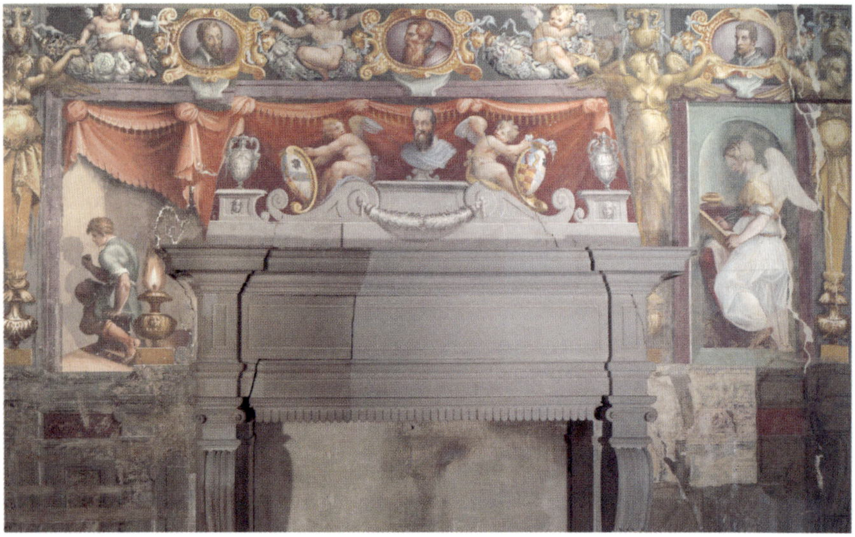

Giorgio Vasari, the fireplace wall of the reception room (detail), after 1569, Casa Vasari, Florence.

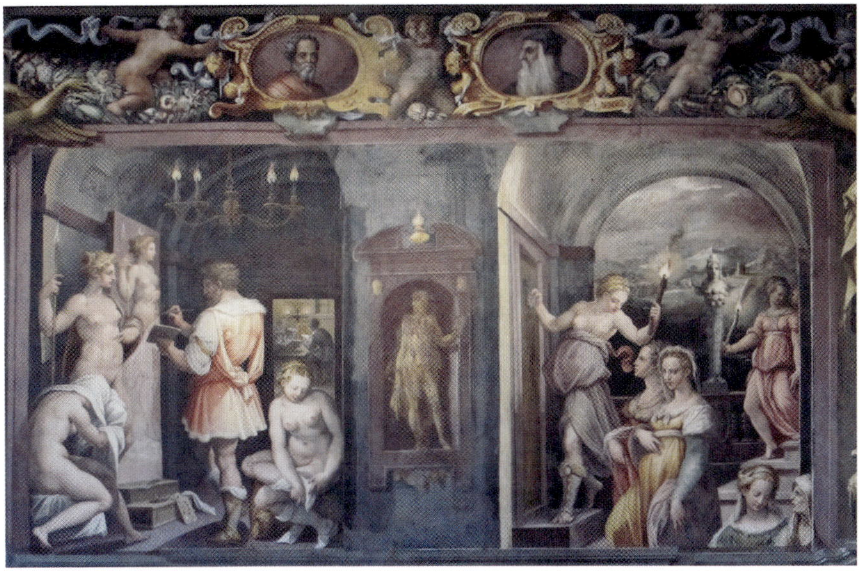

Giorgio Vasari, *The Greek Painter's Studio*, reception room, after 1569, Casa Vasari, Florence.

his own shadow cast by the bloated flame from a brass candlestick. One of his assistants was the Fleming Jan van der Straet, and Flemish painters were famous for fire and night scenes, having pioneered them in the 15th century. But this is Vasari's propaganda.

In the finest nocturnal fresco, a mature male paints a naked female posing as the chaste goddess Diana, while two other models strip off and some more arrive in his porch. The studio is illuminated by an oil lamp (over the statue niche) and a brass chandelier with four candles. Michelangelo, as the pioneer of overhead lighting, is portrayed above the chandelier, with Leonardo, master of chiaroscuro, over the entrance porch. Standing beneath a chandelier was unwise. Large drip pans would cut out downward light and eventually overflow. Actors suffered this indignity on stage, and in the 18th century the seat at the back of the life class at the French Academy was called 'the bucket' because it was below a chandelier, and whoever sat there got dripped on.[32] A bucket of water was usually placed underneath to collect the drips.[33] Vasari's unventilated studio would soon be asphyxiating, sweltering and smoky because of all the people and flames. The ceiling is realistically black from soot, and the torches held by the women outside emit thick smoke. Through a doorway, we see apprentices drawing by triple oil lamp à la Bandinelli. They are oblivious to what's happening out front, when it is they who might most profit from studying the live model. The assistants, who load the painter's palettes and grind his pigment, are not shown.

Vasari is being pulled in several directions. On the one hand, he wants to emphasize the importance of night work for the artist, a practice that was then being institutionalized. He was the driving force behind the founding of the Accademia del Disegno in 1563, presided over by Duke Cosimo. Membership was selective, and after 1571 members no longer had to belong to a trade guild. The Accademia did not replace traditional apprenticeships but put a scientific icing on the educational cake with evening lectures on mathematics, geometry and anatomy. Elected masters of *disegno* gave evening classes in drawing.

On the other hand, Vasari wants to emphasize the importance of live models, even though this contradicts his own practice. He recommended drawing (not painting) from the male and female model, but only at the outset of a career. Daily drawing exercises enabled the young artist to memorize the muscles, so eventually any figure could be drawn without a model present. He gave equal billing to copying figures from great paintings and sculptures, which further marginalized live models. The poses of the three naked models mimic famous antique sculptures, prompting the question of why real women are needed. Less than a tenth of Vasari's surviving drawings are from life.[34]

Drawing from the live male model at the Accademia may have begun only in the 1590s after the founding of the Accademia di San Luca in Rome in 1593. Its president, Federico Zuccaro, had criticized the lack of life classes in Florence, and largely thanks to him they became central to subsequent academic teaching. Even now, live models came last. Novices first drew from drawings and prints, then casts of heads, hands and feet, followed by casts of the antique, and finally the nude model.[35]

The unusual features of Vasari's fresco are partly explained by his wanting to create a festive atmosphere. Night is also the time for glamorous parties such as the one in Castiglione's *The Courtier*. Vasari's fresco is in his reception room. The stream of beautiful women coming to the artist's door at night, and the fact that he *paints* directly from the live model, might have made art lovers think of Titian. In the summer, Titian held torchlit dinner parties in the wonderful garden of his house in Venice. He was renowned for fondling and kissing women at parties, and was rumoured to sleep with his female models (though this has never been proven).[36] The painter's brush hovers above the groin area. The artist's home studio as nocturnal pleasure palace and party venue begins here.

***

Hardly anyone prior to the 20th century would paint from a live model at night because of colour distortion. After the discovery of the early Christian catacombs in Rome in 1578, the poor quality of the wall paintings was attributed to their having been produced 'below ground by candle light'.[37] The two earliest depictions known to me of an artist painting at night are both of Saint Luke painting the Virgin and Child, by the Flemish painters Simon Bening (1521) and Maerten van Heemskerck (1532).[38] But here, divine intervention will correct the colours.

Thomas Gainsborough painted staged landscapes in his studio at night by candlelight, using broccoli as trees, which helped him reduce detail and unify colour. In 1781, Gainsborough and his nephew successfully painted the drapery for a full-length portrait of Queen Charlotte in one night by lamplight. The queen's dress is of gold-spangled silk net over white silk, punctuated by tasselled bunches of gold lace. Gainsborough's nephew also would have spent much of the time tending oil lamps, and the white and gold paint mixtures were sorted out in advance. Goya, much influenced by Gainsborough, applied finishing touches at night with four Michelangelo-style candleholders fixed to the sides of a rigid top hat. This gave a bolder impact to paintings that were often viewed at evening receptions.[39]

Nocturnal painting came of age in the 20th century, precisely because it facilitated anti-naturalism and abstraction. The mythical origins of Futurism were nocturnal, in a setting that recalls Bandinelli's prints. Marinetti's first Futurist manifesto (1909) begins: 'We stayed up all night, my friends and I, under hanging mosque lamps with domes of filigreed brass.' The lamps shone with the 'radiance of an electric heart' as 'we carried our discussion to the farthest limits of logic'. Artificial light helps them defy logic.

Picasso always preferred to paint at night, locked away in his studio. The practice reinforced his penchant for bold, non-naturalistic colours, *grisaille* and monochrome (the Blue and Rose periods). The *Demoiselles d'Avignon* (1907) was painted in a dark, squalid basement without electricity, amid African sculptures, strips of peeled wallpaper, piles of ash from a stove and dusty stacks of canvases.[40] He may have known the French proverb: 'By candlelight a goat resembles a young lady.'[41] Night would play a starring role in the artist-at-work documentary *Le Mystère Picasso* (1955).

Duchamp, in his Cubo-Futurist phase, would paint by gaslight in his New York studio (1910–11): 'You know that gaslight from the old Aver jet is green; I wanted to see what the changing of colours would do. When you paint in green light and then, the next day, you look at it in daylight, it's a lot

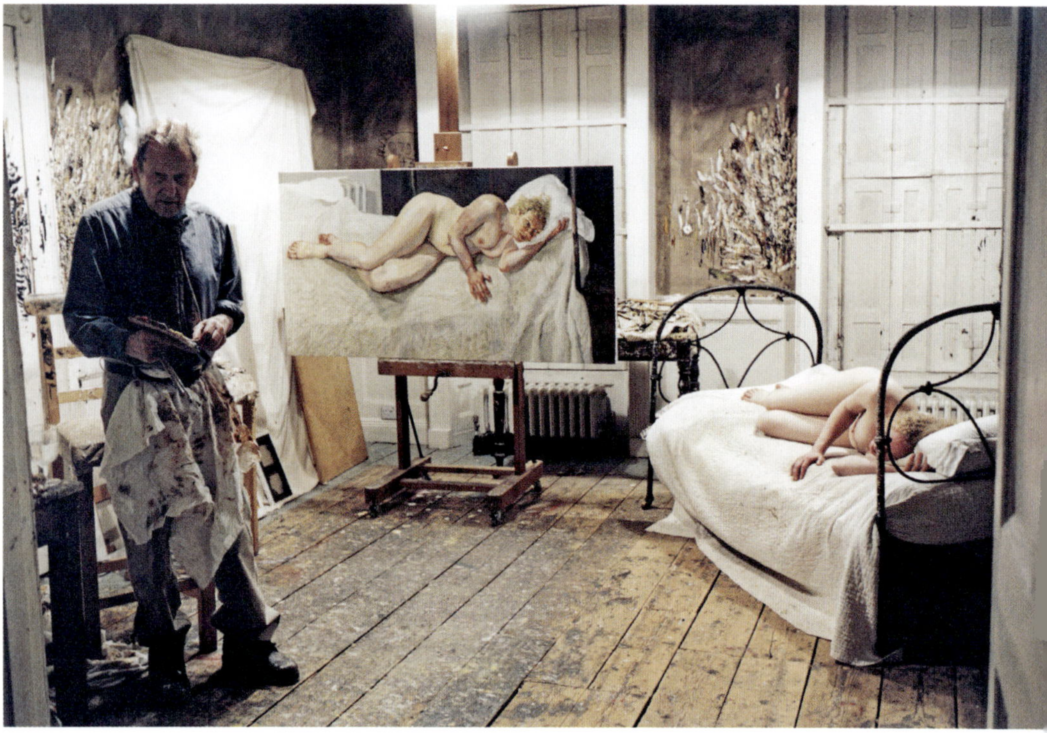

David Dawson, *Lucian Freud Photographed in His Night Studio with Model Ria Kirby*, 2007.

more mauve, grey, and more like what the Cubists were painting at the time. It was an easy way to get a lowering of tones, a *grisaille*.'[42]

Kandinsky's artistic epiphany – and discovery of non-objective art – occurred at dusk: 'I returned home with my painting box having finished a study [in the open air] ... and suddenly saw an indescribably beautiful picture, pervaded by an inner glow .... I could discern only forms and colours ... it was a picture I had painted, standing on its side against the wall. The next day I tried to re-create my impression of the picture from the previous evening by daylight. I only half succeeded, however; even on its side, I constantly recognised objects, and the fine bloom of dusk was missing.'[43]

More recently, Lucian Freud had two studios: a day studio overlooking his garden, lit by natural light from the east, and a night studio, harshly and luridly lit by halogen pendant lights. Pictures were never moved between studios, so there were day pictures and night pictures. The halogen light, which bleached the flesh, was eminently forensic: 'I am a biologist.'[44]

Chapter 10

Making a Spectacle
The Systematic Studio

I suggested earlier that Squarcione's study collection in Padua may have been labelled, because paper *cartellini* feature in his pupils' paintings. This would have been exceptional. Traditionally, libraries and apothecaries were the only places where labelled and classified objects could routinely be found. However, this changed in Europe during the second half of the 16th century with a flurry of theoretical treatises and, starting in Italy, the founding of literary, scientific and artistic academies. Collectors published printed catalogues to inform and entice. Vesalius' illustrated treatise on anatomy set the benchmark. He rejected antique authority, exalting hands-on experience and direct observation. Each anatomical element was labelled with a letter of the alphabet.

The French court ceramicist and pioneering natural historian Bernard Palissy (1510–1590) is a crucial figure. He made moulded platters and grottoes neatly decorated with casts taken from live animals (especially snakes and aquatic creatures) and from humans. Palissy's tin and lead glazes were dazzlingly naturalistic, the product of decades of gruelling experiment. He boasted of becoming emaciated, clothed in rags, of going to bed soiled and sweaty. Once, after six days and nights testing glazes, he ran out of firewood and burned trellises, tables and floorboards. Everyone thought he was mad – including his 'persecutor' wife.

From the 1560s Palissy had a workshop and kiln in the Tuileries, by the Louvre. It may have resembled one of the illustrations from an Italian treatise on the 'secrets' of maiolica composed by the engineer and architect Cipriano Piccolpasso in around 1557 (overleaf). Decoration is being painted onto pots covered in white enamel glaze. Figure drawings and topographical and architectural prints are pinned to the wall – the first depiction of a studio wall collage.[1]

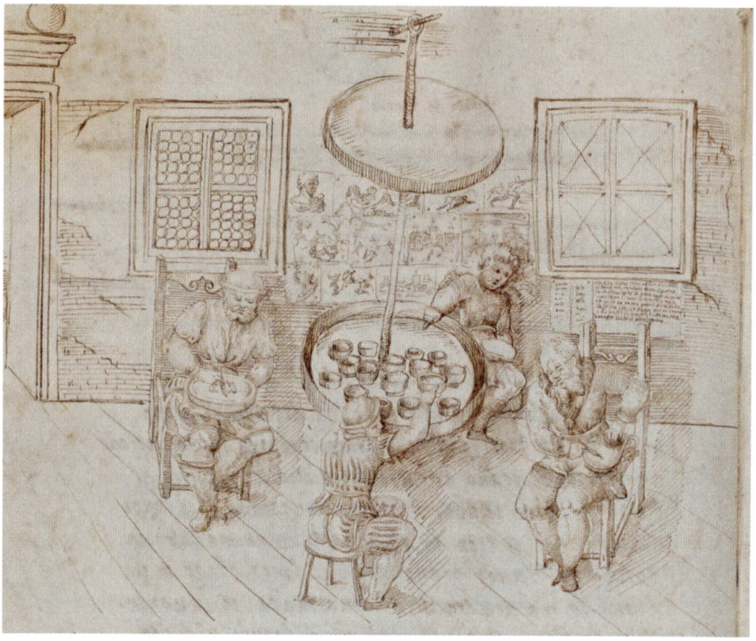

Cipriano Piccolpasso, *Li tre libri dell'arte del vasaio*, 1557, ink on paper.

In 1580, Palissy published a free-flowing autobiographical treatise on fountains, water, clays, glazes, rocks, metals, salt, fossils and agriculture. Modestly entitled *Wonderful Discourses*, it was based on a series of annual lectures delivered in Paris in 1576–84.[2] Palissy put posters on street corners, charging an entrance fee of one crown. Discussion followed, and there were prizes – apparently unclaimed – of four crowns for anyone who refuted his ideas. Palissy boasted that he was a poor artisan, ignorant of Latin, who had learned the truth about nature and glazes from hands-on study and experiment, disproving the theories of ancient and modern thinkers.[3]

Palissy gave a momentous open invitation to his readers: come and visit 'my cabinet in which you will see marvellous things which are placed there to provide testimony and proof of my writings, all arranged in order and on different shelves, with written labels below so that each person can teach themselves'. When people visited his 'little Academy', he claimed, they would 'satisfy the sense of sight, hearing and touch'. As appendices Palissy provided texts from some of the labels, and a dictionary of technical terms. To demonstrate that metals were superheated liquids before cooling and becoming solid in the earth, he displayed one of his vases with the caption: 'I have put

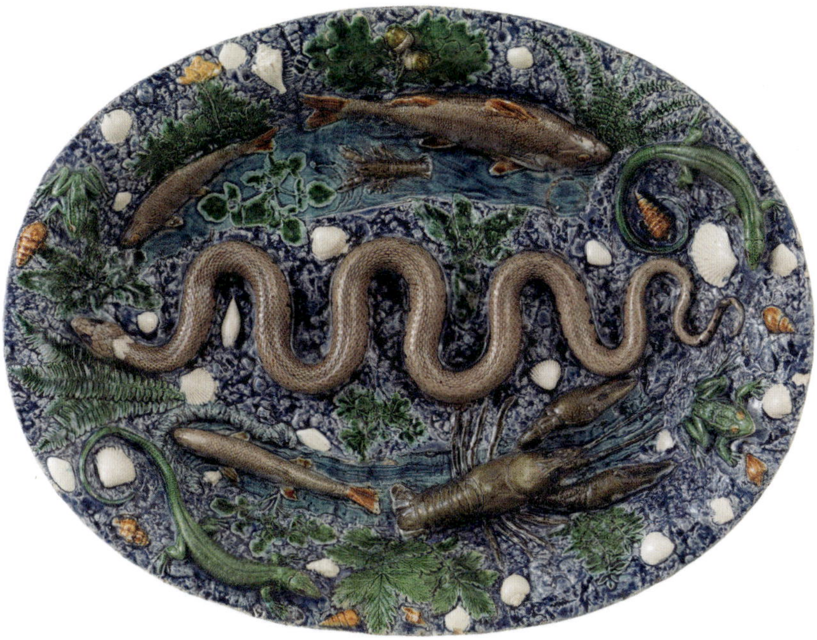

Bernard Palissy, rustic basin, *c.* 1565, glazed clay.

before your eyes this large piece of pottery made in the form of a large vase. But when it was touched by fire, it liquefied and collapsed and entirely lost its form, so that if it had been forged while hot, it would have spread out without breaking, as do malleable things.'[4]

Creating a microcosm of the world's stuff was an endless, Sisyphean task. The beginnings of a consumer society, together with the massive expansion of the known world, meant there were ever more man-made and natural marvels. Ferrante Imperato was a pharmacist in Naples who published a natural history in 1599, with a frontispiece showing his cabinet (overleaf). Ferrante stands nonchalantly by a window while his son Francesco (far left, holding his hat) points something out to two knightly visitors. Two fantasy doggy monsters look on. Ferrante's collection is sublime in its suffocating surfeit. His desire to decorate every surface, and to own a wide variety of fancy display cabinets and storage units, defies logic. Conveniently, only the owner of such a collection can unravel its hidden connections, in the same way that only an astrologer can interpret the zodiac and only Palissy knows the secrets of glazing, firing and casting creepy-crawlies from life (they were stunned by brief immersion in urine or vinegar, then cast).[5]

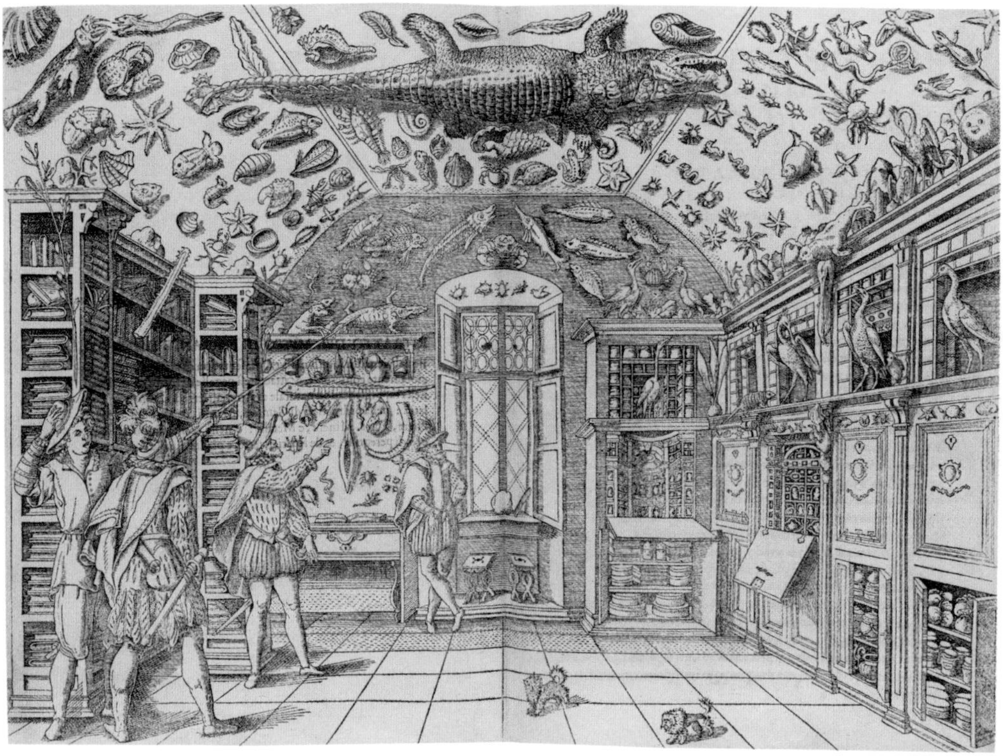

Frontispiece to Ferrante Imperato's *Dell'historia naturale*, Naples 1599.

For the wealthy, there was an expansion in the number of *studioli*, testament in part to the increase in specialized rooms within houses. The sculptors Giambologna in Florence and Alessandro Vittoria in Venice each had two *studioli*, or an office-cum-*studiolo*, fully decorated with easel paintings, sculptures and sculpted models.[6] We don't know how Vasari used the rooms in his houses in Arezzo and Florence, but the Pliny-inspired decor offers up a dizzying rabbit warren of mostly small studios. It is a private 'cabinet' of painted studios, around seven in each house.[7]

This multi-room ideal is celebrated in Raffaele Borghini's dialogue on art and aesthetics, *Il Riposo* (Florence, 1584). Its seriousness is underscored by being prefaced with two alphabetical indexes – the first for artists, the second for topics. Raffaele was a comic playwright and poet. He writes in a leisurely, accessible style. Il Riposo ('Repose') is the country retreat of the Florentine banker, collector and amateur craftsman Bernardo Vecchietto, Giambologna's first patron. Four friends gather on four afternoons/evenings to relax and

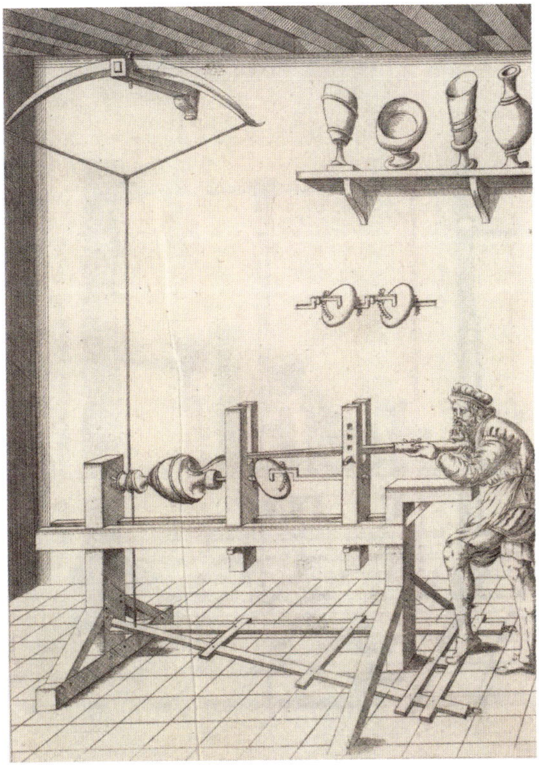

Lathe with oblique cam, from Jacques Besson's *Theatrum instrumentorum et machinarum*, Paris 1582.

discuss art. The work belongs to a new literary genre of art tourism round private houses, artists' studios, churches and town centres. Already on page 14, during a tour of the house, we are told: 'But a great wonder to behold is a *scrittoio* divided into five sections,' all beautifully organized. The contents include statuettes, porcelain vases, rock crystal, stone pyramids, fossils, medals, and 'many new things from India and Turkey that amaze anyone who sees them'. There is a second *scrittoio* further on.

On the floor below are three more rooms: the first is full of artworks, including by Giambologna; the second contains tools, forges and mathematical instruments; the third has a turning lathe with ivory and ebony objects made by Vecchietto. In addition to the drawing and painting recommended by Castiglione in *The Courtier*, turning, metalwork, chemistry and alchemy were fashionable pastimes, providing exercise for hand and brain. In the 1570s, Piccolpasso explained that 'Socrates was not above the practice of jumping, and I believe he did this to keep his body exercised, just as many princes do today when they set their hand to mechanical exercises' – adding that they never 'send their own works to market'.[8] The rise of the amateur artist and artisan further validated the artist's studio.

Lathes, along with bow-drills and potter's wheels, were among the few complex tools known in antiquity, and a workshop for *tornarii* features on the Saint Gall monastery plan. Emperor Maximilian I (1459–1519) and Martin Luther (1483–1546) were notable turners.[9] Tilted cams now permitted the turning of oval and oblique shapes (preceding page), so that some resemble wheel pots that have wobbled or misfired freakishly.[10] Prowess at the lathe could suggest a divinely sanctioned fitness to rule. The first published description of Copernicus' heliocentric model of the solar system (1540) made a comparison with turning: 'The earth, like a ball on a lathe, rotates from west to east, as God's will ordains …'.[11] The fashion for turning helps explain why Saint Joseph, carpenter father of Christ, was now seen as a model for the active and contemplative life, 'ingenious at fashioning every kind of wooden object, howsoever curious'.[12]

Vecchietto's overlord, Grand Duke Francesco I de' Medici (1541–1587), promoted the manufacture of porcelain, stoneware and crystal glass, and had his own private laboratory. He kept a collection of natural and man-made marvels in a sumptuously fitted out *studiolo* partly designed by Vasari (1570–2). Each cabinet door was decorated by a painting relevant to its contents, with depictions of alchemists, jewelers and metalworkers. A medicine cabinet contained antidotes to poison, especially that of Palissy's favourite victims, snakes.

***

Vecchietto's mind-blowing collections are considered therapeutic to body and soul.[13] His is an apothecary where drugs are viewed and touched rather than ingested. But Vecchietto considers the rooms of one of his guests superior. Ridolfo Sirigatti, rich from inherited wealth, was a painter and sculptor. Bernini's father was his best pupil. The spaces in Sirigatti's Florentine house are not just well ordered, but *ordinatissime*, and there are five *stanze*, or rooms, each distinct. The term *stanza* was frequently used for artists' studios and implies an impressive domesticated workspace. A history of Genoese artists (1674) uses *stanza* for the workspaces of liberal artists and *bottega* for artisans' workshops.[14] In Sirigatti's first room, there are 'over a thousand heads, arms, legs, torsos and other parts of statues covering all the walls, and models of horses and other animals'. There are also casts of Michelangelo's Medici Chapel

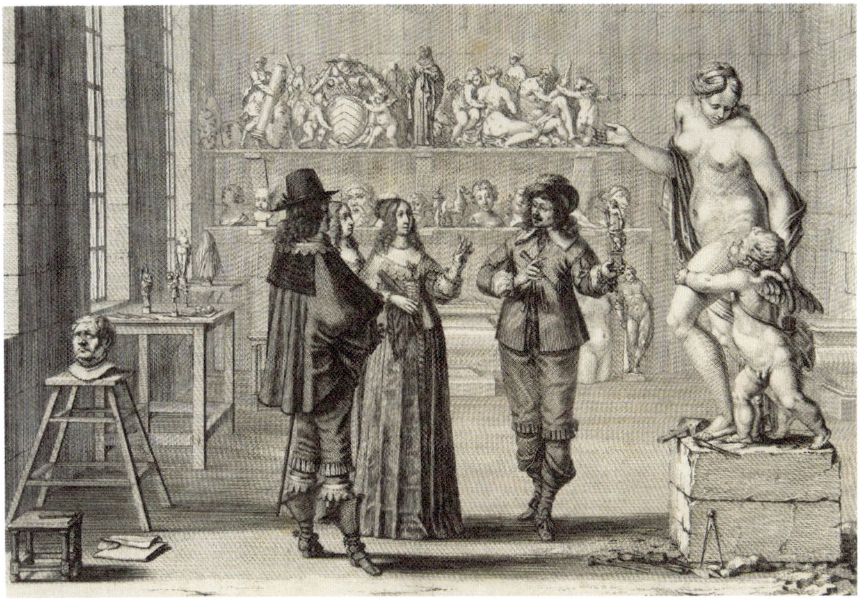

Abraham Bosse, *The Sculptor's Studio*, 1642, etching.

sculptures. The second room contains antique marble fragments, Flemish landscapes, 'a large cartoon by Michelangelo and monstrous dried fish', as well as shells, vases, crystals, musical instruments and more. Vecchietto's favourite room is the third, which contains recent Florentine art. The fourth is a library with busts of philosophers and poets as well as terrestrial and celestial globes.

The fifth and final *stanza* is where Sirigatti 'retires to paint and draw'. It is a place of restorative withdrawal, adorned with 'many drawings, models and a beautiful painting by Andrea del Sarto'. The many works by Sirigatti include vivid portrait busts of his parents – his mother's head marvellously draped in a translucent veil – and a painted portrait of Borghini. Vecchietto knows his stuff: '[Sirigatti] is currently working on a larger than life-size statue of Venus with Cupid at her feet where we can already see that all the limbs will be uncovered with supreme grace. A wax model studied from life shows that the completed statue will be a figure of supreme perfection and beauty.'[15]

The only record of Sirigatti's sculpture is a mediocre print, but the French printmaker Abraham Bosse would illustrate a comparable studio scene.[16] The dapper sculptor, holding a point chisel like a pen, flourishes a wax model for the larger-than-life marble. Assistants are excluded; only the dividers propped against the pedestal indicate how it was scaled up. Venus is lurchingly alive, like Pygmalion's statue, her gesture echoed by that of the female visitor.[17] Tools and a few token marble chippings lie on the ground. At far left, on a stand, is a bust falsely believed to represent the decadent Roman emperor Vitellius, who met a grisly end.[18] Behind it are two modelling tables with trimming knives, the first for wax, the second for clay, with one model covered by a damp cloth. On the shelves is a cast collection, mostly female heads. The sculptor chats urbanely with his visitors. We are a long way from Leonardo's vision of the sculptor's studio.

Sirigatti displayed a Michelangelo cartoon next to a monstrous fish. This hardly sounds *ordinatissimo*, unless you are a Surrealist. Only a few years later the Florentine astronomer Galileo would deride this fashionable type of *studietto* belonging to 'some curious little man' in which you find 'a petrified crab, a dried chameleon, a fly or spider trapped in a piece of amber ... clay figurines ... from the ancient tombs of Egypt, and likewise, in regard to painting, a scribble [*schizzetto*] by Baccio Bandinelli or Parmigianino, or some other trifle'.[19]

Sirigatti would counter-argue that he was striving for universality, rooted in nature, live modelling, and antique and modern art. At just this time, in 1582, the Carracci family of painters founded the Accademia degli Incamminati ('those who are going places') in Bologna. While studying ancient and modern art, members and students were expected 'with admirable frequency to draw living persons, nude entirely or in part, weapons, animals, fruits, and, in short, all things in Creation'.[20] As yet there was no clear distinction between art history and natural history, though Vasari's *Lives* and Galileo's diatribe herald the decline of Pliny's unitary approach in the *Natural History*.[21]

There was also a compelling logic to Sirigatti's *stanza* filled with 'over a thousand heads, arms, legs'. We saw the same kind of display in the box shelves of Lavinia Fontana's *studiolo* (page 111). Art students studied the nude body piecemeal, usually from casts. They could soon follow Odoardo Fialetti's drawing manual, *The True Method and Order in which to Draw All the Parts and Limbs of the Human Body*, which was bound with *All the Parts of the Human Body Divided into More Pieces* (Venice, 1608).[22] Fialetti enabled apprentices and amateurs to learn on their own, from pages of eyes, ears, noses, mouths, profiles and heads.

There is, however, no indication of how to put the jigsaw together. Fialetti assumes that his readers understand proportions and how to synthesize body parts, like Zeuxis when he selected the best bits from the women of Crotona. Michelangelo blithely boasted that 'He who knows how to draw well, and only

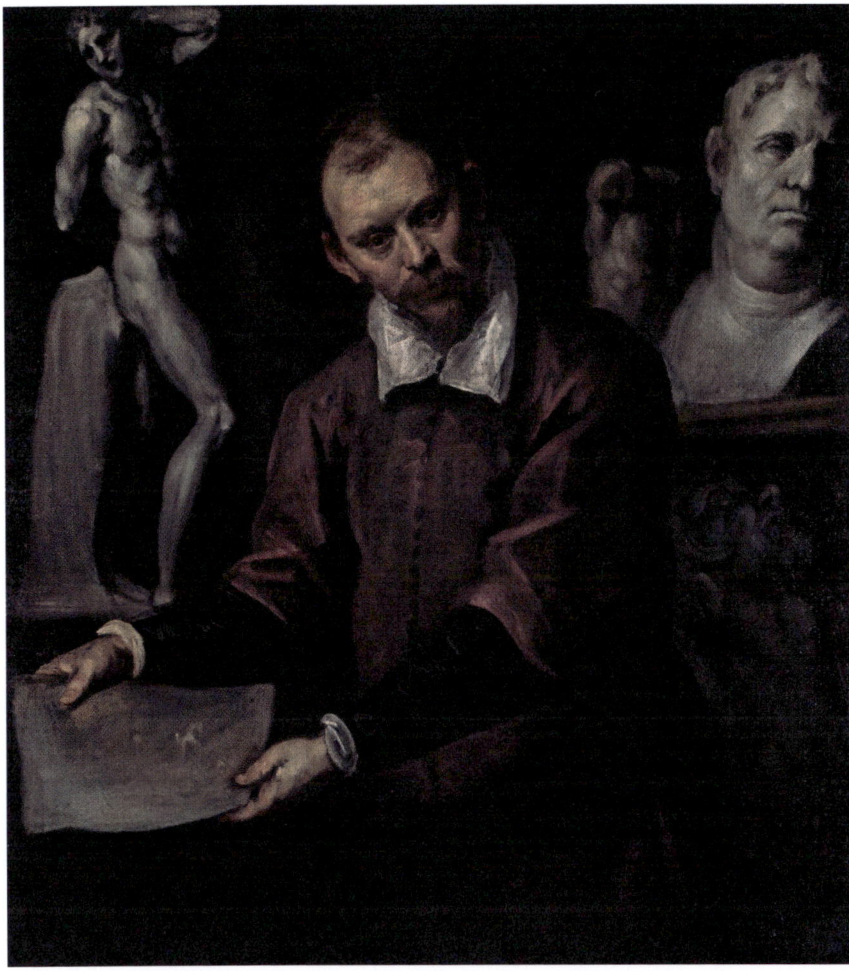

Palma il Giovane, *Portrait of an Artist*, c. 1590–1600, oil on canvas.

makes a foot or a hand or a neck, can paint everything created in this world.'[23] The French painter Pierre Lebrun provided philosophical ballast in the first bluffer's guide to studio visits (1635): 'It is certain that from knowing the proportions one may know Hercules by his footsteps, the lion by his claw, the giant by his thumb, and the whole of a man by a sample of his body. It was thus that Pythagoras, having measured the foot of Hercules, according to the impression which he had left on earth, was enabled to calculate his height.'[24]

The finest demonstration of how profound meaning underlies an apparently random study collection is Palma il Giovane's depiction of an unknown artist in his studio surrounded by casts (*c.* 1590–1600). Palma was one of Titian's last and best pupils. This is a glamorously nocturnal picture with cold lunar lighting – the perfect setting for drawing. In the background, we can just discern a crestfallen Eve. The heads of the four sculptures (the fifth is a headless and armless male torso) all tilt lugubriously in different ways – sideways, back and down. 'How to tilt heads' is an exercise in Fialetti's manual.

The heads evoke what mystics called 'the sweet lean' of Christ's head on the cross, as well as a fashionable melancholia.[25] The artist tilts his head unnaturally sharply down and to one side, echoing the heads of the flanking sculptures. He is emoting sympathetically, trance-like, in a polyphonic dumbshow. He is so moved he has only managed to draw a squiggle, the skimpiest *schizzetto* imaginable – a trademark of the slapdash Tintoretto school. To the sitter's left is bad boy Vitellius, and to the right a model for Vittoria's statue of Saint Sebastian (1561–2); Vittoria, Palma's best friend,[26] kept a bronze version on a table covered with a green cloth in his first-floor *studietto*. In Palma's masterpiece, a doomed obese pagan vies with a doomed slim Christian for the artist's and viewer's sympathy. Here they all have a family resemblance.

Palma's picture conforms to a genre that the Milanese painter and art theorist Giovanni Paolo Lomazzo, in 1585, had called 'intellectual portraits':

> These portraits include as props accurate depictions of artworks expressing the artist's mental concept or Idea. Indeed I have never found that any painter or sculptor, whether old or contemporary, has ever retained in his private studios [*segreti studi*] any drawings or reliefs whose execution and concept did not please and satisfy him.[27]

These are huge claims – first, that all artists throughout history have had a private studio; second, that they have had more than one; third, that these rooms contained only objects that pleased the artist rather than, say, a patron, or God; and fourth, that they represented the artist's mental concept rather than a universally accepted standard. This is the case with Sirigatti's studio insofar as he keeps portrait busts of his parents and of Borghini, and other examples of his work. They are priceless keepsakes and personal favourites rather than merchandise. This was easier for Sirigatti to achieve, as he had inherited wealth.

***

The paragon of the eloquent, universal artist-collector is Peter Paul Rubens (1577–1640), who built a grandiose Italianate studio block by his house in Antwerp – the first of its type (overleaf).[28] The two-storey structure had a richly decorated façade with re-creations of lost pictures described by Pliny, painted in *grisaille* to resemble sculpted reliefs. In a witty reminder of the building's purpose, a mural on the outside of the staircase block showed a vast canvas of Perseus and Andromeda, unframed on its stretcher as though hanging out in the sun to dry; below, a 17th-century engraving depicts a trompe l'oeil balcony where a black servant and a hunting dog straining at the leash keep beady eyes on visitors.

Most impressive were the large expanses of glazed windows, of a type usually found only in churches and civic buildings. This similarity to a church may not be coincidental, as in the Protestant North Netherlands some suppressed monastic buildings had become workshops. After the brutal conquest of Flanders by the armies of King Philip II of Spain in 1584, Protestant refugees from Antwerp set up tapestry-weaving workshops in the Delft convents of Saint Agatha and Saint Anne.[29]

Rubens's father, a Calvinist lawyer, had also fled Antwerp with his family, ending up in Cologne. His father died in 1589 and his mother, the highly educated daughter of a tapestry dealer, returned to Antwerp. Rubens was brought up a Catholic but given a humanist education. Apprenticed at 14 to a local painter, in 1600, like so many Northern artists, he sought out the ancient and modern wonders of Italy. He was soon appointed court painter to Duke Vincenzo I Gonzaga in Mantua, where he could admire the palatial homes of Mantegna and Giulio Romano.

Rubens returned to Antwerp in 1608 after his mother fell ill. The prosperity brought about by the signing of a twelve-year truce with the North Netherlands (1609–21) made this an auspicious time for an ambitious artist. He became court painter to the Habsburg regents, Archdukes Albert and Isabella, and was used for major diplomatic missions. No longer bound by guild regulations, he could take on as many pupils and specialists as he liked. He created a painting factory, turning out works in all genres and sizes. By 1611, he claimed to have refused applications from more than a hundred students.

In 1609 Rubens married Isabella Brant, who brought a big dowry, and the following year acquired a house with extensive grounds in Antwerp's premier residential area. In 1627 he bought adjacent land and buildings. A triple-arched screen divided the courtyard of the property from a garden

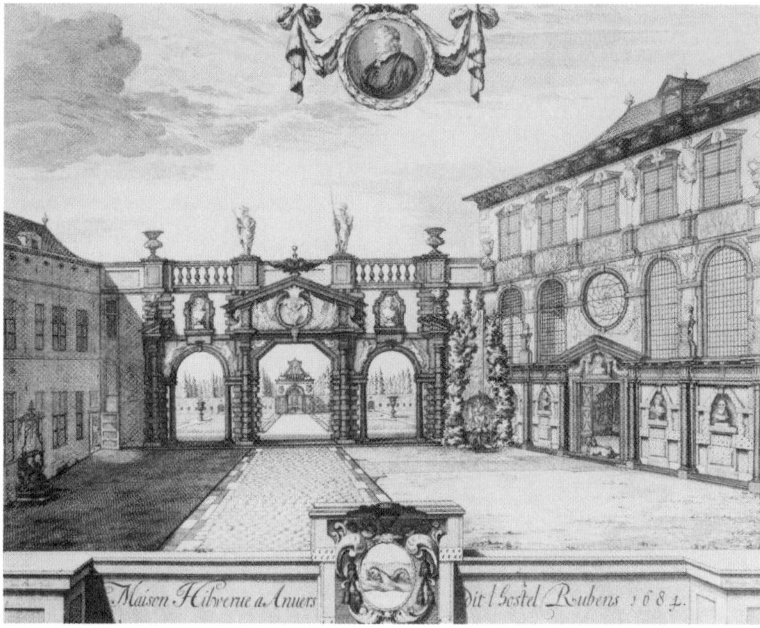

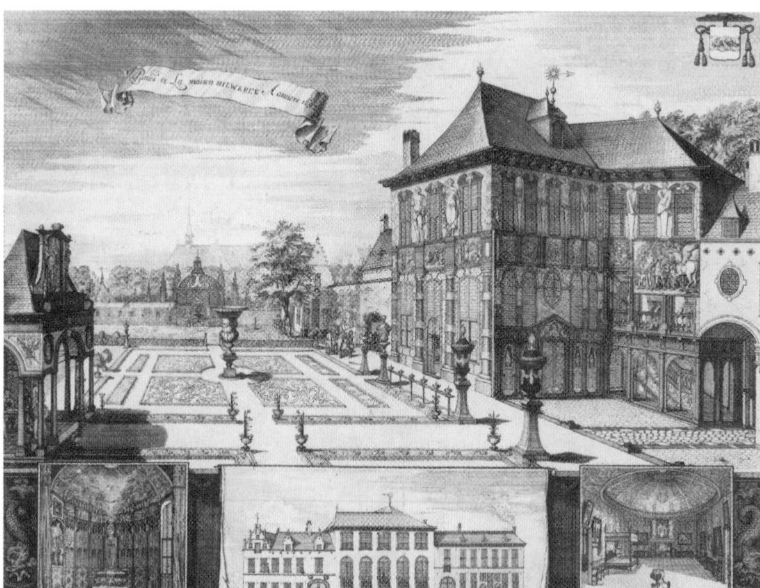

Top Jacobus Harrewijn after Jacques van Croes, *View of Rubens's house (left), the studio block (right) and the garden screen*, 1684, engraving. **Above** Jacobus Harrewijn after Jacques van Croes, *View of Rubens's house in Antwerp*, 1692, engraving.

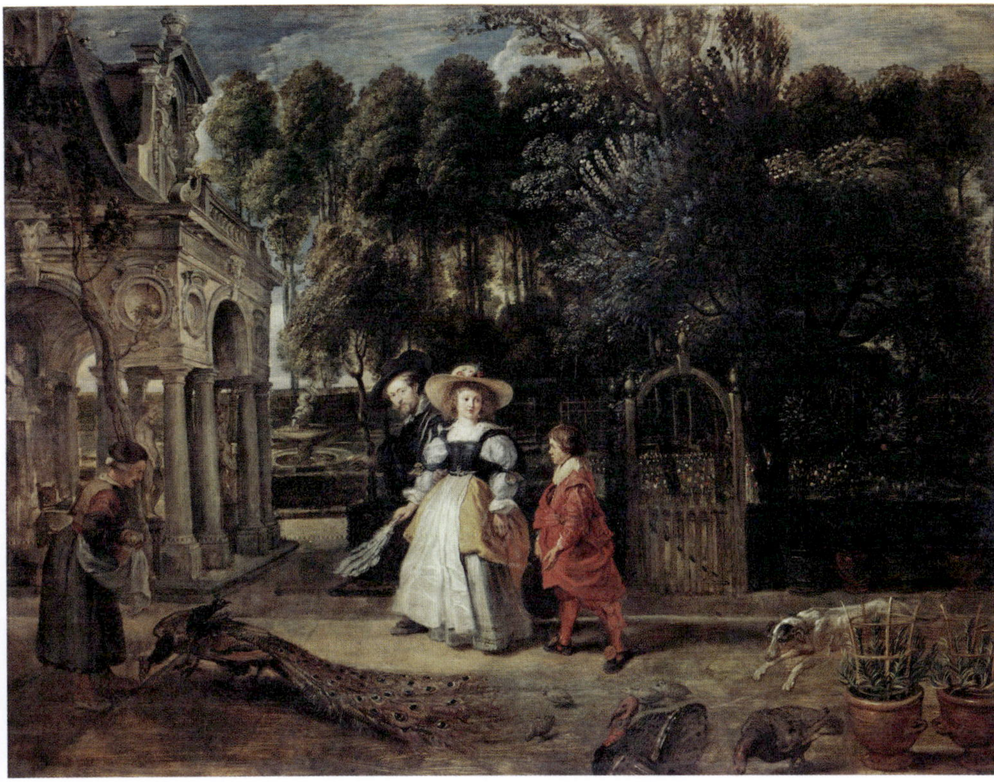

Peter Paul Rubens, *Rubens and Helena Fourment in their Garden*, 1631, oil on wood.

surmounted by statues of Mercury and Minerva, like the grove of an ancient academy. Both beautiful and botanical, the garden contained a wide variety of rare trees, flowers and plants. Rubens bought the latest natural history books and collected shells. He depicted himself in the garden with both his wives (after Isabella's death in 1626, he married the 16-year-old Helena Fourment). He is the only artist prior to Monet for whom his garden was an extension of the studio and of himself. He would later paint landscape 'portraits' of his country house and estate at Het Steen. Health, fertility, ownership and rootedness are writ large. The screen had an inscription from the Roman poet Juvenal: 'One must pray for a healthy mind in a healthy body.'[30] Rubens's day started at 4 a.m. with a visit to Mass. He ate only light vegetarian lunches for fear meat would hamper work, and went for a horse ride at 5 p.m. before dining with erudite friends. It comes as a surprise to learn he died from chronic gout, like a saint dying from syphilis.

The earliest account of Rubens's studio practice is by the Hamburg-born student Otto Sperling, who became physician to the Danish king. He paid a call in April 1621:

> We visited the famous and eminent painter Rubens. The master was working on a canvas while listening to a reading of Tacitus and simultaneously dictating a letter. Since we did not dare interrupt him, he himself addressed us, while continuing to paint, listen to the reading and dictate his letter, as if to give proof of his great ingenuity [*ingenium*].[31]

The layout of the interiors now has to be guessed at, using an 18th-century ground plan and 17th-century reports. The present building, now a museum, is much altered. There were two big painting rooms, the largest taking up the whole of the ground floor of the studio block, with clerestory windows providing angled downlighting (similar to that of the likely destinations for the big picture cycles), and a large fireplace. This is probably where Sperling finds Rubens. He may have been painting an entire picture from scratch or, more likely, completing a work begun by an assistant – but we'll come to that in a moment.

Perhaps by virtue of being a doctor, Sperling is more struck by Rubens's multitasking than by his painting, which he fails to identify. Tacitus was the most profound of the Roman historians, and doubtless helped get him in the mood. Rubens was fluent in Latin, a leading antiquarian, and several sources mention his liking for readings from Roman authors.[32] Later artists, like the sculptor Canova, employed full-time readers.

Rubens's performance is evidently modelled on that of the most celebrated multitasker, Emperor Augustus. The historian Suetonius says in his gossipy and very salacious *Twelve Caesars* – the most popular Roman history book and still unsuitable even for silent reading – that Augustus used to read or write while being shaved and having his hair cut. Portrait series of Suetonius' twelve Caesars were popular, and Rubens contributed portraits to two such series. His patrons included the most powerful European monarchs, so his Augustan behaviour makes him their equal. From his studio in Antwerp, he was managing an art empire and fully acting the part.

Sperling's party are then taken by a servant to see his 'magnificent palace' and his antiquities, 'of which he had a great many'. He had designed an octagonal sculpture gallery, top-lit by an oculus, with niches for portrait

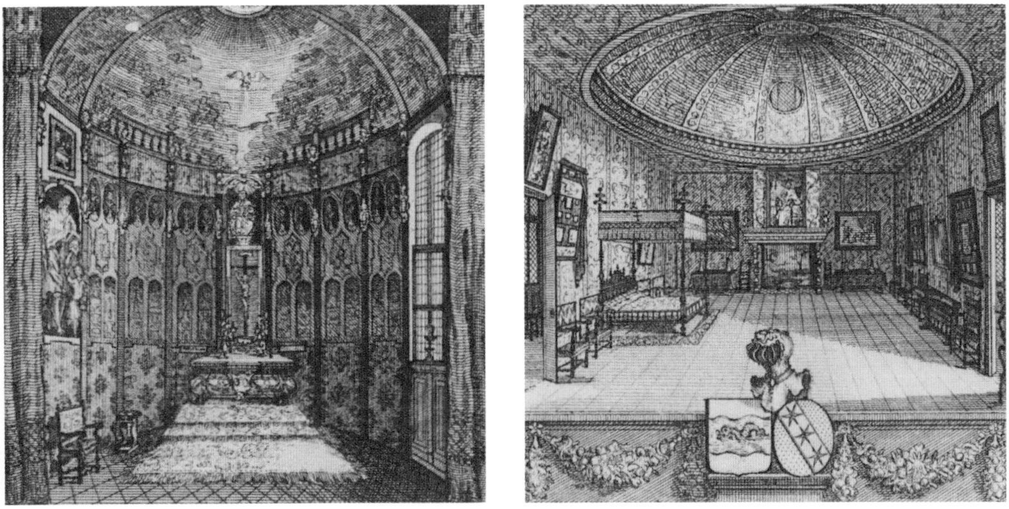

Jacobus Harrewijn after Jacques van Croes, *View of Rubens's house in Antwerp* (details).

busts. It adjoined the main house, on the garden side. Scholars assume it was semicircular because of a contemporary painting and a later engraving from when it was used as a chapel. But they show it in exploded view for legibility. A drawing of the ground plan proves it to be octagonal, with adjoining picture gallery. Both were demolished in the 19th century.[33]

Rubens would have been inspired by studios and galleries in Italy. The sculptor and collector Leone Leoni (*c.* 1509–1590) built an octagonal studio in his palatial house in Milan, top-lit through an oculus in the domed ceiling. It measured 42 square metres (450 square feet), with a single entrance and adjoining *camerino* (small room).[34] Its domed roof was inspired by the Pantheon in Rome. Sebastiano Serlio, in his *Third Book of Architecture* (1540), considered the Pantheon an ideal model for sculpture and picture galleries because of its form and 'celestial light'; the best painters, he strangely claimed, work with light from above. Bernini believed that men and women looked more beautiful in the Pantheon (his French minder demurred, saying French women 'dread nothing like a falling light, which they think gives them hollows round the eyes').[35] Leoni had a superb art collection including casts of the most famous antique and modern sculptures, paintings by Titian and drawings by Leonardo. His studio inspired the octagonal Tribuna of the Uffizi (1584). The Pantheon, and Pantheon-style galleries and studios, were catalysts for the religion of art and artists.

Sperling's account concludes with a visit to the top floor of the studio block, reached by the external stairs:

> We then looked into a large hall without windows but lit through an opening at the centre of the ceiling. There a good number of young painters had gathered, each busy on a different work, for which Rubens had provided a chalk drawing, touched here and there with colour. The young men had to completely execute these paintings, and when they were done, Rubens added the final touches. All this is considered as Rubens' work; thus he has gained a large fortune, and kings and princes have heaped gifts and jewels upon him.

Rubens could do both more and less than this account suggests. In 1622, he contracted to paint all human figures in the huge cycle for Marie de' Medici, and many of his landscapes are autograph; conversely, he sometimes only came up with the basic idea.[36] He had a sliding scale of prices, with wholly autograph work costing around twice that of workshop product. In 1618 he was bargaining with the English ambassador Sir Dudley Carleton, exchanging a selection of his own pictures valued at 6,000 florins for Carleton's antique sculptures, sight unseen. In a letter, Rubens describes and prices twelve works, explaining how much is 'original, by my hand' and how much by assistants or specialist still-life and landscape painters – 'the Eagle done by [Frans] Snyders'. He also identifies copies and retouchings: '600 florins. A picture of an Achilles clothed as a woman, done by the best of my assistants, and the whole retouched by my hand, a most brilliant picture, and full of many beautiful young Girls.'[37] The assistant was Van Dyck, and Carleton knew King James I had just offered Rubens's 'famous *allievo*' (pupil) an annual salary of £100 to come to London. Despite Rubens's eloquence, Carleton wanted wholly autograph pictures, and some tapestries that he knew Rubens collected and designed.

In a 1692 engraving of Rubens's house, the domed painting room is being used as a cavernous bedchamber (preceding page). An opening in the floor would have allowed paintings to be hoisted and lowered. The grandeur of the top-lit studio must have been intended to boost aspiration and inspiration, and to imply it was more than an art factory. Doors on each side lead to smaller rooms, variously identified as a *cantoor* (office) and a 'cabinet'. Rubens also refers to his 'secret *studiolo*'. He most likely made drawings in one or other of these rooms, annotating them with colour notes, and oil sketches. He also liked to 'improve' Old Master drawings. Retouching gave the spark of life.

If his 'secret *studiolo*' was indeed here, at the top of the building, he was still emulating Emperor Augustus, who had lived on the Palatine Hill. According to Suetonius, 'Whenever he wanted to be alone and free of interruptions he could retreat to a study at the top of the house, which he called "Syracuse" and "my little workshop".'[38] Augustus was probably referring to the great inventor Archimedes of Syracuse.

***

Willem van Haecht of Antwerp painted an enchanting evocation of Rubens's studio and gallery, *Apelles Painting Campaspe* (c. 1630, overleaf). This was a new picture type showing idealized galleries, studios and cabinets thronged with visitors. Apelles is a portrait of the red-headed Rubens, and the subject may have been prompted by the fact that his beautiful young wife Helena was modelling nude for him. Rubens's *Battle of Amazons* (c. 1615) hangs directly behind. The old lady disrobing Campaspe is her chaperone or bawd; a younger woman brandishes a print of Rubens's *Judgment of Paris*, perhaps her idea for a group picture. The trio of sculptures over the doorway, centred on a bust of the Farnese *Hercules*, is copied from Rubens's house. The archway leading to the distant sculpture gallery has been enlarged so we can see inside. The adjoining picture gallery leads directly into the garden, just as in Rubens's house.

The displays are organized symmetrically.[39] Italian fashion was to display artworks in series, or as matched pairs, or as a contrived trio.[40] Collectors routinely cut down or enlarged artworks to fit their scheme. Van Haecht alternates symmetry with apparently casual profusion. The head of Hercules forms a trio with the flanking statues, and we see trios of balanced paintings on the wall above Apelles. These echoed the triptych format of medieval altarpieces, still standard in Antwerp, and lent secular and pagan subjects a quasi-spiritual authority.

Paintings, sculptures and, indeed, tapestries that did not fit the galleries were displayed elsewhere. The sale inventory made at Rubens's death listed 324 paintings, so there were plenty to play with. Although Rubens was a wheeler-dealer, he seems to have been the first artist to retain and reacquire works to form an ideal mini-retrospective – something that Turner would

Overleaf Willem van Haecht, *Apelles Painting Campaspe*, c. 1630, oil on panel.

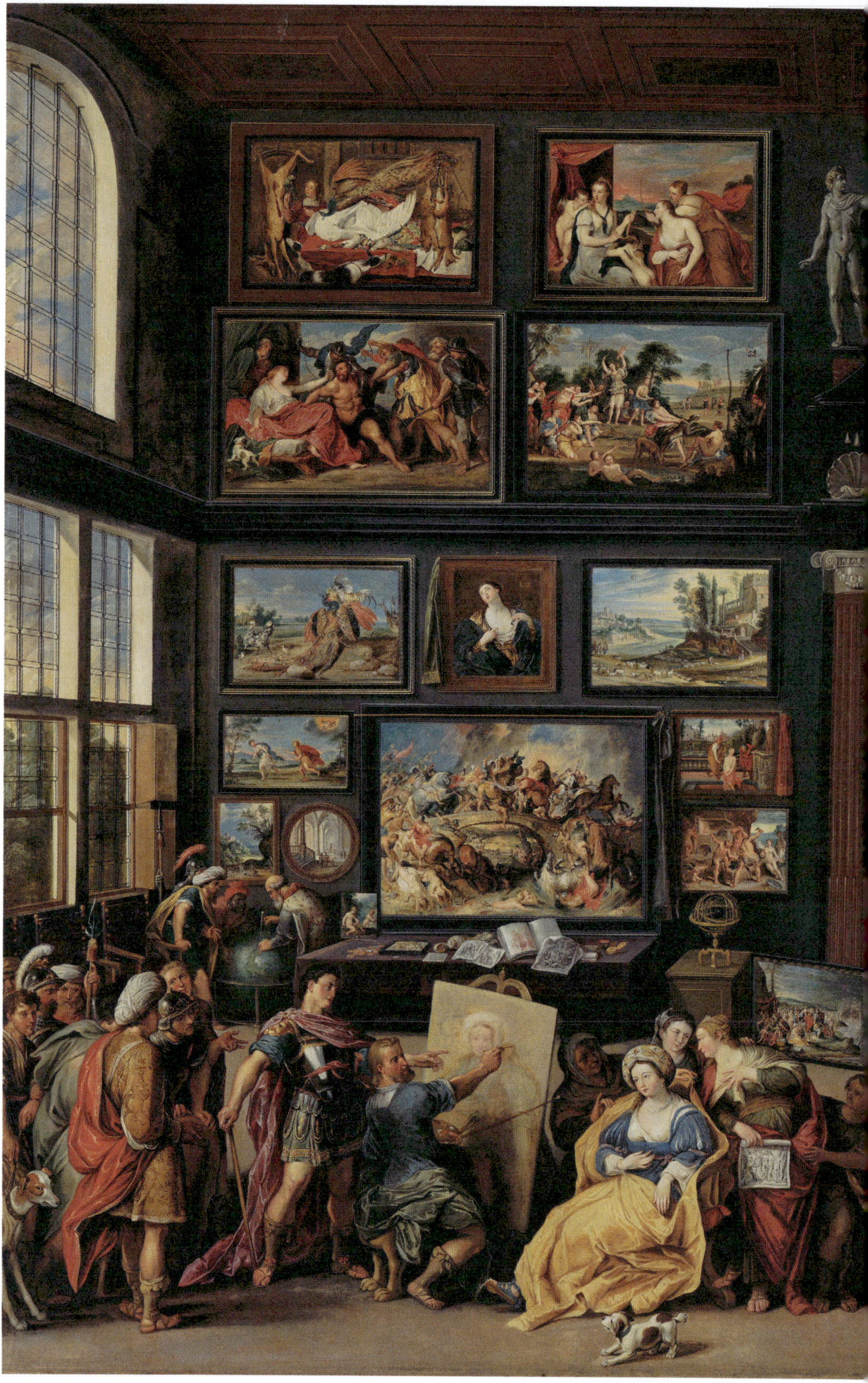

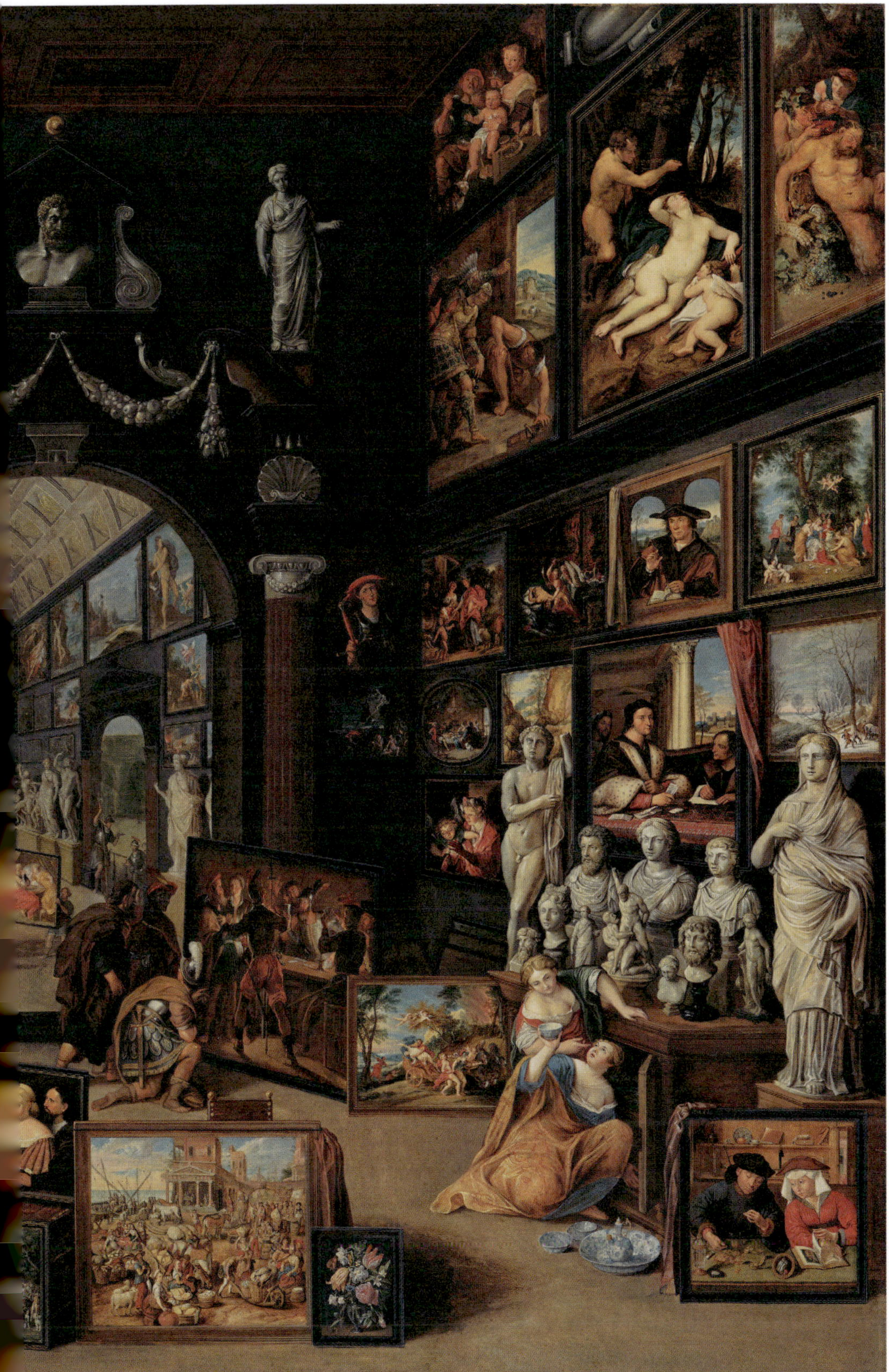

later do. In 1618 he had offered Carleton 'some pictures which I have retained for my own enjoyment; indeed, I have some repurchased for more than I had sold them'.[41]

This type of home studio display first became widespread in Rome in around 1600. The Accademia di San Luca forbade academicians to have or use a shop because their work was 'opera intellettuale'. So they displayed their works, and other artworks in which they dealt, throughout their homes, the best often hung in the *sala* or reception room.[42] The Académie Royale in Paris would go further, banning members from displaying work in their windows.[43] Some Roman artists, such as Bernini, worked in front of visitors, adding to the spectacle.[44] The popularity of studio visits is exemplified by an anecdote about the Spanish lawyer Pedro Montoya. When Montoya mysteriously failed to collect his portrait bust from the studio, Bernini discovered he had left it there on purpose as 'cardinals, ambassadors and prelates stopped their carriages when they saw him in the street to talk to him about it, which pleased and flattered him, as before he had been remarkable in nothing'.[45] Actors and courtesans would leave their portraits in Joshua Reynolds's picture room, to mutual benefit. Many London painters had an entrance charge collected by a footman.[46] Gainsborough used to 'peep & listen through the keyhole' of the door to his splendidly carpeted and wallpapered picture room in Bath.[47] Pierre Subleyras's *The Artist's Studio* (page 23) gives a grand idea of a picture room.

***

Rubens never depicted himself with a paintbrush – we see him touching only a sword hilt or wife, wearing a kid glove. In 1634 he explained he had married a 'young wife of honest but middle-class family' who 'would not blush to see me take my brushes in hand' rather than an aristocrat.[48] But he evidently had no qualms about people seeing him in multitasking action, and his brilliant performances boosted the popularity of studio visits.

To cater for this demand Pierre Lebrun wrote his bluffer's guide, from which I have quoted, explaining the basics of painting and studio etiquette.[49] The *Collection of Essays on the Wonders of Painting* (1635) would have been aimed at patrons and people like Sperling. Lebrun opens with Pliny's famous anecdote about the visit by Alexander the Great to Apelles' studio. When Alexander talked about 'colours and paintings', the boys grinding pigment laughed, so Apelles advised him not to speak about a trade (*mestier*) of which he was ignorant. Lebrun offers a helping hand:

> Reader – my dear friend, I desire to free you from this annoyance, and from the fear that your ignorance should be the subject of derision, when you speak of painting on a flat surface, one of the most noble arts of the world.

Lebrun then gives an itemized list explaining terms. He starts with the mortar for grinding pigment and the 'scaffold or easel' used 'to support the paintings for working', then moves on to tools, colours, shadows, lights, genres, media and proportions. He reveals 'several secrets in paintings', such as recipes and rules, which are not really secrets: 'To imitate a laughing face, the corners of the mouth must be turned up; if they are turned down, the figure will appear sorrowful and weeping.'

Crucial, itemized advice is also given on suitable compliments.[50] I have chosen three, proposing contemporary painters and pictures to whom they could be addressed:

> 'That is not painting, it is nature; and those figures look at the spectators, but with so natural a look that you would swear they were alive.' *Rembrandt's* Night Watch; *Velázquez's* Las Meninas

> 'Is it possible that the brush can have given such softness by such rough touches, and that such apparent carelessness should be so attractive?' *Van Dyck's draperies and backgrounds*

> 'See how well the folds of that drapery are arranged, see those snow white hands, where the veins seem to swell at each beat of the pulse; see how those muscles grow and swell; one may count the ribs .... Is it natural and real, or is it produced by art?' *Rubens's* Judgment of Paris

Chapter 11

Mirroring the Process

Velázquez to Reynolds

One of the intriguing studio developments of the 17th century is the use of mirrors by portrait painters. Traditionally, their main purpose was to increase and direct lighting: a candle or oil lamp placed before a mirror of glass or polished metal is many times brighter. Convex mirrors also magnified.

But now supply and demand greatly increased, and mirrors worked their way down the social scale, frequently placed in bedchambers. Inventories show that artists often had more than one mirror. Larger sizes and different types were made. Abraham Bosse's *Five Senses: Sight* has one of the earliest depictions of a dressing mirror. A larger ebony-framed mirror hangs on the wall, a man uses a telescope (invented in the Netherlands in 1608), and the grotesque head wears spectacles.[1]

Venetian glass-makers, under strict secrecy laws, had dominated the manufacture of mirror glass. But gradually their secrets were spread around Northern Europe thanks to industrial espionage, workers absconding for money and, when all else failed, abduction. Versailles's Hall of Mirrors (1678–84) is the most spectacular consequence, and in the 1680s Parisian glass-makers pioneered cast rather than blown glass, further increasing plate size. In 1697, Venetian makers conceded defeat, thereafter specializing in plates no larger than 104 by 53 cm (48 by 21 inches).[2]

Greater demand for self-portraits, and a vogue for artists to act out their subjects in search of authenticity, made mirrors more desirable. Rembrandt's former pupil Samuel van Hoogstraten urged the artist to 'transform totally into an actor … at best in front of a mirror, where you are simultaneously the performer and beholder. But here a poetic spirit is necessary in order to imagine oneself in another's place.'[3] The Dutch art theorist Gerard de Lairesse

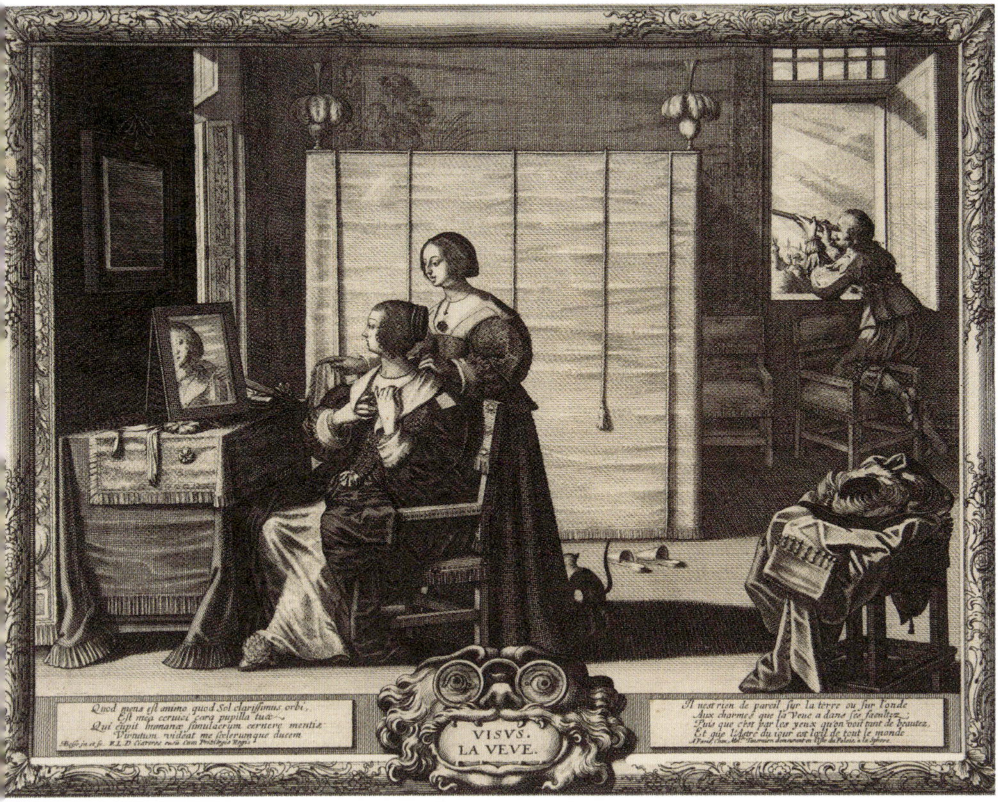

Abraham Bosse, *Five Senses: Sight*, 1635–8, etching.

was more prosaic, saying the artist should sketch the position of their arms, legs and head before the mirror, then pose a mannequin in the same way.[4]

Nonetheless, it is rare to see mirrors depicted in self-portraits and studio scenes.[5] Most would have been kept out of harm's way, with a curtain or drape protecting the surface from dust, scratches and insect excretions. Damp was fatal. Moisture penetration of minute faults in the mercury-impregnated foil backing produced circular grey blooms on the face.[6] The inventory compiled after Vermeer's death in 1676 lists four mirrors, one categorized as 'a bad mirror'; none is located in his first-floor studio.[7] Only one mirror appears in Vermeer's pictures, whereas there are many framed paintings and maps.

As mirror plates grew in size they were competing with paintings for wall space, so it was perhaps best not to advertise the fact. They might equally suggest the artist was vain, or just copying reality and being the proverbial 'ape of nature'. In Vermeer's *The Music Lesson* (c. 1662–4), an ebony-framed

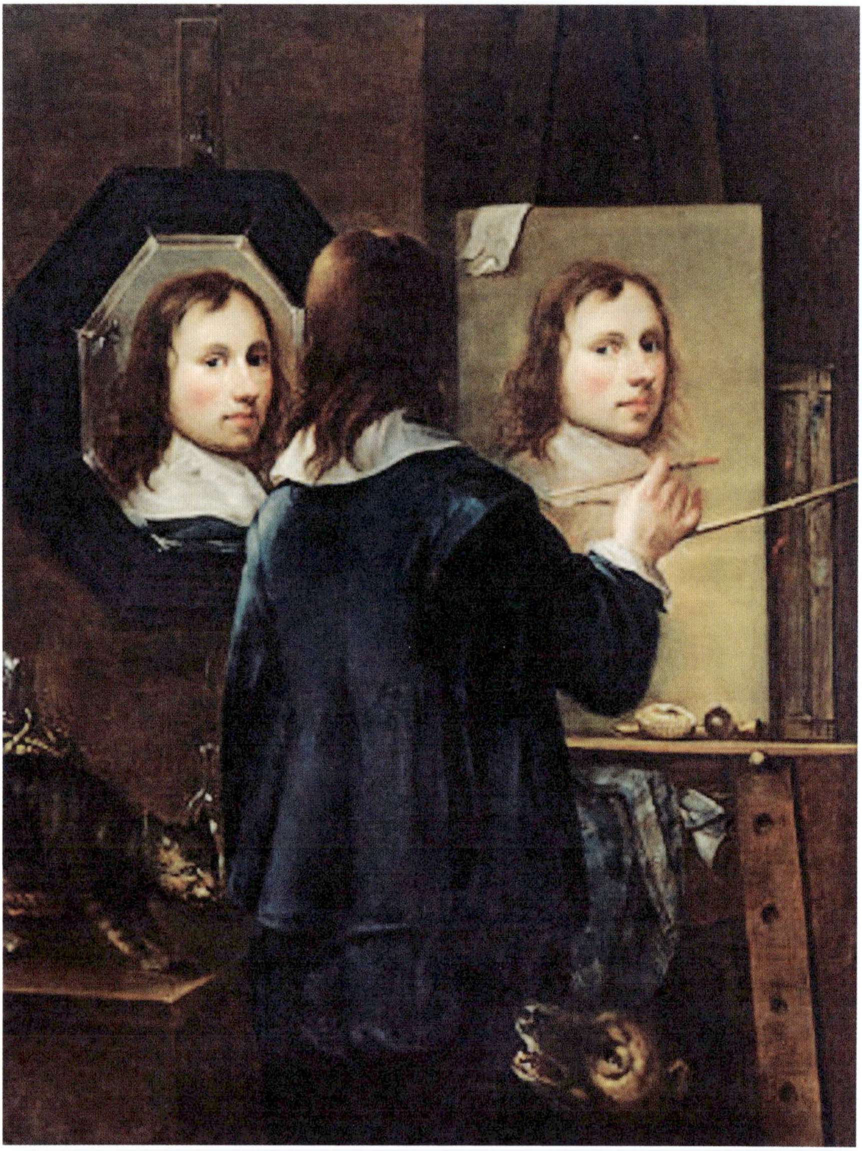

Johannes Gump, *Self-Portrait with Mirror and Easel*, 1646, oil on canvas.

wall mirror reflects the flirting woman's face and the feet of the painter's easel. 'Kiss *my* feet,' Vermeer implies. The Austrian artist Johannes Gump plays with these ideas when he paints his image reflected in an octagonal, ebony-framed mirror. The three likenesses are decidedly comic, and the banality is underlined by the cat and dog squaring up to each other behind the painter – monkey business indeed.

Lairesse had another idea.[8] He recommended placing a mirror in the studio to enable sitters to look their best. Writing on portraiture in *The Great Book on Painting* (1707; English translation 1738; French 1787), Lairesse first warned against unseemly distractions in the studio:

> Another hindrance may be that painting rooms are often hung with such smutty pictures as frequently put females to the blush, or alter their countenances .... In a painting room there ought not to hang the wanton picture of *Mars and Venus caught by Vulcan*; or *Diana's bathing*, though done by Van Dyck .... For though these may hang in a corner, yet when the eye hast once observed them, it will retain them; because their ideas make continual impressions on the mind against its will; and therefore the bare remembrance of such things must put a young and chaste virgin to the blush. Must it not create a longing, to see a picture of two beggar boys fall greedily on ripe fruit, the one eagerly biting a piece of fresh melon, and the other a bunch of grapes, with the juice falling down his chin on his naked breast?[9]

Artworks were believed to affect viewers physically and mentally, with women more susceptible than men, especially when pregnant: a foetus could be transformed in the womb by whatever the mother desired, looked at or imagined. If a pregnant woman imagined an Ethiopian, or a lame man, the foetus would be impressed with those same characteristics.[10] Elisabeth Vigée-Lebrun noted that, in the months before her first child was born in 1780, she painted the portrait of the old, obese, accident-prone Duchesse de Mazarin: 'My daughter had her eyes, and was very like her.'[11] This is why Lairesse singles out female sitters and has conniptions about beggar boys.

Lairesse knew all about studio distractions. In 1664, he had to flee his home town of Liège after an affair with two sisters who modelled for him. Equally

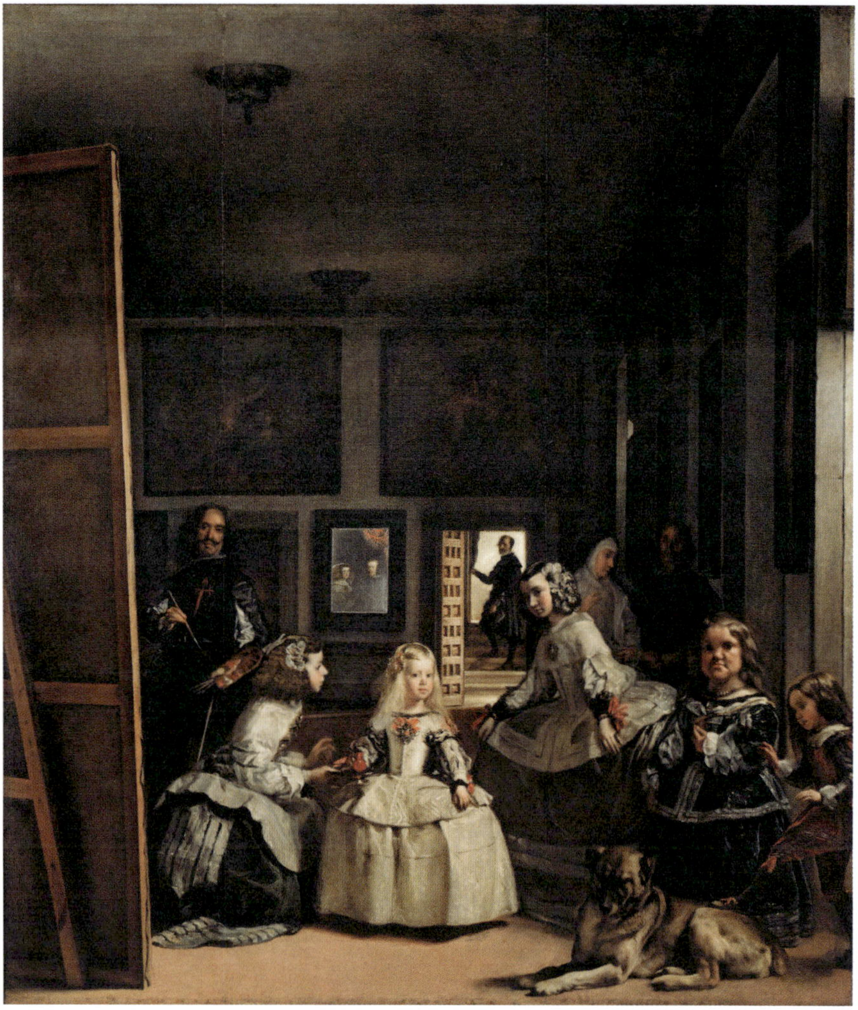

Diego Velázquez, *Las Meninas*, 1656, oil on canvas.

pertinently, he suffered from congenital syphilis. His telltale saddle nose and bloated face are apparent in Rembrandt's moving portrait of *c.* 1665–7. Lairesse had moved permanently to Amsterdam, becoming the leading historical and mythological painter, interrupting work to play his violin. In 1690 syphilis made him blind, so he turned to art theory. Lairesse advocated an erudite classicism, dismissing Rembrandt as someone who threw 'liquid mud' onto the canvas. But we sense a personal investment in keeping the studio clean: liquid mud and juice falling down a chin sound like a leaky, syphilitic face. In order to avoid over-stimulating sitters, Lairesse recommends a different set-up:

> The room should be hung with everything modest, such as fine landscapes and flower pieces, which will amuse the sight without disturbing or tiring the mind, or altering the countenance; fine portraits will also animate a sitter to keep him serene, and make him emulous of their manners: a large looking glass may be likewise of service, if so hung that the sitter may see himself in it; for, thereby discovering any grimace in his look, he will correct himself, in order to have as good an air as he desires; and by such methods as these, a painter may become great.[12]

Lairesse was not a portrait painter, deeming it slavery, so he was probably recommending something he knew about. The mirror is a moral mirror, prompting self-improvement, rather than a vanity mirror. The frontispiece to the conduct book *Mirror of Princes* (Brussels, 1655) showed a prince looking into an ebony-framed mirror held by female personifications of Faith and Justice.[13] In a similar vein, Alberti and Leonardo had recommended looking at a finished painting in a mirror because it supposedly revealed defects. Vigée-Lebrun recommended positioning a mirror 'behind you so that you can see both the model and your painting at the same time'; it is 'the best guide and will show up faults clearly'.[14] Mirror, mirror, on the wall, is this the most perfect pose/portrait of all?

Velázquez's *Las Meninas* (1656) epitomizes Lairesse's desired set-up, except for the copies of wanton paintings by Rubens. It is a fairly accurate depiction of Velázquez's studio, located in the former apartments of the deceased crown prince Balthasar Carlos in the royal palace, the Alcázar. King Philip IV of Spain and his second wife, Mariana of Austria, are reflected in the mirror behind their court painter. Its bulky frame is ebony, with ripple moulding made by a 'waving engine' that used a cam.[15] Ebony was a hardwood imported by the Dutch East India Company, founded in 1602; Vermeer's brother-in-law was a leading ebony dealer and frame-maker. The glass plate was most likely made in Venice or Paris.[16]

If we estimate the open door at 2.7 metres (9 feet) high, the mirror plate is around 1.2 metres (4 feet) high, the largest size available. With its frame, it may be the most expensive item on view, excepting the silver-threaded silk dress of the 5-year-old Infanta Margarita María. It makes for a suitably splendid setting for the royal couple. It is similar in height to, but even wider than, the mirrors with bronze frames in the Alcázar's Hall of Mirrors (begun

1640s), designated a Hall of Princely Virtue – meaning it contained royal portraits and its mirrors reflected the king.[17] Velázquez owned ten mirrors, which suggests both fascination and wealth; this one was probably his own, as no mirror is mentioned in a later inventory of the room's contents. He also owned a large library of 150 books, including titles on perspective, proportion and optics.[18] Anyone interested in optics was interested in mirrors – as Abraham Bosse's etching *Sight* demonstrates.

The studio was south-facing, overlooking a formal garden. The nearest bay provides ample light for the large canvas angled towards it. Velázquez uses only natural light: two light fixings are visible in the ceiling, but no chandeliers. The canvas on its stretcher rests on the floor so the faces can be worked on. Steps would be required to reach the top. Velázquez delights in the fluctuations of light and shade throughout a room densely decorated with pictures in matching ebony frames. They are copies of some of the sixty canvases by Rubens and his workshop illustrating Ovid's *Metamorphoses*, commissioned by the king in 1536–8. They are displayed with the requisite symmetry. While *Las Meninas* was being painted, the royal family and court made frequent visits. Velázquez was Rubens reborn.

Debate continues about what is reflected in the mirror, making this one of the great puzzle pictures. Does it show Velázquez's canvas? The royal couple entering the room? Or posing for their portrait in the place where viewers stand? If it were the first option, Velázquez would block the view of his picture. If the royal couple had just entered, everyone would be bowing. The couple's static, formal portrait pose suggests they are having their portrait painted, facing a mirror to help maintain the pose. The painter leans over to scrutinize them so he can apply the last touches to their faces (he has flesh colours, whites and reds, on his palette). Velázquez's standard practice was in fact to begin a formal portrait by making a bust-length oil study of the sitter from life, possibly in as little as half an hour, which served as a model for the finished work and workshop copies.[19]

Nonetheless, Velázquez keeps us guessing, just as he did in the *The Toilet of Venus* (1647–51), where the ebony-framed mirror held up by Cupid 'incorrectly' shows Venus' face rather than her midriff. Whatever the answer, Velázquez captures the royal visages for eternity in his painted mirror. They have what Lairesse would call a 'good air', and are imbued with mercurial softness and greyness.

***

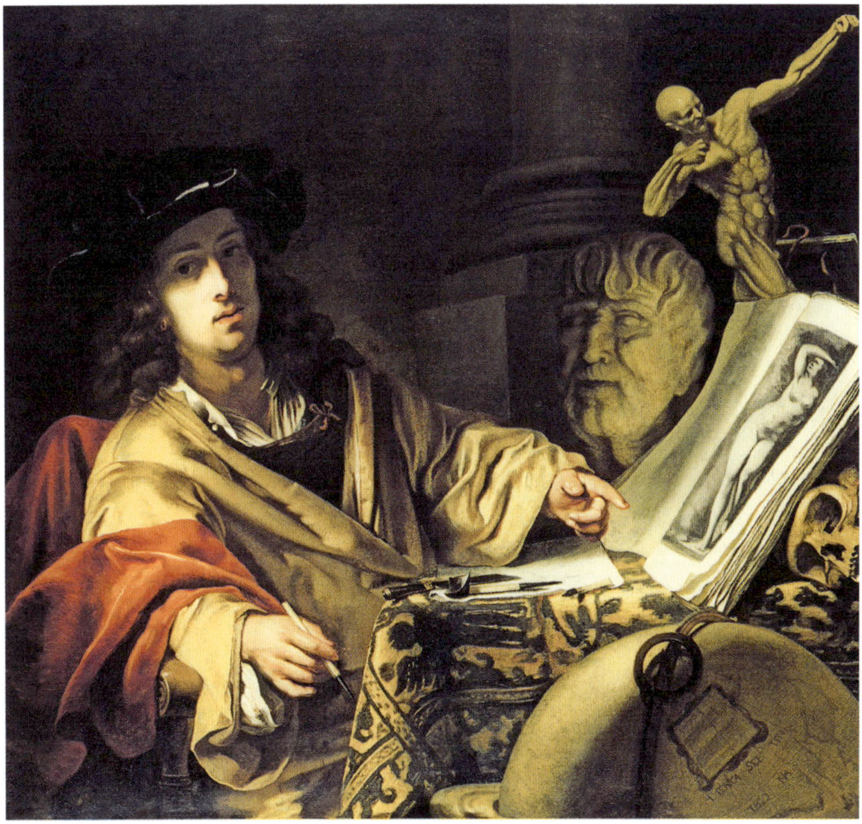

Godfrey Kneller, *Self-Portrait*, c. 1670, oil on canvas.

During the course of his treatise, Lairesse praises three portrait painters who found fame and fortune in London, becoming court painters to British kings: the Fleming Anthony van Dyck (1599–1641), the Dutchman Peter Lely (1618–1680) and the German Godfrey Kneller (1646–1723). Lairesse would have known Kneller, as he lived in Amsterdam from around 1662 to 1672 and, according to one account, initially studied with Rembrandt. In London Kneller became a leading portrait painter, helped by his prodigious charm and productivity. Central to his social and artistic success was the use of two mirrors, which turned a sitting into a double act involving continuous mutual surveillance.

In 1682 Kneller moved into Lely's house – or its neighbour – in Covent Garden Piazza. This pretentiously named square had been developed in the 1630s as a suburb for the nobility. It became the hub of London's art world, and a fruit and vegetable market.[20] Kneller and his workshop painted seven British monarchs and nearly 900 portraits in all. In 1693 Kneller revealed he had '14 Persons sett to him in a day', but some of these sitters had to 'set 10 or 12 times'.[21] Horace Walpole later claimed that, where Kneller 'offered one portrait to fame, he sacrificed twenty to lucre'.[22] But at his best he achieves a cool, compelling intensity – remarkable considering most sitters wore personality-crushing periwigs.

In 1691, Kneller became Principal Painter to the Crown. An eyewitness account gives fascinating details of his 'closet' – the English equivalent of a *cabinet*, *stanza* or *studio*. William Fever, possibly a pupil of Lely, says: 'Mr. Kneller Set 5 feet off the light [window] & the person Set 5 feet off him & 5 feet off the light in a Square.' He positioned 'two looking Glasses behind him, that they could see the Life & ye Pictor'.[23] One mirror lets them see themselves, the other the portrait in progress.

Mirrors made Kneller's sitters feel right at home. England was now a leading producer of mirror glass, thanks to a switch to coal-fired furnaces at the beginning of the century. The Vauxhall Glass Works produced, according to John Evelyn's diary entry of 19 September 1676, looking glasses 'far larger and better than any that come from Venice'. Following French fashion, the elite were creating rooms with unified decor and with mirrors galore. Kneller's full-length portraits of Queen Mary's ladies-in-waiting, the so-called *Hampton Court Beauties* (1690s), hung in the queen's riverside 'Water Gallery', which had closets at the four corners, 'one pannell'd all with jappan [imitation lacquerwork], another with Looking Glass, and two with fine work [embroidery] under pannells of Glass'.[24] The portraits may have been combined with full-length mirrors, as in the Beauty Room at Petworth House.[25]

Kneller's mirrors helped sitters establish and maintain the requisite bearing. They were less likely to flop, fidget and flutter if they were looking into a mirror: the gaze of his static, columnar Beauties is direct and penetrating.[26] Mirrors also allowed the painting process to be viewed continuously, emulating a European trend for public performances of art-making. Closely scrutinizing artists at work was prime court entertainment, and not just in Madrid. In 1665, when Bernini made a portrait bust of Louis XIV in Paris, it was a court event, with Bernini sketching the king as he received the English ambassador, played tennis and conducted meetings. Bernini got down on his knees to draw Louis from below; he quipped that he was 'stealing' the king's face. In his first studio in fine rooms in the Palais Mazarin, he scrutinized the king from so many angles that the younger courtiers 'wanted to giggle'. There were thirteen sittings for the carving of the bust, each of around an hour, with the court in attendance.[27]

In 1678 a public painting contest took place between Lely and Kneller, with both having to paint King Charles II simultaneously. Kneller was 'Young and full of Fire & Ambition' and 'soon show'd how capable he was by readily drawing & Painting the Kings Picture at first sitting'. Everyone was impressed, including Lely, who managed only to lay in his picture 'in a broad manner to finish at other times'.[28] This fiery boy wonder is seen drawing in Kneller's earliest self-portrait (*c.* 1670, page 163). The skull, flayed anatomical figure, female nude inspired by the Belvedere *Apollino*, and bust of Seneca show gravity beneath the gaiety.[29] Lely's magnanimity in defeat must have been because the event was inspired by a public painting contest described in Hoogstraten's art treatise, published that same year. This had involved three landscape painters with distinct styles and methods. The slowest painter, who stops to think, is judged best – the proverbial tortoise triumphing over two hares.[30]

Lely was often criticized for not getting a likeness, and Kneller's hare-like speed and mirrors ensured vividness and accuracy. Gainsborough admired his touch.[31] Allowing sitters to monitor his progress from 'flayed' outline to finished face exuded and inspired confidence. Not everyone welcomed such exposure. In 1715, the portrait painter Jonathan Richardson lamented that portraits were visible when they were not 'fit to be seen, and yet Judg'd of, and Criticis'd upon'.[32] Bernini had been driven to distraction by the French king and courtiers alternating lavish praise of his emergent bust with pernickety criticism of the mouth, pupils, forehead, cheeks, collar, hair and nose: 'Is my nose really a little crooked?' Initially it had been an honour to collaborate – 'The King and I must finish it [together]' – but Bernini eventually became exasperated: 'As soon as the King had gone he threw himself in a chair, put his head between his hands and remained bowed for a long time.'[33]

In his transparency about methods and standards Kneller has something in common with medieval goldsmiths, visible from the street and forbidden to have 'secret' rooms. The clients of Petrus Christus' goldsmith (page 63) stand behind the counter checking as he weighs the jewelry. But Kneller's mirrors involve close scrutiny from beginning to end. This is nearer to the emerging world of scientific experiment and demonstrable proof. King Charles II had his own private laboratory for alchemy and chemistry in Saint James's Palace,

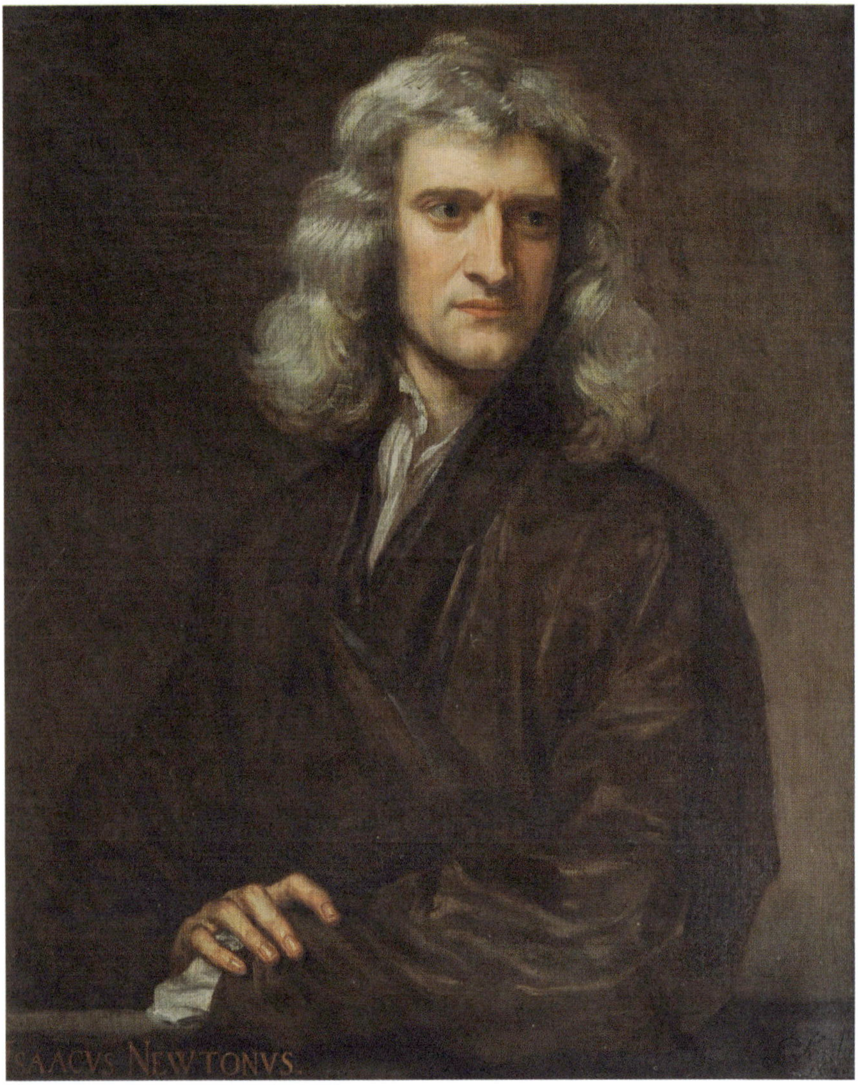

Godfrey Kneller, *Isaac Newton*, 1689, oil on canvas.

and in 1662 he gave a charter to a group of natural philosophers who met to discuss science – thereby forming the Royal Society, with its motto *Nullius in verba* ('Take nobody's word for it'). The curator of experiments Robert Hooke published *Micrographia* (1665): astounding illustrations of insects' compound eyes and plant cells seen through a microscope. In English, the phrase 'experimental method' was first used in 1675.[34] Kneller, son of a surveyor, studied mathematics at Leiden before becoming a painter and would have known some of these ideas. Isaac Newton, whom Kneller portrayed four times, was granted membership of the Royal Society in 1672 for his reflecting telescope. This contained two mirrors rather than lenses, which impaired the image by refracting light.[35] In Kneller's first portrait the magus of light and motion is roughly hewn but sensitive, head and silver hair modelled by an eerie lunar light.

Kneller was later criticized for 'invent(ing) the cold grey-coloured cloths, on which he established his slight expeditious manner'.[36] In other words, he applied a grey priming layer to the canvas that showed through thinly painted upper layers. This is apparent in Newton's portrait. Some painters took their priming paint from the vase of oil in which they put brushes to prevent them drying out, the colour mixture tending towards grey.[37] But instead of being a convenient shortcut, these 'cold grey-coloured cloths' emulate the matt grey look of reflections in a mirror, as in *Las Meninas*. Modern silvering – first developed in 1840 – gives a brighter, harder image.[38]

***

Kneller's studio set-up was emulated by the next two superstar face painters, Joshua Reynolds and Thomas Lawrence, both presidents of the Royal Academy. Lawrence owned two large swing mirrors, at least one of which is known to have been positioned behind him as he worked.[39]

In the octagonal studio in his house in Leicester Square, Reynolds used a mahogany swing mirror, 122 cm (4 feet) tall, converted from a Chippendale firescreen in Chinese style. It survives, as do Reynolds's palette, sitter's chair and spectacles – treasured relics from the emerging cult of English artistic genius. Dr James Beattie, a Scottish moral philosopher conservative in everything except for his loathing for white supremacist views, gave a vivid account of a sitting with the mirror. He had commissioned an unusual allegorical portrait showing himself beside a female personification of Truth who scourges the male vices of Sophism, Scepticism and Infidelity:

> MONDAY 16 AUGUST Rainy & gloomy throughout. Breakfasted with Sir Joshua Reynolds [9 a.m.], who this day began the allegorical picture .... I sate to him five hours, in which time he finished my head, and sketched out the rest of my figure: – the likeness is most striking, and the execution most masterly .... Though I sate five hours, I was not in the

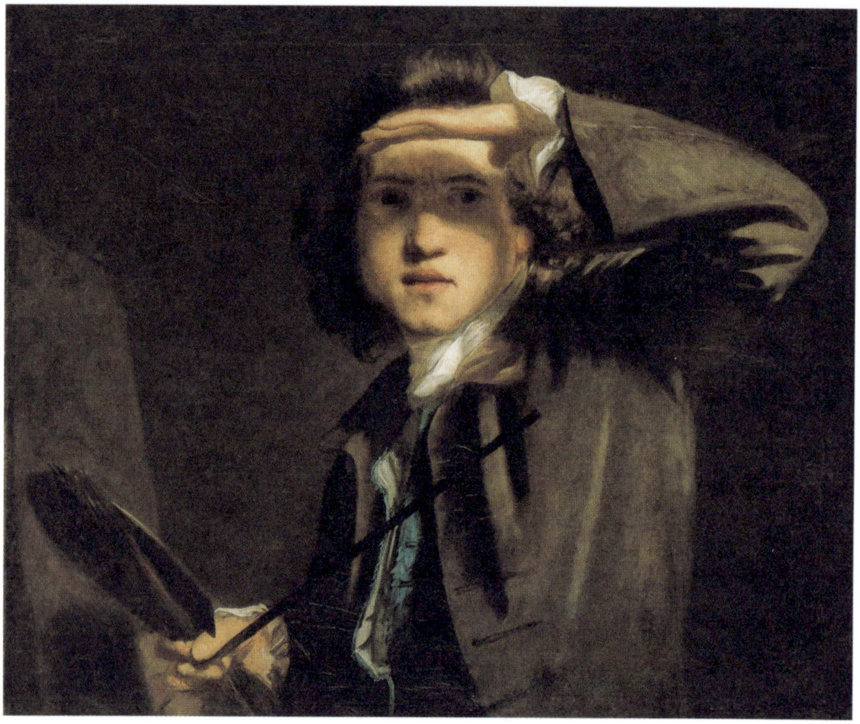

Joshua Reynolds, *Self-Portrait at Easel*, c. 1749, oil on canvas.

> least fatigued; for, by placing a large looking glass opposite to my face, Sir Joshua Reynolds put it in my power to see every stroke of his pencil [brush]; and I was greatly entertained to see the progress of the work, and the easy and masterly manner of the artist, which differs as much from all the other painters I have seen at work, as the execution of Giardini on the violin differs from that of a common fiddler.[40]

With its frame of scrolling and twisting foliage, the mirror was tailor-made to showcase a dancing painting hand (William Blake nicknamed Reynolds 'Sir Sloshua'). Felice Giardini was an Italian famed for his bravura improvised violin solos – 'amazing Rapidity of Execution, and Exuberance of Fancy'.[41] Reynolds's exuberance was flaunted in the only self-portrait to show him at work. His contemporaries credited him with being the first easel painter always to stand, which added considerably to studio theatre.[42]

There is a shift in the late 18th century from the more empirical and pragmatic approach to mirrors espoused by Lairesse and Kneller, to something more evocative and subjective. This coincides with the popularity of the Claude glass, named after the French landscape painter Claude Lorrain (1600–1682): a slightly convex mirror with dark backing that could compress a large view into a small field. It helped in the composition of scenes by reducing detail and lowering tone. Similar methods were used in the studio by Bernini, who, when judging compositional drawings, would wear tinted spectacles, or use magnifying and shrinking glasses, or invert them.[43] In the 18th century, circular, oval or rectangular Claude glasses were made, with velvet-lined lids; so too was glass tinted green, blue and yellow.[44]

Reynolds sought to replicate the effects of the Claude glass in his studio: 'Look at the object from which you are painting, with your eye-lids half closed, which gives breadth to the object, and subdues all the little unimportant parts.'[45] In his self-portrait his eyes are open, but he screens his face and eyes as though outdoors. Imagining himself in the open air made perfect sense, as so many of his portraits were located in landscapes. Reynolds's biographer and pupil James Northcote thought his pictures resembled mirror images because the 'atmosphere of light and shade' imbued them with a 'vagueness that gives them a visionary and romantic character ... like dreams or vivid recollections of persons we have seen'. On seeing a fine Reynolds portrait, 'I almost involuntarily turn back to ascertain if it is not someone behind me reflected in the glass.'[46]

The pinnacle of romantic mirror-play is the home of the architect John Soane (1753–1837) at 12, 13 and 14 Lincoln's Inn Fields, central London (overleaf). His 'Cretan labyrinth'[47] was created over a forty-year period as Soane acquired and rebuilt two neighbouring houses to accommodate his expanding collection of casts, drawings, paintings, architectural models and memorabilia. The first published guide for visitors was entitled *The Union of Architecture, Sculpture and Painting* (1827).

The house showcases Soane's genius as a manipulator of light, dark and space. It contains over 100 convex and flat mirrors and has coloured, frosted and clear glass windows: 'The Mirrors on the Ceiling, and the Looking Glasses ... present an almost infinite succession of those fanciful effects which constitute the poetry of Architecture.'[48] Those fanciful effects were most apparent when he had an opening over three days, from 8 p.m. onwards. The ground floor and basement were lit with over 100 specially ordered lamps, chandeliers and candelabra. The basement was the big draw, with its Gothic-style monk's parlour, cell and cloister, and Egyptian sarcophagus in its own crypt. With his countless flames and mirrors, Soane was architecture's Prometheus Unbound (Shelley's poem was published in 1820).

Soane envisaged a comprehensive study collection for all students and his own pupils, whose drawing office was in a freestanding raised box room, encrusted with casts. In 1833 the house was established as a museum by act of Parliament – one of the first of many such one-artist institutions.[49] In 1828, a Dürer museum had opened in the artist's timber-framed house to mark the tercentenary of his death; but it had no collection and hosted temporary exhibitions, mostly of borrowed prints and contemporary homages.[50]

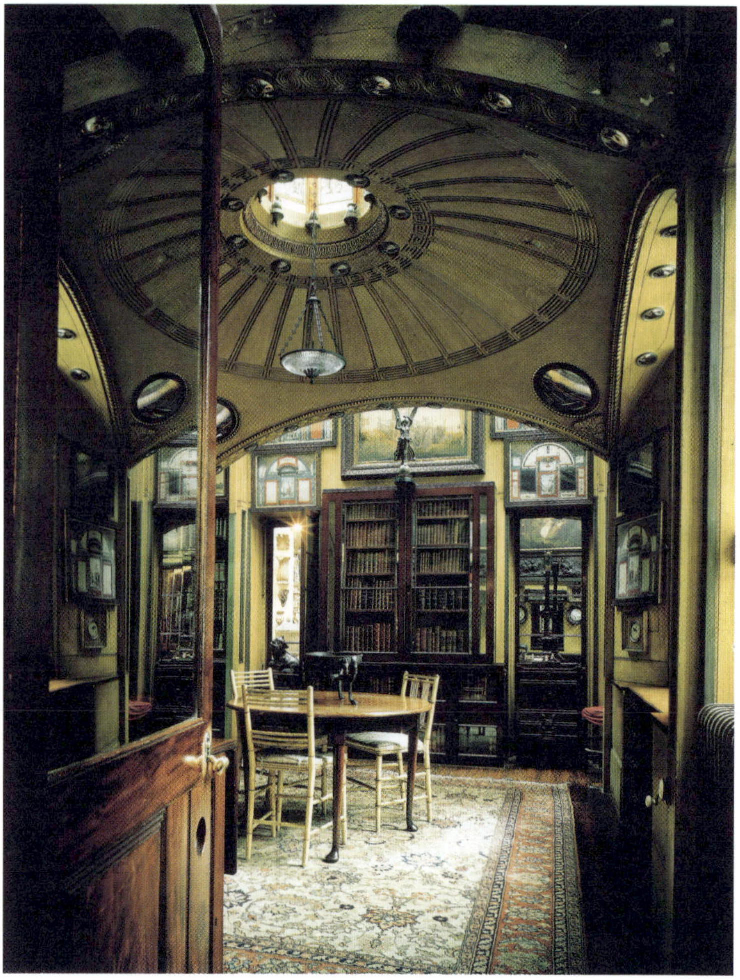

John Soane, breakfast room/study at 13 Lincoln's Inn Fields, 1812–before 1837.

In very few buildings is the universal so rooted in the intensely personal. The convex mirrors that stud the domed ceiling of Soane's breakfast room, where he often worked, were installed in the 1830s when cataracts endangered his sight.[51] Far more than 'fanciful effects', they are guardian constellations of crystal-clear eyes. An artistic super-vigilance reigns here, from breakfast to deep into the artificially lit night. The philosopher earl of Shaftesbury (1671–1713) believed those with self-knowledge acquire 'a peculiar speculative habit, so as virtually to carry about with them a sort of pocket mirror, always ready and in use'.[52] Soane's mirrors are always in use by visitors and by the objects reflected in them.

The museum came about as a consequence of personal tragedy. Soane had hoped his two sons would pursue architecture, creating a dynasty; but his first son died young and he became bitterly estranged from his second. The museum is remedial and compensatory, an inclusive family tree – or forest – of objects that will never die or depart. As such it echoes ideas expressed in Goethe's novel *Elective Affinities* (1808). An architect who is restoring a Gothic chapel asks a young woman to help him repaint the interior. Ottilie, an orphan, notes in her diary the architect's observations on the 'orphaned' status of modern art. When the works of a sculptor are taken from the studio, they 'desert him as the bird deserts the nest in which it was hatched'. But the architect suffers the most: 'How often he employs his whole mind and his whole love in the production of rooms from which he himself must be excluded. It is no wonder that he becomes alienated, since his work, like a child that has been provided for and left home, can no longer have any effect on its father. And how beneficial it must have been for art when it was intended to be concerned almost exclusively with what was public property, and belonged to everybody and therefore also to the artist!'[53]

The Soane Museum remains public property, a permanent mirror of the life of a great architect's mind.

Chapter 12

Women in the Studio

Inspiration, Destitution, Cleaning, Crimes of Passion

The presence of women in studio scenes becomes far more common after 1600: we see them as wives, mistresses, muses, models, patrons, artists and artisans. There's more to this than the provision of titillating eye candy for new picture types. It reflects a basic truth: that women had always played a key role. Wives helped manage the artist's business and household affairs and nurtured children who could contribute. They might also model. Gerard de Lairesse complained that Dutch painters used their wives even if 'ever so ugly, with all her Freckles and Pimples'; by the same token, a 'clownish unmannerly Maid-servant' would model 'a Lady in a Saloon' and a son – 'continually scratching his head, or having a down-look' – would model a lord.[1]

Bernard Palissy shamed his 'persecutor' wife in his treatise because of her refusal to play her allotted role (they were both banned from church for rowing during services). He would have much preferred Hephaestus' 'lovely Charis of the glistening veil', who receives Thetis. The Virgin Mary would have been even better. The Holy Family was increasingly depicted in Joseph's carpentry shop, with Mary sewing or sweeping up – the first appearance of a workshop cleaner.[2]

Palissy might have appreciated Marcus Gheeraerts' drawing of a high-minded painter suffering from what later became known as 'the pram in the hall'. A quotation from Juvenal explains: 'With difficulty shall they emerge whose virtues are obstructed by poverty at home.' Mercury, god of the arts, strikes the threadbare painter with his wand in an effort to supply inspirational Viagra; Minerva, or a model/mistress, has fallen asleep. The studio has an open shop front but no customers. The pigment grinder in the back

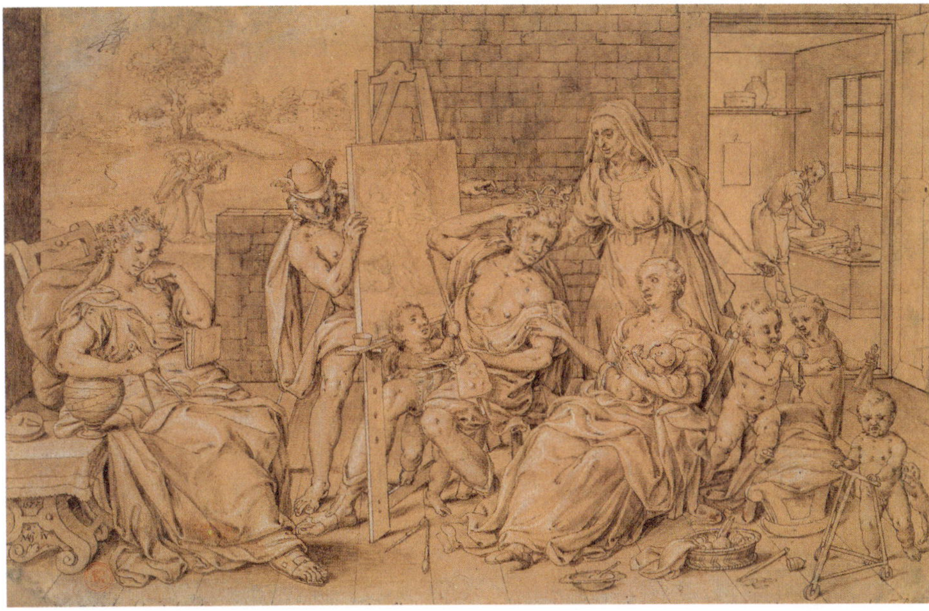

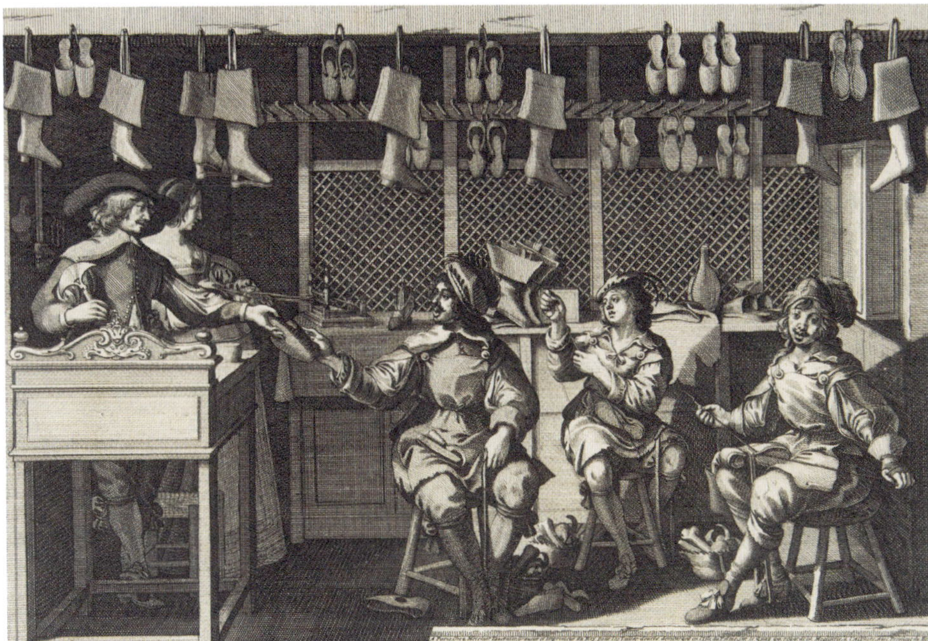

Top Marcus Gheeraerts the Elder, *The Unfortunate Painter and His Family*, 1577, pen and wash on paper. **Above** Abraham Bosse, *The Shoemaker's Shop*, c. 1632–3, etching.

room is an unviable luxury. Gheeraerts, a painter and printmaker, fled to England in 1568 escaping religious persecution but seems to have found success, remarrying after his first wife died. Here he posits the family as central while gleefully implying that bachelordom might be better for some. It was indeed a time of severe economic hardship, with poor harvests and mass migration to cities.[3]

A striking novelty of Abraham Bosse's prints from the 1630s is the high profile of Parisian women as consumers, managers and workers (preceding page). We have already seen Bosse's depiction of a visit by two women to a sculptor's studio (page 141). Elsewhere, a woman takes money from a female customer in a pastry shop; two women separately visit a lawyer; a schoolmistress teaches girls to read; women shop and work alongside men in bookshops and haberdasheries.[4] Parisian tradesmen appreciated having 'the most engaging and pretty' of their womenfolk fronting up the business, and leased attractive girls from poor families. Similar 'box-office' considerations influenced the selection of actresses.[5] The beauty of successful women painters is often extolled as much as their art.

Females were more visible in the public sphere in Northern Europe than in Italy or Spain, where respectable women tended to stay at home, with men doing the shopping and shopkeeping. In 1610 a Frenchman observed that in Florence women 'see the world only from the small openings in their windows'.[6] In Venice, Tintoretto dressed his young daughter Marietta, whom he trained to be a painter, as a boy so he could take her everywhere. In Rome hardly anyone had seen Artemisia Gentileschi (1593–c. 1656) before her rape trial. Her painter father, Orazio, kept her confined at home in the artists' quarter between Piazza di Spagna and Piazza del Popolo.[7] Her only excursions were to church. Orazio hoped she would become a nun and didn't educate her (she learned to write as an adult). Artemisia looked out of the window, however, and wasn't completely isolated: artists and models came to the house, where there was no clear distinction between working and living quarters. The propriety of this became a key issue at the trial.

Conversely, a Venetian traveller to London in 1562 was shocked to find that 'Englishwomen have great freedom to go out of the house without menfolk … [many] serve in the shops.'[8] In the following century, the 'talking, walking' gentlewoman would become a standard London type.[9] The hot-tempered courtesan Margaret Lemon, infuriated by the presence of society ladies in the Blackfriars studio of her lover Van Dyck, threatened to end his career by biting off his thumb.[10]

Bosse offers reassurance that these seductive working women are neither 'independent' nor 'loose' in his stylish depiction of a men's shoe shop.[11] Everyone is a cog in a well-oiled family machine. A well-dressed woman with silk rose planted in an ample cleavage makes multicoloured *nonpareille* ribbon with a mill.[12] It is destined for the shoe on the cabinet, its high heel inspired by Persian male fashions. Louis XIV wore heels wrapped in red silk, raising his 5 foot 4 inch (1.63 metre) frame to more regal heights. The man cuts leather panels to size, a foot-measuring gauge on the wall behind. Three craftsmen, most likely their sons, do the sewing, with baskets of deer bones at their feet for polishing leather. The inscribed verses explain the dynamic:

> The Master and also the Mistress make the common good
> the principal concern of their household./They do not walk
> away from each other, they both keep an eye on their workers
> until they become more diligent at quickly fulfilling their
> requirements./They meanwhile are marvels, asking the boys
> for wine and entertaining themselves with songs/amid their
> cups and bottles.

Here the family unit has become the joyful bedrock of economic, social and moral stability during the Wars of Religion and persecution of witches. Master and Mistress are a perfectly matched pair of shoes, always walking in tandem. The biggest advocates for marital partnerships were King Charles I, head of the Anglican Church, and his French Catholic queen, Henrietta Maria. The 'chaste' love cementing their marriage was held up as a model for government in court masques. Joined as one, 'Carlomaria' ruled by love and example rather than by force.[13] Unlustful marital love would be broadcast in innumerable artist portraits well into the 19th century. The presence of women also crucially underscored the popular myth that art was born of love rather than money.[14]

Bosse's shoemaker scenario could equally be seen as a 'glass half empty', something that reflects the transformation of women into unpaid housewives or low-paid home-workers operating in a 'putting-out' system. From the late Middle Ages women were increasingly squeezed out of the production of cloth and clothing, their traditional domain, as male-only guilds of weavers and cloth-cutters were formed, taking the best-paid skilled jobs. A widow was traditionally entitled to carry on her husband's business if she inherited it.[15] The richest goldsmith recorded in the Paris census of 1292 was a widow

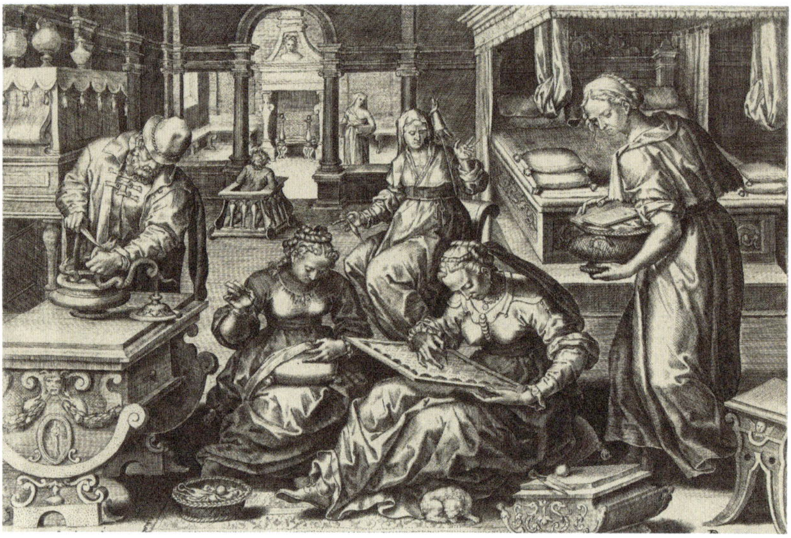

Pieter Jalhea Furnius after Johannes Stradanus, *Cornelia, Mother of the Gracchi, with Female Companions Engaged in Needlework*, c. 1580, engraving.

who had taken over her husband's workshop. But widows were increasingly discriminated against, having limits placed on apprentices and machine tools unless they married a guild member.[16] The emergence of male-only art academies continued a long-term trend. Bosse made prints of the workshops of engravers, painters and sculptors, and they are male-only operations.

The modern woman's main artisanal outlet conformed to Erasmus' recommendations in his treatise *On Christian Marriage* (1526), which echoed biblical precedent: 'The distaff and spindle are in truth the tools of all women and suitable for avoiding idleness.' He did, however, prefer well-born women to study, which 'busies the whole soul' and inculcates virtue.[17] Weaving and embroidery furnished the home and made for attractive gifts (the male equivalent was turning or metalwork). Textile art was often done in the lady's bedchamber: in an engraving made c. 1580, the chamber of Cornelia, mother of two Roman political reformers, has become a female *studiolo*. Her husband kills a snake – a bad omen that results in his death – whereupon Cornelia becomes the exemplary widow, educating her sons (one of the most commonly cited reasons for female education). Most professional embroiderers were men, but the unmarried Leiden embroiderer Catharina Rozee (1632–1682) found fame and fortune depicting scenes in silk thread with such realism they were mistaken for oil paintings. A spider spinning a web in a

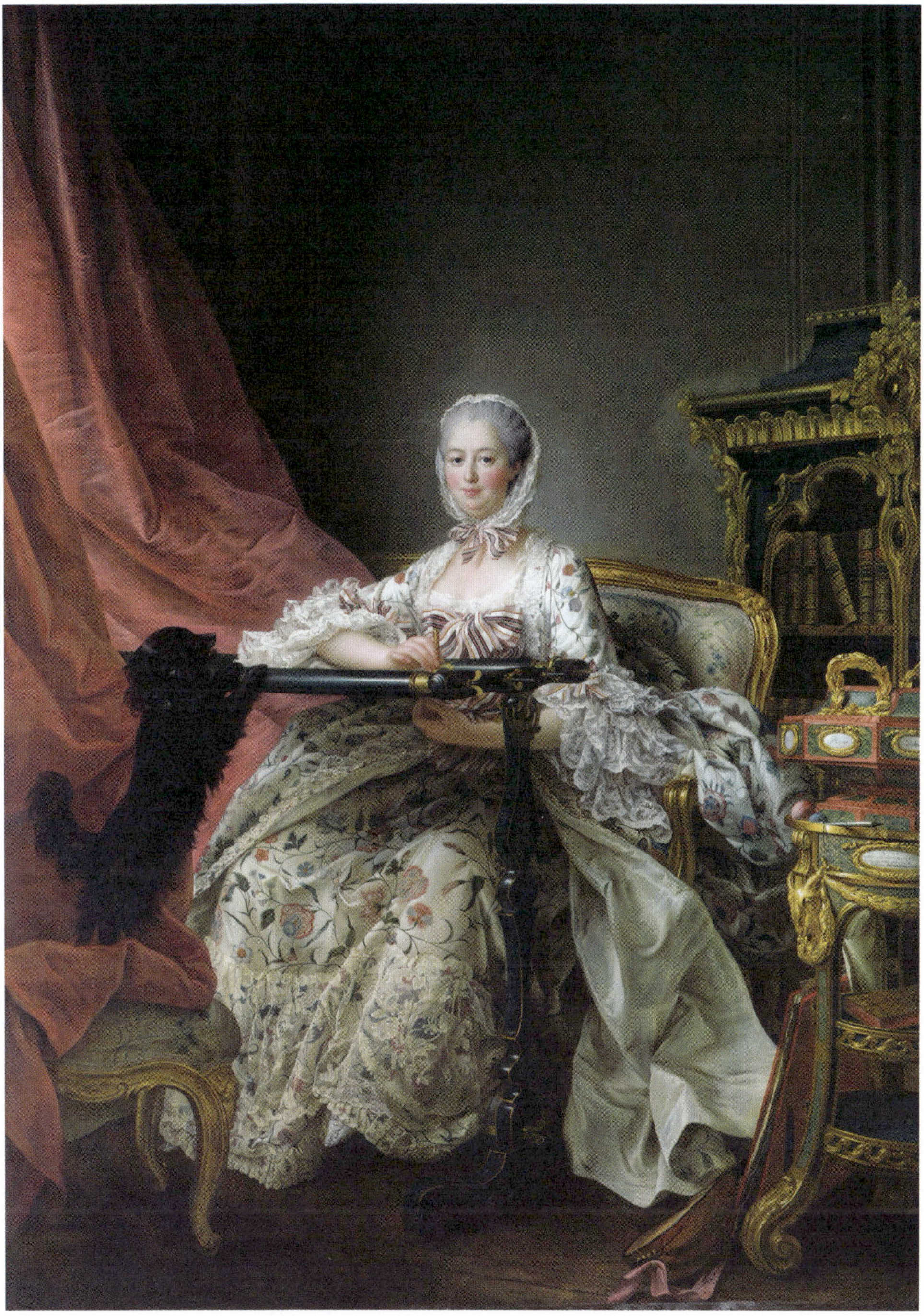

François-Hubert Drouais, *Madame de Pompadour at Her Tambour Frame*, 1763–4, oil on canvas.

tree (a surrogate self-portrait) sold for 500 guilders. Rozee's amazing skill brought accusations of being a witch and sorceress.[18]

The most dazzling affirmation of textile art as a serious pursuit is François-Hubert Drouais's portrait of Louis XV's mistress, then favourite, Madame de Pompadour (1721–1764). An intelligent bourgeoise who married well and seduced brilliantly, Pompadour hosted high-flying salons, orchestrated royal patronage, and was herself an accomplished amateur engraver and intaglio maker with her own drilling machine. Seen in her salon-cum-studio at Versailles (preceding page), she is the glamorous *Gioconda* of textiles. She makes a tapestry with a hooked needle on a large ebony tambour. A courtier noted that in 1756 the marquise had stopped receiving ambassadors in her dressing room but instead received them at her tapestry-frame: 'She went from make-up to making.'[19] After some disastrous political interventions, one would assume she wanted to seem a new Penelope, with her King Charles spaniel 'Milady' symbolizing fidelity.

But this is a big craft mission statement. Pompadour had, after all, revived the fortunes of the Gobelins tapestry factory. Her tambour is the Rolls-Royce of embroidery frames. She is flanked by a sumptuous state-of-the-art worktable with drawers for different coloured threads. Its plaques are from the Sèvres porcelain factory, which she founded. A folio of drawings or engravings and a Neapolitan mandolin lean against it, and a heavy-duty rococo bookcase stands behind. It is a celebration of her hands-on role in nurturing, promoting and practising French luxury arts, and of her ineffable good taste.

***

Depictions of tooled-up women triumphing over sloth and the perceived limitations of their sex became more prevalent in 17th- and 18th-century art. Women not only sew or weave, they draw and paint, as well as read and write. Increased demand for small-scale easel paintings and miniatures, especially portraits, and for copies of paintings, allowed women artists to earn money, though it was usually male relations – like Gentileschi's spendthrift husband – who controlled the purse strings and house keys. In 1678, Samuel van Hoogstraten complained about the fashion for 'childish little things' consumed, but also produced, by 'tidy little women': 'Tidy little Panels, sometimes locked up in little cases, attract the gold from the purse.'[20]

The presence of women in the studio gained credence from the fashion for female personifications of virtue and female heroines.[21] Vasari pioneered female personifications of Painting, Sculpture and Architecture in the decorative schemes of his houses in Arezzo and Florence, adding them to the traditional personifications of the nine liberal arts such as music, history and poetry (see Chapter 9).[22] He mentions only one female artist in the 1550 edition of the *Lives* – the Bolognese sculptor Properzia de' Rossi – but thirteen are mentioned in the 1568 edition. Cesare Ripa's *Iconologia* (1593/1603), an illustrated iconographic handbook for artists, gives pointers to many more personifications, with three-quarters of the *c.* 600 examples being female. Hoogstraten's art treatise has nine chapters named after the ancient muses, but now embodying different aspects of painting. They are 'nine mistresses' who seduce young men, making them fall in love with painting and teaching them the rudiments.

Gentileschi depicted herself as *Pittura* (*c.* 1638–9), her attributes derived from Ripa – including dishevelled hair, a symbol of imagination and poetic *furor* (overleaf). Despite this iconographic dependency, it is hard to exaggerate the picture's originality. It was painted in London, where she had gone to assist her father, court painter to Queen Henrietta Maria. Artemisia doesn't stand still like Ripa's personification of painting, or sit like Saint Luke. She models herself on Michelangelo's airborne Creator on the Sistine Ceiling, throwing herself into her work body and soul. Ten years later she wrote to a Sicilian patron: 'You will find the spirit of Caesar in this soul of a woman.'[23] Her studio is cell-like and windowless, but in Caesar style she is crossing a cultural Rubicon. The limits are unclear as she breaks through the closed 'window' of the picture frame.

Gentileschi was the first woman to gain membership of the Accademia in Florence, in 1619. She was following in the footsteps of Sofonisba Anguissola, whose fame persuaded the Accademia di San Luca in Rome to change its rules in 1609 and allow female members – though women could not attend meetings. Anguissola had been ennobled after teaching painting to the Spanish queen, Elizabeth of Valois.

According to Bernini in Paris, all the accolades given to 'girls who painted' irritated his great patron, Pope Urban VIII (r. 1623–44). The pope must also have been referring to Lavinia Fontana, the first woman to win public commissions, who moved from Bologna to Rome in 1603.[24] Bernini cites the pope's complaint after Guillaume Château, who made reproductive prints, came to his studio and 'showed him the copy that a girl had made in miniature of a *Virgin* by Charles Lebrun'. The unnamed girl was almost certainly his daughter. Bernini 'thought it quite good', but then relayed the pope's complaint: 'It

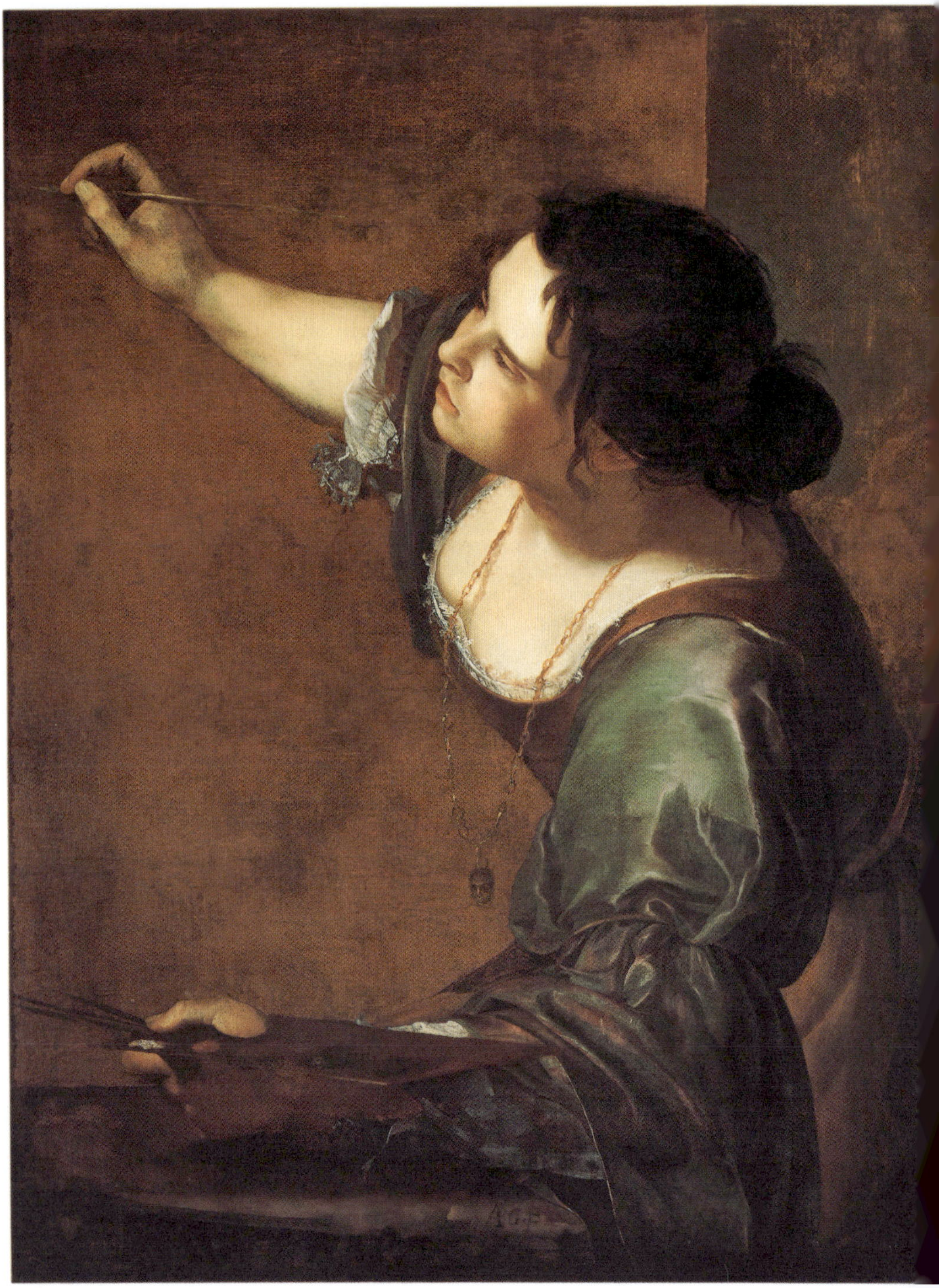

Artemisia Gentileschi, *Allegory of Painting*, *c*. 1638–9, oil on canvas.

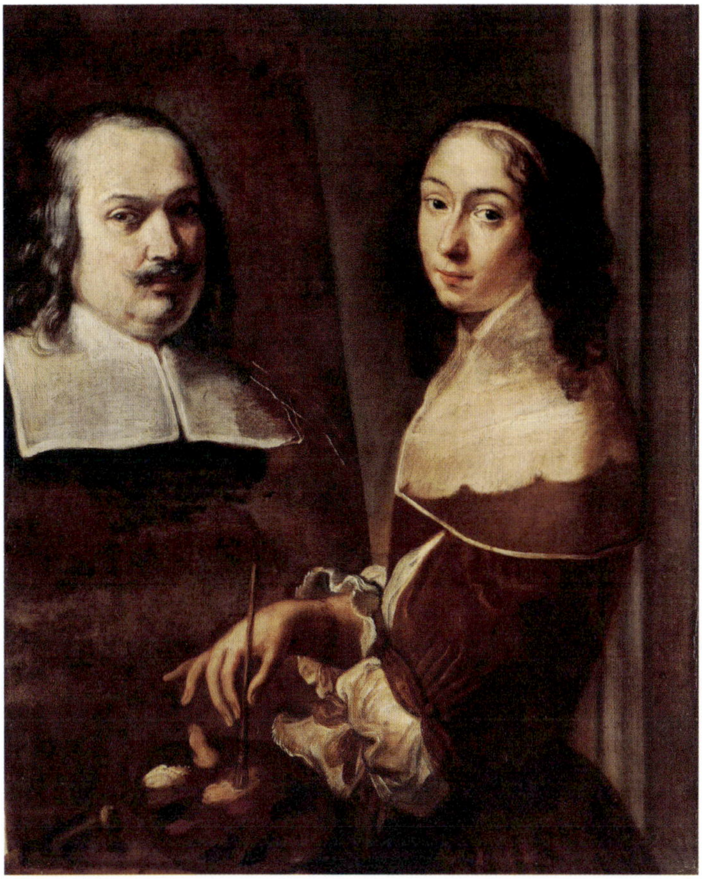

Elisabetta Sirani, *Self-Portrait Painting Her Father*, c. 1665, oil on canvas.

was very rare for [women] to do any good, as from the moment they began they got so much praise, that they early on had had far too high an opinion of themselves. Anyway they could never draw as well as men, as it was against propriety for them to draw from the nude; the best advice one could give them was to choose only the best examples to copy.'[25] The popularity of female personifications, heroines and nudes meant that not being able to draw the male nude was becoming less of a handicap.

In 1665, the female painter who would most readily have come to Bernini's tactless mind was the Bolognese Elisabetta Sirani (1638–1665), who plays an important role in the history of the artist's studio. Sirani died suddenly just before Bernini left for France and was given a quasi-state funeral. Bologna was the only Italian city with walking, talking, working, writing gentlewomen. The presence of the oldest university in Europe made education more widely valued, even if women could not attend. There was a significant group of women writers and musical composers. Thirty-five professional women painters, five printmakers and four embroiderers are recorded in the 17th century.[26] Sirani's father, Giovanni Andrea, had worked for the great Bolognese Baroque painter Guido Reni (1575–1642). He trained his three daughters to be his assistants, while giving them a literary education.

In a besotted biography, the culmination of a history of Bolognese painting, Count Carlo Cesare Malvasia (1616–1693) identified women painters as a unique feature of the city. Sirani painted in a 'virile and grand manner' superior to any man; she was 'the scorn of nature, the prodigy of art, the glory of the female sex, the gem of Italy, the sun of Europe' – and, of course, very beautiful.[27] In 1662, when her father became bedridden and unable to paint because of arthritic gout, Elisabetta took over the running of studio and household, never marrying. She established the first secular art school for girls (medieval nuns ran illumination 'schools' in convents). At least two pupils were from non-artist families. Increasing numbers of women were taking art lessons, which gave them a marketable skill that could count towards a dowry. Private art lessons provided a reliable source of income for professional artists and drawing masters.[28]

Sirani was famously fast, able to paint a head in less than an hour. The head of her father has just been completed in this self-portrait, one of two versions painted for Bolognese patrons. Both surrogate and successor, she turns wistfully towards her sitter/viewer, an elegant painting hand positioned where her father's deformed hands would be if his body were painted. A fluted pilaster rises behind her, showing she now supports her family. Portraying her father reassures us that she represents continuity, not rupture with patriarchy. A later French artist, Adélaïde Labille-Guiard, included a dowdy portrait bust of her father in an otherwise supremely glamorous studio scene with two female pupils (1785; opposite). Labille-Guiard had recently been admitted to the Académie Royale as one of four female members (the maximum allowed). Everyone smiles, including Papa.[29]

Malvasia published Sirani's fascinating work diary, *Record of the Paintings Made by Me, Elisabetta Sirani*, which shows she completed over 200 canvases and 15 prints in a decade (around 120 works by Gentileschi are known from a much longer career). Even her drawings were collected, a first for a female artist.[30] Malvasia stresses that her earnings were put to the 'common benefit of the household'. Many of her pictures were of heroic females,

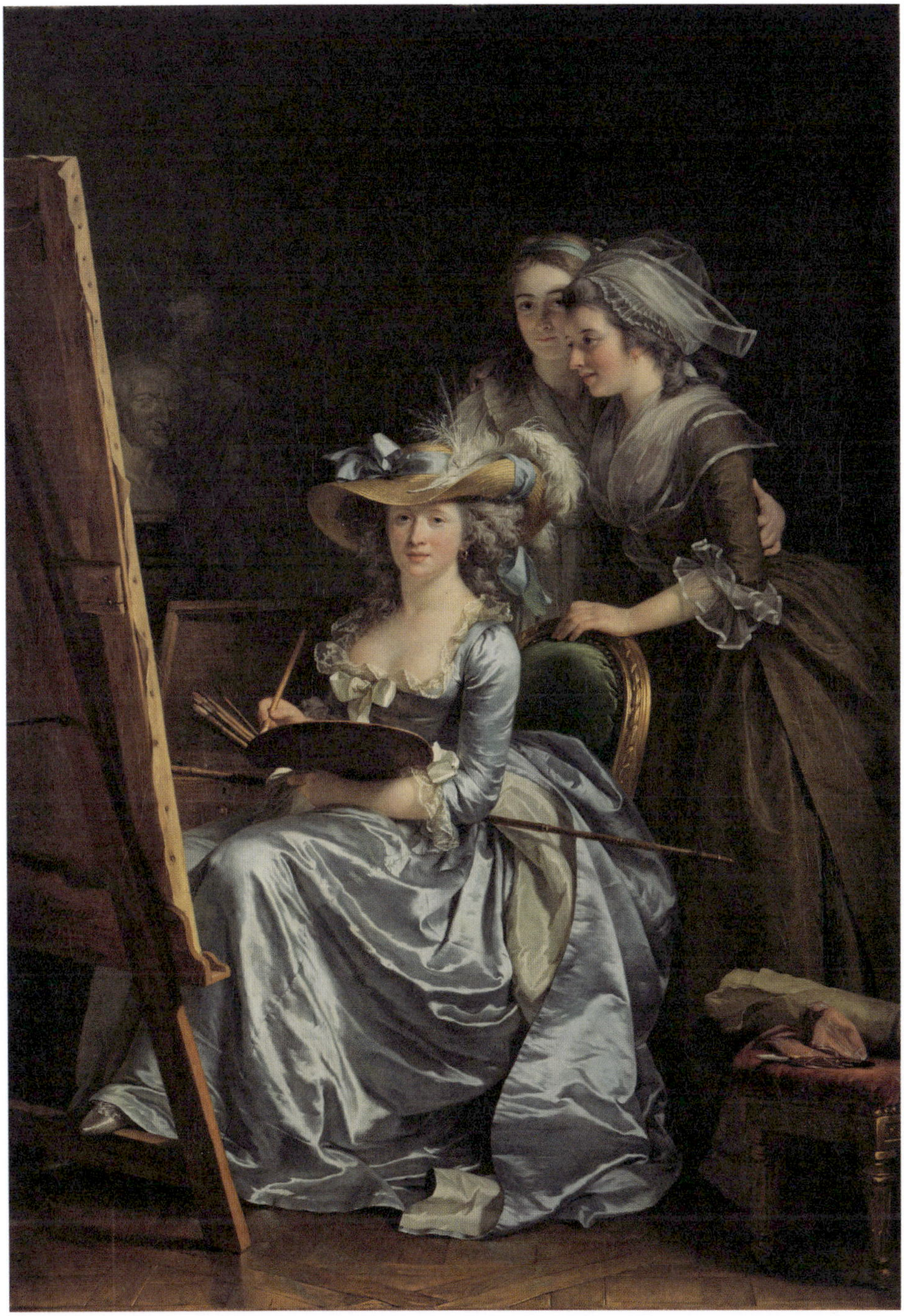

Adélaïde Labille-Guiard, *Self-Portrait with Two Pupils, Marie Gabrielle Capet and Marie Marguerite Carreaux de Rosemond*, 1785, oil on canvas.

including Portia stabbing herself with an embroidery needle (an ironic dig?) and many female personifications. Like Gentileschi, Sirani portrayed herself as *Pittura*, but now flanked by two big books placed under an inkwell, like an alumna of Bologna University.

By carefully documenting her work, Sirani helped counter rumours that her disabled father painted her pictures.[31] For similar reasons, she signed about two-thirds of her works, often 'embroidering' her name onto painted fabrics, wittily alluding to more traditional female arts. Most conclusively of all, she allowed patrons to witness her in action. On 13 May 1664,

> the most Serene Cosimo Grand Prince of Tuscany came into our house to see my paintings, and in his presence I worked on a painting for his uncle Prince Leopoldo in which I personified three virtues of his great family – Justice assisted by Charity and Prudence. I quickly sketched out all of the child that is feeding from the breast of Charity, and at the end of the visit he ordered a BV [Blessed Virgin] for himself, which I executed immediately so it was ready by the time he returned to Florence.[32]

Sirani knew how to tempt clients. She painted the convulsive breastfeeding zone in this famously puritanical man's presence, rather than a pious face, hand or bit of drapery. She signed it by 'sewing' one letter of her name on each of Justice's silk buttons. Leopoldo was delighted, sending her a crucifix encrusted with fifty-six diamonds, which she put in her *studiolo* with other prized possessions (money transactions were for tradesmen). Sirani died at age 27 in the summer of 1665, believed poisoned by her female cook, but more likely from peritonitis. Her last notebook entry records that during the spring every prince, princess and VIP visiting Bologna had come to see her in her studio.

Sirani's performances were celebrated at her funeral in the basilica of San Domenico, Bologna, where a temporary structure made from fictive marble was erected in the transept under the dome. It was designed by the painter Matteo Borboni, who in 1659 had commissioned a small half-length figure of Saint Francis to go in his *stanza*.[33] Inspired by the Temple of Honour in ancient Rome, the monument to Sirani was immortalized in a print reproduced in Malvasia's biography. It is an open-sided elongated octagon, the domed roof supported by eight columns. Malvasia's measuring scale shows it is 21 metres

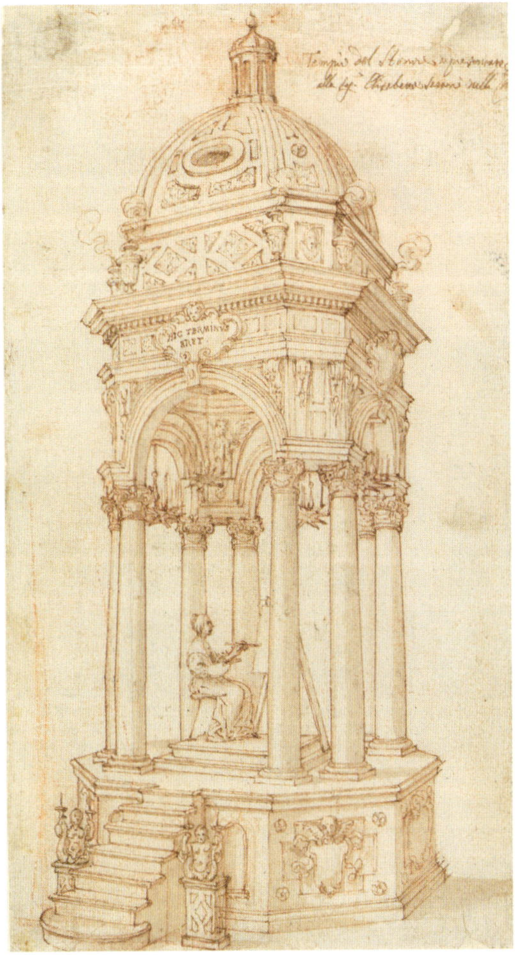

Matteo Borboni, *Catafalque of Elisabetta Sirani*, 1665, brown ink and wash over red chalk on paper.

(70 feet) high and 9 metres (30 feet) wide. The octagon enshrines a colossal wax statue of Sirani 'masterfully sitting' before her easel painting a BV. Four chandeliers hang from the dome, their circle of drips kept well clear of the statue. The chandeliers suggest Sirani worked at night to meet tight deadlines.

This seems to be the first statue of an artist, the next being the bronze statue of Dürer erected in Nuremberg in 1840, which gave no indication of his profession. The flight of steps suggests visitors climbed up, watching Sirani at work in death as they had in life. Beside the steps was one of several emblematic inscriptions: VELOX NON TARDA ('Fast, not slow'). It functions as

Sirani's motto and as a warning to keep traffic moving round the statue. Sirani is both person and personification. Malvasia would entitle his history *Felsina pittrice* –'Bologna Paintress'.[34]

Astonishingly, Sirani was then buried in Guido Reni's tomb. Her father would join them in 1670, with all three having a joint epitaph. Reni, reputedly a virgin but probably homosexual, would have turned away in his grave. According to Malvasia, Reni could not endure women in his house, especially detesting old women, and was never alone with a female model: 'he always feared sorcery and poisoning', and suspected sorcery when he found a woman's blouse among his laundry.[35] But the shared tomb served a higher purpose, becoming a celebration of artistic lineages and chaste heterosexual marriages. 'Guideliza' is an artist counterpart to 'Carlomaria'. In death, they 'do not walk away from each other' and they serve 'the common good'.

***

In Northern Europe, women would play such a significant role as tastemakers that 'feminine' styles would be identified. The power of women as patrons was demonstrated during and after the regencies of two widowed queens of France, the Florentine Marie de' Medici (1610–17) and Anne of Austria (1643–51). Marie and Anne helped create a vogue for images of *femmes fortes* (strong women), historical, biblical, mythological and allegorical.[36]

The prominent role of women is one of the most striking features of Bernini's visit to Paris (June to October 1665). Bernini had been recommended to the king as an architect by Christina, former queen of Sweden. In 1654 she had shocked Christendom by first abdicating, then converting to Catholicism after moving to Rome. She had entered Rome in a carved wooden carriage designed by Bernini and immediately visited his studio. He greeted her in his working clothes, since he 'considered it to be the most worthy possible garment in which to receive that great lady'. Christina appreciated the 'beautiful subtlety' of Bernini's gesture and wished to 'touch the garment with her own hand'.[37] Having made her wooden carriage, he may have wanted to appear like the carpenter Saint Joseph. Bernini declared in Paris that she 'knew as much about the mysteries of art as those whose profession it was'.[38]

Bernini was struck by the sophistication and independence of Parisian women, far exceeding the women he knew in Rome. His guide Chantelou tells him the French court is a 'woman's paradise'. There was a constant stream of female visitors to his studio. The queen sat down and 'stayed there to watch him working', then got up to take a closer look; the Duchesse de Nemours 'stayed an hour, going back and forth between the portrait and the *Christ Child* [a marble relief]; from time to time she watched Marot [a printmaker] drawing'.[39] The scene in Bernini's studio is paralleled by Velázquez's *Las Meninas* (1655). Protocols in Madrid for women were similar to those in Florence, but Velázquez – perhaps influenced by French fashion – allows female visitors to dominate, with the infanta and her entourage taking centre stage.

When the Duchesse d'Aiguillon dropped by with her lifelong friend Madame du Vigean, Bernini 'replied with wit and gallantry to the praises of these two ladies'. Madame d'Aiguillon, then in her sixties, was niece and heir to Cardinal Richelieu. Merrily widowed in 1622 from a husband 'she could not stand', according to her enemies she enjoyed a passionate lesbian relationship with Vigean.[40] She hosted salons for leading writers, artists and scientists. She told Bernini 'she was convinced that the bust surpassed anything done in modern or ancient times, although antiquity reached such high standards of perfection'. This is as formulaic as the compliments listed in Pierre Lebrun's *Essays on the Wonders of Painting*, but Chantelou has extracted something quotable from a long conversation.

The moralist Jean de la Bruyère (1645–1696) believed women like d'Aiguillon should be like beautifully polished weapons, 'a cabinet piece [*pièce de cabinet*] that one shows to the curious, but which is not to be used'.[41] Similar qualms prompted some monks to tell Bernini a bon mot of King Henri IV: 'It may be my wife [Marie de' Medici] who builds the convent church of the Feuillants, but she builds it with my money.'[42] These exchanges were all part of the so-called *querelle des femmes* or 'woman question', with the feminist camp arguing that women's brains functioned as well as men's, while their physical delicacy gave them greater subtlety, sensitivity and speed of thought. Their greater leisure time and solitude should be spent on study and cultivation. Women's heightened sensitivity is manifest in the long, wavy fingers of the Roman Cornelia and Sirani, and in the raised hand of the woman in Bosse's sculptor's studio: the slashed fingertips of her kid gloves turn her hands into tremulous live coral. The Jesuit Nicolas Caussin (1583–1651) warned against creating 'Sibyls [female prophets] and Muses' while neglecting religious studies and tradition.[43]

Gendered concepts of media and styles were also being formulated. Willem van Haecht's *Apelles Painting Campaspe* dramatizes gendered artistic taste in the studio (pages 152–3). Campaspe, wearing the turban of a sibyl or muse, and her female entourage bring in a drawing of the *Judgment of Paris*, presumably the basis for Apelles' next picture with them as models and judges of the finished work. At far right, two women closely examine pieces of Chinese blue-and-white porcelain, prized imports of the Dutch East India Company. Women from ruling families in the Netherlands started a European trend of having an Asian-style porcelain room or cabinet, lined with silk or lacquered wood panels and, later, with mirrors.[44] Van Haecht's picture celebrates female expertise in art and beauty, and female power over a great artist. Antwerp, where he lived, was ruled by the Archduchess Isabella, a major patron of Rubens and repeat visitor to his studio.

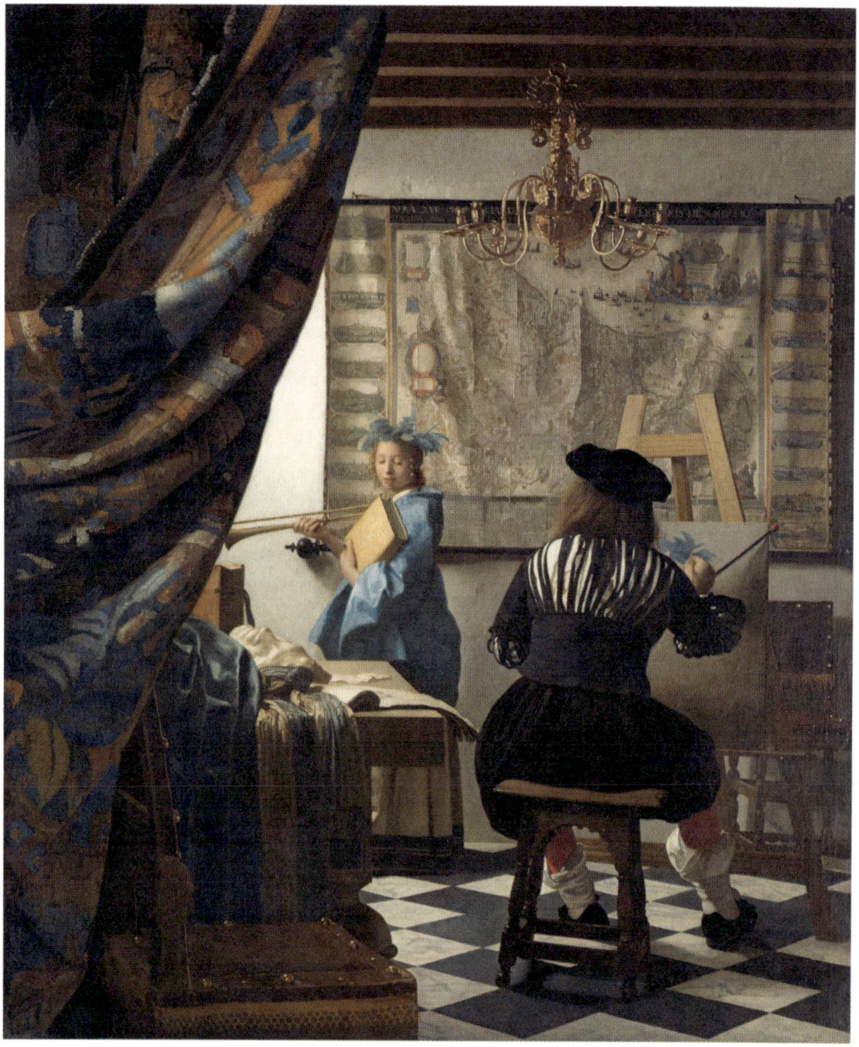

Johannes Vermeer, *The Art of Painting*, 1666–8, oil on canvas.

Bernini caused outrage after complaining that the king's bedchamber and anterooms were 'designed to the taste of ladies'. Gold-embroidered velvet covered the walls, and there were ornate cabinets, chandeliers and silver vases filled with roses. The first rooms through which he had passed, 'with their statues and busts', were superior, 'more masculine in character'. Chantelou later explained that 'the cabinets and cut-glass had been put there at the time of the Regency [of Louis's mother, Anne of Austria], which was a government feminine in character'. The English architect Christopher Wren, visiting Paris at the same time, found Versailles too feminine: 'The Women, as they make here the Language and Fashions, and meddle with Politicks and Philosophy, so they sway also in Architecture, Works of Filigrand [fine ornamental work], and little Knacks.'[45] Gendered concepts of media and styles would intensify with Edmund Burke's 1757 classification of the Sublime as male and the beautiful as female, and in the denigration of Rococo art as 'Pompadour' (*c.* 1800).

Vermeer's *The Art of Painting* (1666–8) shows how an artist's studio might become 'feminine in character' in this period. It is a *cabinet* of patterned fabrics and clothes, plus brass chandelier, draw-leaf table with turned legs, marble floor tiles, elaborate hand-coloured map and walnut chairs decorated with velvet, silk and lace. Apart from the deluxe chandelier, most of these props appear in other pictures, so we can assume they were household items. The immaculate tiles, costly and heavy, are never likely to be found in a studio, or on a first floor. The same tiles appear in other pictures, arranged in different patterns. The foppish artist models a stylish slashed doublet, painter's beret, bloated breeches, velvet shoes. In the absence of his face, we dwell on his egg-shaped hand as it hatches one of Van Hoogstraten's 'tidy little Panels'. The female model, dressed as Clio, muse of history, is the human centre of attention, moist lips quivering in sunlight. Van Hoogstraten observed that Darius, king of the Persians, wore his golden sword-belt in a 'loose and feminine' way. Looseness is a striking feature of the clothing, draperies, rucked map and crinkled sheets of paper. Vermeer's father had been a maker of patterned satin fabrics.[46]

Apart from *The Astronomer* and *The Geographer*, Vermeer's paintings have female protagonists. The absence of children is striking, not least because Vermeer was survived by ten offspring whose upkeep contributed to his financial ruin and death. Because we cannot tell if Vermeer's women are married or mothers, they are more available for imaginative projection. He grants them the leisure and solitude to become 'Sibyls and Muses', or just to daydream. Clio's eyelids are lowered not out of virgin modesty, but for meditation.

The plaster cast bathed in light must be Vermeer's invention; it is too craggy to be Apollo, god of light, as has been claimed. The headband and the proximity of the big book suggest it was inspired by a print of the venerable Cumaean Sibyl on Michelangelo's Sistine Ceiling.

Vermeer's life was shaped by women. His widowed mother ran the family inn in Delft, and after his marriage to a Catholic woman, Catharina Bolnes, he lived in the house of his wealthy mother-in-law, Maria Thins, legally separated from her violent picture-dealer husband. The inn and marital home were on opposite sides of the market square, with a Protestant church in the middle. He probably had a studio in the inn before transferring to a first-floor, north-facing studio across the square. The width of both buildings was around 7 metres (23 feet) – slightly bigger than average – meaning that Vermeer's studio would have been a comfortable 6.5 metres (21 feet) wide. The proportions were similar to those in many of his depicted rooms.[47]

The studio *mise-en-scène* is misleading in several ways. Unlike in *The Astronomer* and *The Geographer*, Vermeer's painter has few visible tools – no palette, spare brushes, bottles or pigment (some scholars think he should have a *camera obscura*). No model could hold that pose for long. He would have made separate drawn studies, and dressed a mannequin. Any painter would have started with the face rather than the wreath, symbol of fame. This is redolent of canvas-work embroidery, where you start anywhere.

Vermeer gives us something unprecedented: a faceless painter painting a faceless head. So while giving us a glimpse into the artist's studio, he insists that crucial aspects should remain secret and private. We stand, as it were, in the anteroom to the chamber of the king of painters. He communes with his mistress-muse, and with his art. He does not offer us a chair.

***

Female models who were not members of the household remained the exception. They were expensive, difficult to find and persuade, disappointingly real and alive. They were first widely used in art academies and schools in the 19th century, the change brought about by the desire for greater naturalism, mass migration of job-seeking young women from country to city, and competition between art schools. Modelling became professionalized, and not just a sideline for sex workers, family and servants.

Paris had a 'model market' on Monday mornings outside the Ecole des Beaux-Arts. Auditions were held. Trilby O'Ferrall, the Irish laundress heroine

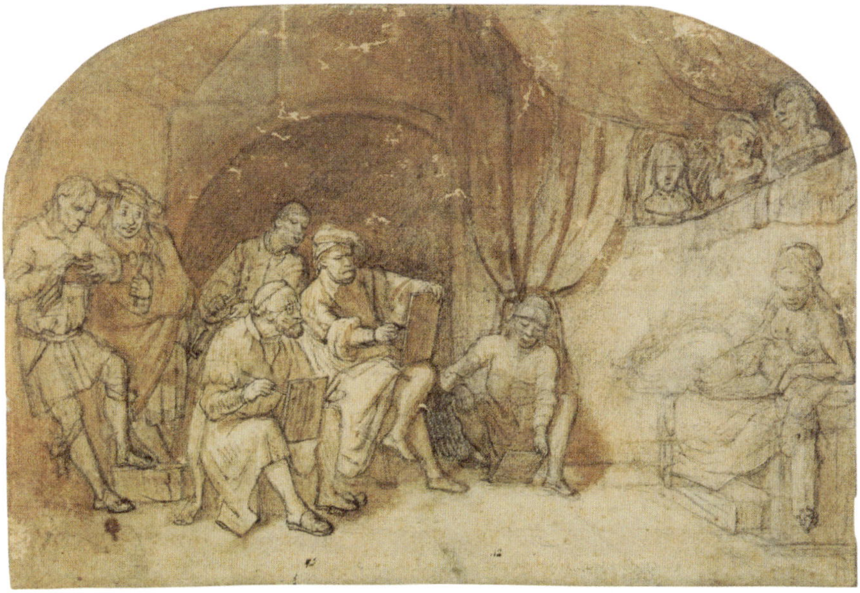

Constantijn Daniel van Renesse, *Rembrandt and His Pupils Drawing from a Nude Model*, c. 1650, pen and wash over chalk.

of George du Maurier's bohemian novel *Trilby* (1894), displays her assets to an artist: '"That's my foot," she said, kicking off her big slipper and stretching out the limb. "It's the handsomest foot in Paris. There's only one in all Paris to match it, and here it is" ... and [she] stuck out the other.' Trilby adds for good measure that she poses for *l'ensemble*, 'head, hands, and feet – everything'.[48] She thereby refutes one of Lairesse's major objections to female models: 'There is always a tiny smudge that fogs the clear glass of her mirror .... To put it bluntly, none will charm in public: except with borrowed enticements, or purchased teeth. This one has attracted everyone with a pleasing face, but is deformed by a crooked back, and has a bosom like a full food bag.'[49] Lairesse recommended artists use 'fine Plaister faces, which are to be had in Abundance'.[50] Plaster Venuses and prints, especially after Raphael, were easy options for bodies.

Rembrandt seems to have used paid female models only after about 1650, when he ran a lucrative private school at the top of his large house in the Breestraat, Amsterdam. The above drawing is by an amateur artist who took lessons there. Even now a shelf of casts provides an overbearing corrective to the model reclining in a draped, tented space.[51] Plaster chaperones and polices flesh. Rembrandt had extensive art and costume collections. As seen here, he

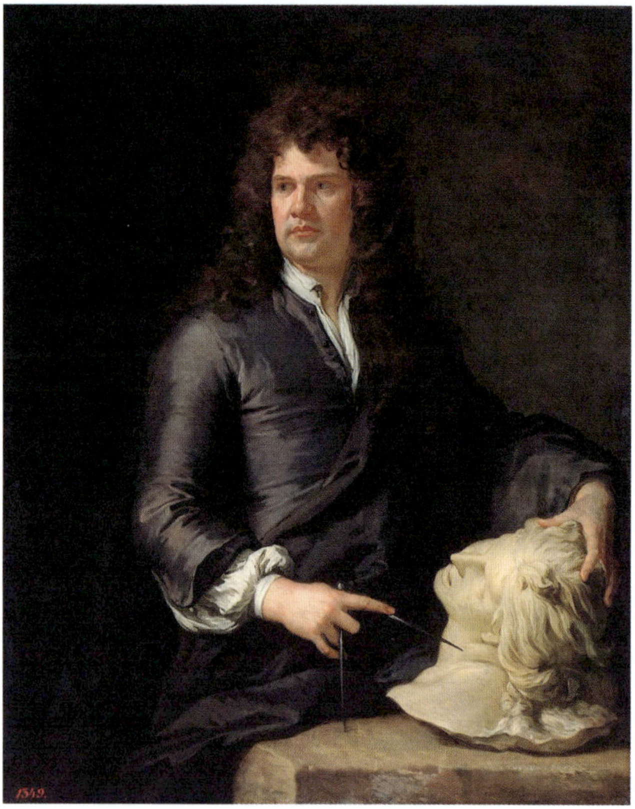

Godfrey Kneller, *Grinling Gibbons*, 1680s, oil on canvas.

dressed casts in textiles. But big trouble is brewing. The second student from the left ogles rather than draws the model. A possibly apocryphal anecdote has Rembrandt overhearing a student say to a female model inside his study cubicle: 'Here we are naked like Adam and Eve in the Garden.' He promptly expelled them from Eden, driving them out of the house.[52]

Guido Reni studied the heads of ancient statues, especially Niobe and her daughters, for eight years.[53] More shockingly, on being asked who the female model was for his beautiful Madonnas and Magdalens, 'he ordered his colour-grinder, who had the ugly mug of a criminal, to sit down and look up at the sky, and with him as model he produced a little head of a female saint, the sight of which was so wondrous that it seemed ... made by magic'.[54] The Flemish painter Peter Angelis, when studying in Rome in the 1720s, dressed a 'rustick ill shapd' male model in women's clothes, thereby causing 'much sport and laughter to his companions'.[55]

From around 1600, male artists were often portrayed manhandling the plaster heads of distressed females, flaunting in eroticized form the male artist's godlike power over life and death, their mastery of emotional expression, and the irrelevance of live women in the serious studio. The most popular female fetish heads were the Medici *Venus*, surprised by peeping Toms as she bathes, and Bernini's *Proserpine* being abducted by Pluto, god of the underworld. The Niobe group was discovered in 1583 and displayed until 1769 as a thrilling tableau in Villa Medici, Rome.[56] Niobe was punished for her parental pride by having her seven daughters (and seven sons) strafed by arrows. The heads of the crying and dying female figures were available as plasters. Five distressed female heads are displayed on the shelves in Bosse's print of the sculptor's studio. Intense expressions were hard for a human model to hold, as were raised heads.

In Kneller's sumptuous silver-grey portrait of Grinling Gibbons, the decorative wood-carver and sculptor grasps Proserpine's hair and places the pointed tip of his compass against her neck with exquisite sadism. Our queasiness is intensified by her lifelikeness. The mindset is encapsulated by Bernini's comment on Veronese's painting of *Susannah and the Elders*: 'Anyone who pricked [Susannah's] arm would draw blood.'[57] Expressive female heads die repeatedly – in mythical life, in plaster life through decapitation, and in their studio afterlives.

***

The Royal Academy in London, founded in 1768 under George III's patronage, was the first state-sponsored institution to use female models. Initially located in the royal palace at Old Somerset House, it followed the lead of the St Martin's Lane Academy, a private art school founded by William Hogarth in 1735. Hogarth, with typical candour, admitted using female models 'to make it more inviting to subscribers'.[58] The RA was also a pioneer in having female founder members: the flower painter Mary Moser and portrait painter Angelica Kaufmann. The Académie Royale in Paris had only ever admitted one woman, the still-life painter Marie-Thérèse Reboul in 1757.

However, in Johann Zoffany's nocturnal group portrait (overleaf) the two female members are present only as unfinished, unframed bust-length canvases, dowdy disembodied muses hung at the same height as the shelved plaster casts and chandelier. They don't look into the room. Moser's husband George, enamel painter and Keeper, blocks her view as he places a supporting

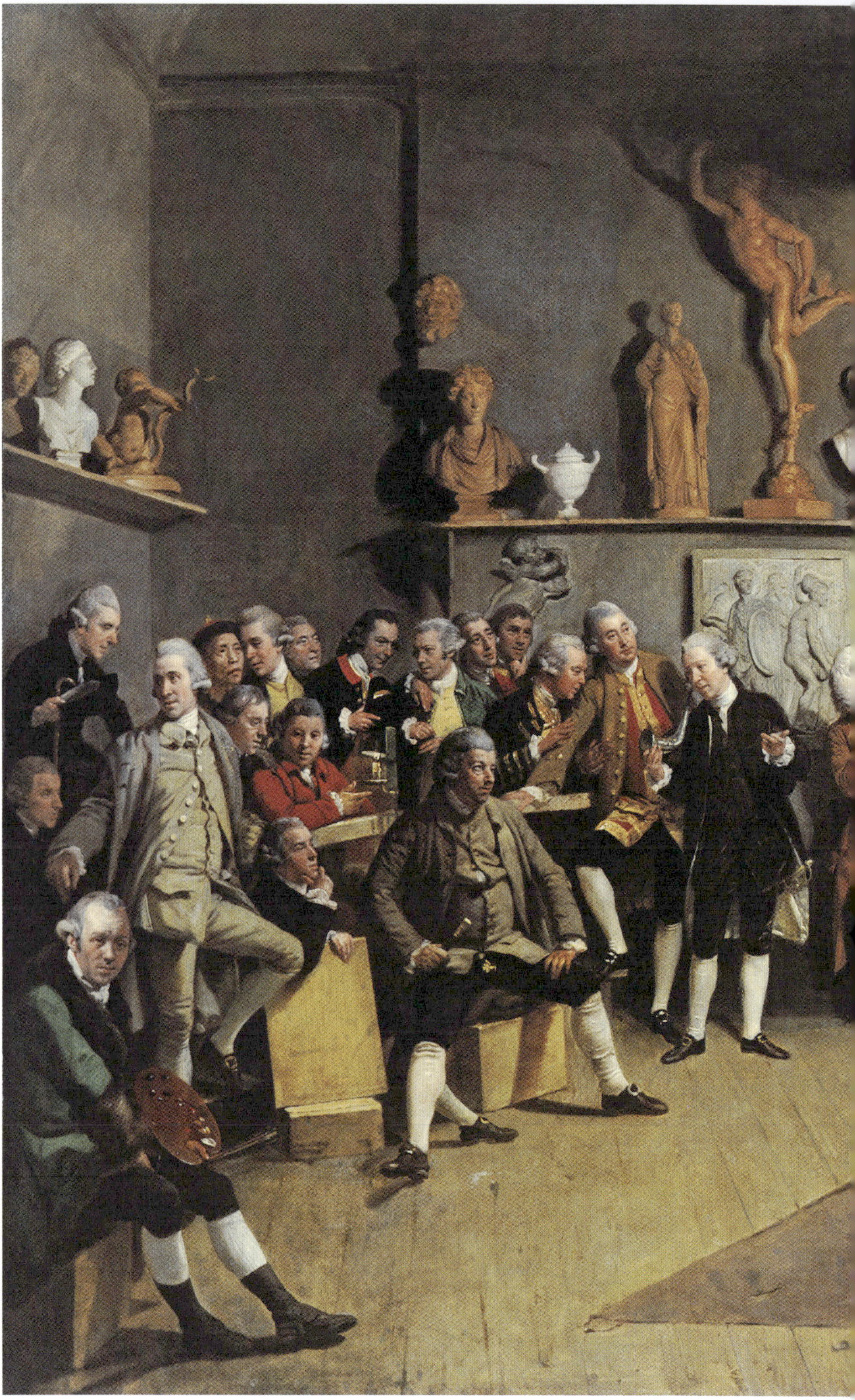

Johann Zoffany, *The Academicians of the Royal Academy*, 1771–2, oil on canvas.

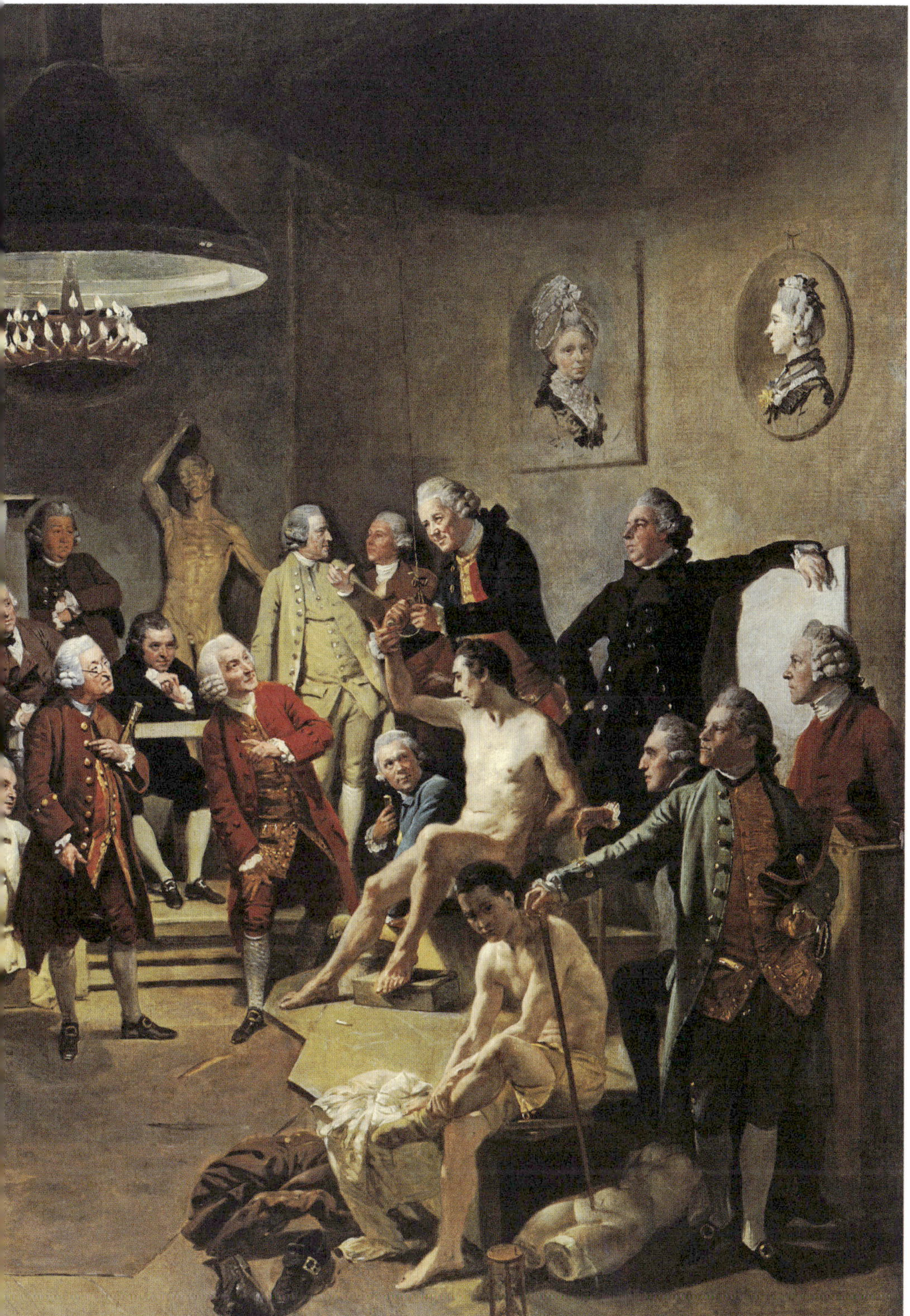

rope round the male model's hand. Kaufmann had painted supremely glamorous self-portraits, but one of these might have been too attention-grabbing, prompting further gossip (she was rumoured to be Reynolds's lover).[59]

The portraits are usually seen as a compromise, since women were not allowed in the life room with male models. But they could have been present

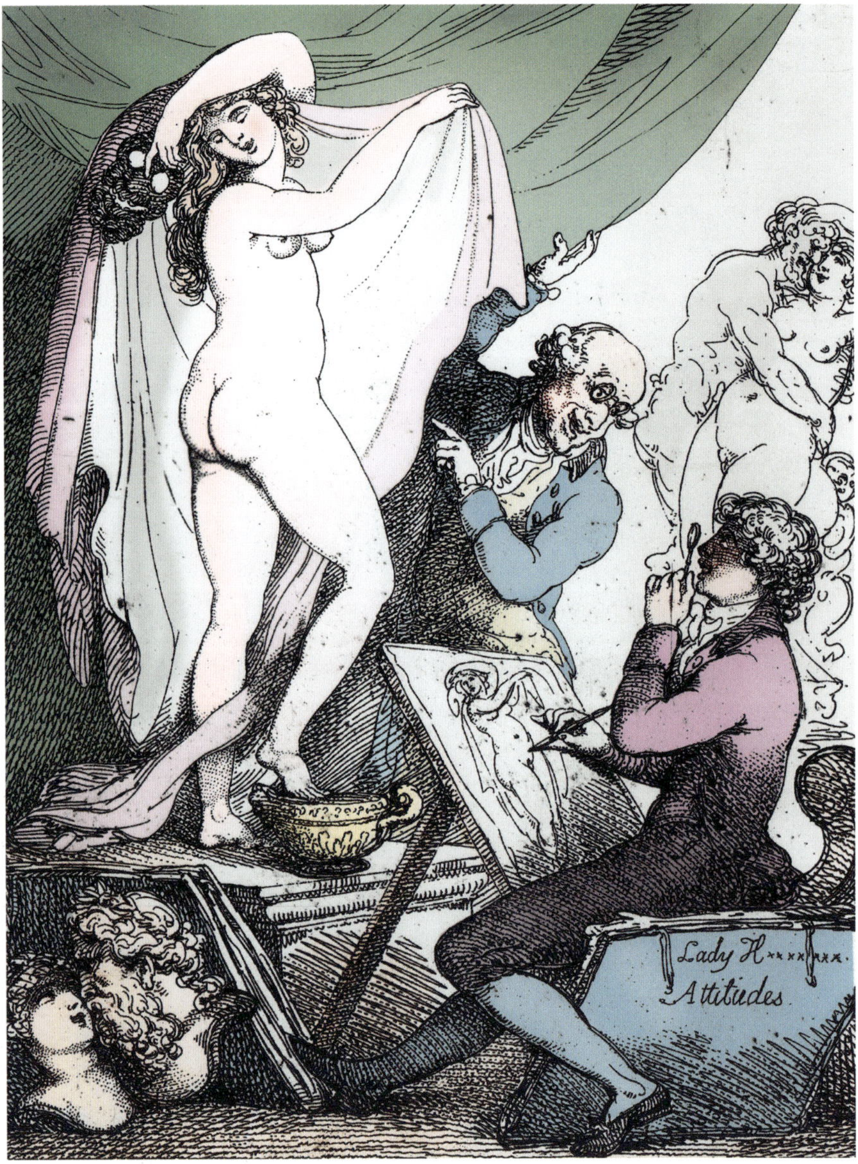

Thomas Rowlandson, *Lady H******* Attitudes*, c. 1791, hand-coloured etching.

if the members had been drawing casts. Zoffany (bottom left) was determined to exclude the female body entirely. Lying on the floor in the shadows at bottom right is a grubby cast of a female torso, evidently a Venus fragment. The portrait painter and dandy Richard Cosway slots his stick into the navel, a variant on 'pricking' with compass. Thirty-two founder members are present and identifiable, plus the visiting Cantonese sculptor Tan-Che-Qua (back left) and Dr William Hunter, professor of anatomy (the white-wigged man in the middle, stroking his chin). The foremost model strikes the pose of the antique *Spinario* (thorn-puller), while the male *écorché* figure used by Hunter lurks at the back. Reynolds stands below the chandelier on a mat stained by oil drips. As in Paris, student tuition was free, financed by profits from sales at the Summer Exhibition.

Despite some female participation in exhibitions, no more female academicians were admitted until the 20th century. The first female student was enrolled in 1860, when Laura Herford applied as L. Herford and the assessors assumed she was male. Realizing their error, they were dismayed to find no written rule excluding women. Others followed, but women were not allowed to draw male models until 1893, when a man was supplied with a baggy length of fabric wrapped around his bathing trunks.[60]

At the outset, four male models were employed, plus the Academy's porter, and a female model for 'three nights a week, every other week'.[61] Male models were often prizefighters or soldiers. Two hours was the standard shift, measured with an hourglass. Female models were paid more than the males, to compensate for reputational damage and harassment. The future cartoonist Thomas Rowlandson was nearly expelled for blowing a peashooter at a female model. No unmarried man under the age of 20 was allowed to draw them. Sex workers were the most convenient source for private use, and many academicians used them. The sculptor Joseph Nollekens (1737–1823) got his models from Mrs Lobb, who ran a brothel near Shaftesbury Avenue. James Northcote was dismayed when a 'battered courtesan' sat for Reynolds's *Cimon and Iphegenia*. Courtesans who modelled, he claimed, 'looked upon it as an additional disgrace to what their profession imposed upon them, and as something unnatural, one even wearing a mask'. Some insisted on being paid in cash to preserve their anonymity.[62]

Female modelling came of age with Emma Hart (1765–1815), the first artist's supermodel since Campaspe and the Virgin Mary. Hart, daughter of a blacksmith, had a priapic rise from actress's maid to wife of the ambassador to Naples, Sir William Hamilton (1730–1803). She was simultaneously the lover of Lord Nelson, living with him and Hamilton in a *ménage à trois*. Her international celebrity stemmed from theatrical 'attitudes', dances in which she struck a series of statue-like poses wearing gossamer-thin white muslin dresses without stays.[63] Long, flowing hair and swirling shawls added to the effect. She performed in the evening, with dramatic lighting. Goethe visited Naples in 1787: 'The old knight [Hamilton] holds up the light.' Hart proudly wrote: 'I left some dying, some crying, and some in despair. Mind you, [they] was all nobility, as proud as the devil. But we humbled them.' Hamilton collected Greek antiquities, but she was no Pygmalion's statue come to life. She was an artist in her own right, a sensational self-sculptor, admired for her art and wit as well as her beauty.

Hart wrote to Hamilton's nephew, her former lover, explaining that Sir William had set up a studio in Naples: 'The house is ful of painters painting me. He as now got nine pictures of me, and 2 a painting [me]. [Nathaniel] Marchant is cuting my head in stone, that is in cameo for a ring. There is another man modeling me in wax, and another in clay. All the artists is come from Rome to study from me, that Sir William is fitted up a room that is calld the painting-room.'[64]

Hart had already been portrayed by many artists in London, and it was said she modelled for the life class at the RA. George Romney painted his 'Divine Emma' over seventy times, and he and Reynolds depicted her as a Bacchante, a dancing devotee of the wine god Bacchus. Rowlandson's *Lady H******* Attitudes* (c. 1791) shows Sir William as a cheerleading pimp surrounded by fornicating antique sculptures. His wife stands on a podium (page 196).[65] Cartoons spread the word that artists' studios were exciting places. First published when the couple returned to England in 1791 for their wedding, it was later included in a set of thirty-seven erotic prints. The Niobe head on the floor is now in a happy clinch with a river god. The pen of the 'humbled' young artist hovers over Hart's sex, which he magnifies. She rests her foot on one of her husband's Greek vases, Venus emerging from the shell. This is the *ne plus ultra* of the feminized studio, and of unchaste marital love.

Chapter 13

Chaste Space

Friedrich to Mondrian

From around 1500 we have seen the typical contents of the artist's studio change, in ways that broadly track the emergence of consumer society and the use of material possessions to position oneself socially and culturally. Among the most egregious survivors are Vermeer's *Art of Painting*, Drouais's *Madame de Pompadour* and the Soane Museum.

The accumulative tendency would intensify, becoming deliriously eclectic, during the last third of the 19th century, with deluxe studios now bursting at the seams with trophies of empire. The Viennese studio of the self-styled sybaritic heir to Rubens, Hans Makart (1840–1884), who died from syphilis, featured oriental rugs and metalwork, exotic animal skins, African weapons and 'palms, palms, palms' (overleaf).[1] Visitors paid to watch him from a balcony. Victorian *horror vacui* – fear of empty space – would be itemized in deceptively sombre form by a new arrival, and rival: the camera.

What the aesthete Edmond de Goncourt praised as fetishistic *bricabracomania* and Rodin derided as 'conglomeration style'[2] would reach its outlandish, parodic zenith with Kurt Schwitters's studio-based encrustation installation *Cathedral of Erotic Misery* (1920–37, frontispiece), which expanded into the house, forcing his family out. Then there is post-war Picasso, simply buying another house for the 'forest of new arrivals'.[3] Francis Bacon's anti-type to conglomeration style is the studio as skip, its contents landfill – or, for now, museumfill.

From around 1800 there is a reaction against the overstocked studio, and the emergence of what I call chaste studio space. This more spartan environment is devoid of commodities, 'feminine' decor and 'comfort'. Until the 18th century, the word *comfort* had referred to spiritual and medical succour, but now it took on its modern meaning of general physical wellbeing.

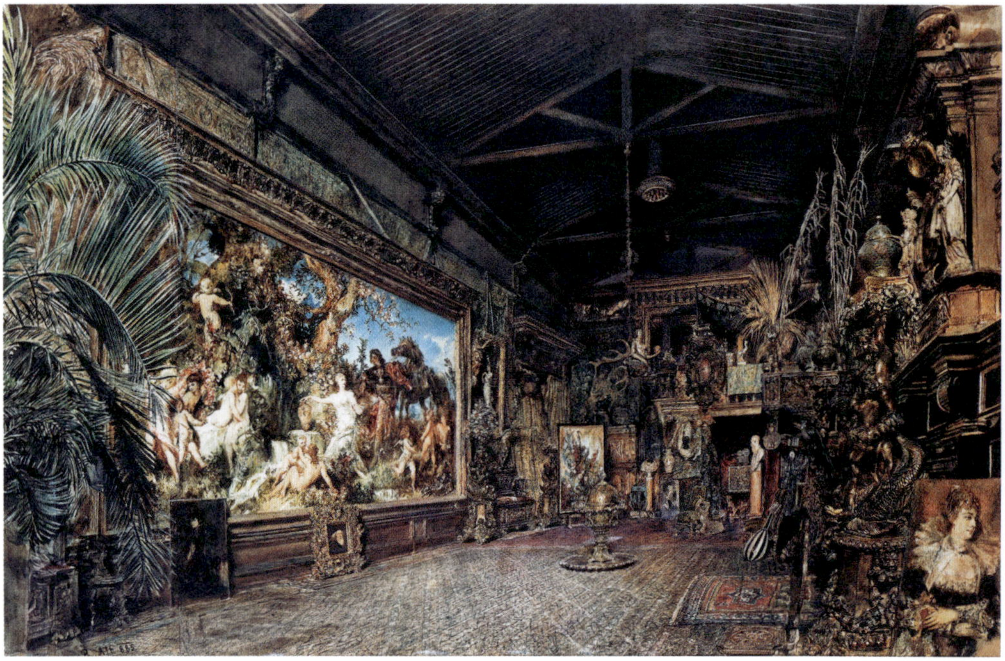

Rudolf von Alt, *The Studio of Hans Makart in Gusshausstrasse, Vienna*, 1885, watercolour.

Upholstery, interior decoration and the science of ergonomics came of age. New furniture types, properly padded so as to remain un-lumpy, yet light enough to be moved around into intimate groupings, catered to a more informal leisure society in which women played a prominent part. The historical-novelist Sir Walter Scott, builder of Abbotsford, a medieval-style writer's retreat, concluded his description of a castle interior in *Ivanhoe* (1820) with a penetrating aperçu: 'of comfort there was little, and, being unknown, it was unmissed'.[4] For generations of avant-garde artists, not only must discomfort be cultivated, but comfort must not be missed.

The German landscape painter Caspar David Friedrich (1774–1840) is exemplary. He lived and worked in a riverside house in Dresden, where he moved in 1802. It was described by the son of his portrait painter friend Gerhard von Kügelgen: 'Friedrich's studio … held nothing but the easel, a chair and a table, above which hung the room's only ornament, a T-square, although no one could understand why it was so honoured. Even the justifiable paintbox, phials of oil and paint rags were banished to the next room, for Friedrich was of the opinion that all external objects disturb the pictured world within.'[5]

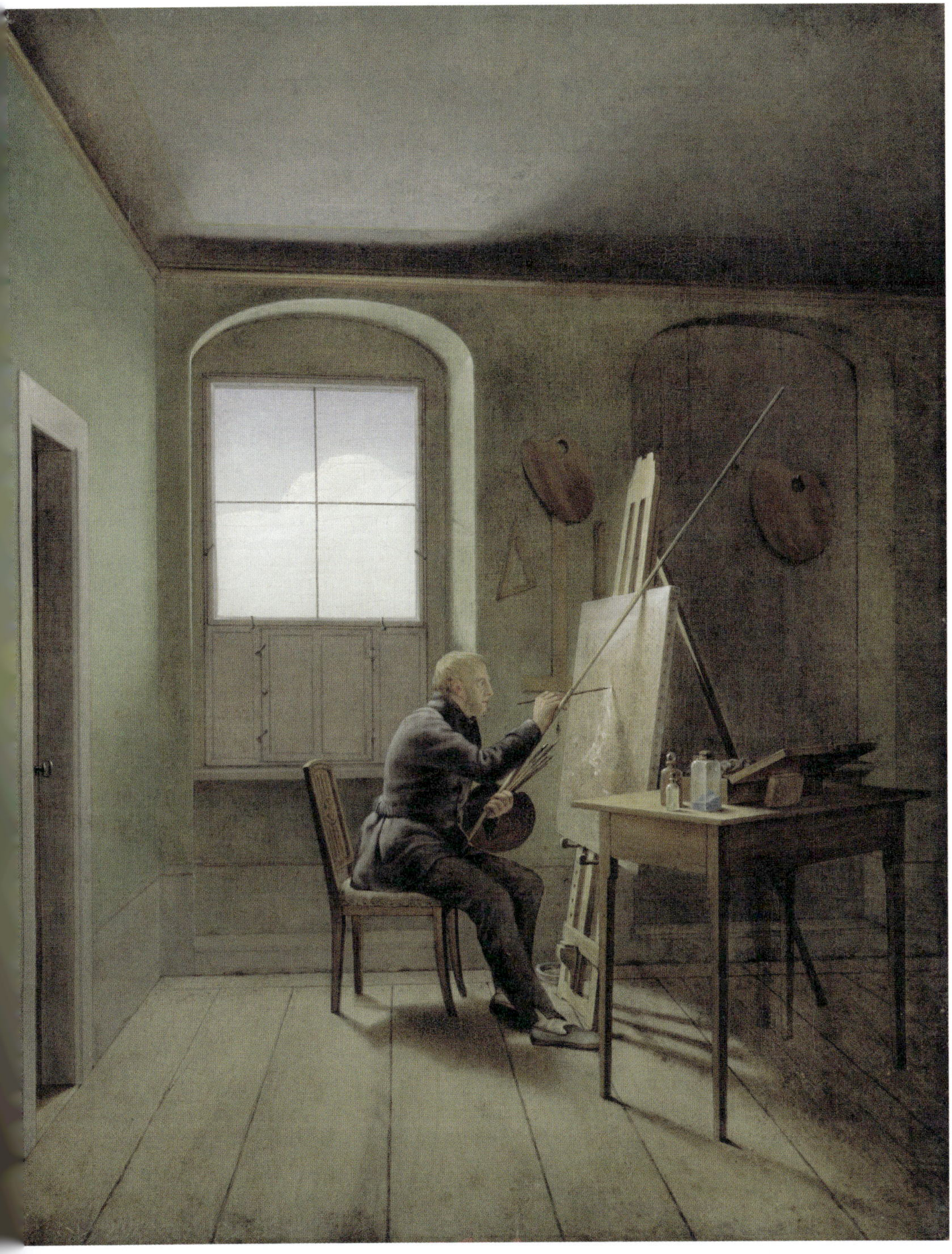

Georg Kersting, *Caspar David Friedrich in His Studio*, 1811, oil on canvas.

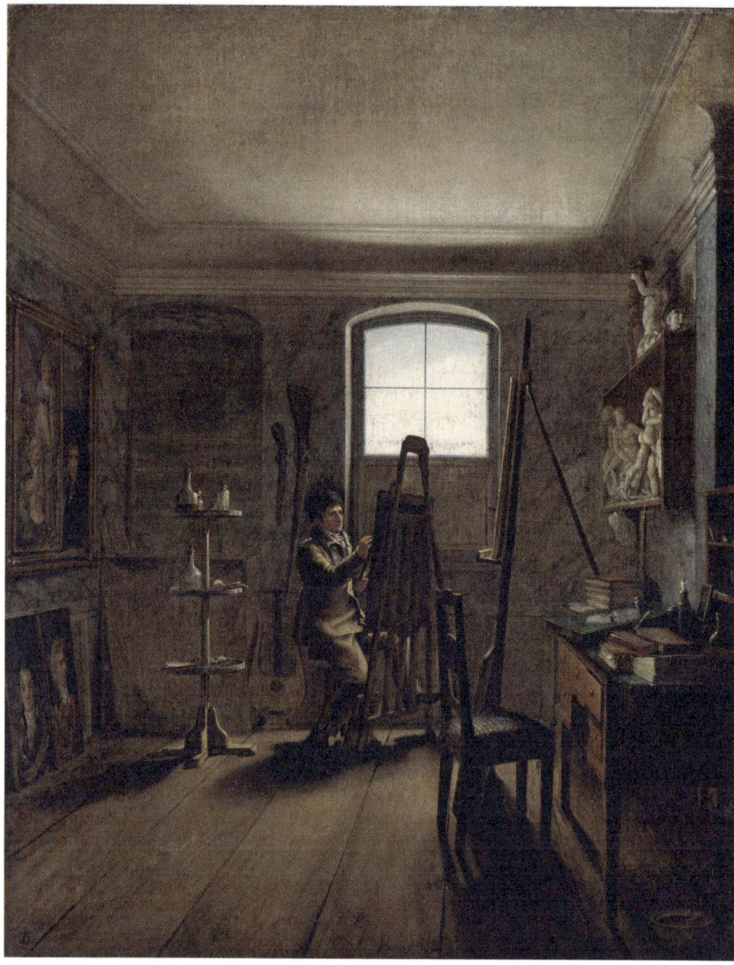

Georg Kersting, *Gerhard von Kügelgen in His Studio*, 1811, oil on canvas.

Corroboration comes from Georg Friedrich Kersting's limpid portrait of 1811 showing Friedrich at work (preceding page). The room is – as a local newspaper would observe – 'strange and inhospitable', with nowhere for visitors to sit.[6] The shuttered lower window prevents a view of the busy commercial river. Friedrich's T-square can be seen on the back wall, but with palette, set square and ruler for company. An open paintbox and various bottles are on the table, but still no paint rags.

Kersting depicted Kügelgen's studio simultaneously, and the pictures were shown together – almost certainly the first time such a studio pairing had been created and exhibited. Kügelgen's is similar architecturally, but cluttered with furniture, shelving, casts, books, lyre (symbol of Apollo), duelling pistol and hunting rifle. The walls have painted marbleized decoration, the mahogany sideboard-cum-desk is covered in green baize. Flattering gilt-framed portraits of formally dressed men and children line the walls, and there are two easels, suggestive of efficient multitasking and a steady flow of commissions. Kügelgen is socialized, a man of the world. Rooms like these prompted Friedrich to object to 'large numbers of pictures displayed or stored up like merchandise in a room in such a way that it is no longer possible to look at any one picture without seeing half of four others at the same time'.[7]

After a strict Lutheran upbringing, Friedrich attended the renowned Academy in Copenhagen, his education beginning with prints and casts and ending with the live male model. But there is no evidence here of any education or religion, no study collection or books. Friedrich went on sketching expeditions, often with Kersting, drawing views and details in pencil and watercolour, but no sketches are to hand as he paints the waterfall in an unidentified mountain scene. The landscape has apparently been memorized and imagined, emerging fully formed from within.

Critics often compare Friedrich's studio to a monk's cell. He did indeed believe artists should aspire to 'pious simplicity'[8] and portrayed himself in rough, monkish garb in a hallucinatory drawing of 1810. Here Friedrich wears a padded felt coat and thick trousers. Wilhelm Wackenroder's *Confessions from the Heart of an Art-Loving Friar* (1796), purportedly written from the 'solitude of a monastic life', had made artistic piety fashionable – great art should involve emotional meditation rather than being a 'frivolous plaything of the senses'.[9] Gothic churches, sometimes ruined, and wayside crosses frequently star in Friedrich's pantheistic landscapes. *Cross in the Mountains* (1808), the first landscape altarpiece, was unveiled to the public in his studio, done up like a gloomy chapel.[10]

***

Friedrich's cell-like studio coincided with a vogue for artists to occupy former religious buildings, just as they would occupy disused industrial buildings with religious fervour in the late 20th century. Since the atheistical French Revolution of 1789 and the Napoleonic conquest of Continental Europe, studios had been set up in former religious buildings left empty after suppression.[11] In Paris, the convent church of Les Feuillants was nationalized, and the great Neoclassical painter Jacques-Louis David used the nave as a studio to paint the vast *Oath of the Tennis Court* (1790–4). Documenting a key moment in the Revolution, David held portrait sittings there for the deputies of the Third Estate. David later used the former church of the Collège de Cluny to paint *The Coronation of Napoleon as Emperor* (1805–8). New gods seamlessly replaced the old.

Some of David's pupils moved into a convent in 1801, forming a utopian male commune called variously the 'Primitifs' (Primitives), 'Méditateurs' (Meditators), and 'Barbus' (Bearded Ones), thereby becoming the first avant-garde movement. Disillusioned by David's new painting, the *Intervention of the Sabine Women* (completed 1799), they denounced it as too sophisticated and feminine: 'Pompadour'. They preferred the more manly purity and simplicity of archaic Greek vases and early Renaissance art. When Napoleon asked one of them why he wore a distinctive white 'Phrygian' tunic and cap that separated him from the world, he replied: 'To separate me from the world.' The *Journal des Arts* explained that 'practical study means nothing [to them]; meditation is all'.[12]

The Primitifs occupied the Convent of the Visitation de Sainte Marie, founded in 1651 in the Parisian suburb of Chaillot. A munitions explosion had destroyed part of it, and its new owner let it decay further. The artists performed strange rituals inspired by Oriental and Western religions, and by masonic rites. They wore ancient Greek clothing, grew their hair long, practised vegetarianism, and believed in reincarnation and pantheism.[13] They had all gone their separate ways or died by 1803. Charles Nodier, their leading writer, summarized their aims in *Meditations from the Cloister* (1803), giving an upper-case, Marinetti-style call to arms: 'THIS GENERATION IS RISING AND IS DEMANDING CLOISTERS.'[14]

Yes, you did read that last word correctly. Nodier calls on artists to replace the clergy, giving new moral and cultural direction.

Jean Broc's massive life-size *School of Apelles* (1800) evokes the severe but limpid Neoclassical ambience they were after, though the crowds of inspired young men – some are group members – are hyperactive rather than meditative. After the Revolution in 1789, the Académie Royale had been dissolved and artists had formed new, informal groupings celebrated in studio portraits.[15] At first sight, Broc's school is anti-academic, with no study collection. The contour drawing on the canvas – a sketch for the *Calumny of Apelles*, a repudiation of a charge of sedition – is the sole visual aid, and the reason for the uproar. In fact, even when incensed, the artists instinctively live, breathe and model high art, no less than Emma Hamilton during her

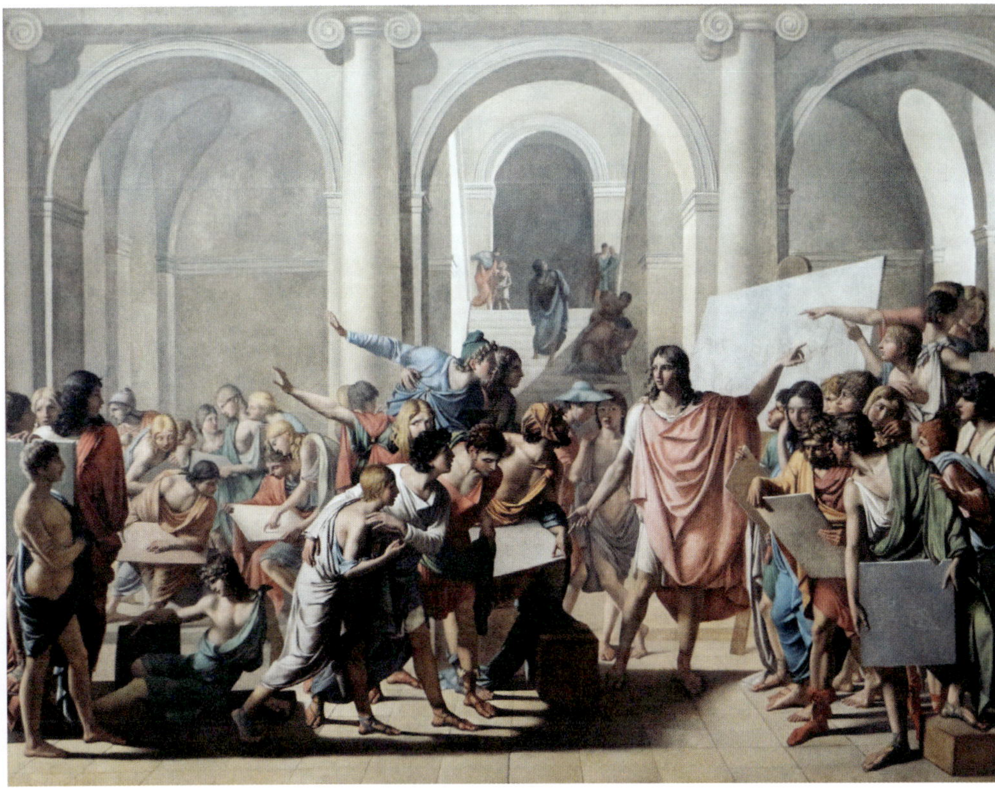

Jean Broc, *School of Apelles*, 1800, oil on canvas.

'attitudes'. Apelles' pose derives from his near namesake the *Apollo Belvedere*, while his head and much of the rest is adapted from Raphael's *School of Athens* (critics accused Broc of plagiarism, rather missing the point).[16] Women in general, and Campaspe in particular, are conspicuous by their absence. Those who did wish to become artists were trained separately from men with private tutors and, from the 1870s, in private schools.[17] It took until 1897 for women to gain entry to the Ecole des Beaux-Arts, founded in 1648, by open competition. But who needs women anyway when so many of the boys, and the long-haired Apelles, are delightfully androgynous?

More long-lived and influential were the Christian Lukasbrüder (Brotherhood of Saint Luke), a spiritual and artistic fraternity founded in Vienna in 1809 by six German, Swiss and Austrian students associated with the Vienna Academy. They called each other 'Apostles'. In 1810 the Lukasbrüder shifted their centre of operations to Rome, hoping to revive Christian fresco painting in the 'simple and pure' style of Perugino and Raphael. They secured cheap lodgings in the monastery of Sant'Isidoro a Capo le Case, remaining there until the expiry of the lease in 1812. They then moved elsewhere in Rome. The monastery had been suppressed when Napoleon conquered Italy but, like the Convent of the Visitation, would become a monastery again after his downfall. In around 1817 the group became known as the 'Nazarenes', an initially dismissive critical reference to their monastic lifestyle and biblical subject matter as well as their uniform of long, flowing cloaks and hair. At Sant'Isidoro they shared household tasks, with each living and working in their own cell. In the evenings, they read and drew from a male model in the refectory, followed by heavy drinking.

Not all convent cultists were humourless prigs. In 1824 the francophile John Soane, who idolized Napoleon, performed his own act of revolutionary self-cloistering. He built a Monk's Yard and Parlour – or 'Parloir of Padre Giovanni' (Father John) – in the basement of 14 Lincoln's Inn Fields, filling it with medieval fragments from the Palace of Westminster (which he was rebuilding), stained glass, illuminated manuscripts and the tomb of his wife's lapdog. The guidebook found it 'admirably adapted for seclusion and study'.[18] Padre Giovanni took tea there with bemused friends.

***

So Friedrich was not alone in cultivating a monkish workspace, nor in developing a personal religion with mystical tendencies. But there are key differences – over and above the fact that he specialized in small-scale landscapes, didn't belong to a group, and hated history painting in fancy dress: art should be of its own time, not an 'ape' of the past.[19]

The most distinctive aspect of Friedrich's studio is its decoration with measuring tools, including the T-square that so baffled contemporaries. His veneration of tools rejects the romantic notion of unfettered genius in favour of 'honest' craftsmanship. It challenges Michelangelo's credo that compasses should be in the artist's eye, not in the hand. In other words, a mixture of experience and personal judgment should determine proportions, rather than mechanical instruments or rules. A plumb line hangs from Friedrich's painting hand, which rests on the longest mahlstick in art history. It is aligned with the base of the T-square, as if touching it. In *Winter Landscape* (c. 1811) Friedrich depicts a lame man in a snowy landscape, praying before a crucifix. He has just discarded his crutches. These tools are Freidrich's own crutches and prosthetic limbs. They were indeed vital, as he used bilateral symmetry and painted bolt-upright forests, crosses, Gothic churches and ships' masts. He saw no difference between mechanical and sacred geometry.

Friedrich's studio resembles an artisan's workshop as much as a monk's cell. The criss-crossing lines of easel, table, floorboards and tools suggest he operates an intricate painting machine made of finely carpentered wood. Kügelgen's comparison to a 'gutted corpse' suggests a stripped-down, diagrammatic quality with T-square as spine, kidney-shaped palettes, etc. The furniture is plain wood, simple in form and light in colour (unlike Kügelgen's mahogany desk and other furniture). The sunlight further bleaches it. A European fashion had started for *bois clair* – light, unstained woods – and for native woods such as ash, walnut, sycamore, beech, elm, pear and cherry.[20] This trend, which would become known as Biedermeier style in Germany and Austria, intensified with the economic crises and blockades during the Napoleonic wars, and with increased nationalism. Friedrich railed against Italophile critics and artists who were 'no longer satisfied' with German sun, rocks, trees, plants and so on.[21] His studio celebrated 'honest' German wood, craft and light.

Friedrich had a lifelong artistic 'brotherhood' with his own brother Christian, a carpenter who executed wood engravings for him. Friedrich himself designed furniture – a desk for his sister-in-law, a complete set of fittings for Christian's shop, an easel for a painter friend, and a frame for *Cross in the Mountains*.[22] The brothers drew up plans to renovate a church interior, designing the layout so 'all distinctions of rank' would disappear.[23] Kersting, the son of a glazier, evidently also enjoyed simple craftsmanship: see the devotion to detail on the shutters and the spare elegance of the window frame. The top of Friedrich's chair-back aligns with the centre of the shutters.

One might assume that the grizzled Lutheran is aligning himself with the carpenter Saint Joseph, who had been transformed by Catholic propaganda into a carpenter-architect. But there was a more potent catalyst in Diderot and d'Alembert's great *Encyclopedia*, subtitled *Systematic Dictionary of the Sciences, Arts and Trades*. The Paris folio edition (1751–72) comprised seventeen volumes of text and eleven volumes of plates, the most striking of which depict, with astonishing detail and clarity, workshops, tools and machines.[24] Many have a functional austerity similar to that of Friedrich's studio (overleaf). The entry for 'Peuple' (people) gives sympathetic accounts of the gruelling lives of labourers who are 'sober, just, faithful, religious'.[25] Their moral rectitude means rulers should obtain the people's consent through a social contract. These arguments helped lay the intellectual foundations for the French Revolution.

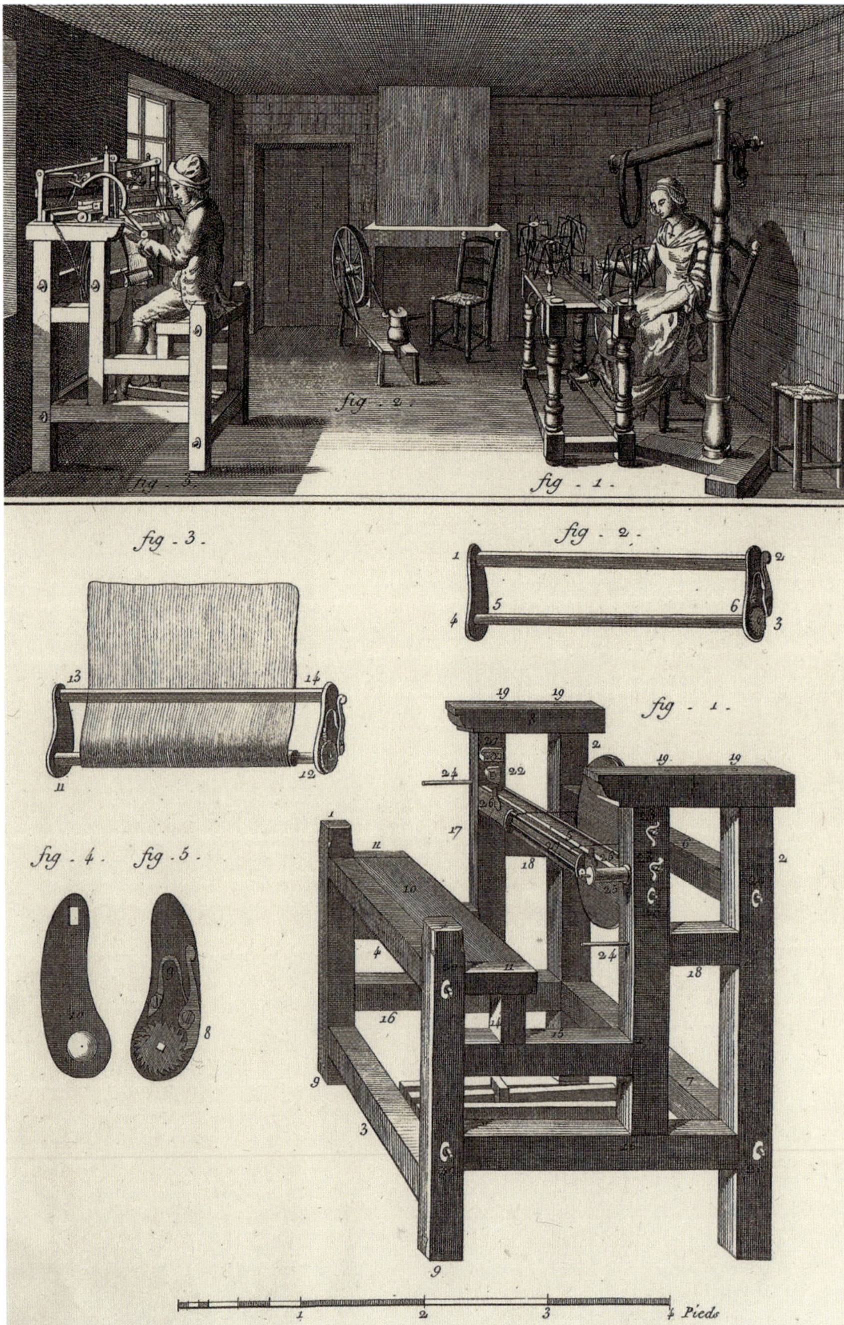

Diderot and d'Alembert, *Encyclopedia, or a Systematic Dictionary of the Sciences, Arts and Trades*, 1751–65, vol. 2, plate 1, 'Silk Stocking Frame'.

Diderot, son of a master cutler, took responsibility for the descriptions of crafts and manufacturing processes. He replicated the actions of his beloved Socrates, visiting workshops to observe and interview craftsmen.[26] Some suspected he was after trade 'secrets' – which turned out not to be secrets at all. He learned how to use machines that were impossible to describe.[27] In his entry for 'Art', he derided the prejudice that prevented the elite studying and practising mechanical arts. Liberal artists 'have sung their own praise long enough; they should now raise their voice in praise of the mechanical arts'. More respect and wider knowledge would lead to better pay, patronage and innovation: 'Let us teach them to think better of themselves, only then can we obtain more perfect products from them!'[28] Craftsmen are essential keyworkers. Pompadour's shift from 'make-up to making' in 1756 was an early response.

The illustrations do for arts and trades what Vesalius had done for anatomy, and Hooke for fleas. The workshops are mostly bare and clean, devoid of models or plans. The workers use instinct and experience, implicitly trusting their tools. Of course, we could think of them all as automata, slaves to their machines, but Diderot wants their diligence and dexterity to garner respect. It is a new religion of work.

Jean-Jacques Rousseau (1712–1778), who contributed the article on political economy, would go in an anti-luxury direction in his educational treatise for boys, *Emile* (1762). Rousseau advocated 'simple' furniture, few possessions, and definitely no picture gallery or library.[29] Manual workers came closest to the state of nature, and if anyone 'is ashamed to be seen wearing a leather apron or handling a plane', he is 'a mere slave of public opinion'. Carpentry is best for Emile: 'It is clean and useful; it may be carried on at home; it gives enough exercise; it calls for skill and industry, and while fashioning articles for everyday use, there is scope for elegance and taste .... Peter the Great was a ship's carpenter.' Emile must take nothing for granted: 'If he sees the pieces of a chest put together, he will want to know how the tree was cut down. When at work he will say of each tool, "If I had not got this, how could I make one like it, or how could I get along without it?"'[30] Friedrich is the first in a long line of modern 'carpenter' artists. Marcel Duchamp, who was a fine craftsman, would claim that Seurat was the only artist he respected because he 'made his large paintings like a carpenter, like an artisan'.[31]

In 1802, the *Encyclopédie* (as it is commonly known) had taken on three-dimensional form with the opening of the Musée des Arts et Métiers in Paris. It was a 'temple' of technology in the former monastery of Saint-Martin-des-Champs. The founding collection came from Jacques de Vaucanson, maker of

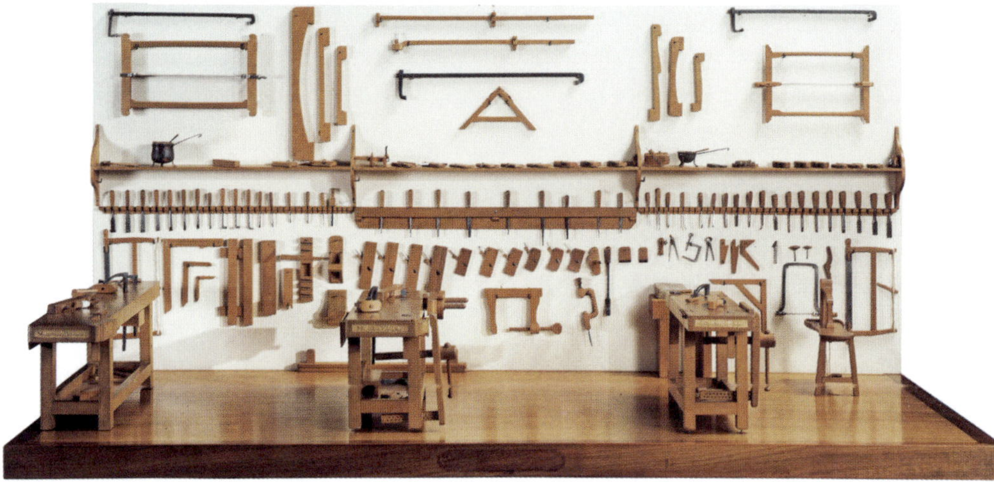

François-Étienne Calla, *Carpenter's Workshop*, 1783, scale model in wood and metal.

automata and machines: his metal-cutting lathe (1765) had been described in the *Encyclopédie*. Seventeen finely crafted models of artisans' workshops at one-eighth scale were also exhibited, inspired by the *Encyclopédie* illustrations. They were commissioned in the 1780s as educational aids by the governess and educational reformer Madame de Genlis, who painted and reputedly had skill in fifty-two handicrafts. She took children to artisans' workshops and artists' studios, reading beforehand the relevant sections in the *Encyclopédie*.[32]

Friedrich's studio was very much a bachelor's domain not open to intrusive Madames. But in 1818 he surprised everyone by marrying Caroline Bonner, daughter of a local blue-dye warehouse manager, an uneducated 'woman of the people' half his age.[33] A week after his marriage he informed his family, and we see him balancing Caroline's cleaning skills against the onslaught of modern knick-knacks and creature comforts: 'It's a droll business, when a fellow has a wife .... Only in the room where I work is everything still as it was. Everywhere else, window curtains are now required. The following are also now needed: coffee roaster, coffee grinder, coffee strainer, coffee bag, coffee pot, coffee cups, everything – everything is now needed. Everything has changed; formerly my room was my spittoon, now I am directed to spit in little dishes put there for the purpose. But my love of cleanliness and neatness is happy to comply.'[34]

***

The spartan studio ideal was taken to exciting new extremes by Henry Murger in his semi-autobiographical *Scènes de la vie de bohème* (1851), initially published as short magazine stories. Murger charted with affectionate irony the lives, lodgings and loves of artists, writers and musicians living in garrets in Paris's Latin Quarter. He turned it into a play, which inspired Puccini's opera *La bohème* (1896). In the preface to the stories Murger explained: 'They are the race of obstinate dreamers for whom art has remained a faith and not a profession .... They live, so to say, on the outskirts of life, in isolation and inertia .... They die, for the most part, decimated by that disease to which science does not dare give its real name, want.'[35]

The first story opens with the composer Schaunard, who 'took the art of borrowing to the perfection of a science', being evicted from a room on the sixth storey. The new tenant appears, without furniture. The landlord assumes it has not yet arrived. But the young man, Marcel, points to a large folding screen that he opens, 'displaying to the view of the astonished landlord a magnificent interior of a palace, with jasper columns, bas-reliefs, and paintings of old masters'. Unimpressed, the landlord demands 'real chairs and tables in solid mahogany' as security for rent. Marcel ruefully retorts:

> 'Alas! Neither gold nor mahogany makes us happy,
> as the ancient poet well says. And I can't bear mahogany;
> it's too common a wood. Everybody has it.'
> 'But surely sir, you must have some sort of furniture.'
> 'No, it takes up too much room. You are stuck full
> of chairs, and have no place to sit down.'
> 'But at any rate, you have a bed. What do you sleep on?'
> 'On a good conscience, sir.'[36]

Marcel's furniture phobia is explained when the landlord discovers his profession. An easel arrives: '"I was sure he was an artist!" exclaimed the landlord, the hair of his wig standing up in affright, "a painter!!"' Marcel can stay only if he pays in advance, 25 francs per month. He pulls out a 500-franc note. The dumbfounded landlord nearly falls over. The joke is that a rich kid is slumming it in order to live the bohemian life. He is footloose and furniture-free; we later discover he uses a leather boot as chamber pot.

Bohemians were anti-materialist heirs to the Cynic philosopher Diogenes living in his tub (actually an amphora). Tragically, Murger died in poverty

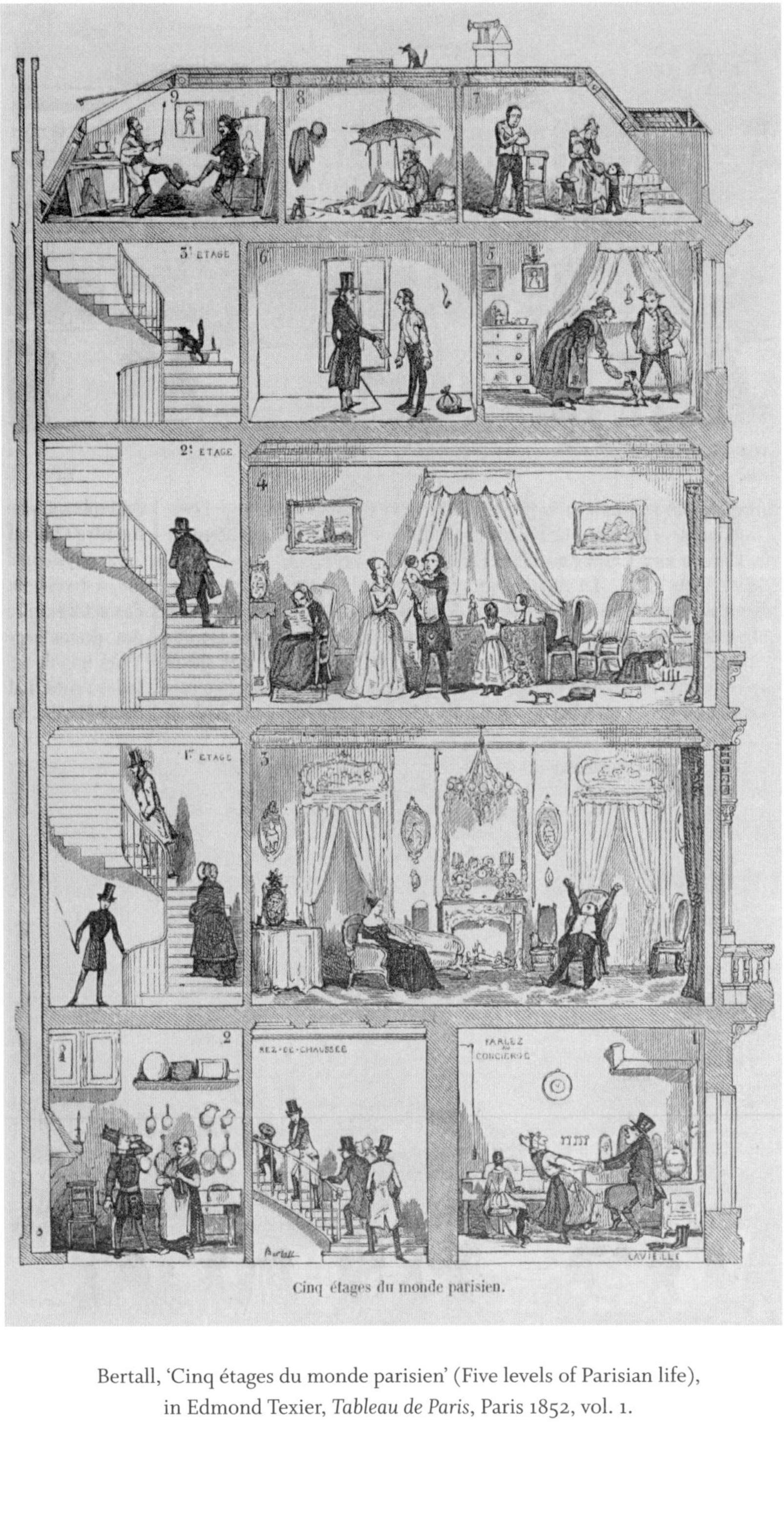

Bertall, 'Cinq étages du monde parisien' (Five levels of Parisian life), in Edmond Texier, *Tableau de Paris*, Paris 1852, vol. 1.

aged 39; a friend's gift of 500 francs for medical help came too late. Sadly for hardcore romantics, he is not necessarily representative of his type. A study of students at London's Royal Academy has shown their life expectancy was the same as that of other professional classes, and artists were no more likely to commit suicide.[37]

Furniture-free life looms large in cartoonist Bertall's cross section of a new apartment block in the Boulevard Saint-Martin. It illustrates an essay on the 'five levels of Parisian life' in Edmond Texier's *Tableau de Paris* (1852). The practically destitute family of four on the right (no. 7) have a chair, bed and table. But the philosopher beneath an umbrella is furniture-free (no. 8), and so too the flat-sharing 'brother' artists doing a Cossack dance – their water jug and bowl sit on unsold canvases (no. 9). The furniture-free bachelor on the floor below (no. 6) is being evicted. Texier's laconic commentary explains: 'The painter stamps his feet to reignite his inspiration' (and to keep warm?). The philosopher is 'meditating on a work about palingenesis', the Stoic concept of perpetual rebirth and regeneration. Just as 'the summit encloses the most noble part of man, the organ of thought', so 'in the capital of the arts and civilization, genius, industry and application occupy the most elevated region. There the painter creates in silence.'[38] And in soot – the skylight opens onto a wall.

Many young artists aspired to live the furniture-free life. James McNeill Whistler, who arrived in Paris in 1855, memorized Murger, whom he met. He and his English friends lived as spartanly as possible, and one of them made drawings of fine furniture on the walls of an otherwise empty garret. (Drawing, painting and daubing on dilapidated studio walls would become a trademark of modern bohemians like Giacometti, Bacon and Freud.) During his four years in Paris, Whistler lived at nine different addresses in the Latin Quarter. In 1857 he occupied a room on the tenth floor that had a camp bed, chair, basin and pitcher. His one luxury – apart from dandyish clothes – was his prized collection of oriental blue-and-white china.[39] He wouldn't, therefore, have been short of a chamber pot.

When Van Gogh rented a room in The Hague in the winter of 1881, he was determined to keep things simple: 'I'll be moving into the studio around 1 January. Regarding furniture, I'll take the very simplest, a wooden table, a couple of chairs. For a bed, I'd be content with a woollen blanket and the floor.' This was the middle of a Dutch winter.[40]

***

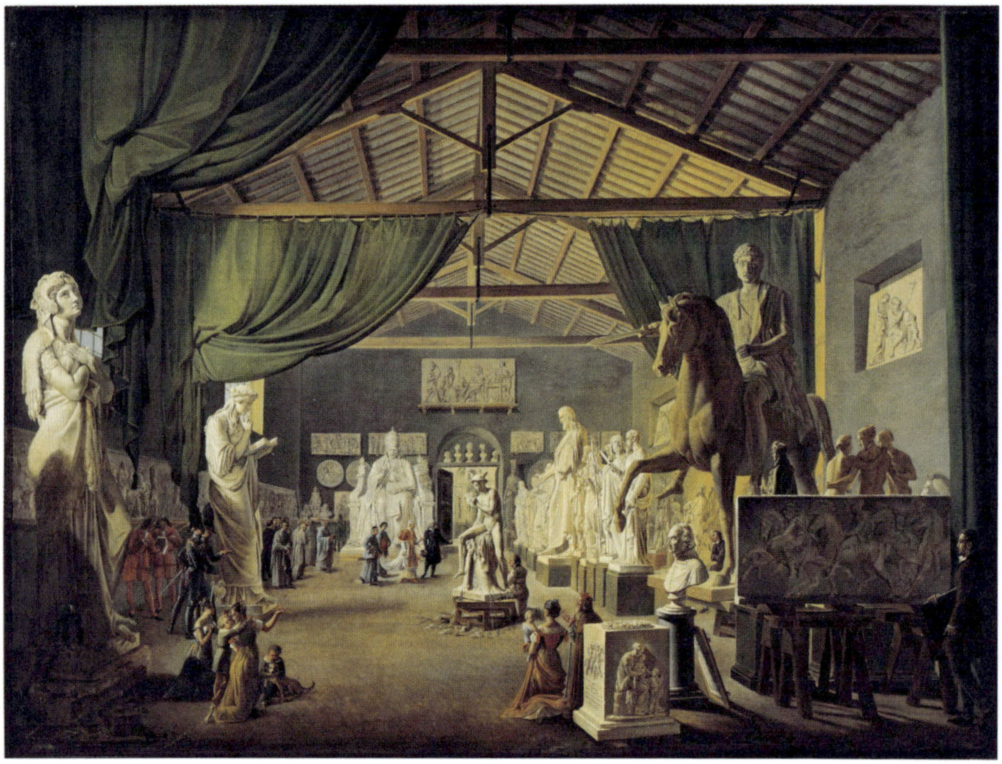

Ditlev Martens, *Pope Leo XII Visits Thorvaldsen's Studio near the Piazza Barberini, Rome, on Saint Luke's Day, 18 October 1826*, 1830, oil on canvas.

Creating chaste studio space was in some respects easier for 19th-century sculptors because of their dazzling displays of plaster casts taken from full-sized clay models. The Rome-based sculptor Antonio Canova (1757–1822) pioneered this procedure. Any number of marble versions could be made from these casts by assistants using pointing machines. The 'original plaster' remained a studio property, creating a complete archive which ultimately enabled Canova to establish his own museum in his home town in Northern Italy. The retention of the original plaster countered Goethe's complaint that the works of a sculptor 'desert him as the bird deserts the nest in which it was hatched' and can no longer affect him. Canova limited himself to making clay models and applying the finishing touches to marbles. Many later sculptors simply made a small clay model, and left the rest to assistants.

After Canova's death, the big draw in Rome was the studio of his Danish Protestant rival Bertel Thorvaldsen (1768/70–1844). Thorvaldsen's 'original casts' were displayed in his basilica-like studio showroom near Palazzo Barberini. The painter who recorded the pope's visit in 1826 relegates him to the background, so it initially looks as though the visiting families are art idolators kneeling before Thorvaldsen's sculptures. The comprehensiveness of the cast collection made it feasible for Thorvaldsen to publish two illustrated catalogues in 1833, one appended to a biography. He too would set up a museum, in Copenhagen.[41]

It was standard practice to display 'original plasters' of large new sculptures at public exhibitions such as the Paris Salon, hoping for a commission to copy the work in marble or bronze – though critics like Baudelaire became 'wearied by the monotonous whiteness'.[42] Rodin (1840–1917), a specialist in bronze, even cast his clay sketch models in plaster, and reworked his plasters. So there was a radical dichotomy between what visitors saw in his studio and the darker, more complex patinas of the completed bronzes, and of the sooty photogravures that were used to reproduce photographs in print media (engravings were often preferred). Courbet complained that a photograph of one of his pictures looked 'burned and dark'.[43]

From the 1880s, Rodin's studios became the most photographed of his era and, unusually for the time, many showed unfinished works (overleaf). He would often have clay and plaster models photographed, and would then sketch revisions onto the print. He took a special interest in studio staging and lighting. He liked unforgiving lighting that bleached.[44] In 1896, he showed photographs alongside sculptures and drawings at an exhibition in Geneva. He had recently appointed Eugène Druet to be his official photographer, a post he held until 1903. Druet accidentally discovered the technique of solarization while developing a photograph of *The Age of Bronze*; it produced a stark, spectral effect that Rodin appreciated.

On 2 September 1902, the young Austrian poet Rainer Maria Rilke wrote about a visit to Rodin's studio at the Villa des Brillants in Meudon, a twenty-minute train ride from Paris. The villa had been acquired in 1895, and a studio added to it. Rilke had been commissioned to write a book on Rodin and from 1903–6 would be Rodin's secretary. He described his visit in a letter to his wife, Clara Westhoff, a sculptor whom he had met in an artist's colony at Worpswede, Germany. Westhoff, like Camille Claudel, had been Rodin's pupil.

Rodin's international fame had been secured by his retrospective in a purpose-built pavilion at the Universal Exhibition of 1900. The display was almost entirely of plasters, along with drawings and seventy-one photographs.

Rilke describes the pavilion, now re-erected at Meudon: 'His big pavilion … has been transported into his garden which it seems to fill completely,

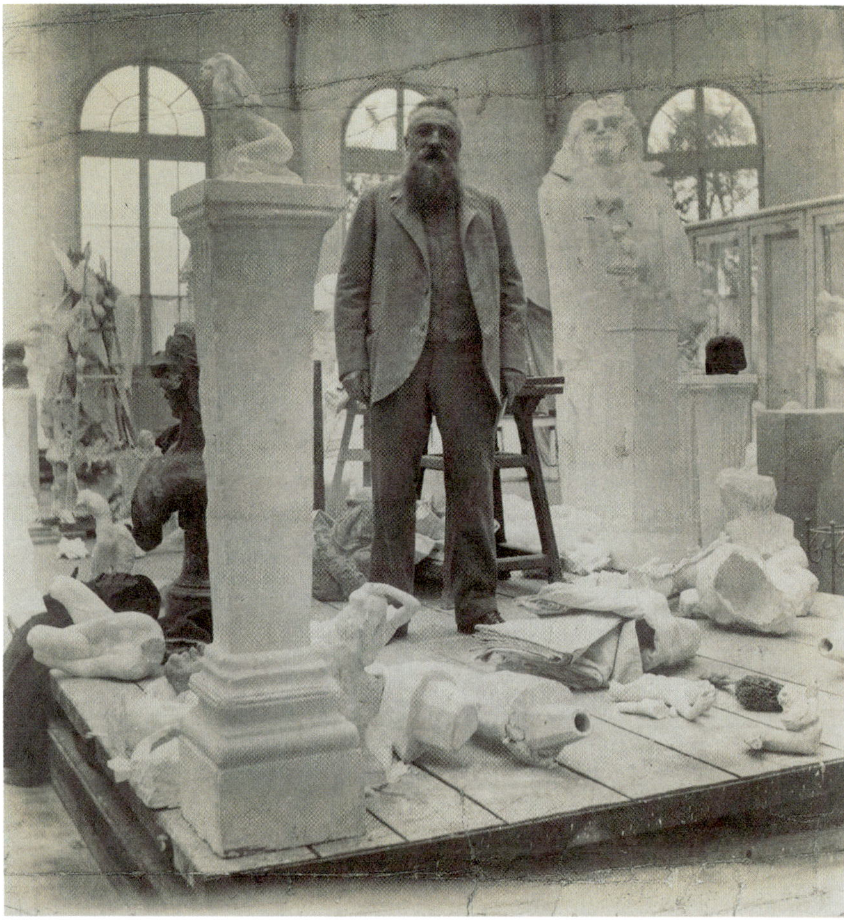

Eugène Druet, *Rodin in his Pavilion Studio*, c. 1902.

along with several more studios in which are stonecutters and in which he himself works. Then there are in addition rooms for baking clay and for all kinds of manual work. It is an immensely great and strange impression, this great, light hall with all its white, dazzling figures looking out of the many high glass doors like the inhabitants of an aquarium .... What a lot is there, everything, everything ... it is fearfully taxing in the first place because of the quantity, secondly, because everything is white; one goes about among the many dazzling plaster casts in the very bright pavilion as through snow. My eyes are hurting me, my hands too.'[45] This is – to adapt the title of Robert Hughes' television series – 'the shock of the new plaster'. The debilitating dazzle of 'white cube' spaces is prefigured here.

In his hagiographic book of 1903, Rilke would compare Rodin's less frequented studios to 'cells, bare, poor and grey with dust'. The comparison was a decades-old cliché, first used about his main studio in the Dépôt des Marbres, Paris, which was situated near the university on the Left Bank and housed sculptors engaged on government projects. Rodin had moved here in 1880 so he could make bronze doors for a new museum of decorative arts – the *Gates of Hell*. He eventually occupied three units, and after 1895 commuted from Meudon. In 1882 Henri Thurat had published the first evocation in *Art populaire*: 'The studio is poor, severe, but big. No refinements. You would think yourself in a monk's cell. This ascetic lair demands respect.'[46]

A later visitor, Paul Gsell, ran with the idea in *Art* (1911), a book of edited interviews with Rodin that may well be the first publication in this format. Gsell opened with a tour de force about the Dépôt: 'A little artist city, marvellously tranquil, it seems the fraternity house of a new order. Rodin occupies two of these cells.'[47]

Rodin had in fact been a lay monk. In 1862 he joined a religious order after the death of his beloved elder sister, who had just become a nun. Between 1852 and 1862, 982 new religious congregations were approved in France thanks to Emperor Napoleon III's cynical support for the Catholic Church after his *coup d'état*. Rodin joined the Congregation of the Blessed Sacrament, founded by Father Pierre-Julien Eymard (he was canonized in 1962). Many hours were spent kneeling in silence, meditating on the Passion. Eymard gave Rodin a studio and commissioned a portrait bust, but the sculptor left after a few months for unknown reasons.[48] Towards the end of his life, in 1908, Rodin returned to a convent. He took four rooms in the Hôtel Biron, which had been the Couvent des Dames du Sacré-Coeur until 1904, when the republican government suppressed all religious houses; the last nun had left in 1907. Matisse, whom Rodin had met and influenced in 1900, was already in residence; in December 1907 he had moved into the whitewashed refectory, and the nuns' visitor reception area had become his wife's salon. He had previously been living at the suppressed Couvent des Oiseaux, where he had started an art school.[49] Rodin, when he moved in, immediately bought a phonograph and played 'some old Gregorian chants which nobody likes and which ... nobody possesses but the Pope'.[50]

The 'monk's cell' studio was a myth masking the reality of an artist whose private life and art were and still are often considered scandalous. When Rilke arrived on the scene, Rodin had been living unmarried since 1864 with his former model, the seamstress Rose Beuret, and their brain-damaged son, whom he refused to acknowledge. He was embarking on his latest relationship with a model, the English painter Gwen John. She called him 'mon maître' and considered him godlike. Every pretty woman he came across was fair game, including Monet's daughters, who had to leave the family dinner table because Rodin was ogling them. Beuret kept the heating low at Meudon to dampen ardour, but she had no control over the temperature in the Dépôt des Marbres.[51]

But in *fin-de-siècle* France the difference between church and brothel, monk and beast, Saint Luke and Pygmalion, was blurred. A source of inspiration was the self-styled Abbé Boullan (1824–1893), a Catholic priest who undertook the spiritual education of Adèle Chevalier in 1856. In 1859, now lovers, they founded a penitential religious community (one of the 982), where they developed scandalous practices. Two years later, they were jailed for embezzlement and indecency, and in 1876 they were excommunicated. Undeterred, Boullan claimed to be the reincarnation of Saint John the Baptist, insisting that the Fall had been caused by a sinful act of love and could be reversed only by acts of love accomplished in a religious environment. He established a new community in Lyon, offering penitential sex and astral sex with incubi.[52] Boullan was the model for the satanist Canon Docre in Huysmans's decadent novel *Là-Bas* (1891). Docre orchestrates a climactic orgy in a chapel in a suppressed convent. Satanism was fashionable because of the romantic cult of the persecuted and repressed outsider. The *Gates of Hell*, with the adulterous sinners Paolo and Francesca, in the Dépôt des Marbres studio provided the perfect backdrop for Gwen John's ecstasies with the Great Art God. After Rodin ended their affair, John converted to Catholicism.

At just this time (1905), Fernande Olivier moved in with a possessive young Spanish painter, Pablo Picasso. He was living in a dilapidated studio complex, the Bateau-Lavoir. She was surprised to find a chapel dedicated to her in an alcove in his squalid studio. The 'altar' was a packing case covered in the white lawn blouse she had worn at their first meeting, with two cerulean blue vases filled with artificial flowers. The 'altarpiece' consisted of a drawing of her made after their first encounter, presumably nude. It was mounted on material cut from a blue nightdress she had left behind.[53]

***

Rodin took the idea of chaste studio space mainstream. Negotiations started in 1909 for a bequest of his collections to the French state. This was conditional on the Hôtel Biron being acquired and turned into a museum. Agreement was reached in 1916, a year before his death, and in 1919 museums opened in Paris and Meudon. Altogether there are around 6,600 sculptures (mostly plasters and terracottas), 8,000 drawings, and c. 25,000 photographs.

Simultaneously, the Romanian-born sculptor Constantin Brancusi (1876–1957) began to choreograph every aspect of his Parisian studio while cultivating the persona of a monkish peasant (page 221).[54] In 1916, Brancusi moved into a new home studio in the Impasse Ronsin, a cul-de-sac off the rue de Vaugirard in Montparnasse. It had no plumbing and a single communal toilet in the yard that stank.[55] In the 19th century Montparnasse had been popular with academic artists because of the proximity of the Ecole des Beaux-Arts, founded in 1648 as the teaching wing of the Académie Royale. But it was now full of artists who could not afford Montmartre. Chagall, Picasso, Léger, Mondrian, Rivera and Van Dongen had studios there.[56] In 1927, Brancusi's studio was flooded and he moved to one opposite. By 1941 he had five interconnecting spaces. Like Rodin, Brancusi would eventually donate his studio and its contents to the French state. In 1997, it was partially recreated in a slick Renzo Piano building outside the Pompidou Centre.

Visitors often compared Brancusi's whitewashed studio to a monk's cell or monastery, whether Eastern (Tibetan) or Western (Benedictine). He wore white overalls and hat, with white beard and hair. From 1921 he had a white dog. Man Ray, who helped him buy a camera and make a darkroom in a corner of the studio, recalled his first visit: 'I was more impressed than in any cathedral. I was overwhelmed with its whiteness and lightness .... [It] was like entering another world – the whiteness, which, after all, is a synthesis of all the colours of the spectrum, this whiteness extended to the home-built brick stove and long stovepipe – here and there emphasized by a rough-hewn piece of oak or the golden metallic gleam of a polished dynamic form on a pedestal. There was nothing in the studio that might have come out of a shop, no chairs or furniture. A solid white plaster cylinder six feet in diameter, cast on the floor of the studio, served as a table, with a couple of hollowed out logs to sit on .... Brancusi lived like a hermit, in his studio in the heart of Paris.'[57]

Although Brancusi lived alone, he wasn't a hermit, and he did exhibit, mostly in New York. He gave excellent dinner parties and had a succession of relationships with much younger women. He took many glass plate photographs of them posing and dancing in the studio: Galateas come to life. He gave false reassurance to two Romanian students: 'I would not dare touch beautiful girls like you even with a flower.' Flowers were in fact central to Brancusi's courtship rituals.

Brancusi was alluding to the belief that artists should channel their libido into their art. In Henrik Ibsen's *When We Dead Wake* (1899), the sculptor Professor Rubek believes that if he touches his model, or even desires her sensually, his artistic vision will be lost.[58] Cézanne ordered his housekeeper to make sure her dress never brushed him. Brancusi's portraits of women, notably *Princess X – Portrait of Princess Marie Bonaparte* (1915–16), are indeed vials of sublimated sexual energy: they resemble sex toys. His credo was: 'It is pure joy that I offer you,' with the emphasis on *pure*.

Brancusi's studio was a cathedral of self-created stuff, and as such it claimed a unique integrity. In 1916 Brancusi, who left Rodin after only a month because 'nothing grows under a great tree', started to use oak in addition to his usual materials of stone, marble and bronze. He was a skilled carpenter who had made his own violin as an adolescent. As well as employing wood for sculptures he made stools, chairs, benches and a conspicuously uncomfortable chaise longue. 'Feminine' comforts were excluded. (Gauguin had helped make wood an avant-garde material. In his journal *Noa Noa* – Tahitian for 'rosewood' – first published in 1924, he registered his joy at cutting rosewood with an axe, ecstatically proclaiming: 'Farewell painting! My home shall be of carved wood.'[59]) Many of Brancusi's components were used interchangeably, so bits of furniture could be incorporated into his assemblages or could revert to being furniture. He was constantly reconfiguring his sculptures, which he called 'mobile groups'. They are close-knit families of objects at home in the studio.

Despite his peasant demeanour, Brancusi was fascinated by modern technology – photography, film, phonographs, aviation – and used power tools for polishing and cutting, concealing them from visitors. Electric motors made his polished metal sculptures rotate, catching the light and reflections. For visitors, spectacular lighting effects were created with concealed lamps (rather like those at the Soane Museum) and mirror bases. Dust-cloths were removed with a flourish. However, his own photographs were conspicuously crude and included the surrounding studio. Man Ray noted ruefully: 'They were out of focus, over or under exposed, scratched and spotty. This, he said, was how his work should be reproduced.'[60] Brancusi brought to photography the 'fantastic ignorance' that John Ruskin discerned in medieval sculptors. Their work's imperfection was a sign of 'life and liberty' that gave it 'uncouth animation'.[61] Brancusi's uncouth photographs

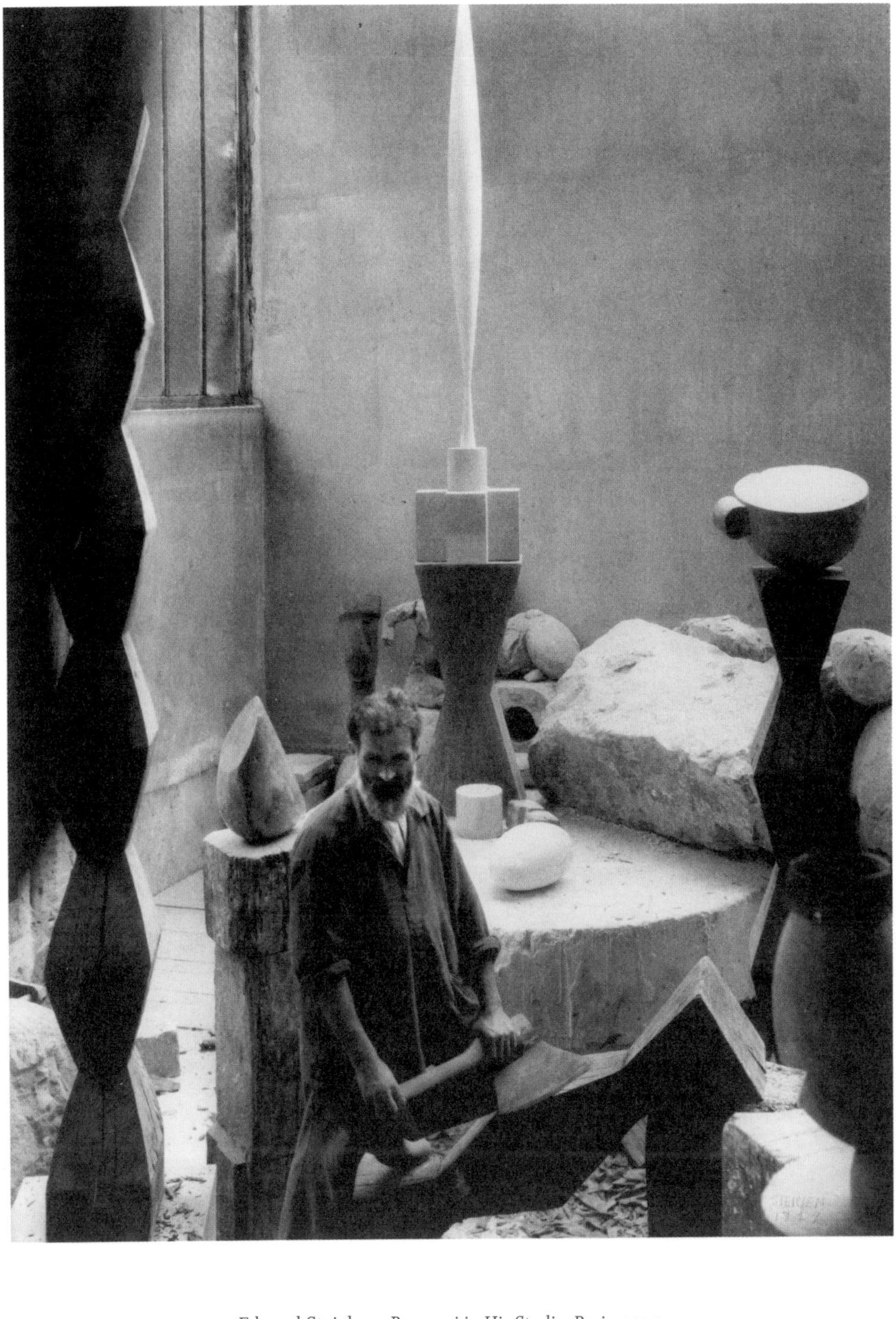

Edward Steichen, *Brancusi in His Studio, Paris*, 1925.

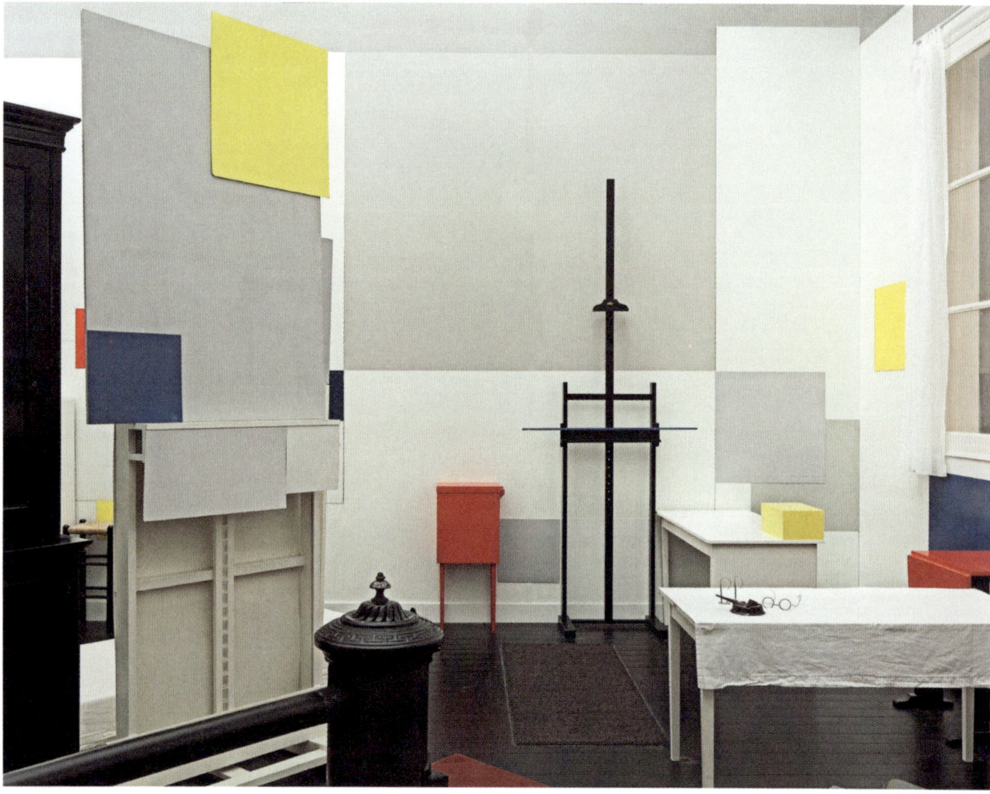

Frans Postma, *Reconstruction of Mondrian's Studio Based on Paul Delbo's 1926 Photograph.*

animated sculpture and studio through chance effects, while lack of clarity preserved their mystery.

More refined ensembles were being created by the Dutch painter Piet Mondrian (1872–1944), who lived nearby, firstly in rue de Coulmiers (1919–21) and then in a large studio block at rue du Départ (1921–36). His home studio was irregularly shaped, roughly pentagonal, because it bridged the gap between three buildings. Mondrian was the most persistent micro-manager of studio space, with new incarnations being frequently photographed for publicity purposes. This habit started early, in a whitewashed attic studio in Amsterdam in 1905.[62]

Mondrian started out as a Symbolist landscape painter, but in 1917, after encountering Cubism in Paris, he co-founded the De Stijl movement. His non-representational 'neo-plastic' paintings, pared down intuitively to a few rectilinear components and colours, were utopian expressions of cosmic order. Painting, furniture and architecture were integrated into an endlessly evolving studio environment. Painted cardboard panels were fixed to the walls. Eventually, easel paintings would be rendered obsolete in a seamless neo-plastic world. Mondrian's greatest influence would be on modernist architecture and design; individual pictures can look orphaned when exhibited alone in galleries.

The Dutch journalist W. F. A. Röell wrote four articles between 1920 and 1932 based on studio visits. The post-Rodin clichés come thick and fast. In 1920 the overall-clad painter, 'deaf to the Whitsuntide jollity [in the streets] around him, grapples with his materials in monk-like solitude in his quest for his lofty, highly controversial ideal'. Röell takes refuge in a 'cubic cane chair', but later: 'In desperation I clutch at an oriental cushion decorated with arabesques on the divan.' He has just been praising Kees van Dongen's nearby studio, where 'one is staggered by a drunken riot of colours and cushions'.[63] Van Dongen's fancy-dress balls were legendary.

Röell repeats the Mondrian/Van Dongen contrast in 1926, but is now delighted to discern 'an element of natural weakness in Mondrian' – a round vase with a flower. The painter explains, only half apologetically: 'I needed something to symbolise feminine grace and charm. But take a good look: my flower is artificial, and what is more, I whitewashed the leaves in order to banish that impossibly naturalistic green from my interior.'[64]

This is as near as Mondrian ever came to a joke, but he was deadly serious. Using theosophical ideas derived from the Pythagorean 'table of opposites', Mondrian believed the world comprised female and male elements. Curved lines were female, straight were male: the straight is the 'intensification of the curved'. The curved is natural and individual; the straight spiritual and universal.[65] The cast-iron stove was the snake in the grass. Mondrian loathed its roundness. It projected bulbously into the centre of his room and could not be painted.[66] The female had to be suppressed, even in his stage-set designs: 'If I had my way I'd put the actresses behind screens so that the audience wouldn't have to look at them and could just follow the text.'[67]

The painter's easel was the crucial piece of furniture, more important than any painting. Easels were ideal sculptural and architectural elements.[68] The easel was placed against the external wall with no picture on it, or only a small one, so we see it as a cross. Mondrian removed the back legs to get it flush with the wall. After 1928, he painted it white. Until the end of 1927, a large easel bearing a virtually blank canvas was used to screen his single bed. No paint stains disfigured his easels or floor. Most scholars think he worked standing at a table, placing stretchers flat on a tablecloth made from waxed canvas. He operated like an artisan at a workbench.

The English Aesthetic Movement had made easels into essential items of furniture for elegant interiors, thereby creating an arty studio ambience (and lethal trip hazards) in smarter homes.[69] As a student, Oscar Wilde had 'carelessly' placed an unfinished painting on an easel in his rooms. In 1879 he rented a floor of Thames House, off the Strand. This had a long, panelled reception room, which he painted white. Fashionable taste and medical opinion had turned against sombre wall colours: white dispelled gloom and revealed dirt.[70] At the far end, Wilde gave pride of place to Edward Poynter's portrait of the actress Lillie Langtry in a yellow dress. Her easel was surrounded by white lilies – or lillies.[71] It was the high altar in a temple of beauty.

Mondrian's easels were altars too, but they did not showcase curvaceous feminine beauty. Still, the fact that Mondrian painted his artificial flower white ironically demonstrates his debt to the Aesthetic Movement. Wilde famously quipped, 'I find it harder and harder every day to live up to my blue china.'[72] Mondrian and his visitors had to live up to a far stricter studio rule. In 1932 Röell observed: 'The creator of the Neo-Plastic evangelism lives in monk-like sobriety. There is nothing around him to titillate his senses. When he puts mirrors on the walls to enrich them, it is forbidden to mirror oneself in them.'[73] One could not even take refuge in narcissism.

***

Being overwhelmed by a studio's lightness and whiteness would soon be the rule rather than the exception. The 'white cube' studio and gallery is the most long-lived of modern design conventions.[74] Search 'contemporary artist's studio' and you find identikit white-walled rooms – logically enough, as the artworks are destined for identikit white-walled galleries and private homes. The draconian 'Law of Ripolin', devised in 1925 for male property owners by the modernist architect Le Corbusier, remains in force. Having called on the police to enforce a decree for 'all rooms in Paris to be given a coat of white-wash', Corbusier elaborated: 'Every citizen is required to replace his hangings, his damasks, his wall-papers, his stencils, with a plain coat of white ripolin. *His home* is made clean. There are no more dirty, dark corners. *Everything is shown as it is.* Then comes *inner* cleanness, for the course adopted leads to refusal to allow anything at all which is not correct, authorized, intended, desired, thought-out: no action before thought. When you are surrounded

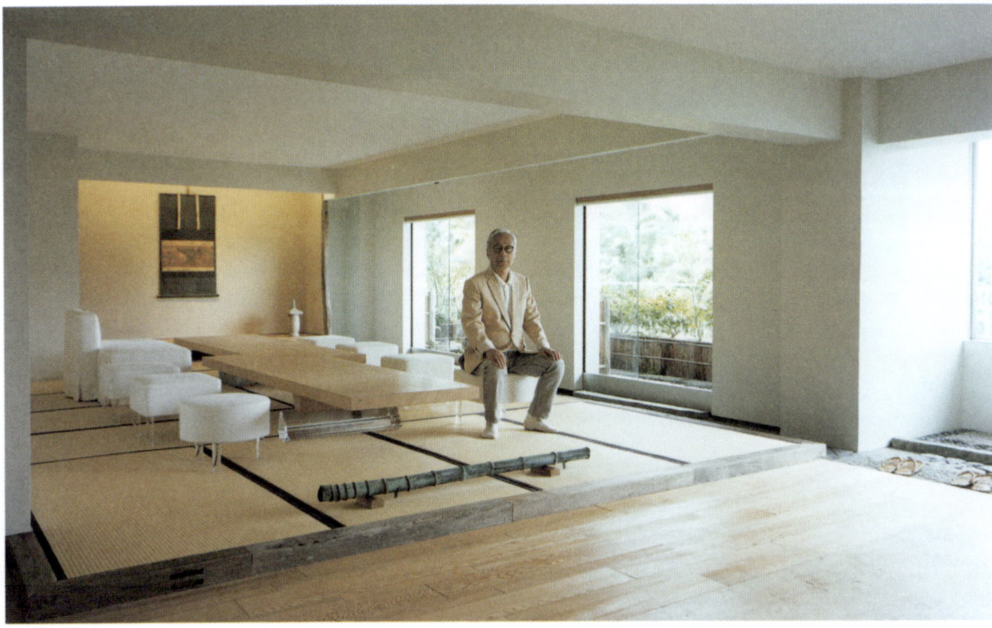

Yasutomo Ebisu, *Hiroshi Sugimoto in His Tokyo Home Studio*, 2019.

with shadows and dark corners you are at home only as far as the hazy edges of the darkness your eyes cannot penetrate. You are not master in your own house. Once you have put ripolin on your walls you will be *master of yourself*.'[75] The law of the medieval workshop that outlawed secret places is here updated and applied to domestic interiors. We almost yearn for Hans Makart's palm-infested pleasure palace.

The Japanese photographer and architect Hiroshi Sugimoto (b. 1948) has tried to steer a poetic course between modernist austerity and crafted variety in his Tokyo home studio.[76] The walls of the penthouse apartment are coated with white Japanese *shikkui* plaster, which Sugimoto considers the finest surface on which to view shadows – presumably subtle rather than Bandinellian. The interior and balcony garden evoke a Japanese teahouse and tea garden. Sugimoto learned carpentry as a child and makes and designs his own furniture, using a range of old and new materials. The hallway is paved with stone beams from old temples: 'The material usually comes first, and then I think about the design.' It is a minimalist monk's parlour, with green tea.

Chapter 14

Eliminating Easels

Workshop and Factory

The 20th-century shift towards artists occupying industrial spaces such as factories and warehouses is strikingly illustrated by the Bauhaus, founded as a school of art and design by Walter Gropius in 1919. Over its fourteen-year existence in three different locations (Weimar 1919–25; Dessau 1925–32; Berlin 1932–3), it helped redefine the nature of art. The Dessau campus, designed by Gropius and fitted out by his colleagues and students, became the world's most visited workshop complex.

Gropius, an architect, was a founder member of the Deutscher Werkbund (1907), which sought to unite fine art and industry by embracing modern materials and mass production. But the war temporarily turned him against machines and a machine aesthetic. So initially, in Weimar, Gropius idealized the Middle Ages in the manner of the Arts and Crafts Movement – and of Goethe, Weimar's most celebrated resident.[1] Since Goethe's essay celebrating Strasbourg Cathedral, medieval cathedrals had been considered total works of art, living organisms made with spiritual purpose by a large community. The name 'Bauhaus' derived from the medieval *Bauhütten*, masons' lodges. The first Bauhaus manifesto featured an Expressionist woodcut of a Gothic cathedral by Lyonel Feininger, head of the print department. Its three spires – signifying painting, architecture and sculpture – were haloed by starbursts.

Gropius amalgamated the School of Arts and Crafts in Weimar with the Academy of Fine Art in order to create 'a new guild of craftsmen' that would build 'the crystal symbol of a new faith'. There were to be no class, status or gender distinctions (the latter were reinstated after a year, with most women – about half the intake of 150 – ushered towards weaving, which

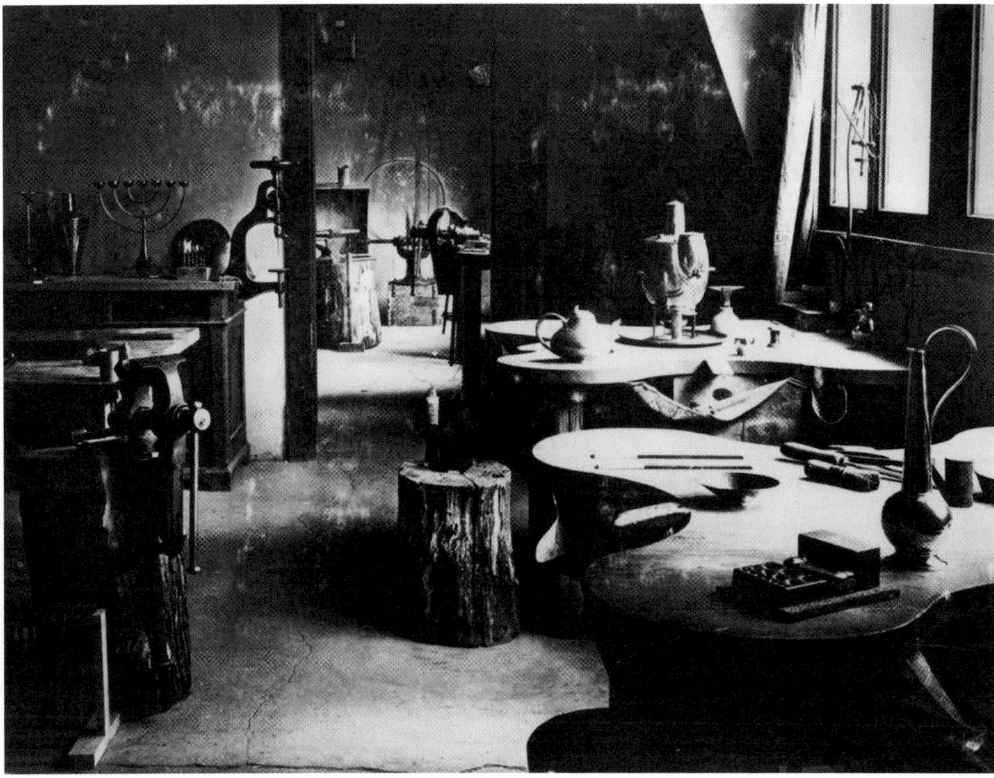

Metal Workshop, Bauhaus, Weimar, 1923.

ironically became the most profitable department).[2] Each workshop was initially run jointly by an artist, a *Meister der Form* – most of these were painters – and a craftsman, a *Meister des Handwerks*. Creative 'ambidexterity' would soon demolish the 'arrogant wall between artist and artisan'.[3] Students took the now celebrated preliminary course devised by deputy director Johannes Itten, a charismatic shaven-headed mystic with his own monkish uniform. Itten had a studio in a Gothic-style garden 'church' designed by Goethe in Weimar's landscaped park. It was called the Tempelherrenhaus, after four life-size sculptures of Templar knights on the roof.

Itten's course involved creating contrasts and harmonies of colour, form and texture. In drawing lessons, students had to distil still-life objects, live models and Old Master paintings into expressive arrangements of lines and geometrical shapes. Empathy, intuition, self-expression and sexual abstinence were stressed. Yoga-style stretching, breathing and chanting exercises were part of the pre-class routine, sometimes conducted in the park outside Itten's studio. What Paul Klee, another Master of Form, dubbed 'a kind of body massage to train the machine to function with feeling' may also have been prompted by Cennini's insistence on massage: a German translation of *The Book of Art* appeared in 1916.[4]

The workshops were in the former school of arts and crafts, a two-storey building designed by the Belgian Art Nouveau architect Henry van de Velde.[5] He was school director until wartime xenophobia forced him out. Gropius ran the carpentry workshop, and wood was a key material in picturesque Weimar, as it was for Gauguin and Brancusi. Faculty and students collaborated on making a house from reclaimed teak in Berlin (Sommerfeld House, 1920–1). Even in the metal workshop on the first floor, run by Itten, chunky wooden furniture, exposed beams and tree-trunk tables dominated (preceding page). The undulating goldsmiths' tables with attached leather aprons for catching filings were identical to those used by the jewelers in Diderot's *Encyclopédie*.[6] Artefacts were curvaceous, organic-looking, with proportions based on the Greek golden section; the Hungarian Gyula Papa's seven-branch brass candelabra and Carl Jakob Jucker's silver-plated brass samovar were traditional luxury goods, unsuited to mass production.[7] No machine tools were visible. Theophilus would soon have felt at home in this cosily folksy, pseudo-monastic room.

At the end of 1922 Itten, more interested in self-realization than end products, resigned. Gropius wanted the Bauhaus to embrace mass production and commercial tie-ups. Facing severe financial shortfalls, and now influenced by Russian Constructivism and Dutch De Stijl (Mondrian's co-founder Theo van Doesburg had been giving private lessons in Weimar since February 1922), Gropius heralded a new age of industrial designers and hi-tech architects. In 1923 he announced this seismic change in a lecture, 'Art and Technology: A New Unity'.

Right-wing political hostility and draconian budget cuts persuaded him to relocate to the industrial and mining town of Dessau, 110 kilometres (70 miles) to the north. It was home to Junkers, the 'all metal' aircraft and boiler manufacturer, and IG Farben chemicals. The offer of land and money to build a brand-new campus was irresistible. Using reinforced concrete, steel, plate glass and brick infill, Gropius designed an asymmetrical, centrifugal constellation of three main blocks linked by bridging structures (1925–6). Lacking a façade or obvious main entrance, it had to be circumnavigated to 'grasp its corporeality and the function of its elements'.[8] Perambulation was standard in English-style informal gardens and in picturesque architecture, such as the Tempelherrenhaus and park. But Gropius applied these ideas to

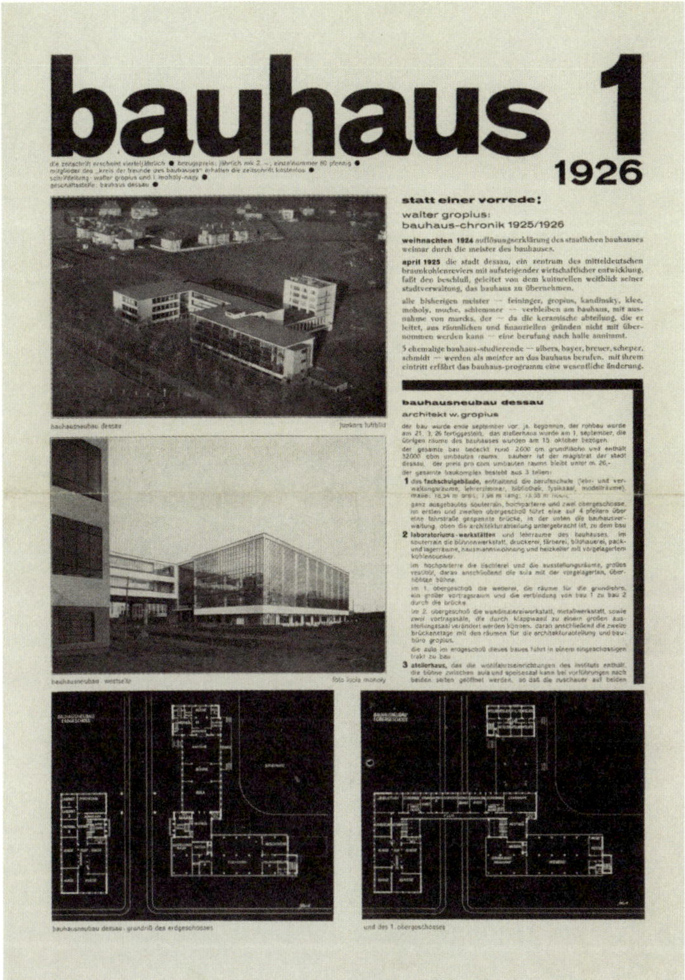

Cover for the *Bauhaus magazine*, no. 1, 1926.

a large institutional building, using the latest materials and stark geometrical forms with flat roofs. The lack of conventional architectural markers was in line with Bauhaus typography: capital letters were abolished in 1925. An English journalist, Lilian T. Mowrer, thought the building far superior to a mere factory – it was 'as sleek and free from ornament as a racing car'.[9] The main decorative feature was the subtly varied patterning of the steel window-frames. Dessau's mayor proudly boasted that between 1927 and 1930 over 20,000 visitors came, from Europe and beyond. Critics complained about high heating bills.

The building's beating heart was the four-storey middle block with its open-plan 'laboratory workshops'. This quasi-scientific term derived from Soviet Russia. A state-sponsored art and technology college, Vkhutemas, had been founded in Moscow in 1920 with Constructivists on the staff. Aleksey Gan proclaimed: 'Taking a scientific and hypothetical approach to its task, the group asserts the necessity to fuse the ideological component with the formal component in order to achieve a real transition from laboratory experiments to practical activity.'[10] The Russian Expressionist painter Wassily Kandinsky, who taught in both institutions, was an important link. Gropius adopted the formal and technological elements but tried to keep the Bauhaus politically neutral.

Gropius turned the workshop block into a giant fish tank by wrapping it in a curtain wall of glass (courtesy of the German Plate Glass Association) that continued round the corners: 'Glass, glass and more glass, radiating dazzling white light from every wall.' Passers-by could see inside, and at night it glowed magically like 'a giant light cube'.[11] It meant that, in winter especially, there was no shortage of natural light even in a polluted industrial city (Dessau was plagued by smog, as it sits on a flood plain where the river Mulde flows into the Elbe). In London, from the 1880s, successful painters built all-glass 'winter' studios to make work possible on dark, smoggy days.[12] Photographers frequently occupied all-glass rooftop studios added to existing buildings on major shopping streets; this improved the quality and duration of natural light. With the coming of electricity, they advertised their studios by leaving lights on at night so they glowed.[13] Ironically, a photography studio was established in Dessau only in 1929, after Gropius's departure. Lucia Moholy (1894–1989), who took most of the official Bauhaus photographs, made a darkroom in the basement of the master's house she shared with her husband, the Hungarian Constructivist painter-photographer László Moholy-Nagy.

The art critic and perceptual psychologist Rudolf Arnheim saw the glass in moral terms: 'You can look in from the outside through the large windows and see the people at work as well as the private lives of those taking a rest. Every object shows its construction .... It is tempting to judge this honesty from a moral point of view.'[14] There is a latent medievalism to this 'modernist' transparency (no secret spaces for dishonest activity). There is also a superficial similarity with Jeremy Bentham's 'panopticon', a layout for prisons and factories that enabled surveillance. More pertinently, it turned the whole building into a stage. Theatre, dance and yoga were components of the Bauhaus curriculum, often performed on roofs and balconies. Oskar

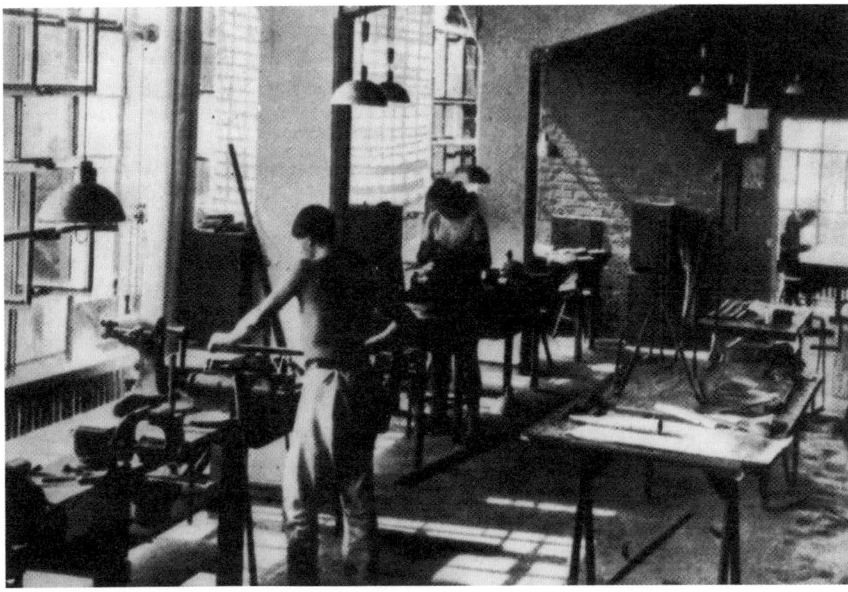

Marianne Brandt, *Metal Workshop, Bauhaus, Dessau*, c. 1928, gelatin silver print.

Schlemmer, Master of Theatre, orchestrated mechanized movements by silent masked performers.[15] Man, machine and building were in sync.

The metal workshop and the preliminary course had been taken over after Itten's departure by Moholy-Nagy (it was he who eradicated capital letters). In stark contrast to Itten, he wore red workman's overalls, actually a Breton fisherman's outfit. A cult of the male worker had taken hold in late 19th-century Europe and America, prompted by both economic rivalry and nationalism as well as by socialism and a belief in the dignity of labour, whether industrial, agricultural or artisanal.[16] Brass candlesticks were out; sleek electric lights made from ferrous metals, nickel and chromium were in.[17] Marianne Brandt (1893–1983), one of the few female Bauhaus apprentices allowed to escape weaving, was Master of Metalwork from May 1928 until July 1929. Her lights were used throughout the Dessau complex. A spherical ceiling light was made from pressed aluminium and frosted glass, the bottom half flashed with opal glass. The domed lights are made from nickel-plated sheet brass.[18] In 1924, Bauhaus lighting had been laughed at by manufacturers at the Leipzig trade fair for looking like cheap machine products while being expensively handmade, but by 1928 models were being made under licence by a lighting company.

A photo of the workshop at this point shows it has been partially re-equipped, though there are still few power tools (preceding page). On the right are Marcel Breuer's new drafting tables, supported by tubular steel sawhorses. Breuer, an apprentice who became Master of Carpentry, pioneered the use of tubular steel for furniture. Yet mysticism and medievalism are not eradicated. The constellations of pendant lights give a cosmic feel, while the angled 'braces' on the ceiling beams recall medieval barns and halls.

The wall painting workshop, run by Hinnerk Scheper, designed coloured decoration for architecture, furniture and toys, with the most profitable product being wallpaper. Easels were conspicuous by their absence. The students worked on large trestle tables.[19] They decorated the Bauhaus in their 'haus' style of square and rectangular patches of a single colour on predominantly white or off-white walls. Bold colour accents were put on ceiling beams and staircases.

Easels were largely confined to the studios of the painters, who were among the earliest (and most famous) Masters of Form. The seven masters were accommodated in state-of-the-art villas designed by Gropius in a small pine wood nearby. There were three pairs of semi-detached houses and a detached house for Gropius and his wife, Ilse. The star painters Klee and Kandinsky were neighbours, just as they had been before the war in Munich. They demanded compensation for their huge heating bills. A sheepish Paul Klee was photographed in his *atelier* – the French loanword used in German for studio – keeping close to the Junkers radiator. The cold, blunt wall colour plan drawn up by Fritz Kuhr for Klee's atelier was modified: the long expanse of curtain was white, and the wall against which he sits yellow, complementing the blue.

Klee's atelier has been decluttered. His natural history specimens, including seaweed sandwiched between plates of glass, children's drawings and non-Western carvings, are nowhere to be seen. He had a washing line for drying watercolours. Photographs of his studio in Weimar show the floor space packed with angled easels on which small pictures are displayed – five easels in one, four in another. They attest to his astonishing productivity (he left over 10,000 works) but also give the false impression he could not bear to part with them and created dense family gatherings of easels and art. Klee cocooned his canvases in thick homemade wooden frames; in Dessau, easels and frames were minimized and marginalized, so the pictures were better integrated with the wall. Neat horizontal and vertical patterns were created. Klee was devising colour theories that could be used to create patterns for textiles.

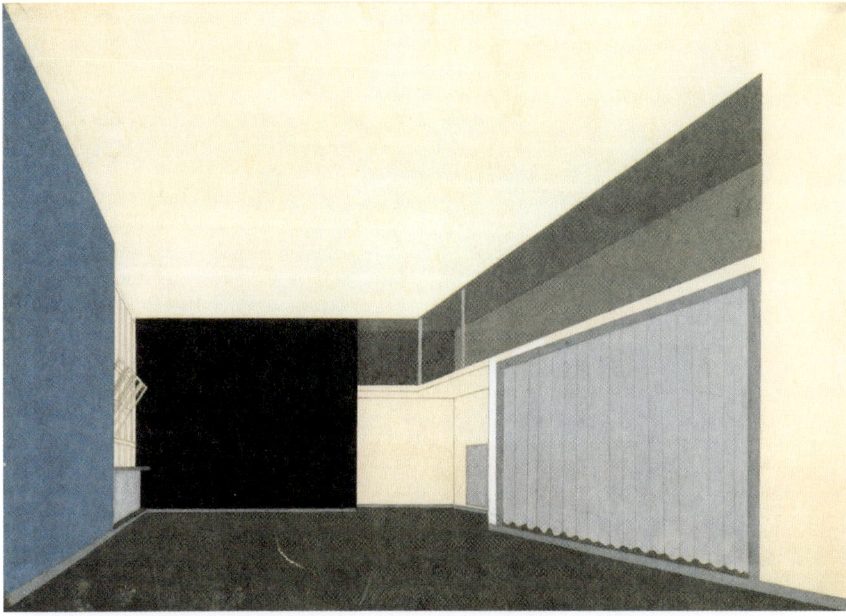

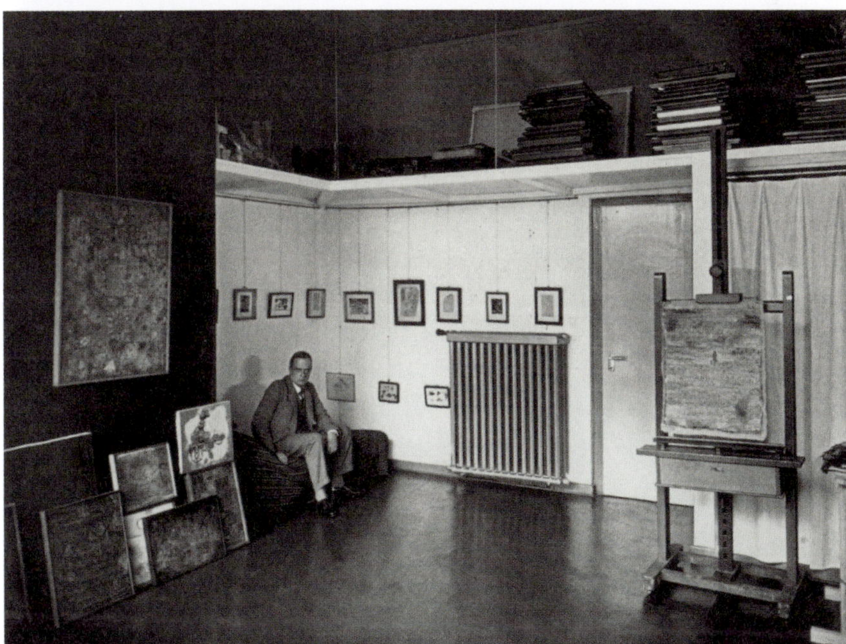

Top Fritz Kuhr, *Wall-Painting Scheme for the Atelier of Paul Klee's Master House*, 1926, tempera, silver bronze and pencil on paper. **Above** Lucia Moholy, *Paul Klee in His Atelier*, 1926, gelatin silver print.

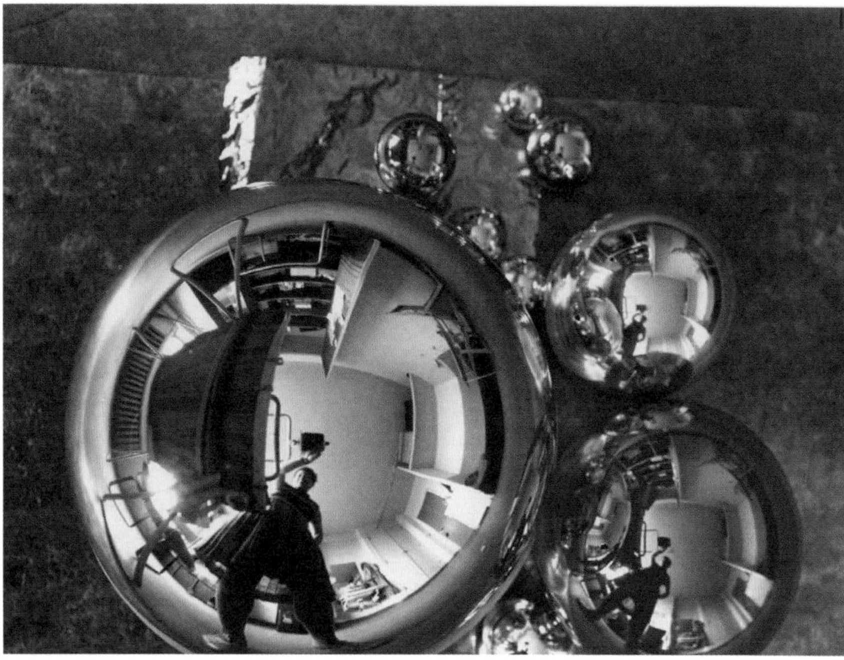

Marianne Brandt, *Self-Portrait in Atelier*, 1928–9, gelatin silver print.

Gropius called each of the twenty-eight student bedsits in the residential block an 'atelier', but at 5.17 by 4.5 metres (17 by 15 feet), they were more like cells. They had built-in furniture, with bedspreads, cushions and fabric for the Breuer stools provided by the weaving workshop. (From 1926 this was run by Gunta Stöltz, the first female Master.[20]) There was a Breuer worktable before a large window and balcony – but no easel. The underside of the table and the side of the tubular metal stool are visible in Marianne Brandt's ballsy self-portrait. This is Alice through the (stainless-steel) Looking-Glass. The multiple reflections show Brandt's sense of herself as mass producer and master manipulator of form. Her atelier is a laboratory where all manner of shape- and size-shifting takes place.

In 1927, after frequent appeals by Klee and Kandinsky, 'free' painting classes were allowed to take place, and they persisted until the final closure of the Bauhaus in 1933. But Klee, Kandinsky and Georg Muche were no longer in charge of workshops. Ilse Gropius believed 'the days of the painter at the Bauhaus to be truly over'.[21] When Walter Gropius resigned in 1928, he recommended the architect Hannes Meyer as his successor. Meyer restructured the school, amalgamating metalwork, carpentry and wall painting into an interior design department making popular household goods. 'Elimination of painters' was one of his aims.

In 1930 Meyer was in turn forced to resign because of his communist sympathies. He was replaced by modernist architect Mies van der Rohe, who had agreed to keep out of politics, like Gropius. Political activity and smoking were banned, and many leftist activists expelled. But the following year, the Nazi Party won nineteen of thirty-six seats in Dessau, and the Bauhaus was dubbed Bolshevist and un-German; in August 1932 it was forced to close. Mies transferred the Bauhaus to Berlin, where it reopened in October in the Steglitz district as a private architecture and interior design school. It now occupied a former telephone factory, the walls whitewashed. Mies was a refined aesthete, and a dilapidated factory in brick and glass is unlikely to have been his ideal location. But the Bauhaus would help establish the factory-style laboratory workshop and the former factory as model workplaces.

In April 1933 the Nazis came to search for communist literature and sealed the building. They demanded the sacking of Kandinsky and other staff members, as well as a ban on Jews. Mies and his colleagues dissolved the Bauhaus in July.[22] Paradoxically, its closure only increased its influence by scattering its teachers and students around the world, especially to the United States. In 1938, the Museum of Modern Art in New York mounted 'Bauhaus: 1919–28', accompanied by a lavishly illustrated catalogue.

***

Although the Bauhaus was the most impressive model for the factory-style space, it was not the first or only one. Successful 19th-century sculptors had worked in large proto-factories, as we saw with Thorvaldsen in Rome. Mural painters also used functional 'non-art' spaces. At Giverny during the First World War, Monet had a hangar-like studio constructed so he could work on the waterlily murals (overleaf). Measuring 15 metres (49 feet) high, 12 metres (39 feet) wide and 23 metres (75 feet) long, it had a large window and skylight on the north side. He was rightly appalled by its appearance, far worse than the large space upriver at Neuilly-sur-Seine built by the mural painter Puvis de Chavannes (1824–1898): 'They've gone and built me something revolting, and I'm ashamed at being responsible for it, when I'm always grumbling about the people who uglify Giverny.'[23] After Monet's death, twenty-two panels were installed in the Musée de l'Orangerie in Paris. The remainder stayed in the studio until

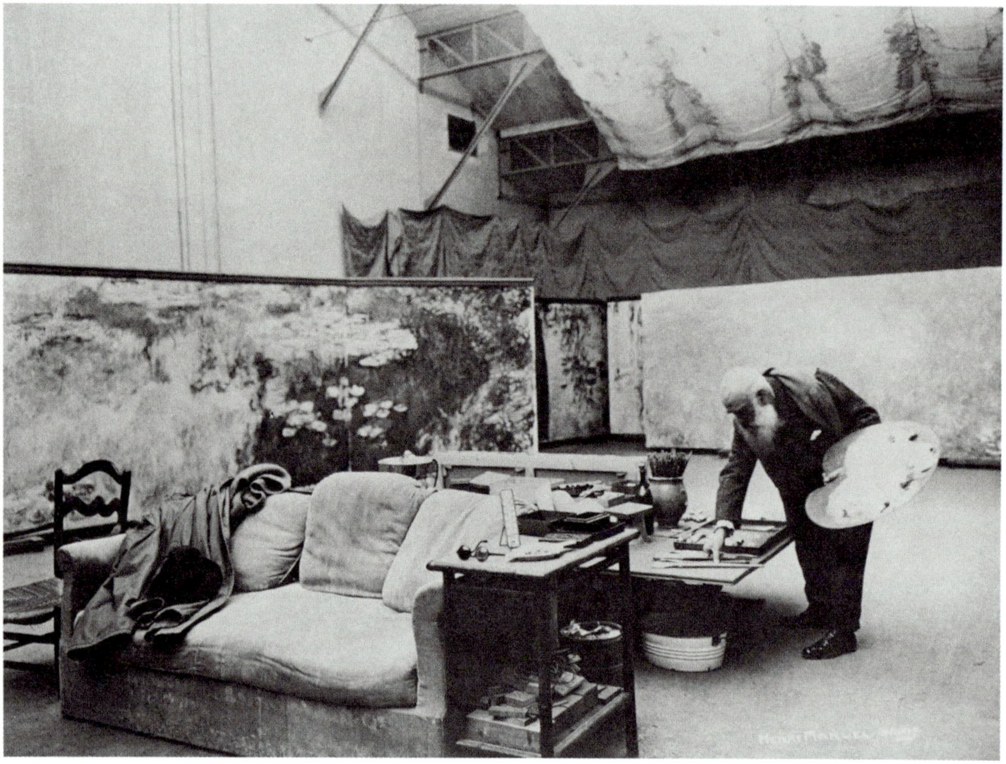

Henri Manuel, *Monet in His Studio in Front of 'Morning'*, c. 1924–5, photograph.

the late 1940s, when collectors and curators began to take an interest and visited Giverny, attracted by the canvases' panoramic size, serialism and abstraction.[24]

With the rise of communism and fascism, and especially after the Wall Street crash of 1929, there was far greater emphasis on creating grandiose public art projects, and these too required vast studios. At the Paris World's Fair of 1937, competing nations adorned their pavilions with colossal artworks. Raoul Dufy's 600-square-metre (6,458-square-foot) panorama *The Electricity Fairy*, for the Electricity Pavilion, was made in a hangar outside Paris. It comprised 250 panels of canvas on plywood.[25] Electric lighting and power tools facilitated the expansion of studios. Josef Thorak's *Comradeship*, a 6.7-metre (22-foot) bronze trio of beefcakes (two men and a woman), guarded the Nazi pavilion. Thorak had an atelier (oddly, the Nazis still used the French word) near Munich designed by Albert Speer. Claimed as the world's largest studio, it was supposedly big enough to accommodate a Zeppelin.[26]

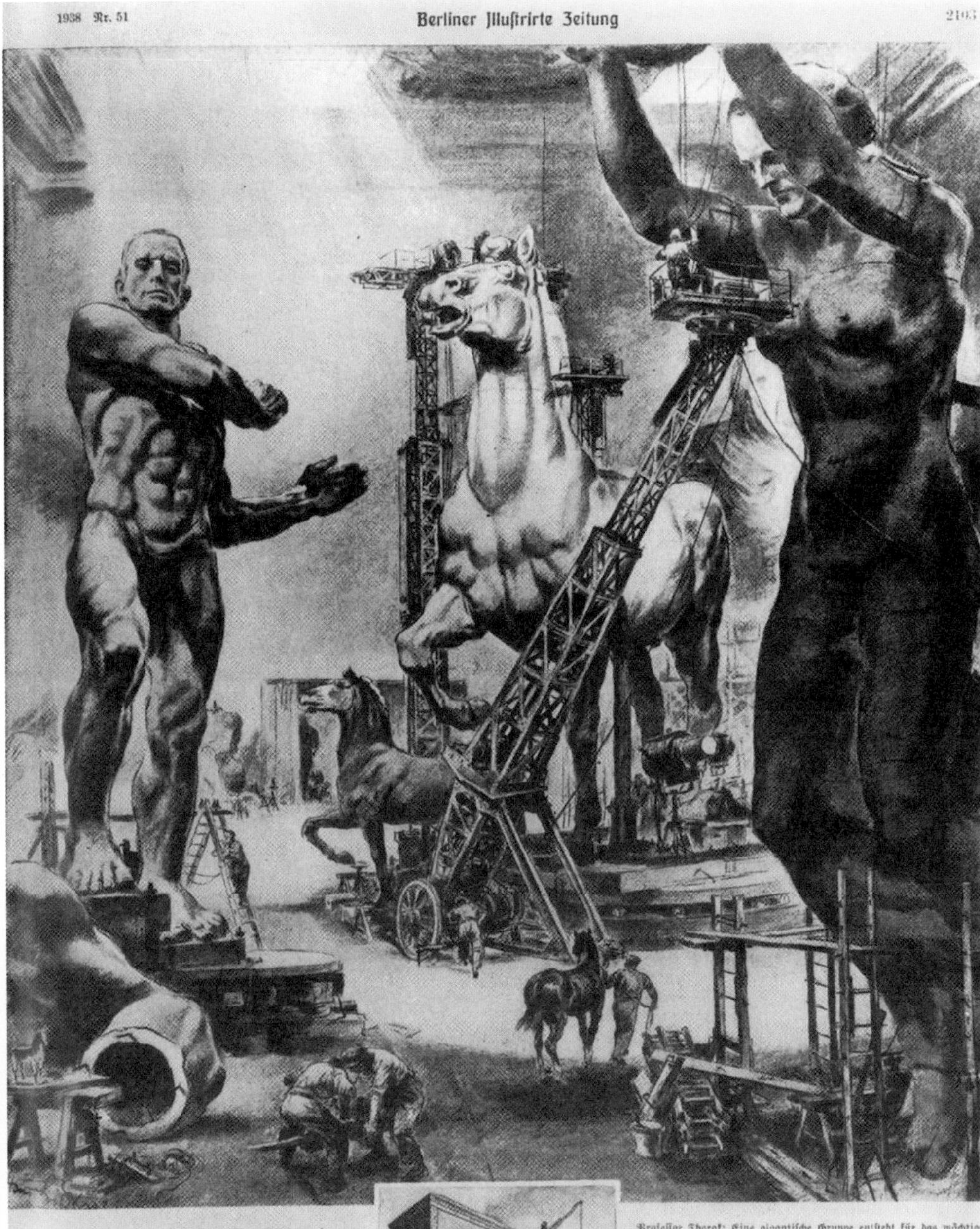

1938 Nr. 51 Berliner Illustrirte Zeitung 2103

Im größten Atelier der Welt

„Professor Thorak schreitet mit mir", so erzählt Hans Liska, „durch sein riesiges Atelier in Baldham bei München, das im Auftrag des Führers nach einem Entwurf von Professor Albert Speer erbaut wurde, und spricht von seinen Werken und Gesichten, von vollendeten und zukünftigen Dingen. Das Glück eines Künstlers ist bestimmt durch die Größe seiner Zeit, und gewaltig ist die neue Aufgabe für Professor Thorak: Eine gigantische Gruppe entsteht für das mächtige März-Feld in Nürnberg. Nach dem lebenden Modell (z. B. einem Pferde) wird eine kleine Ton-Skizze geschaffen, die sich dann zu einer vier Meter hohen Modellform wandelt. Nach dieser entsteht dann endgültig die Riesenplastik. Scheinwerfer leuchten die Figuren aus, die Licht-Effekte werden geprüft, auf hohen Arbeitskränen werden die Feinheiten vom Künstler selbst herausgearbeitet. Dann rollen die Standbilder, von Treckern gezogen, aus dem Atelier zum Gleisanschluß, wo Kräne die gewaltigen Einzelteile der Kolossalfiguren auf Waggons verladen."

'In the World's Largest Atelier', *Berliner Illustrirte Zeitung*, 1938.

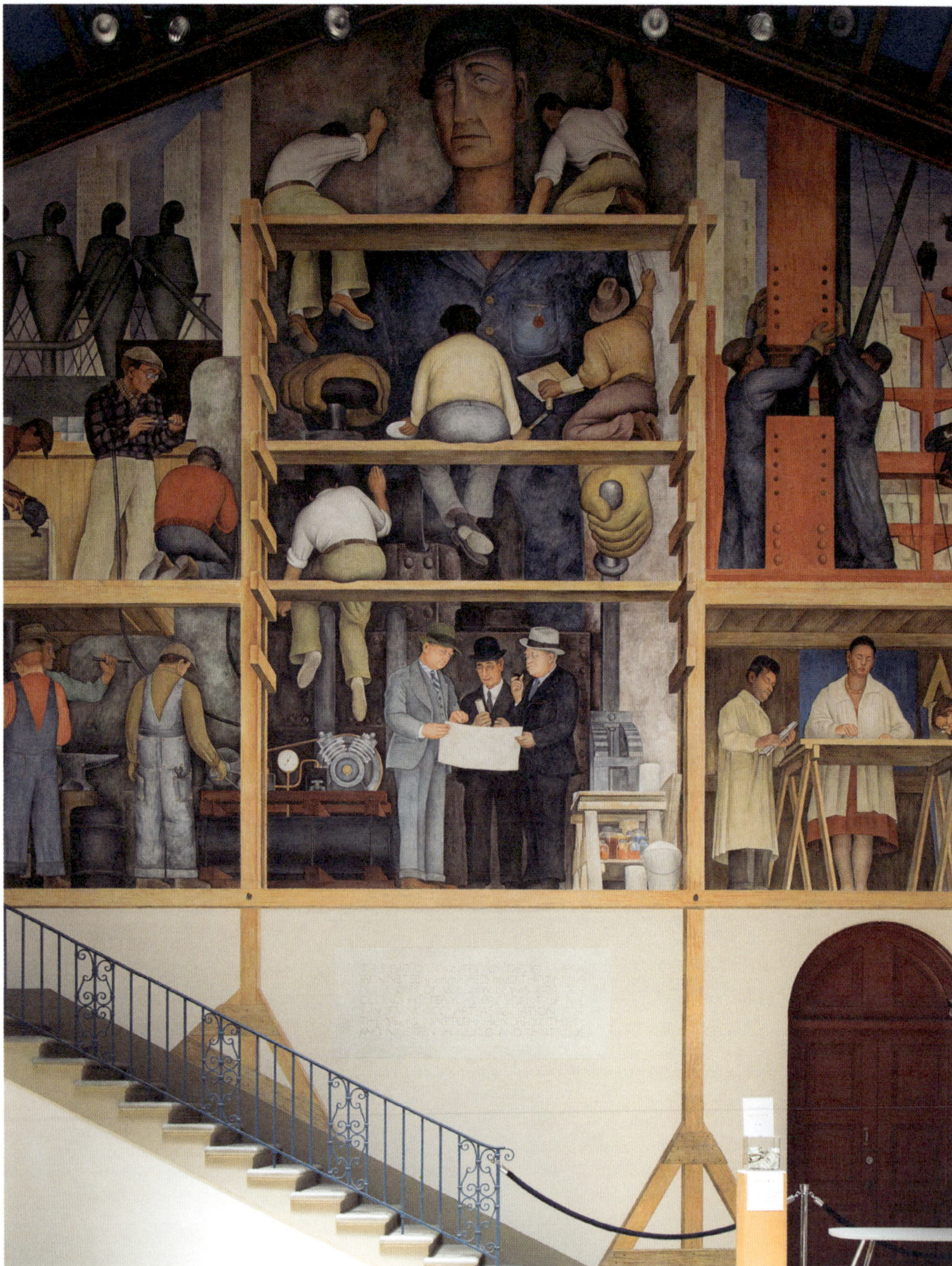

Diego Rivera, *The Making of a Fresco Showing the Building of a City*, 1931, fresco, San Francisco Art Institute.

There was a flurry of public murals, especially in Mexico and the United States. Diego Rivera's *The Making of a Fresco Showing the Building of a City* (1931) blurred the boundaries between factory and studio, architecture and art, modern and old.[27] Located in the gallery of the San Francisco Art Institute, it was painted in front of spectators in an Art-Deco-meets-Giotto style, generating huge press coverage. The wooden scaffold with compartments evokes a medieval mason's lodge. The communist Rivera and his team are painting a godlike factory worker. Four assistants prepare the surface of the fresco; to the left, sculptors use power tools and goggles to carve an Easter Island-style head – an ironic nod to Gutzon Borglum's Mount Rushmore (1927–41), carved by abseiling workers using pneumatic drills. Below the painters, two architects and the mural's patron examine plans drawn up by the glamorous female draughtsman on the right. At top right, construction workers ease an I-beam into place. Rivera is singled out: the man seen in rear view at dead centre with his 'well known amplitude'[28] is the only worker who has paused for some old-fashioned solitary musing.

***

In the documentary film *Painters Painting* (1970–2), the American abstract painter Robert Motherwell explained why so many post-war Americans had studios in former factories:

> The scale of America is different. I don't mean that one goes out and looks at the desert. Most painters live in cities. I would say that most American painters work in what were once small factories, whereas European artists work either in apartments or studios that were designed in terms of the scale of easel painting. There's … a *heroic* impulse as compared with the intimacy of a French painting.[29]

Motherwell is referring to artists' occupation of lofts formerly used for light industrial purposes. In Depression-era New York it became easier to find cheap lofts, even if they were not legally residences and rarely had hot water. In 1935, Willem de Kooning vacated his first loft space in the industrial district of Chelsea after a few weeks because of the smell from the downstairs bakery, but moved straight into another loft next door.[30] After the war, availability increased with the relocation of industrial production to sites outside cities, or abroad. The critic Thomas Hess claimed that, once whitewashed, a loft could become 'a room as serene as the nave of a Cistercian chapel'.[31]

Motherwell's '*heroic* impulse' was in fact a legacy of 1930s muralism. But his statement about not going to the desert in search of space was topical, a reference to land artists Walter De Maria and Michael Heizer, who made site-specific work in the Mojave Desert. Nonetheless, Motherwell seems to imagine the factory studio as a desert with roof and ribbon windows, inspiring precisely because of its emptiness, barrenness and expansiveness. Motherwell's ideal artist is a hermit in a deserted factory, not a collaborator in the style of the Bauhaus or Rivera. The architecture critic Robert Harbison drily noted: 'Because they are so uncommunicative for long stretches, one attributes absolute integrity to industrial structures .... The aesthete is seldom more credulous than when presented with the brute facts of labour.'[32]

The heroic impulse in American art would be inflected in various ways by Andy Warhol's Factory (1964–8) on the fourth floor of a building at 231 East 47th Street.[33] Built in 1887, it is usually assumed to have been a hat factory prior to Warhol, but may have been an upholsterer's.[34] It was 12 metres (40 feet) wide, and estimates for the length range from 23 to 30 metres (75 to a 100 feet) – a similar footprint to Monet's studio. It was dilapidated. The exposed brick walls were crumbling, the concrete floor broken, the south-facing windows blacked out. There were two jerry-built toilets, male and female. Exposed wires dangled from the barrel-vaulted ceiling.

By christening it The Factory, Warhol claimed continuity with the building's past. This was reinforced with statements about wanting to be a machine and to delegate work, and by screen-printing with professionally made photo-stencils. The myth did not entirely correspond to reality, as there was initially arduous manual work that wouldn't have been out of place in Diderot's *Encyclopédie*. The first new project involved Warhol and assistant Gerard Malanga painting and screen-printing around 400 plywood boxes with the livery of Campbell's soups, Brillo pads, etc. They worked on the floor, round the clock, for about three months. Malanga said he had never worked harder. According to one observer, it looked like 'a production line in a surrealist sweat shop'.[35] The production process wasn't totally streamlined, however, and Warhol exploited chance effects and controlled accident. Warhol is easier to understand as a printmaker like Rembrandt, creating multiples in many different states, than as a painter. However, Rembrandt didn't work on the floor or have a Malanga, and for the later portraits Warhol rarely did more than take a photograph.

The Factory decor was Janus-faced too, looking camply backwards as well as futuristically forward. Warhol had gone to 'haircutting parties' at the apartment-cum-salon of hairdresser and theatre lighting designer Billy Linich (later Billy Name).[36] Every surface was covered in tinfoil and silver spray paint, and there was strobe lighting. Warhol made a series of *Haircut* films and asked Name to decorate The Factory, turning it into the Silver Factory: 'It must have been the amphetamine but it was the perfect time to think silver. Silver was the future, it was spacey – the astronauts .... And silver was also the past – the Silver Screen .... And maybe more than anything else, silver was narcissism – mirrors were backed with silver.'[37] It was a windowless hall of mirrors, a beatnik Versailles. As in Bandinelli's Belvedere academy, the beautiful views were inside. It was a perpetual night studio, with non-naturalistic screen-printing done by artificial light. More prosaically, silver foil insulated a cold building, just as silver suits insulated astronauts.

There had long been crossover between artists' studios and hairdressing salons (a French term anglicized in around 1900). In 1917, Harrods Hairdressing Salons were advertised as 'enshrined in an atmosphere of refinement and artistic comfort'.[38] The hairdresser as an artist of genius, a Pygmalion sculpting the heads of modern Galateas, goes back to the late 18th century, when French hairdressers called their shops *académies de coiffure* – an upstart move that the fine-artist members of the Académie Royale tried to ban.[39] The rapidly balding Warhol would not have required a haircut from Name, as he wore toupees and then wigs from the mid-1950s onwards. He was being a voyeur of haircuts, and his silver salon-studio may have represented a lost paradise. He wore silver wigs to match his decor, self-sculpting his head, and in the 1980s gave a wig to graffiti artist Jean-Michel Basquiat as a work of art. The critic David Bourdon considered Warhol 'a combination of hairdresser, make-up man and studio photographer' who transformed his sitters into 'glamorous apparitions'.[40]

Name also supplied the red velvet sofa in Art Deco style that became the most famous piece of furnishing in any artist's studio (overleaf). He found it dumped in the street and rolled it into the Factory freight lift. It stars in many photographs and films from the Silver Factory era, including the pornographic *Couch*, and was often used as a bed. It too undermined the heroic, all-American factory ideal. Comfy sofas sometimes appear in male artists' studios, but they are never usually depicted using them – the idea being that they are for female models and visitors. Monet doesn't touch his in Henri Manuel's famous photographs, whereas Madame de Pompadour sits happily

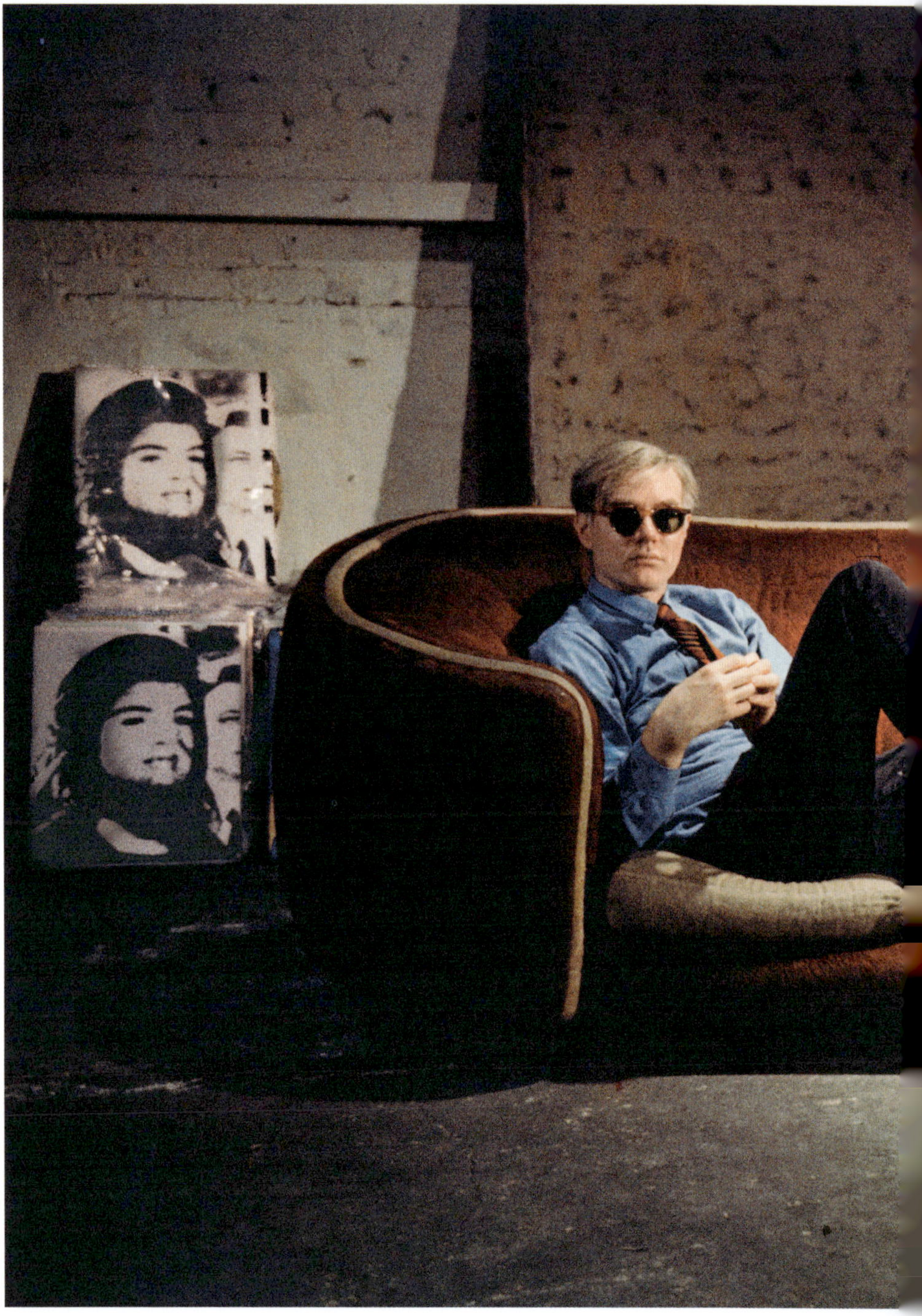

Bob Adelman, *Andy Warhol on the Red Couch at The Factory*, New York City, 1964.

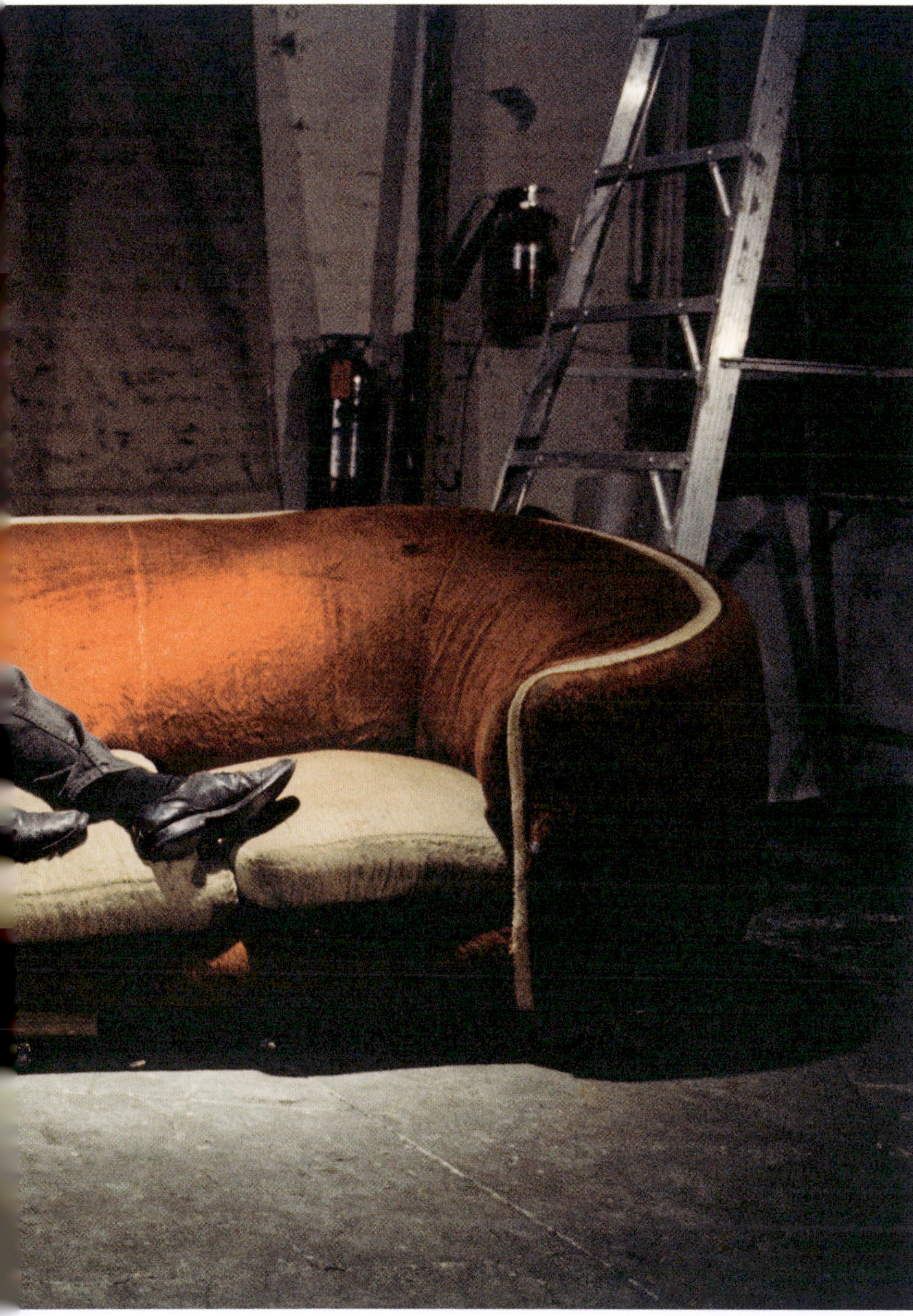

on hers in Drouais's portrait. In 1953, Thomas Hess derided those artists that 'like to work from an easy chair which is riveted to a concrete slab which is anchored to the center of the earth. Others, and among them De Kooning, prefer to keep off-balance.'[41]

It was in fact Pompadour-era Rococo designers who first made sofas with arms that curved inwards.[42] Sofas were immediately gendered as female. William Cowper's moralizing anti-luxury poem *The Task* (1785) was written after a lady's request for a poem extolling the virtues of sofas. Cowper instead claimed sofas had been invented to gratify ladies and libertines: 'The sofa suits/the gouty limb' (1: 107–8). So when Warhol casually reclined on his sofa, wearing a French sailor shirt, he challenged ingrained stereotypes about gender, nationality and status. He also allowed himself to be photographed lying on the floor. Warhol was in fact a workaholic who did not live or sleep in The Factory.

Warhol had to vacate The Factory on 31 October 1967, prior to the building's demolition. He moved downtown to Union Square, to the sixth floor of a 19th-century building with Moorish trimmings. The couch was lost in transit. There were three tall windows at the front of the new premises, providing natural light for rubber plants and cacti, and polished wood floors. The emphasis now was on swanky office space, with large desks at the front, their baize tops covered in glass. There were white telephones. Employees wore black suits. Warhol wanted the space to be called a studio rather than The Factory: it was described as 'an office, or more like a funeral parlour'.[43] In the spring of 1968, he announced: 'The new art is business.' The office was the new factory, symbolized by the white telephone (at the Bauhaus, Moholy-Nagy had claimed to have ordered a series of porcelain enamel paintings from a local factory entirely over the phone). Now full of computers, the office today remains an essential component of the vast subcontracting empires of Jeff Koons and Damien Hirst.

Chapter 15

Inside/Outside

Studios for Nomads

In October 1849, Gustave Courbet (1819–1877) was planning his next big-hitting Salon shockers, *The Stonebreakers* and *Burial at Ornans*. He intended to paint them in his beloved home town of Ornans, using local people and landscapes. But he needed a larger studio, more like his new one in Paris. The latter was located at the apse end of the former chapel of the Collège des Prémontrés (1618), near the Sorbonne on the Left Bank. After the Revolution, the chapel had been sold and converted into a two-storey building. There were three apartments above, usually occupied by artists, and a café below. A friend called it Courbet's 'legendary studio … that temple of the new artistic religion'.[1] Courbet had previously occupied the nearby chapel of the Collège Narbonne, which became damp during the winter, forcing him to replace the inefficient sheet-iron stove with a second-hand ceramic one.[2]

Ornans was a small agricultural town in the fiercely independent Franche-Comté region, on the border with Switzerland. Courbet's father was a wealthy landowner, and the artist often went home for the summer. Asserting regional identity and dignity would be a central feature of his boldly painted, epic-scale narratives. In Paris, he brought country to city by playing up his provincial accent and adopting a gauche manner. He insisted on his independent and nomadic nature, while not being a lazy dilettante or fraud.[3]

This meant breaking out of the confines of the studio. In one of his many self-dramatizing self-portraits, Courbet is a high-flying young genius lording it over Ornans and the viewer (overleaf). Dressed as a Parisian dandy, with his cute English spaniel, pipe and sketchpad, he is on the lookout for subjects and scenes. Emile Zola's comment about Monet's picnicking pictures is apt: 'Like a true Parisian he takes Paris with him to the countryside.'[4] Courbet

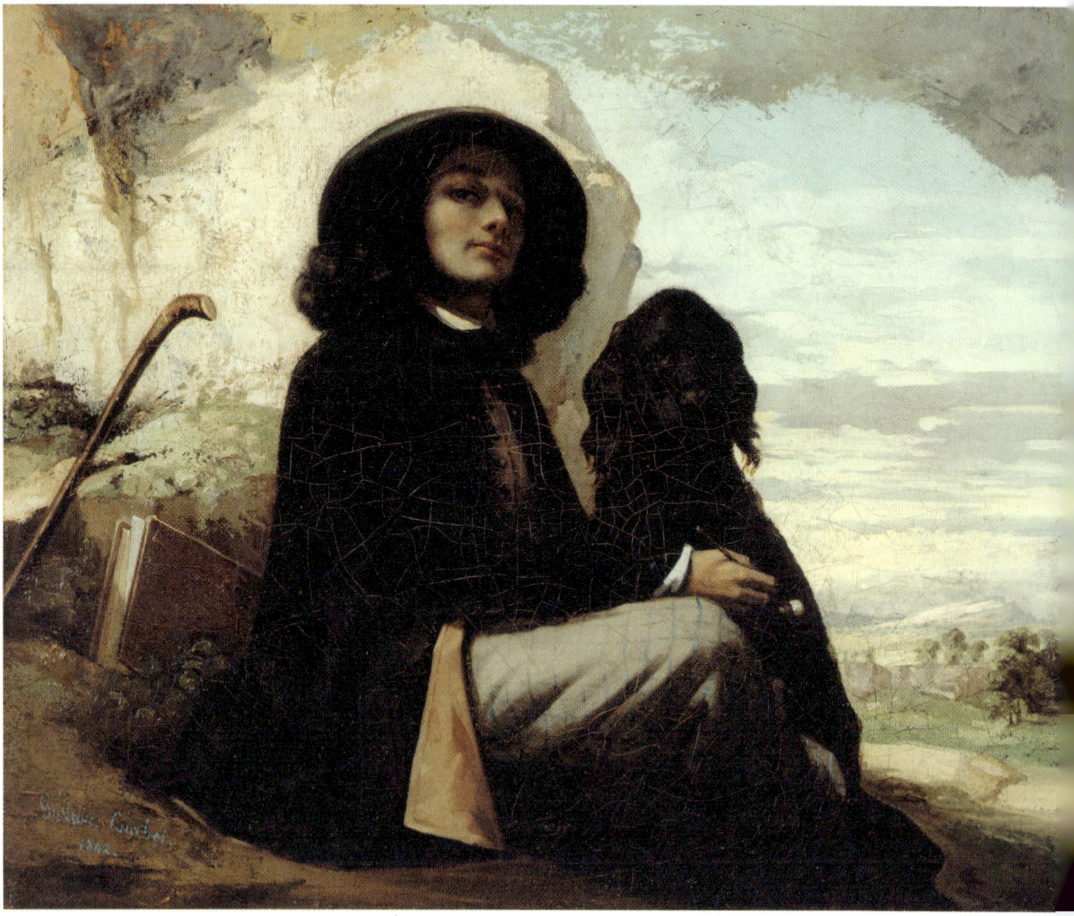

Gustave Courbet, *Self-Portrait with Black Dog*, 1842, oil on canvas.

equally epitomizes advice given to jaded urbanites seeking 'sacred dialogue' with nature: 'Do not worry about staining your new trousers, Monsieur, or about turning your beautiful silk dress green, Madame, stretch out on the thick green grass of this secluded clearing.'[5] Courbet will gladly chafe his clothing on the limestone rocks that halo him. He is an heir to Rousseau, who could work only while walking in the countryside 'with my little paper book and a pencil'; the Forest of Montmorency, north of Paris, was his only 'cabinet and study'.[6]

Courbet's new studio in Ornans would be a literal manifestation of his insider/outsider persona, and of his inside/outside painting practice. It was located in a two-storey laundry inherited by his mother in 1848. He was allowed to convert it, inserting a large window and skylight on the north side: 'Now you can see as clearly as in the street.' The walls were painted 'sombre' greeny-yellow relieved by 'sombre' red, with white window embrasures. The high ceiling and upper quarter of the walls were sky blue: 'That makes for a fantastic effect.'[7] It was like being in the open air.

Because of the vast dimensions of the *Burial* (3.15 by 6.6 metres, or roughly 10 by 22 feet), which had more than forty over-life-size figures, Courbet still complained about the new studio's size, 'only' 5 metres longer than the painting. The studio's 4-metre width made it difficult to stand back to view. He had to find space for his models, whom he painted one at a time: 'Here models are to be had for the asking; everyone wants to appear in the *Burial*.'[8] Ten years later he found a much bigger space, converting a foundry on the outskirts of Ornans. He painted two frescoes of river scenes in a frieze on the upper walls, and this time the sky-blue ceiling was traversed by clouds and swallows.

Courbet's decor chimed with a fashion for airy interiors that evoked open landscapes and skies rather than asserting solid architectural enclosure. From around 1750 it had become fashionable to paint ceilings to resemble a sky with fluffy clouds, sometimes continuing the illusion down the walls into a Chinese-style landscape with figures, open pavilions and kiosks. In around 1800, such schemes fell out of fashion, superseded by a style evoking Pompeian wall decoration with large areas of plain colour (as in the Soane Museum) and contrasting bright borders – hence the distinctive colour scheme in Courbet's first Ornans studio.[9] Sky-blue ceilings, sometimes with clouds and birds, were given new currency with the publication of John Nash's full-colour *Views of the Royal Pavilion, Brighton* (1827), the sybaritic Prince Regent's Chinese-style pleasure palace. The swallows that traversed Courbet's second Ornans studio were one of the most popular bird motifs in Oriental art.[10] Théophile Gautier's love poem 'Chinoiserie' (1838) included the immortal lines, 'She passes her head through the trellis, and is touched by the flying swallow.'[11] When Courbet said the effect of his Ornans ceiling was *fantastique*, he alluded to just such interiors.[12]

***

Courbet's transformation of his studio into a permeable pavilion reflects his working procedure, for he often painted and drew landscapes in the open air, sheltered by an umbrella. He roughly laid them in with a palette knife, then finished them off in the studio. The knife was a conspicuous part of his painter's armoury in a way not seen since the medieval scriptorium. A sculptor friend described the gestation of a Courbet landscape (mid-1860s): he took a 1-metre (3-foot) canvas with him to the site, and a painting box containing four bottles of paint: white, red, yellow and blue. Having mixed them on the palette, he scraped them on with his knife: 'We were stunned by that speed of execution! Barely two hours of work to cover a one-meter canvas.'[13] He could also paint specific landscapes from memory, and loved to demonstrate his skill with the palette knife in front of a studio audience.[14]

Painting outdoors first became common in Italy in the 17th century when Northern European artists went on sketching expeditions in the countryside outside Rome, using their drawings as studies for landscapes and landscape backgrounds to be painted later in the studio. Outdoor painting in oil was attempted in the 1630s but did not become widespread until the end of the 18th century.[15] Specialist portable equipment such as the Claude glass, painting box, drawing frame (similar to Leonardo's in Chapter 7), camera obscura and camera lucida were developed.[16] Parasols or 'sketching umbrellas', sun hats and revolvers (for robbers, snakes, wolves and dinner) were also crucial. Oil paint could be stored ready-mixed in bottles or bags made from sections of pig's bladder and, from the 1840s, in glass syringes and collapsible metal tubes that prevented the paint drying out.

The caravans of foreign artists in the Roman countryside were caricatured by the Swedish watercolourist Carl Jacob Lindström: the long-haired, floppy-clothed German Nazarene (opposite) has come all this way with his painting box to paint a single flower, in keeping with Wackenroder's belief that art is 'the flower of human emotion'.[17] His more worldly mountain dog keeps watch for predators.

The rise of the 'umbrella studio' necessitated a demonstrable increase in the physical exertion of painters. As such, it usefully countered John Locke's complaints in his influential treatise *Some Thoughts Concerning Education* (1693) that learning to paint is a waste of 'Time, Pains and Money' for a gentleman because it is 'a sedentary Recreation, which more employs the Mind than the Body'. Locke recommended 'Gardening or husbandry' and 'working in wood, as a carpenter, joiner, or turner'. Amateur painting and drawing in Britain became a female preserve.[18] Locke's criticism transformed painting practice inside as well as outside the studio, giving rise to conspicuously non-sedentary painters such as Joshua Reynolds, esteemed as the first easel painter to always stand. He continuously walked backwards and forwards, which was only appropriate as many of his full-length portraits had landscape

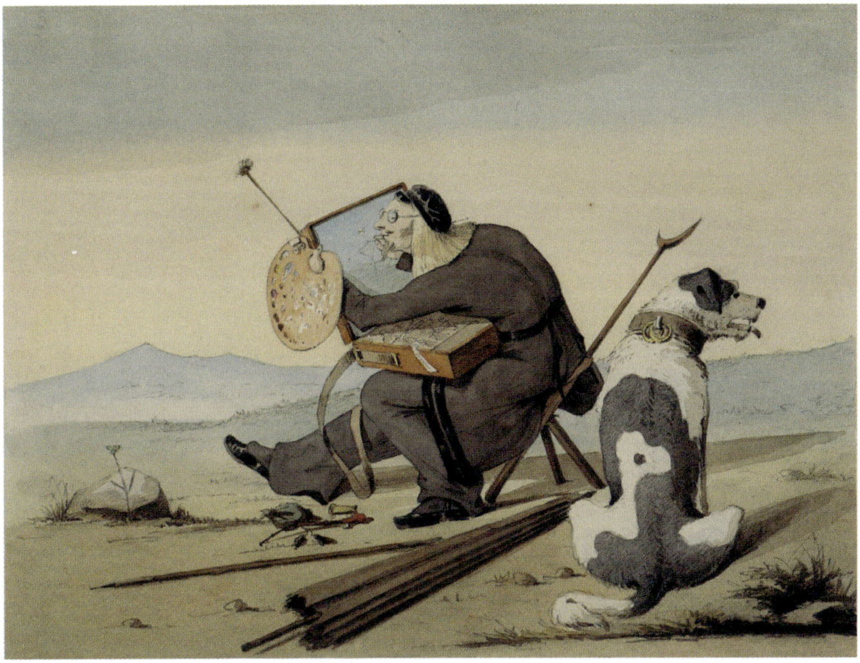

Carl Jacob Lindström, *The German Painter*, 1840, watercolour.

settings. Whistler and John Singer Sargent were equally energetic in the studio, as well as working in the open air.[19]

With the rise of tourism and nationalism, interest had grown in depictions of local scenery. The French Revolutionary and Napoleonic Wars (1792–1815), which made Rome less accessible, only intensified this trend.[20] Guidebooks told artists where to go in regions including the Lake District (from 1773) and the Forest of Fontainebleau (from 1837). The latter was 63 kilometres (39 miles) from Paris – from 1849, an hour's train journey. Its primordial, chaotic array of sandstone boulders and oak trees became the new cast collections and Roman ruins. It was 'a vast atelier of our young artists', according to a guidebook of 1839.[21] The peripatetic peasant painter Jules Breton memorably captured the scene: 'Every morning we set out to make the conquest of some new motif, and our umbrellas were seen like a crop of gigantic mushrooms, dotting the field in the sunshine.'[22] The Barbizon School of landscape and peasant painters was named after a village on the edge of the forest where an artists' colony was established in 1843. It was there that Eugène Bléry pioneered etching from nature by cutting directly onto a copper plate, a method that Whistler would make his own.[23]

Nature had also invaded some studios. The animal painter Rosa Bonheur acquired a château on the edge of the forest in 1860. Living there with her long-term female companion, she dressed in men's clothing and took a gun with her on painting expeditions. She had brought a 'Noah's Art' of animals with her from Paris that included horses, goats, lapwings and monkeys (below). A squirrel lived 'like a hermit' inside a plaster cast of the goddess Diana, an iconoclastic indication of changed priorities.[24] She even acquired some lions. In 1861–2 cows, bulls and peasants modelled in Courbet's short-lived Realist art school in Montparnasse.[25]

Franche-Comté comes to Paris and stages a coup in Courbet's great manifesto picture, *The Painter's Studio: A Real Allegory Summing up a Seven-Year Phase of My Artistic Life* (1854–5; opposite).[26] It is set in his Paris chapel studio but was painted in Ornans. Courbet loved to paint in a party atmosphere. A friend wrote that he 'was pleased to surround himself with large groups of idlers; he would keep on painting, smoke his pipe and, from time to time,

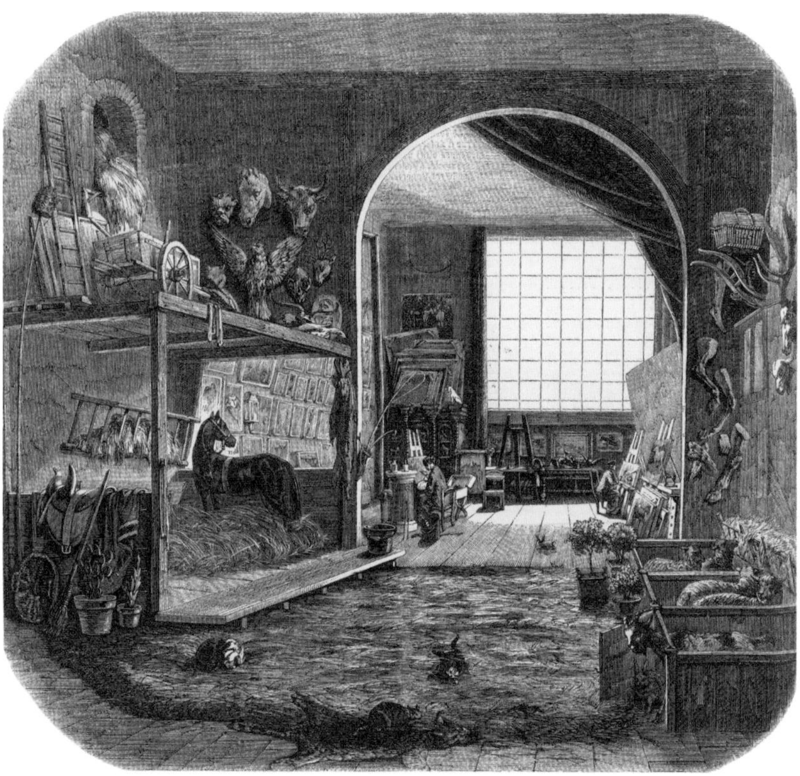

The Studio of Rosa Bonheur, engraving from *L'Illustration*, 1 May 1852.

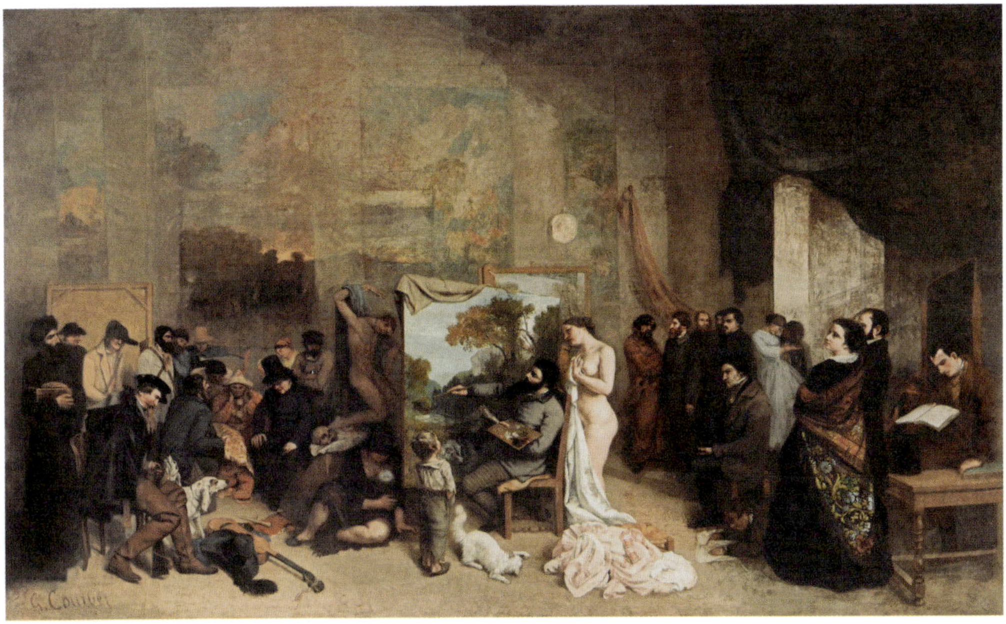

Gustave Courbet, *The Painter's Studio : A Real Allegory Summing up a Seven-Year Phase of My Artistic Life*, 1854–5, oil on canvas.

drink some beer'. Another mentions him singing 'with his falsetto voice'.[27] But here the Prince of Painters occupies a peaceful Franche-Comté realm, seemingly oblivious to his twenty-eight visitors as he puts finishing touches to a landscape. The back partition wall dissolves into clouds, sky, rocks and trees. Courbet initially planned to depict some of his pictures stacked and hung against the wall, but lack of time and an inspired change of mind persuaded him to leave the images unframed, incomplete, evanescent, their skies overflowing, engulfing everything.

When this work was first shown in Courbet's self-financed Pavilion of Realism at the Universal Exhibition in Paris, Delacroix was so impressed he stayed an hour. But one thing perplexed him: 'It looks a though there were a *real sky* in the middle of the painting.'[28] Critic Paul Mantz complained that Courbet assumed that buildings 'had neither roof nor walls'. It is, of course, an *effet fantastique*, and the pavilion itself, designed by the architect Léon Isabey, had Chinese-style trelliswork and a garden with lilacs at the entrance.[29] We don't know if Courbet was able to paint any sky decoration in his rented Paris studio – he had it whitewashed in the spring of 1855[30] – or if its 'Ornanisation' was pure wish-fulfilment.

Courbet acknowledges and overturns many studio conventions in this work. The *mise-en-scène* resembles a triptych altarpiece, only appropriate in a former chapel. The thumbhole of Courbet's palette, and his knife, are dead centre, emphasizing his firm grasp and physical engagement. On the right are his cultured friends, 'the people who serve me, support me in my ideas, and take part in my actions'.[31] They include Baudelaire, engrossed in a book, and a child on the floor, drawing. The portrait heads (including his own) were mostly derived from existing portraits. The figures on the left represented 'the other world of trivial life, the people, misery, poverty, wealth, the exploited and the exploiters, the people who live off death'. These include a Jewish moneylender, Irish beggar-woman with baby, Asian man, priest, clown and hunter. 'It is the world that comes to me to be painted,' he boasted, while also conceding that 'it is fairly mysterious, it will keep people guessing'. This human Noah's Ark is a combined limbo, hell, purgatory and paradise, with Courbet as Dante or God. 'Courbet saving the world,' Baudelaire observed in his notebook.[32]

The studio is a chaste space, with minimal seating, few drapes, no upholstery or knick-knacks. Courbet turns his back on the female model. The most prominent studio property is a mannequin posed like Saint Sebastian. Courbet considered himself a martyr to the cause of art and leftist politics, so this must be an ironic alter ego rather than an obsolete academic helpmate (he used mannequins throughout his career). Critics and cartoonists mocked the doll-like stiffness of Courbet's figures, including the peasant picture behind the mannequin.[33] The nude female model – much admired by Delacroix – was based on a photograph and fond memories. At far right, behind Baudelaire, looms a large swing mirror with the dark backing of a Claude glass. Initially Baudelaire's mixed-race mistress Jeanne Duval, his 'black Venus', was depicted gazing into it, but Courbet painted her out. The mirror sets the tone. Only a few areas of the foreground are brightly lit, and the background has had the tone lowered and detail reduced as if filtered through a Claude glass.

Courbet initially planned to include several casts, but only one made it into the final picture. At first sight, the roughly octagonal white object suspended from a nail on the back wall resembles one of those bullet-hole Turner suns, surrounded by misty landscape traces. It is in fact a low-relief sculpture of a female head in the style of Bernini's *Proserpine*, the goddess of winter and spring, who looks up and back over her shoulder as she is dragged off to the underworld. 'Proserpine' appears to look up at a thin vertical strip of trees and sky comparable to an Oriental hanging scroll. We can adapt Gautier: 'She passes her head through the wall, and is touched by the trees and sky.' Courbet tries to enter the spring landscape that he is finishing. He presses his body up against his canvas so his leg seems almost to step into it.[34] His paintbrush touches the thatched roof of a riverside hut, an ideal studio for a modern nature painter, and for the innocent child of nature at Courbet's side. It is a primitive counterpart to Protogenes' garden cottage and to Rousseau's purpose-built house in the Forest of Montmorency called the Hermitage.

Even the silver-grey window embrasure on the far right has become a primordial landscape: the undulating shape made by the draped curtain resembles the summit of a famous 'obelisk' rock on the river Meuse that Courbet painted the following year.[35] It is not just humanity that comes to his studio to be painted; mountains and sky move there too, making it a true microcosm.

***

Working in nature's 'vast atelier' was demanding – but that only added to the attraction.[36] Van Gogh's *The Painter on the Road to Tarascon* (1888; destroyed 1945) is a classic image of extreme art tourism: a Northern urban artist strives to immerse himself in Mediterranean nature and culture (overleaf). Van Gogh had gone to the rural backwater of Arles to establish a male artists' colony, along the lines of the Nazarenes. The ground-floor studio room in the Yellow House, his 'studio of the south', had whitewashed walls decorated with Japanese prints and paintings of sunflowers.

Van Gogh is not simply 'laden with boxes, sticks, a canvas, on the sunny Tarascon road', as he explained in a letter to his brother, Theo. He is an art soldier on campaign, flanked and framed by two tree trunks that create a natural studio. They form a picture-shaped window without walls or glass. His walking stick – and his leg – are given a sabre's curve. Van Gogh believed that the 'souls of places' entered the souls of men and, to this end, 'I plough on my canvases as they do in their fields.'[37] His black shadow ploughs the ground (no other shadows are shown). He sometimes lost the battle: 'I went to Tarascon one day, unfortunately there was so much sun and dust [blown by the cold Mistral wind] that day that I came home empty-handed.'[38] But he will win the war, as this picture attests.

Three years earlier, while living in Nuenen, the Netherlands, Van Gogh had laid his open-air exploits on thick for Theo:

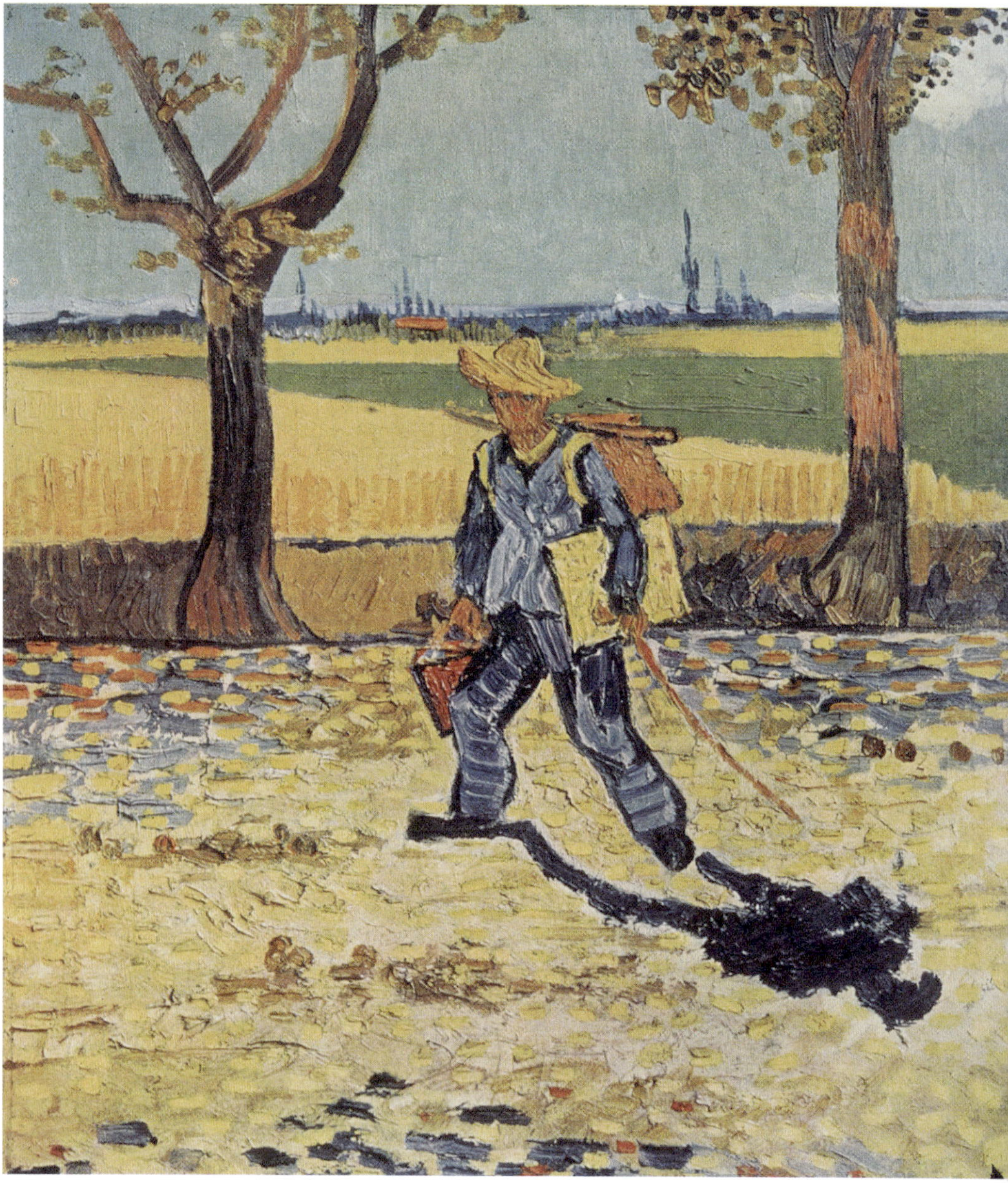

Vincent van Gogh, *The Painter on the Road to Tarascon*, 1888, oil on canvas. Presumed destroyed 1945.

> But just go and sit outdoors, painting on the spot itself! Then all sorts of things like the following happen – I must have picked a good hundred flies and more off the 4 canvases that you'll be getting, not to mention dust and sand &c. – not to mention that, when one carries them across the heath and through hedgerows for a few hours, the odd branch or two scrapes across them &c. Not to mention that when one arrives on the heath after a couple of hours' walk in this weather, one is tired and hot ...[39]

Not to mention, we should add, that oil paints reflect sunlight, blinding the painter; not to mention that there can be wind and rain ...[40] For Van Gogh and many other open-air artists, their chosen vocation was penitential hard labour, just as work had been after the Fall of Man.

For the less diehard or youthful, booking a room with a view, or renting a studio with a view, became a convenient shortcut as long as it wasn't a fleapit. Studio scenes with a nice view through a window were a new 19th-century genre.[41] From the windows of Whistler's Chelsea studio on the river Thames in the 1860s, he could 'paint what he wanted. Only the road separated the house from the river; opposite was Battersea Church and a group of factory chimneys; old Battersea Bridge stretched across, and at night he could see the lights of Cremorne [Gardens].'[42] During the winter, the American landscape painter Winslow Homer (1836–1910) painted from the balcony of his converted seaside carriage house in Prouts Neck, Maine. When Van Gogh first arrived in Arles, he used a canopied roof terrace at the Hotel-Restaurant Carrel as a studio.[43]

Boats were used as mobile studios. Willem van de Velde (1611–1693) had been the great pioneer, going to sea to record Dutch naval battles, becoming the first war artist. He drew the Battle of Scheveningen in 1653 from the deck of his galliot, a small Dutch sailing vessel. But boat studios became far more common in the 19th century. In 1838, the Russian Chernetsov brothers travelled down the Volga on a barge, making landscape sketches for a 700-metres (nearly half a mile) long panorama that they gave to Tsar Nicholas I.[44] J. M. W. Turner first used a converted rowing boat along the Thames and its tributaries in 1805–6.[45] More alarmingly, in 1842 he claimed he had had himself tied to a ship's mast for four hours to observe a snowstorm.[46] Scholars are sceptical because Turner was 67, and in 1822 the battle painter Horace Vernet had painted a picture illustrating a similar story told about

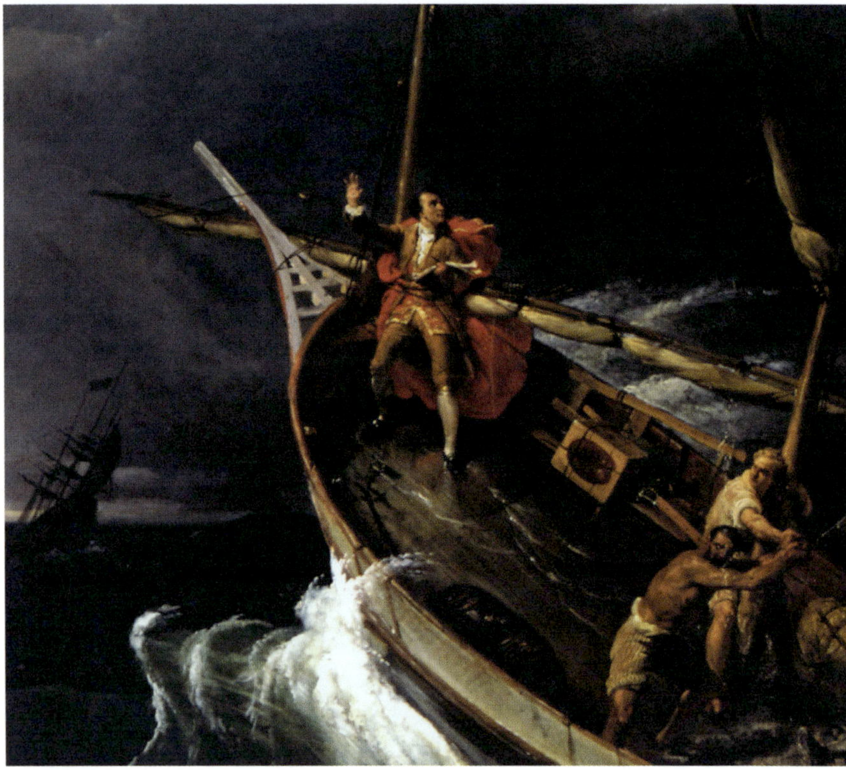

Horace Vernet, *Joseph Vernet Tied to a Mast in a Storm* (detail), c. 1822, oil on canvas.

his landscape-painter grandfather. During a storm at sea, 'contemplating with rapture the terrible scene unfolding in front of his eyes, he entrusted both to his memory and to his notebook the fleeting effects of a stormy sky and of a raging sea'.[47] The embattled artist, whose painting box and easel lie on the deck out of reach, resembles mezzotint prints of David Garrick acting King Lear on the heath. This even beats Bernini burning his thigh on the studio stove. The previous year, Vernet had depicted himself fencing in his own studio while holding palette and brushes, the acme of the non-sedentary painter.[48]

The best-documented boat studio is that of the Barbizon painter Charles-François Daubigny (1817–1878). In 1857 he equipped an 8.5-metre (28-foot) ferry boat with a cabin studio, baptizing it *Le Bottin*, and rowed along the rivers Oise, Marne and Seine. He was probably inspired by Roger Fenton's famous 'photographic van', a converted wine-merchant's van. Accompanied by an assistant, photographer Marcus Sparling, Fenton had shipped this vehicle to the Crimea in 1855 crammed with thirty-six boxes of equipment and glass photographic plates. It had areas for cooking, living and sleeping, and a darkroom that became unbearably hot and dangerously fumy because it had to be sealed. The van was conspicuous, drawing Russian fire. A reproductive engraving derived from one of Fenton's photographs was printed in the *Illustrated London News* in 1855, when the war photographs were exhibited in London. The accompanying article called it 'the studio of battle' and praised Fenton's exertions for proving that photography was no easy, soft option. Fenton had photographed Britain's French allies, and was immediately asked to visit Emperor Napoleon III.[49]

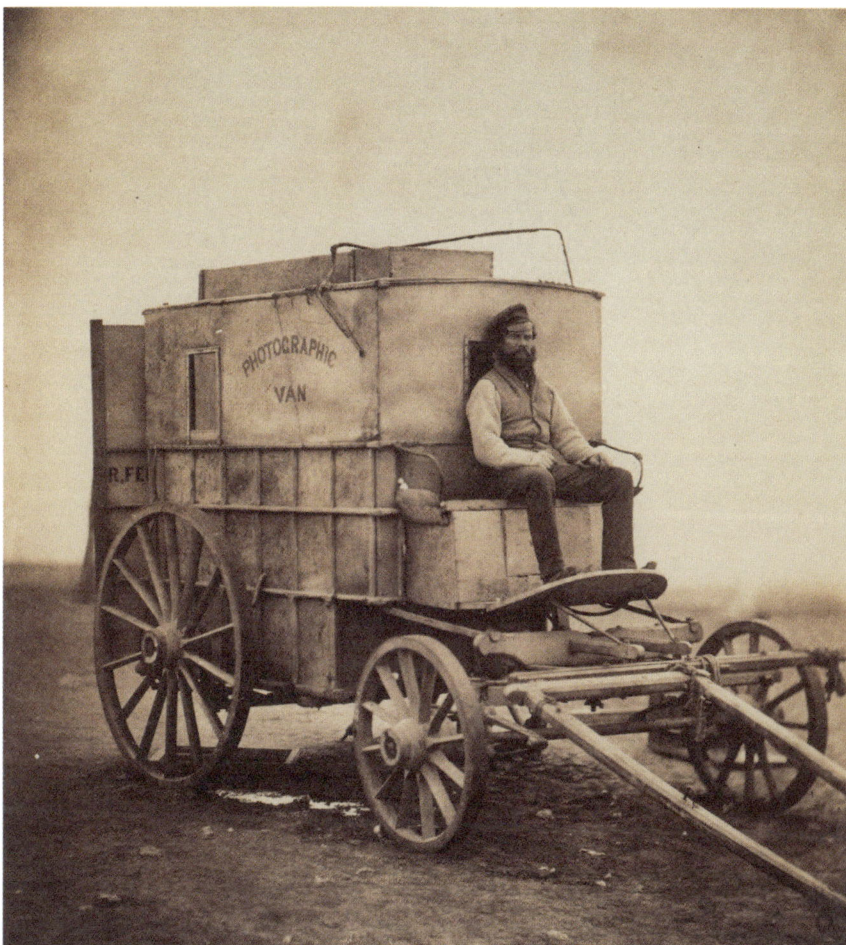

Roger Fenton, *Photographic Van, with Marcus Sparling*, 1855, albumen print.

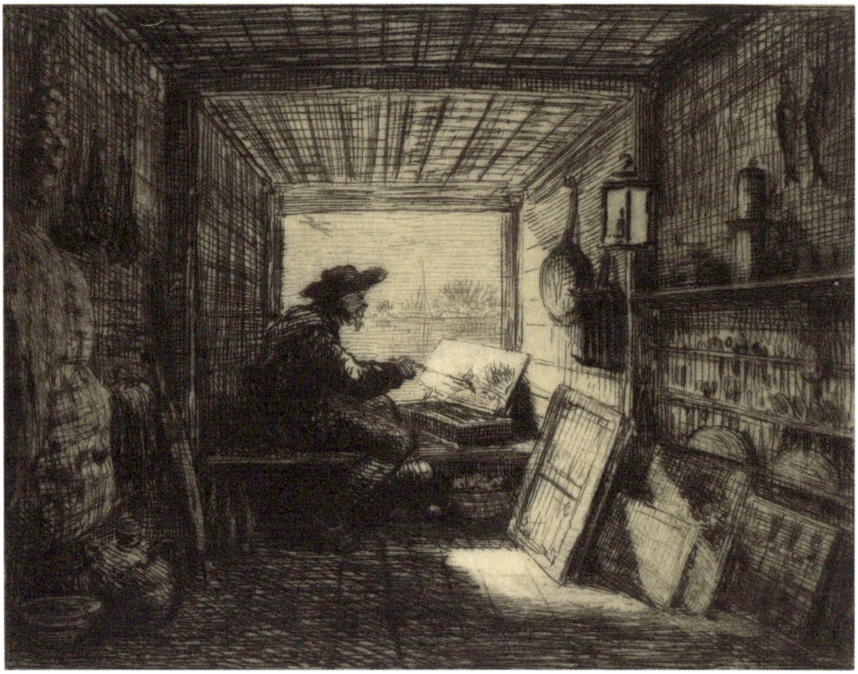

Charles-François Daubigny, *The Boat Studio*, from the series *The Boat Trip*, 1862, etching.

In 1862, Daubigny celebrated and mythologized his slightly less perilous boating expeditions in a series of fifteen Rembrandtian etchings, with his son Karl as cabin boy.[50] Their campaign lasted several days and included comic episodes: on-board boozing, a cowherd doing a moony at them, bird shoots, shoals of fish (their main food) jumping for joy when they leave. There are mundane episodes of meals, sleep, fishing and peasant life, and a dramatic Vernet-style incident when *Le Bottin* is nearly capsized by a passing steamboat. Some scenes are sketched in, others more densely worked, suggesting different times of day, moods and speeds. There are four nocturnal scenes lit by lanterns.

Daubigny twice depicts himself painting, alone and intensely absorbed (he doesn't depict the moment when he fell overboard after stepping back to look at a canvas). There is a loosely drawn panorama, with the artist a tiny speck on deck before his easel; and a densely worked, plunging perspectival view of the cabin interior, with the painter before his painting box. The doors have been thrown open, creating a square prospect. It is a self-contained grotto-cum-garret, with canvases, tools, bottles, food and cooking utensils lining the walls. Daubigny's clothes and wide-brimmed hat look Dutch Golden Age.

Even at his most intense, Daubigny doesn't forget his sense of humour. The canvas at bottom right consists of three identically spaced trees, echoing the items in the racks above. It has 'realisme' inscribed on it in childish letters, taunting critics who complained of the monotony and banality of his 'impressionistic' work.[51] This gives a clue as to why he called his boat *Le Bottin*.[52] A 'bottin' is the French word for a commercial directory, named after the statistician Sébastien Bottin. Daubigny is creating an illustrated directory of nature.[53] The print would be reproduced in the *Gazette des Beaux Arts* in March 1874, just before the April opening of the first Impressionist exhibition.

***

On 6 November 1886, a regional newspaper reported strange goings on Belle-Isle, 14 kilometres (9 miles) off the coast of Brittany: 'Breton fishermen are astonished to see a man, dressed like them, in oilskins, heavy boots, and sou'wester, stubbornly painting, during the storm, upon canvases fixed to an easel lashed to the rocks with ropes. Often a gust will rip palette and brushes from the hands of the painter, who begins over again without ever becoming discouraged. This is Claude Monet, seeking fleeting splendours of the storm. With the same aim, Vernet had himself attached to the mast of a ship.'[54]

A critic added that 'he goes to his work as if going into battle'.[55] That same winter of 1886–7 Monet (1840–1926), who admired Daubigny, would paint in deep snow at Honfleur, wearing three coats and three pairs of gloves. A year earlier, in November 1885, he had been swept away by a wave on the beach at Etretat after misreading the tides, losing everything except his palette, which stuck to his face.[56] These exertions helped compensate for the fact that he was – until the late waterlily canvases – producing what his favourite author Delacroix called 'miserable little pictures' for 'mean little dwellings'.[57] Like the workaholic Emperor Augustus, he got a barber to cut his hair while he painted away in the Creuse in 1889.

The idea that Monet never had a studio was central to his mystique throughout his career, and to the other Impressionists in their early years. 'My studio! But I have never had a studio!' he insisted to a journalist in 1880. 'I don't understand shutting oneself away in a room,' he claimed at his first solo exhibition. A catalogue essay in 1889 concluded: 'The open air is his only studio.' This was patently false, as he always had some sort of studio, and almost always put finishing touches to work indoors after due reflection, in a way that Titian – not to mention Courbet – might have understood:

'I always need a moment of peace and quiet before I can do the final touches,' he confided to his dealer. He signed and dated pictures when they were finished, often a year later.[58]

At Giverny, on the Seine, Monet eventually had four studios, two of which were hung from floor to ceiling with his work. The third studio, constructed at great expense in the garden from 1914–16, was reserved for work on the waterlily pictures. But his largest studio was the Japanese-style garden he meticulously tended and modified. He claimed that painting and gardening were his only two interests. No artist since Rubens had made their own garden central to their identity. A German art historian explained: 'Monet reveals himself best … in the garden he has planted about his country house. He has made it on the same principle as his pictures …. Every individual blossom contributes to the mass of colour.'[59]

Technically, therefore it was true that Monet never had *a* studio, *a* room. Monet had innumerable studios, indoors and out, and frequently had recourse to a 'room with a view'. He rented rooms opposite Rouen Cathedral in 1892–3 and managed to work simultaneously on fourteen canvases; they were completed at Giverny in 1894, when there were over thirty. In London in 1900, he painted views from a luxurious suite at the Savoy Hotel: 'I had up to a hundred canvases under way – of a single subject. By searching feverishly among the sketches, I would choose one which wasn't too far away from what I could see.'[60] He made sure he never gave the game away by letting a window, door frame, or balcony railing intrude on the image.

Monet also had a boat studio, probably on Daubigny's recommendation. He acquired an old fishing boat in 1872, shortly after moving to Argenteuil (1871–8) on the Seine: 'A fair wind had brought me just enough money in one go to buy a boat and have a wooden cabin built on it just big enough to set up an easel.' He made day trips, and took it with him when he moved further down river. In 1883, it accompanied him to Giverny, but after 1890 he got a larger 'broad-bottomed boat fitted with grooves to hold a number of canvases', and sufficient room in the cabin to sleep.[61]

Monet painted his first boat studio five times in the mid-1870s – the only occasion he painted any of his studios – but none of these works shows him painting. Only one image reveals the boat's interior, and it is a longways view redolent of Daubigny. It is seen from a distance, with the lilac cabin doors open at both ends. It is like peering into a camera box. There are no palettes, brushes or canvas to identify the dark figure seated inside, but it must be Monet in one of those quiet, reflective moments.

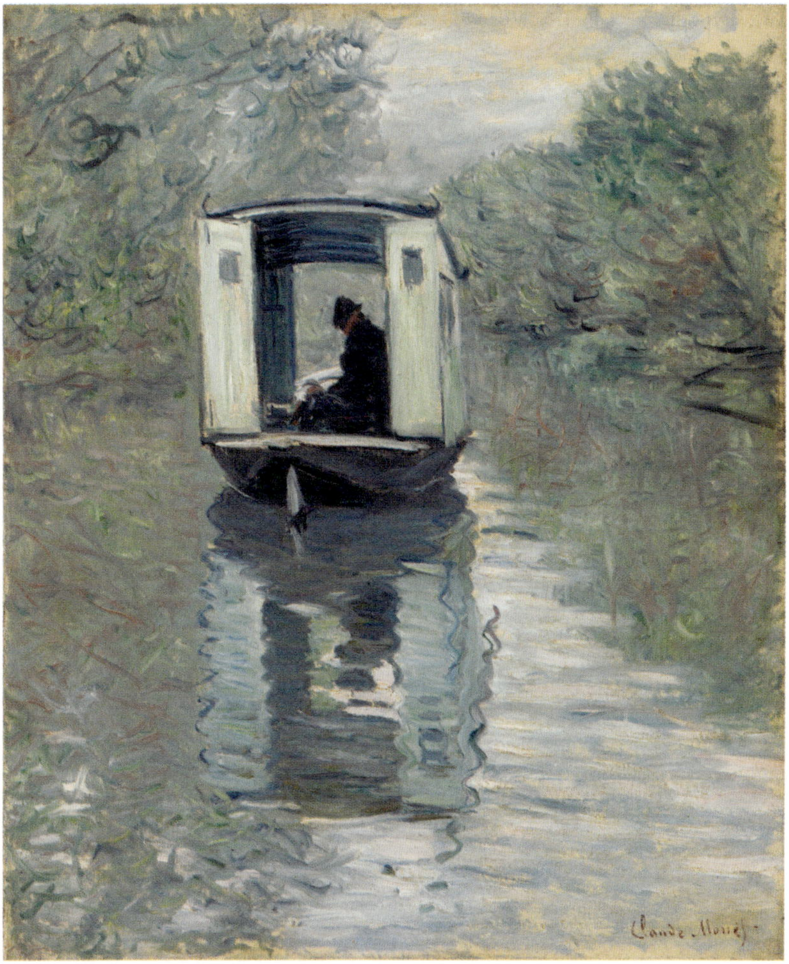

Claude Monet, *The Studio Boat*, 1876, oil on canvas.

This is one of Monet's earliest works to have a mystery at its core (only from around 1890 was Monet's work discussed in relation to Symbolist poetry).[62] Whereas in the four other pictures the boat is under control – being rowed, or moored to poles – here it drifts. The anchor remains on board, its curved arms summarily indicated next to his leg; the rudder is apparently untouched. The boat has drifted disconcertingly off centre on the canvas. Monet did sometimes paint with his boat drifting, thereby turning himself into an aquatic *flâneur*, a dandyish observer of nature rather than of society. The boat's reflection is a series of untethered ropey ripples. Rimbaud's Symbolist dream poem 'Le Bateau ivre' (Drunken Boat, 1871) comes to mind.

The 'impassive rivers' let the poet sail where he wants but then, having reached the sea, his anchor and rudder are lost: 'And from then on I bathed in the Poem/Of the Sea, infused with stars, and lactescent,/Devouring the azure verses; where, like a pale elated/Piece of flotsam, a pensive drowned figure sometimes sinks ...'.[63]

Monet's picture celebrates his ecstatic escape from the prison of the static urban studio.

***

In the wake of Courbet's skyscape studios, the blue-grey studio would become a trademark of Realist-Impressionist painters. Frédéric Bazille's depiction of the studio in Paris that he shared with Renoir (opposite) has sky-blue walls, dark blue curtains and a pale grey floor and ceiling – impossibly eggshell-smooth, like modern polished concrete. These echo the colours of sky and buildings seen through the enormous window.[64]

Floor-to-ceiling windows increased the 'open-air-ness' of painters' studios. Light no longer came channelled from on high, spiritualized. And why should it, when artists were painting 'everyday' secular subjects? Bazille's curtains do not allow part-closure of the window's lower section. Massive windows like Bazille's and Rosa Bonheur's were made possible by advances in the manufacture of sheet glass. French glass-makers had provided much of the knowhow for the Crystal Palace at London's 1851 Great Exhibition.[65] In England, repeal of the dreaded window tax in the same year further fuelled the boom. Prefab garden studios in iron and glass were pioneered by Bellhouse & Co. of Manchester in 1855.[66] The Bauhaus would be the Crystal Palace of studio-workshops.

Manet is the bowler-hatted man discussing Bazille's latest open-air picture. The identities of the three figures on the left are much debated. Monet probably stands behind Manet, with Renoir seated and Zola on the stairs. Bazille did not initially depict himself, so Manet took his paintbrush and added the tall, willowy figure with a palette. It is a double-edged tribute because Manet's portrait sketch obliterates Bazille's own picture, *View of the Village*, with a girl in a pink dress sitting on a hillside. Manet had mixed feelings about being imitated by his many followers, and was exasperated at being confused with Monet because of the similarity of their names, subjects and styles.[67] But individuality is here largely subsumed under a collective identity.

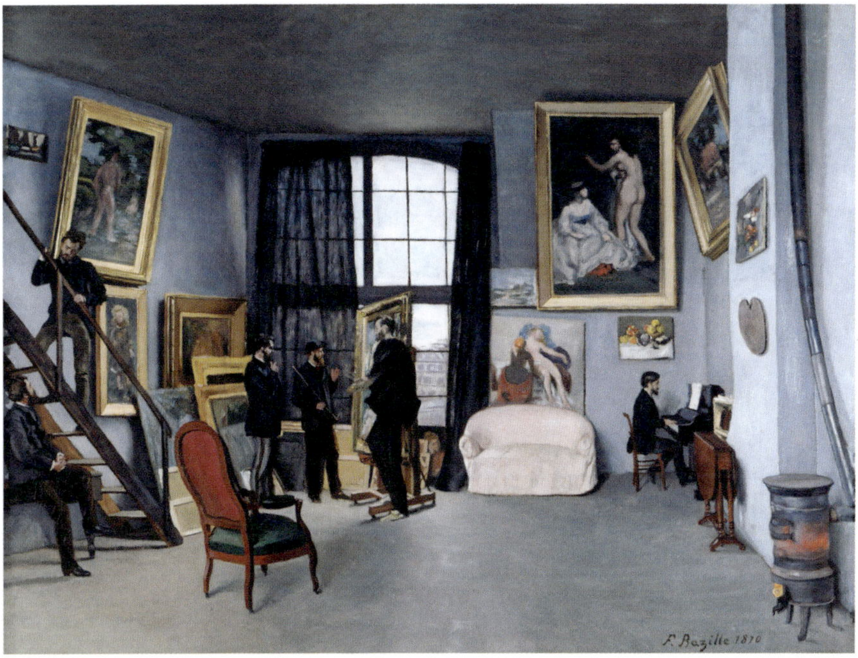

Frédéric Bazille, *Bazille's Studio*, 1870, oil on canvas.

Many of the figure paintings, including Renoir's *Landscape with Two Women* at top right, had been turned down for the Salon. All bar one are set in the open air, and the models strike the 'natural' poses advocated in a series of manuals by the reformer of art education Horace Lecoq de Boisbaudron (1802–1897).[68] Boisbaudron recommended dispensing with the life-room podium and ropes, and letting clothed and nude models walk freely, not just around the room but outdoors in the countryside. He devised a series of techniques whereby the artist could memorize usable but fleeting natural positions and expressions.[69] His former student Rodin told his roving models to freeze when they chanced upon a good position and often used amateur models, like Camille Claudel and Gwen John. The men in Bazille's studio are a masterclass in Boisbaudronism as all seem animated in an unselfconscious way, thereby echoing the uninhibited, mobile ethos of the pictures.

Everything in the studio except the green armchair is pushed against the walls to encourage perambulation and discourage social sitting. The armchair and flesh-pink sofa face each other, elegant elephants in the room, symbols of upholstered 'feminine' comfort that every self-respecting man avoids in public. The reclining nude in Bazille's unfinished *La Toilette* is the same colour as the sofa below it, underlining their affinity. The armchair, which Bazille considered his 'only luxury',[70] is an 18th-century type called a *fauteuil à la reine* (queen's armchair).

Renoir perches on the edge of a table, ready to spring into action. He chats to Zola as he climbs the stairs. No one seeks refuge near the glowing stove.

***

Painting from nature went out of avant-garde fashion in the wake of Cubism and non-objective art, though traditional open-air painters could now make use of cars. In the 1930s, Laura Knight set up her easel in the back of a huge Rolls-Royce parked at various English racecourses, the door propped open framing a view.[71] But the inside/outside studio took on a new lease of life after 1945.

Jackson Pollock's Long Island barn, now a museum, was a unique attempt to unify nature and art. Artist and studio became famous because of a striking series of photographs taken by Hans Namuth in 1950 and a ten-minute film made by Namuth and Paul Falkenberg in 1950–1. The Museum of Modern Art in New York had had a film programme from its founding in the 1930s, but the 1950s would see a significant increase in documentaries, notably Henri-Georges Clouzot's *Le Mystère Picasso* (1955).[72] This was followed by the Technicolor Van Gogh biopic *Lust for Life* (1956). Pollock immediately regretted allowing Namuth in, vulgarizing his methods and dispelling the mystery. He started binge drinking again after a long dry period.

In 1945 Pollock's partner, the painter Lee Krasner (1908–1984), had proposed they leave New York and buy a permanent home in the country.[73] They married in the autumn and bought a clapboard farmhouse with five acres of land in a small fishing village. They painted the interiors white. There was a barn full of farm tools; after eight months, they moved it to allow views of the marshes and bay from the house. A raised wooden floor was then installed in the repositioned barn (6.4 by 6.4 metres, or 21 by 21 feet), but no electricity or heating. Large gaps in the clapboard walls made it resemble a torn architectural carcass. Cold, wind, rain and light could cut through. There were no screens on the high windows. When Namuth arrived to take photographs, 'Blinding shafts of sunlight hit the wet canvas, making its surface hard to see.' Warhol would later mock the fact that Pollock 'was still following the tradition of wanting to get out there alone in the woods'.[74] Only later did Pollock have it insulated.

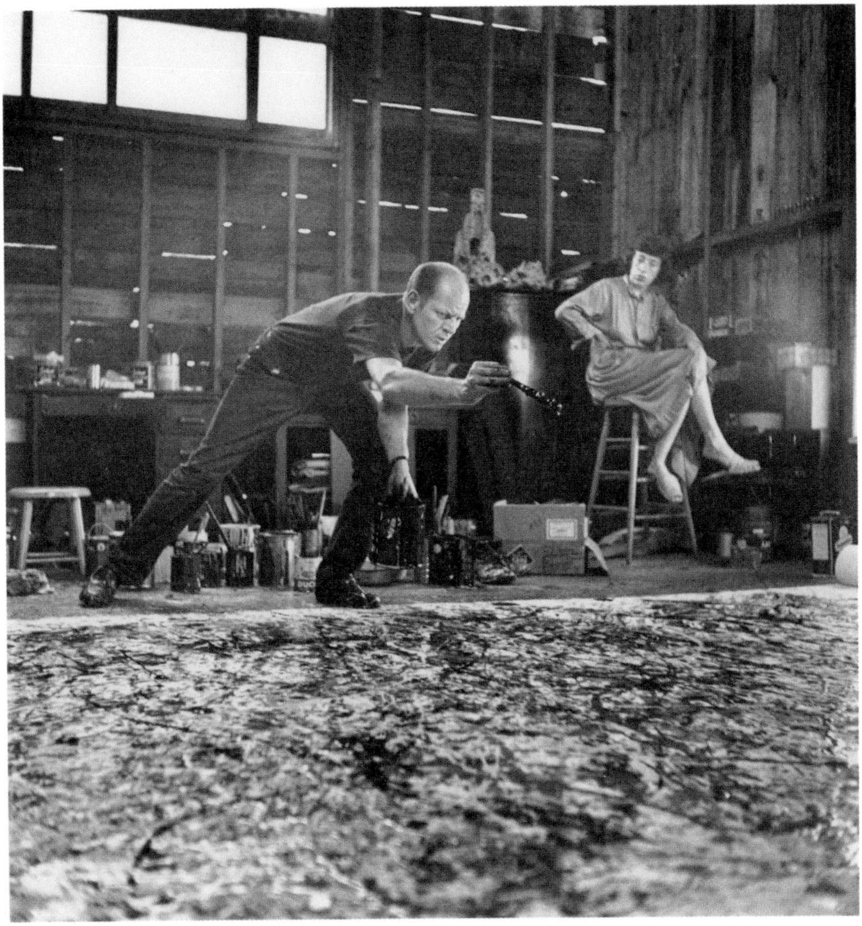

Hans Namuth, *Jackson Pollock and Lee Krasner*, 1950, gelatin silver print.

In the 1930s Pollock had been hugely impressed by the Mexican muralists, and by Gutzon Borglum's exploits on Mount Rushmore. He rejected easel painting, palette and paintbrush: 'My painting does not come from the easel .... I prefer to tack the unstretched canvas to the hard wall or floor. I need the resistance of a hard surface.'[75] To this end he also hoped to make sculpture in his new home, collecting scrap iron and rocks. Moving all around his canvas like a sculptor, he was, as it were, 'painting in the round'.

With its hardness and exposure to the elements, this was a 'studio of battle'. Resistance was an important concept in avant-garde circles, the idea being that unfamiliar materials, tools and situations prevented any academic slickness. In 1948, Picasso explained the development of collage: 'We sought to express reality with materials we did not know how to handle.' Louise Bourgeois's later shift from wood to marble came about because wood 'offers no resistance'. Artists now had to collaborate with truant materials. Pollock used sticks, trowels, knives and house paint and aluminium radiator paint dripped straight from the can, adding sand, broken glass, string, gauze and even cigarette butts. Only if there was 'an easy give and take' could his paintings come out well.[76]

Namuth's photograph is conventional insofar as we have a seated woman and a standing man. But Krasner is above the crouching Pollock, alert and perched in an unusual twisting pose similar to Michelangelo's *ignudi* and the cross-legged Erythraean Sibyl. Pollock and Krasner both admired Michelangelo and made drawings after the *ignudi* in the 1930s. Krasner had adapted the sibyl's pose for a nude life drawing.[77] The carefully contrived, supremely witty set-up suggests this is America's Sistine studio, with Pollock a down-to-earth New World art god creating light and dark.

Namuth filmed Pollock painting outside in the farmyard on a wooden platform, and from below, painting on glass. He thereby upstaged Picasso, who had painted on a Plexiglas panel in his barn studio at Vallauris for the documentary *Visite à Picasso* (1949).

***

From the mid-1950s, many artists were inspired by photographs and films of painters at work to stage dynamic neo-Dadaist performances of art-making in a range of indoor and outdoor spaces. The Pollock-inspired Japanese Gutai group (meaning 'body tool'), founded in 1954, were pioneers in this area. Saburo Murakami ran through paper screens; Kazuo Shiraga rolled around in mud; Murakami Saburo and Shozo Shimamoto threw ink and paint. From 1958, the French artist Yves Klein staged events with 'living paintbrushes': paid female models who undressed in front of an invited audience, covered themselves in blue paint and then pressed their bodies against large canvases or sheets of paper.

The New York artist Allan Kaprow simultaneously claimed Pollock as the progenitor of interactive Happenings. Pollock's dance of 'diaristic gesture' and his embrace of non-art materials and tools meant we must 'become preoccupied with and even dazzled by the space and objects of our everyday lives, either our bodies, clothes, rooms, or, if need be, the vastness of Forty-Second Street'.[78] Multimedia performances implied that artists should now work in New York's 'vast atelier' rather than in private studios, though many of these events took place in specially revamped galleries. In 1964, Lucas Samaras actually rebuilt his 6 by 13 foot (1.8 by 4 metre) bedsit studio inside the Green Gallery in New York, calling it *Room #1*. It found no buyer. Marina Abramović has claimed: 'Good art is never made in studio. Good art I make in life.'[79] Mostly, though, her performances occur in museums and galleries.

In 1968, the land artist Robert Smithson (1938–1973) announced the 'fall of the studio':[80] 'The modern artist in his "studio", working out an abstract grammar within the limits of his "craft", is trapped in but another snare. When the fissures between mind and matter multiply into an infinity of gaps, the studio begins to crumble and fall like the House of Usher ...'.[81]

Edgar Allan Poe's short story of 1839 centres on Roderick Usher, an invalided male painter whom the narrator finds lying at full length on a sofa in a profusely furnished and draped studio. The Gothic windows are too high to look out of or to open, and admit only 'feeble gleams of encrimsoned light'. Usher, his studio and sofa are the epitome of diseased decadence.

Perhaps inspired by the 'infinity of gaps' in Pollock's clapboard barn, Smithson wanted to make art an integral part of natural and material history. Conceptually, it was an industrial-age counterpart to Pliny's *Natural History* and Palissy's *cabinet*. Smithson urged artists to collaborate with contractors and industry in making site-specific 'earthworks'. He made mock-heroic photographic travelogues, traipsing around industrial wastelands and quarries, treating them as the new Rome, and exhibiting quarried rock and documentation in galleries. The fall of the studio was a new Fall of Man, a fortunate expulsion from the safety of the studio into a wilderness that inspired gargantuan levels of creativity (the nascent environmental movement was not impressed). Ironically, Smithson shared an immaculate whitewashed loft studio with his artist wife Nancy Holt on Greenwich Street, New York City.

The 'fall of the studio' has had its most pharaonic incarnation in the German painter-sculptor Anselm Kiefer's 100-acre (40-hectare) studio complex near Barjac in the Cévennes (overleaf).[82] Kiefer moved there in 1992, with seventy lorries bringing the contents of his previous studio, a former brickyard in Germany. This included some old lead from Cologne Cathedral. Kiefer makes vast mixed-media landscape paintings, assemblages and architectural sculptures, all meditations on German history and the passage of time. Using lead, concrete, plant matter, old clothes and assorted detritus, he creates ruins and follies: 'I do not consider ruins as something disastrous; on the contrary they mark the beginning of the reconstruction of a cycle, of circular time.'[83]

The Barjac estate was a silk factory, with a stone manor house and barns where the silk was processed. Kiefer added large pavilions and glasshouses, so there are now over seventy buildings filled with large-scale installations. Some planting was done, and paths laid. He also dug out a labyrinthine underworld of interconnecting tunnels, caves and crypts. These subterranean studios, like purgatorial pit-houses (see page 54), threaten to undermine and dissect the buildings above. 'My tools are not just the brush and the palette knife,' Kiefer says. 'I call upon all kinds of machines, such as cranes, trucks, excavators.'[84] Barjac was a studio, artwork and landscape in perpetual progress. In 2007 Kiefer established a new, main studio in a former department-store warehouse near Paris. However, the Barjac complex remains open for guided tours.

***

Having traced the history of the artist's workplace from ancient Greece to the present day, I am struck by what a hydra-headed creature it is. When Leonardo disavowed dirt and disorder, up popped Michelangelo to heroize mess and sweat. Just as Academicians were creating luxurious temples to high art, Diderot celebrated the empty workshops of 'mere' artisans.

Throughout, there has been a symbiotic relationship between the studio and other spaces, whether they be workshops and scholars' studies or the street, landscape, river, sea and sky. What the future holds is anyone's guess. With carbon footprints coming into the equation, the ideal of the globe-trotting artist (and artwork) is being called into question. On the other hand, in the era of pandemics, the rooted home studio – which may now just be a kitchen table – can feel like a prison. The only certainty is that there will be many more incarnations, and that not all the studios of the future will be swallowed up inside a laptop, smartphone or metaverse.

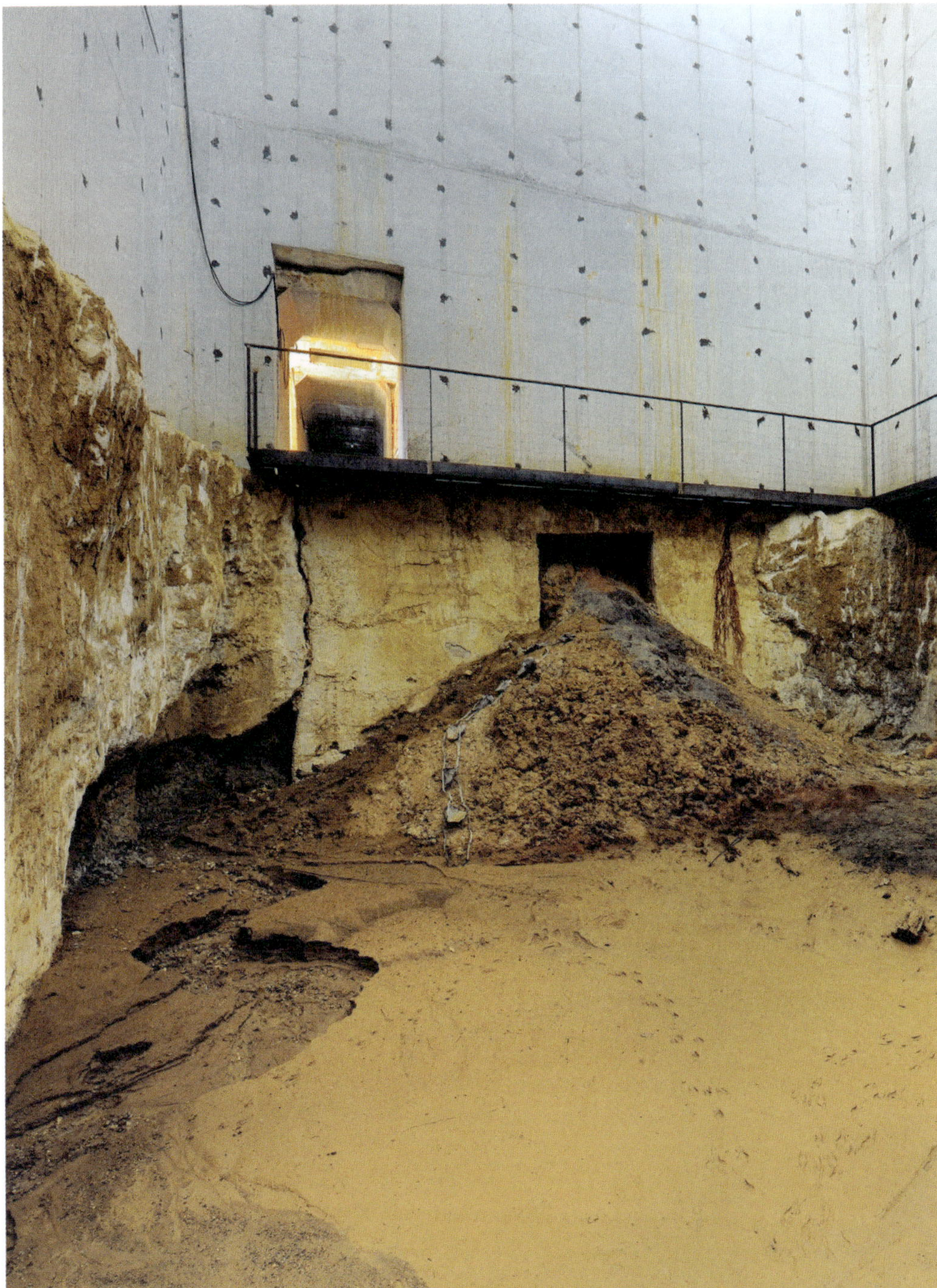

Charles Duprat, *Anselm Kiefer's studio in Barjac, France*, 2011.

Notes

Introduction

1. P. Ogden and J. Edwards, *7 Reece Mews: Francis Bacon's Studio*, London 2001, 13.
2. D. J. Getsy, 'The Reconstruction of Francis Bacon's Studio', *The Studio Reader*, ed. M. J. Jacob and M. Grabner, Chicago 2010, 99–103.
3. P. Thornton, *Authentic Decor*, London 2000.
4. P. F. de Chantelou, *Diary of the Cavaliere Bernini's Visit to France*, ed. A. Blunt et al., Princeton 1985 (hereafter 'Chantelou'), 57, 145, 192, 206.
5. Many of Nauman's videos document actions performed in the studio.
6. *Oxford English Dictionary* (hereafter *OED*), 'Studio'. M. Cole and M. Pardo, *Inventions of the Studio*, Chapel Hill 2005, 3–6.
7. *Trésor de la Langue Française informatisé*: 'Atelier'.
8. *OED*, 'Design C1'.
9. The first major American studio picture is Matthew Pratt, *The American School*, 1765, which shows Benjamin West's London studio. See https://www.metmuseum.org/art/collection/search/11797.
10. E. Kris and O. Kurz, *Legend, Myth and Magic in the Image of the Artist*, New Haven 1979, 38ff.
11. M. McCormick, *The Tale of Genji: A Visual Companion*, Princeton 2018, 89–91.
12. C. Clunas, *Chinese Painting and Its Audiences*, Princeton 2017, 37–83.
13. *Ibid.* 70.
14. Royal Academy inv. 04/502. P. Sohm, 'Palettes as Signatures', *Art History* (November 2017), 1002, for Annibale Carracci's lost self-portrait on a palette.
15. See https://www.theguardian.com/artanddesign/2015/jun/18/marina-abramovic-the-planet-is-dying-we-have-to-be-warriors.

Chapter 1

1. S. P. Morris, *Daidalos and the Origins of Greek Art*, Princeton 1992, 9–15.
2. There are superficial similarities with the Semitic smithy god Kothar. Morris, 80–1.
3. S. Lewis, 'Images of Craft on Athenian Pottery', *Bollettino di Archeologia online* C 4 (2010); E. Z. Dembin, 'Voicing the Past: The Implications of Craft-Referential Pottery', in *The Adventure of the Illustrious Scholar*, Leiden 2018, 537–63.
4. The temple was shared with Athena, another maker god. A. Burford, *Craftsmen in Greek and Roman Society*, London 1972, 82, 166–7, 244, n. 462; F. Brommer, *Hephaistos*, Mainz 1978, 75–90. M. Detienne and J. P. Vernant, *Cunning Intelligence in Greek Culture and Society*, Hassocks 1978, 175–276.
5. M. Delcourt, *Héphaistos*, Paris 1957.
6. A. F. Stewart, *Greek Sculpture: An Exploration*, New Haven 1990, 36.
7. Homer, *The Iliad*, trans. A. Verity, Oxford 2011; subsequent quoted lines from the *Iliad* use the same source. I use 'lame' for Verity's 'crook-footed', l. 371.
8. The Greek word is ἀστερόεντα.
9. Stewart 6; Burford 43.
10. Stewart 6.
11. Burford 28–36.
12. Xenophon, *On Household Management*, 6.3–5.
13. Burford 206.
14. Phidias was also a painter.
15. Stewart 66–7. Pliny, *Natural History*, 24.37, for Lysippos' earnings.
16. Burford 137.
17. Pliny 35.58–9; J. J. Pollitt, *The Art of Ancient Greece: Sources and Documents*, Cambridge 1990, 126.
18. Stewart 33; Pollitt 58–63 for descriptions.
19. Plutarch, *Life of Pericles*, 13.4–9, 31.2–5; Pollitt 53–4.
20. B. Kemp, *The City of Amarna and Nefertiti*, London 2012, 59–60, for thieving.
21. There are many variants – see *Iliad* 1.590 ff.
22. P. Kidson, 'The Figural Arts', in *The Legacy of Greece*, ed. M. I. Finlay, Oxford 1984, 401–28.
23. B. Ramazzini, *Diseases of Workers*, trans. W. Wright, Birmingham, AL 1983, 31, 33, 63, 77, 275–7, 327, 437–9.
24. Ramazzini 17.
25. Kemp 227.
26. Burford 91–2; J. J. Pollitt, *The Art of Rome: Sources and Documents*, Cambridge 1983, 175–6.
27. *The Autobiography of Benvenuto Cellini*, Harmondsworth 1958, 360.
28. *The Treatises of Benvenuto Cellini on Goldsmithing and Sculpture*, London 1898, 95, §25. B. Gopnik, *Warhol*, London 2020, 849–51.
29. Xenophon 4.2–3.
30. R. and M. Wittkower, *Born under Saturn*, New York 1963, 4–6.
31. K. Lapatin, *Luxus: The Sumptuous Arts of Greece and Rome*, Los Angeles 2018.
32. Burford 196–7.
33. Stewart 25, 40–1. N. Penny, *The Materials of Sculpture*, New Haven 1993, 226–30.
34. P. Hills, 'Titian's Fire', *Oxford Art Journal* 30:2 (2007), 194.
35. E. Kris and O. Kurz, *Legend, Myth, and Magic in the Image of the Artist*, New Haven 1979, 39.
36. N. Spivey, *Greek Art*, London 1997, 5.
37. J. Hall, *The Sinister Side*, Oxford 2008, 15; Stewart 54–5, for praise/blame.
38. For a revisionist view, H. Silverblank and M. Ward, 'Why Does Classical Reception Need Disability Studies?', *Classical Receptions Journal* 12:4 (2020), 502–30.
39. O. Michel and P. Rosenberg, *Subleyras 1699–1749*, Paris 1987, 26–7, 96.
40. His eldest son was born in 1742, so too young to be the boy painter in the picture. The toddler's hair may have darkened.
41. 'Vita di Pietro Subleyras', *Memorie per le Belle Arti* 2 (February 1786), 33.
42. See *The Iliad*, 23.740–4.
43. Morris 12.
44. Morris 13–14 stresses that a god is here influenced by a human's work.
45. M. Vidale, 'Le diverse nature del tornio da vasaio nelle immagini della ceramica greca (VI–IV secolo A.C)', *Ocnus* 6 (1998), 117–35.
46. C. Mattusch, 'The Berlin Foundry Cup', *American Journal of Archaeology* 84 (1980), 435–44.
47. Penny 227–8; 41–2, for multi-part marble statues. G. M. A. Richter, *The Sculpture and Sculptors of the Greeks*, New Haven 1970, 114–34.

Chapter 2

1. A. Burford, *Craftsmen in Greek and Roman Society*, London 1972, 167–8.
2. *Ibid.*, 122.
3. For Socrates' changing views, R. Parry, 'Episteme and Techne', *Stanford Encyclopedia of Philosophy*, https://plato.stanford.edu/archives/fall2020/entries/episteme-techne/.
4. J. J. Pollitt, *The Art of Ancient Greece: Sources and Documents*, Cambridge 1990, 75, 15; Diodorus 1.97.5–6.
5. Xenophon, *Memorabilia*, 4.2.33.
6. *Ibid.* 3.10.1.
7. *Ibid.* 4.2.1.
8. *Ibid.* 1.2.37.
9. *Ibid.* 2.1.20, citing Hesiod and Prodicus.

10. See also Plato's *Euthydemus* (280b–281c).
11. M. Barasch, *Theories of Art: From Plato to Winckelmann*, New York 1985, 8–9.
12. Burford 156.
13. Diogenes Laërtius, *Lives and Opinions of Eminent Philosophers*, 2.123; R. F. Hock (1976), 'Simon the Shoemaker as an Ideal Cynic', *Greek, Roman and Byzantine Studies* 17, 41–53; J. Sellars (2003), 'Simon the Shoemaker and the Problem of Socrates', *Classical Philology* 98, 207–16.
14. D. B. Thompson, 'The House of Simon the Shoemaker', *Archeology* 13 (1960), 234–40; J. McCamp, *The Athenian Agora: Excavations in the Heart of the Classical City*, Cambridge 2001, 177–81.
15. *Socratic Epistle* 12 to Aristippus, in A. J. Malherbe, *The Cynic Epistles: A Study Edition*, Missoula, MO 1977, 251. Aristippus is 'forbidden to go to the craftsmen' (*Epistle* 9, 247).
16. O. Lau, *Schuster und Schusterhandwerk in der griechisch-römischen Literatur und Kunst*, Bonn 1967. See also the supremely meditative marble funeral *stele* for Xanthippos, c. 420, British Museum, 1805,0703.183.
17. R. and M. Wittkower, *Born under Saturn*, New York 1963, 4 gives a misleadingly negative account of Socrates' attitude.
18. Pliny 35.69.
19. Aelian, *Varia Historia*, 14.8; Pollitt 79.
20. For praise of sectoral competition, with beggar competing against beggar, poet against poet, etc., Hesiod, *Works and Days*, trans. R. Lattimore, 21.24–6.
21. Roman depictions of workshops are few and meagre. Burford 176.
22. F. de Angelis, 'Playful Workers: The Cupid Frieze in the Casa dei Vettii', in *Pompeii: Art, Industry and Infrastructure*, ed. E. Poehler et al., Oxford 2011, 62–73. For a Byzantine example, K. Weitzmann, *Antique and Early Christian Book Illustration*, London 1977, 60–1.

Chapter 3

1. W. Horn and E. Born, *The Plan of St Gall*, Berkeley 1979, 1: 147.
2. D. Ganz, 'The Preconditions for Caroline Minuscule', *Viator* 18 (1987), 33; 30–1, 33 for writing and reading as 'ploughing'. For Isidor's poems, C. H. Beeson, *Isidor-studien*, Munich 1913, 166; J. Janzen, https://medievalfragments.wordpress.com/2013/01/25/pondering-the-physical-scriptorium/.
3. C. de Hamel, *Scribes and Illuminators*, London 1992, 8–16.
4. *Ibid.* 29.
5. Illuminators only exceptionally made their own parchment. R. Branner, *Manuscript Painting in Paris during the Reign of St. Louis*, Berkeley 1977, 7 and n. 30, 31.
6. *St Mark* in MS. Auct.D.2.16. Oxford, Bodleian Library.
7. J. G. Alexander, *Medieval Illuminators and Their Methods of Work*, New Haven 1992, 35–6.
8. B. M. Metzger, 'When Did Scribes Begin to Use Writing Desks?', in *New Testament Tools and Studies VIII*, Leiden 1968, 123–37. E. Clayton, 'Workplaces for Writing', in *Pen in Hand: Medieval Scribal Portraits*, ed. M. Gullick, Walkern 2006, 1–18.
9. C. de Hamel, *Meetings with Remarkable Manuscripts*, London 2016, 279.
10. D. F. Ruggles, *Islamic Art and Visual Culture*, Oxford 2011, 28.
11. *Ibid.* 44.
12. Beeson 166.
13. See Chapter 4.
14. M. Gullick, 'Self-Referential Portraits', in *Pen in Hand*, 99.
15. Alexander 12.
16. Horn and Born 1: 147.

Chapter 4

1. Theophilus, *On Diverse Arts*, ed. and trans. C. R. Dodwell, London 1961, bk 1, Preface.
2. E. R. Curtius, *European Literature and the Latin Middle Ages*, London 1953, 83–5, 407–13.
3. Theophilus, bk 3, Preface; Exodus 31: 1–6; 35: 30–5.
4. S. Kroustallis, 'Theophilus Matters', in *Zwischen Kunsthandwerk und Kunst*, ed. A. Speer, Berlin 2014, 54–5.
5. J. Van Engen, 'Theophilus Presbyter and Rupert of Deutz', *Viator* 11 (1980), 152.
6. Theophilus xl, for a list.
7. Theophilus was identified as 'Roger' in a copy of the treatise. H. C. Gearhart, *Theophilus and the Theory and Practice of Medieval Art*, University Park, PA 2017, 94–5. Plates 8–9, 13–30 for Roger's work.
8. Kroustallis 57–63.
9. J. Cherry, *Medieval Goldsmiths*, London 2011, 6. J. Bärsch in *Goldene Pracht*, Munich 2012, 59–67, 112–33.
10. Cherry 28–33.
11. Theophilus 64–5.
12. E. Fernie, *Romanesque Architecture*, New Haven 2014, 206 and passim; N. Coldstream, *Masons and Sculptors*, London 1991, 37; W. Horn and E. Born, *The Plan of St Gall*, Berkeley 1979, 1: 127.
13. Horn and Born 2: 189–99.
14. *Ibid.* 2: 195. They give the measurements as 27½ × 26⅔ feet.
15. Alberti, *On the Art of Building*, trans. J. Rykwert et al., Cambridge, MA 1988, 28–9. Bk 1.12.17–19.
16. Theophilus 65.
17. S. Nash, *Northern Renaissance Art*, Oxford 2008, 184, fig. 126.
18. V. Babucke, *Grubenhaus und Brettchenweber*, Likias 2005.
19. A. Thomas, *The Painter's Practice in Renaissance Tuscany*, Cambridge 1995, 38–9; E. Goldring, *Nicholas Hilliard*, New Haven 2019, 71.
20. E. MacCurdy, *The Notebooks of Leonardo da Vinci*, London 1954, no. 511.
21. *A Diderot Pictorial Encyclopedia*, ed. C. C. Gillispie, New York 1959, 2: 408, 412. A leather 'apron' is fitted to the table to catch particles.
22. Gearhart, 60–4, for mining.
23. He is adapting Matthew 13: 44–5.
24. J. Le Goff, *The Birth of Purgatory*, London 1984, 17–44; 54, 59–60, 101, 103, 142–3.
25. Gearhart 3.
26. But see E. Brepohl, *Theophilus Presbyter und die mittelalterliche Kunsthandwerk*, 2 vols, Cologne 1999.
27. Theophilus xix; Gearhart 43. M. Gullick, 'A Bibliography of Medieval Painting Treatises', in *Making the Medieval Book*, ed. L. L. Brownrigg, London 1995, 241–4.
28. R. Branner, *Manuscript Painting in Paris during the Reign of St. Louis*, Berkeley 1977, 8–9.
29. Hugh of St Victor, *Didascalion*, trans. J. Taylor, New York 1961, 56 (1.9). See also Van Engen 147–63.
30. Trans. John Sturdy, 1964, typescript, Warburg Institute, 24 (ch. 11).
31. Richard of Saint Victor, *The Book of the Patriarchs…*, trans. G. Zinn, London 1979, 309 (5.1); 302 (4.22); 186 (2.9); 220 (3.1). God is the 'supreme Artisan', 213 (2.24); 250 (3.20).
32. Richard of Saint Victor, 266 (4.6). C. J. Hahn, *Strange Beauty*, University Park, PA 2012, 242. This idea echoes the 'self-sculpting' – in

marble – recommended by Plotinus, *Enneads*, 1.6.9. See the miraculous workshop in H. Schlunk, 'The Crosses of Oviedo', *Art Bulletin* 32 (1950), 110–11; Hahn 81, figs 36–7.

33. Michelangelo, *The Poems*, trans. C. Ryan, London 1996, no. 62, ll. 6–7.
34. R. Lightbown, *Secular Goldsmiths' Work in Medieval France*, London 1978, 4, with a description by Alexander Neckam; V. W. Egbert, *The Medieval Artist at Work*, Princeton 1967, 58.
35. H. Géraud, *Paris sous Philippe-le-Bel*, Paris 1837.
36. Nash 199–200.
37. D. Gaborit-Chopin, 'Guillaume Julien "et compagnie"', *Studi di oreficeria*, ed. A. R. Calderoni, Rome 1996, 71–84.
38. See https://www.frieze.com/article/tracey-emin-and-sarah-lucas-shop, no. 220.
39. C. W. Platts, in *Florence at the Dawn of the Renaissance: Painting and Illumination 1300–1650*, Los Angeles 2012, 304–5, no. 46.
40. J. Henderson, *The Renaissance Hospital*, New Haven 2006, 117–35.
41. *Ibid.* 120.
42. E. Welch, *Shopping in the Renaissance*, New Haven 2005, 135–7.
43. K. Prajda, 'Goldsmiths, Goldbeaters and Other Goldworkers in Early Renaissance Florence', in *Craftsmen and Guilds in the Medieval and Early Modern Periods*, ed. E. Jullien and M. Pauly, Stuttgart 2016, 199 and 301.
44. Prajda 195–220.
45. A. Thomas, *The Painter's Practice in Renaissance Tuscany*, Cambridge 1995, 64, 57. Cennini, *The Craftsman's Handbook*, trans. D. V. Thompson, New York 1960, 86.
46. Alberti 152. Welch 2005, 125.
47. Welch 134.
48. Prajda 202–3, 205–6; R. Goldthwaite, *The Economy of Renaissance Florence*, 358–9.
49. G. Davies, 'The Organisation of the Goldsmiths' Trade in Trecento Siena', in *Orfèvrerie gothique en Europe*, Rome 2016, 15.
50. Welch 79.
51. Welch 158, for the inventory of a Sienese goldsmith.
52. H. Van der Velden, 'Defrocking St Eloy: Petrus Christus's "Vocational Portrait of a Goldsmith"', *Simiolus* 26:4 (1998), 243–76.
53. Compare the depiction of Vincent of Beauvais with convex mirror in *The Mirror of History*, British Library Royal 14 E 1 f. 3r, c. 1479. Clayton, 5, fig. 7.
54. Lightbown 85.
55. Welch 151. Cherry fig. 67 for a draped counter of a goldsmith/moneylender.
56. *Goldene Pracht* no. 149 for a similar but smaller (21.3 cm) hammer made from steel.
57. Brepohl 2: 43 for illustration of nine types of hammer.
58. Lightbown 4.
59. J. C. Schmitt, *Les rythmes au Moyen Âge*, Paris 2016.
60. M. Baxandall, *Giotto and the Orators*, Oxford 1971, 74, 56.
61. Cennini 2, 65, 86.
62. Cennini 42–3.

Chapter 5

1. M. Kemp, *Behind the Picture*, New Haven 1997, 84–90.
2. A. Bolland, 'Art and Humanism in Early Renaissance Padua', *Renaissance Quarterly* 49 (Autumn 1996), 469–87.
3. A. Thomas, *Painting in the Italian Renaissance Workshop*, Cambridge 1999, 66–71.
4. D. Gordon, 'A Sienese Verre Eglomisé and its Setting', *Burlington Magazine* (March 1981), 148–53.
5. L. Bourdua, 'Displaying the Bodily Remains of Saint Anthony of Padua', in *Bild und Körper im Mittelalter*, Paderborn 2006, 243–55; F. Lucchini, 'The Making of a Legend', in *Franciscans and Preaching*, ed. T. J. Johnson, Leiden 2012, 451–84.
6. Cennini, *Il libro dell'arte*, ed. and trans. L. Broecke, London 2015, §200.
7. D. Thornton, *The Scholar in his Study*, New Haven 1997.
8. *Ibid.* 43–4.
9. Broecke 1–2.
10. Thornton 9–11.
11. *The Earliest Lives of Dante*, trans. J. R. Smith, New Haven 1901, 24–5.
12. D. Radcliff-Umstead, 'Petrarch and the Freedom to Be Alone', in *Francis Petrarch, Six Centuries Later: A Symposium*, Chapel Hill 1975, ed. A. Scaglione, 236–48. Thornton 9.
13. J. Brantley, *Reading in the Wilderness*, Chicago 2007, 37–9.
14. R. J. Quinones, *The Renaissance Discovery of Time*, Cambridge, MA 1972, 117. M. Bishop, *Letters from Petrarch*, Bloomington 1966, 68.
15. L. B. Alberti, *On the Art of Building*, trans. J. Rykwert et al., Cambridge, MA 1988, 223. Bk 7.12.127.
16. *Antoine de Pise: l'art du vitrail vers 1400*, ed. C. Lautier and D. Sandron, Paris 2008, 44–5. He recommends nipping out to churches to check the colours of saints' robes.
17. The Arena Chapel, and lost cycles in the basilica of St Anthony and Palazzo della Ragione.
18. Underdrawings for frescoes can also appear 'sketchy', notably Spinello Aretino's, but are painted over. U. Procacci, *Sinopie e Affreschi*, Milan 1961, nos 58 and 60.
19. A. Grafton, *Leon Battista Alberti*, London 2000, 43–4.
20. See vol. 1 of M. P. Merrifield, *Original Treatises*, 2 vols, London 1849.
21. C. M. Cipolla, *Clocks and Culture, 1300–1700*, New York 1978.
22. J. Le Goff, *Time, Work, and Culture in the Middle Ages*, Chicago 1980, 43–52.
23. T. Pesenti, 'Dondi dall'Orologio, Iacopo', in *Dizionario Biografico degli Italiani*, 1992, vol. 41.
24. S. Cohen, *Transformations of Time and Temporality in Medieval and Renaissance Art*, Leiden 2014, 52.
25. Quinones 114.
26. Quinones 148.
27. E. Gallo, *The Poetria Nova*, The Hague 1971, 17, ll. 43–70. M. Carruthers, 'The Poet as Master Builder', *New Literary History* 24 (1993), 881–904.
28. Quintilian, *Institutes of Oratory*, 10.3.7, 10.4.2. See also Horace, *Ars Poetica*, l. 388. For Petrarch's approving comment, M. A. Lanzillotta, *Le postille del Petrarca a Quintiliano*, Florence 1988, nos 836, 898.
29. Murasaki Shikibu, *The Tale of Genji*, trans. R. Tyler, New York 2001, 323, ch. 17.
30. M. Weidner et al., *Views from the Jade Terrace: Chinese Women Artists*, Indianapolis 1988, 141–4, 212. W. Cheng, 'What to Remember Her By? A Case of a Female Effigy Portrait in the Qing Dynasty (1644–1912)', *Ming Qing Yanjiu* 25:1 (2021), 55–97.
31. K. Clark, *Leonardo da Vinci*, London 1989, 146 (Bandello); R. and M. Wittkower, *Born Under Saturn*, London 1969, 40–1.
32. Suetonius, *Lives of the Caesars*.
33. S. Hale, *Titian: His Life*, London 2012, 673.
34. P. Conisbee et al., *In the Light of Nature: Corot and Early Open Air Painting*, Washington, DC 1996, 103.

35. C. Tomkins, *Duchamp: A Biography*, London 1997, 399–400.
36. See also T. B. Hess, 'De Kooning Paints a Picture (1953)', *Reading Abstract Expressionism*, ed. R. Pipes, New Haven 1991, 172–80.
37. Suggestion from Laura Jacobus. R. G. G. Mercer, *The Teaching of Gasparino Barzizza*, London 1979.
38. L. Monnas, *Renaissance Velvet*, London 2012, 15.
39. *Ibid.* 32.
40. F. Ames-Lewis, *The Intellectual Life of the Early Renaissance Artist*, New Haven 2000, 70–4.
41. Thomas 58–9.
42. G. Tagliaferro and B. Aikema, *Le Botteghe di Tiziano*, Florence 2009, 56–7.
43. Hale 644.

Chapter 6

1. J. O. Schaefer, 'Saint Luke as Painter: From Saint to Artisan to Artist', in *Artistes, artisans et production artistique au Moyen Âge*, ed. X. Barral i Altet, Paris 1986, 1: 413–27.
2. M. Bacci, *Il Pennello dell'Evangelista*, Pisa 1998, 87–96.
3. M. Clarke, *The Art of All Colours: Medieval Recipe Books for Painters and Illuminators*, London 2001, 12.
4. Bacci; G. Kraut, *Lukas Malt die Madonna*, Worms 1986.
5. *Luca Evangelista*, ed. G. Canova Mariani, Padua 2000, 31–4, and passim.
6. Jacobus de Voragine, *The Golden Legend*, trans. W. G. Ryan, Princeton 1993, 2: 252–4.
7. E. Welch, *Shopping in the Renaissance*, New Haven 2005, 151–8; 97, fig. 90, for late 14th-c. pharmacy.
8. J. H. Marrow, 'Artistic Identity in Early Netherlandish Painting', in *Rogier van der Weyden: St Luke Painting the Virgin*, ed. C. Purtle, Boston 1997, 53.
9. For later examples, Welch, figs 111, 122–4, 138–9, 141–2, 156.
10. H. Chapman and M. Faietti, *Fra Angelico to Leonardo: Italian Renaissance Drawings*, London 2010, 39–41.
11. E. van der Wetering, *Rembrandt: The Painter at Work*, Berkeley 2009, 47–69. *Drawing in Silver and Gold: From Leonardo to Jasper Johns*, Hugo Chapman, Stacey Sell, p. 173, pl. 65.

Chapter 7

1. R. Lightbown, *Andrea Mantegna*, Oxford 1986, 15–29; *Francesco Squarcione*, ed. A. De Nicolò Salmazo, Padua 1999.
2. C. E. Gilbert, *Italian Art 1400–1500*, Evanston 1980, 34.
3. *Ibid.* 34.
4. H. Chapman and M. Faietti, *Fra Angelico to Leonardo: Italian Renaissance Drawings*, London 2010, 38.
5. E. van der Wetering, *Rembrandt: The Painter at Work*, Berkeley 2009, 47–69.
6. L. Melli, *Maso Finiguerra*, Florence 1995.
7. F. Ames-Lewis, *Drawing in Early Renaissance Italy*, New Haven 2000, 4.
8. D. Thornton, *The Scholar in his Study*, New Haven 1997, 136.
9. J. Fletcher, 'I Bellini', in *La bottega dell'artista tra Medioevo e Rinascimento*, ed. R. Cassanelli, Milan 1998, 131. S. Nash, *Northern Renaissance Art*, Oxford 2008, 179–89.
10. *Ibid.* 16.
11. Nash 159–60.
12. Lightbown 18.
13. P. F. Brown, *Venice and Antiquity*, New Haven 1996, 191.
14. See Ghirlandaio's *Saint Jerome in his Study* (1480). Thornton, 40.
15. Lightbown 16.
16. Lightbown 20–1.
17. Probably only Martin Kemp has truly understood perspective.
18. *Albrecht Dürer: Documentary Biography*, ed. J. Ashcroft, New Haven 2017, 168.
19. M. Kemp, *The Science of Art*, New Haven 1990, 53–4.
20. *Leonardo on Painting*, ed. and trans. M. Kemp and M. Walker, New Haven 1989, 58–68.
21. Kemp 170–2.
22. It is too large to be glass, as Kemp 170 claims (following Leonardo).
23. *Leonardo on Painting*, 114.
24. N. Coldstream, *Medieval Craftsmen: Masons and Sculptors*, London 1991, 18.
25. M. Conway, *The Literary Remains of Dürer*, London 1889, 65.
26. Fletcher 133.
27. *Leonardo* 199.
28. Vasari, *Lives of the Painters, Sculptors and Architects*, trans. G. du C. de Vere, London 1996 (hereafter 'Vasari'), 2.560, for Vasari and Salviati's visits to baths.
29. Ames-Lewis; Chapman and Faietti, 60–4; J. Burke, *The Italian Renaissance Nude*, New Haven 2018, 33–48. For a much earlier instance, T. A. Heslop in *Age of Chivalry*, ed. J. Alexander and P. Binski, London 1987, 27–9.
30. A. Wright, *The Pollaiuolo Brothers*, New Haven 2005, 158–62.
31. Chantelou 280, 285.
32. I. Bignamini and M. Postle, *The Artist's Model*, Nottingham 1991, 80, n. 68.
33. *Subleyras 1699–1749*, Paris 1987, 67. A life class with stove first appears in Crispijn [van] de Passe, *La prima-[quinta] parte della luce del dipingere et disegnare*, Amsterdam 1643–4.
34. *Letters of Courbet*, ed. and trans. P. Chu, Chicago 1992, 119, nn. 53–7.
35. J. Munro, *Silent Partners: Artist and Mannequin from Function to Fetish*, New Haven 2014.
36. P. Nuttall, 'Reconsidering the Nude: Northern Tradition and Venetian Innovation', in S. M. Lindquist (ed.), *The Meanings of Nudity in Medieval Art*, Farnham 2012, 299–318. D. Wolfthal, in T. Kren et al., *The Renaissance Nude*, Los Angeles 2018, 81–119.
37. Cellini, *Autobiography*, trans. G. Bull, Harmondsworth 1956, 101, 279, 288.
38. Ames-Lewis 104–10.
39. J. Guiffrey, 'Histoire de l'Académie de St-Luc', *Archives de l'art français* 9 (1915), 62.
40. Vasari 2.649.
41. P. O. Long, *Openness, Secrecy, Authorship*, Baltimore 2004.
42. R. Signorini, *A Casa di Andrea Mantegna*, Mantua 2006; G. Sacchi, *Mantegna Archipictor*, Mantua 2000. H.-P. Schwartz, *Das Künstlerhaus*, Braunschweig 1990, says it was preceded by the Florentine houses of Mino da Fiesole, Giuliano and Antonio da Sangallo and Perugino.
43. F. Ames-Lewis, *The Intellectual Life of the Early Renaissance Artist*, New Haven 2000, 66–70. Woodworkers, who made architectural models, also became architects.
44. This changed in Florence under Duke Cosimo I de' Medici, who stopped courtiers having shops in their *palazzi*.
45. P. Kristeller, *Andrea Mantegna*, Berlin 1902, 541 doc. 86.
46. Vulcan appears in *Parnassus* (1497), painted for Isabella d'Este, the duke's wife.
47. Lightbown 53–5.
48. R. Dugoni, 'Sul lago di Garda', in *Andrea Mantegna e i Gonzaga*, ed. F. Trevisani, Milan 2002, 268–71. Some scholars doubt it happened.
49. For Macchiavelli's dressing up, D. Thornton, *The Scholar in his Study*, New Haven 1997, 32.
50. J. Woods-Marsden, *Renaissance Self-Portraiture*, New Haven 1999, 85–95.

51. For naked self-portrait busts, Woods-Marsden, 98–100.
52. Leonardo, *Treatise on Painting*, trans. A. P. McMahon, Princeton 1956, no. 520.
53. F. P. Fiore, 'La Casa di Andrea Mantegna a Mantova', in *Andrea Mantegna: Impronta del Genio*, Florence 2010, 2: 580 and n. 12. Sacchi 25, 33.

Chapter 8

1. See Hesiod, *Works and Days*, 21: 24–6.
2. *Leonardo on Painting*, ed. and trans. M. Kemp and M. Walker, New Haven 1989, 38–9.
3. F. Ames-Lewis, *The Intellectual Life of the Early Renaissance Artist*, New Haven 1998, 79–87.
4. B. Ramazzini, *Diseases of Workers*, trans. W. Wright, Birmingham, AL 1983, 69.
5. C. Bambach, *Leonardo da Vinci Rediscovered*, New Haven 2019, 3.397–490.
6. *Ibid.* 3.398.
7. *Ibid.* 3.443–7.
8. *Ibid.* 3.398, 4.372 n. 1.
9. Vasari 1.635–6.
10. L. Campbell, *Renaissance Portraits*, New Haven 1990, 178–80.
11. A. Martindale, *The Rise of the Artist*, London 1972, 50–2; J. Hall, *The Self-Portrait*, London 2014, 104.
12. Nicholas Hilliard, *A Treatise Concerning the Arte of Limning…*, ed. R. K. R. Thornton and T. G. S. Cain, Ashington 1981.
13. Campbell 170–1, 174–5.
14. Campbell 151–7, 182; Vasari, 2.1024; Chantelou 57, 146, 187, 205, 207, 327.
15. *Leonardo on Painting* 39.
16. B. Read, *Victorian Sculpture*, New Haven 1982, 50.
17. A. Liebermann, *The Artist in His Studio*, New York 1988, 202.
18. Leonardo, *Treatise on Painting*, trans. A. P. McMahon, Princeton 1956, n. 512.
19. S. Nash, *Northern Renaissance Art*, Oxford 2008, 165–6.
20. *The Journal of Eugène Delacroix*, ed. W. Pach, New York 1937, 525.
21. Vasari 2.151.
22. J. Hall, *Michelangelo*, London 2005, 214, 205.
23. Vasari 2.743; S. Alpers, *The Vexations of Art*, New Haven 2005, 22.
24. Michelangelo, *The Poems*, trans. C. Ryan, London 1996, nos 5, F3 and 4.
25. Filarete, *Trattato di Architettura*, ed. A. Finoli and L. Grassi, Milan 1972, 2: 533 ff., 561, pl. 115.
26. K. Herrmann-Fiore, 'Il tema "Labor"', in M. Winner (ed.), *Der Künstler über sich in seinem Werk*, Weinheim 1992, 245–89.
27. I. Lavin, 'David's Sling and Michelangelo's Bow', *Past-Present*, Berkeley 1993, 29–62.
28. The standard English translations make no sense.
29. B. Degenhart, 'Dante, Leonardo und Sangallo…', *Römisches Jahrbuch für Kunstgeschichte* 7 (1955), 101–287.
30. Michelangelo, *Poems*, nos 248 (l. 12) and 250.
31. It is similar to the still-to-be-discovered relief depiction of Aeneas on the Ara Pacis in Rome.
32. See also the nude figure to the right of Joseph in the Doni *Tondo* (1503–4).
33. G. A. Johnson, 'Michelangelo, Fortunetelling and the Formation of Artistic Canons in Fanti's Triompho di Fortuna', in *Coming About … A Festschrift for John Shearman*, Cambridge, MA 2001, 199–205.
34. Hall, *Michelangelo*, 89–97.
35. P. Barocchi, *Scritti d'arte del Cinquecento*, Milano 1971, I: 3, 10–13, 1098–1101.
36. *Michelangelo: Selected Readings*, ed. W. Wallace, New York 1999, 636.
37. D. Parker, *Michelangelo and the Art of Letter-Writing*, Cambridge 2010, 5–7.
38. F. Calafati, 'I disegni di Michelangelo per L'Altopascio', in G. Maurer and A. Nova, *Michelangelo e il linguaggio dei disegni di architettura*, Venice 2012, 179–91.
39. G. Corti, 'Two Early Seventeenth-Century Inventories Involving Giambologna', *Burlington Magazine* 118:882 (September 1976), 629–34.
40. C. Avery, *Giambologna*, London 1987, 215–17.

Chapter 9

1. *Baccio Bandinelli: Scultore e Maestro*, ed. D. Heikamp and B. P. Strozzi, Florence 2014, 242–69 (T. Mozzati).
2. The term *stanze* is used. C. Bambach, *Leonardo da Vinci Rediscovered*, New Haven 2019, 3.321–3, 495.
3. Bambach, 3.493–8. N. Pevsner, *Academies of Art*, Cambridge 2014.
4. B. Thomas, 'The Academy of Baccio Bandinelli', *Print Quarterly* 22:1 (March 2005), 8.
5. D. Thornton, *The Scholar in his Study*, New Haven 1998, 33.
6. J. Le Goff, *Time, Work, and Culture in the Middle Ages*, Chicago 1980, 43–52.
7. Vasari 1.142–5, citing Sacchetti's *Trecentonovelle*, nos 191–2. P. Barolsky, *Why Mona Lisa Smiles*, University Park, PA 1991, 14–31.
8. W. T. O'Dea, *The Social History of Lighting*, London 1958, 8.
9. *Leonardo on Painting*, ed. and trans. M. Kemp and M. Walker, New Haven 1989, 224–5.
10. S. Foister et al., *Dürer's Journeys*, London 2021.
11. A. Laing, *Lighting*, London 1982, 41. For Venetian nightlife, P. Hills, 'Titian's Fire', *Oxford Art Journal* 30:2 (2007), 185–204.
12. P. Burke, *The Fortunes of the Courtier*, Cambridge 1995, 39–40.
13. *Ibid.* 46.
14. Pliny, *Natural History*, 35.151.
15. Michelangelo, *The Poems*, trans. C. Ryan, London 1996, no. 103.
16. A similar Prometheus, albeit clothed, appears in the *Florentine Picture Chronicle*.
17. O. Raggio, 'The Myth of Prometheus', *Journal of the Warburg and Courtauld Institutes* 21 (1958), 44–62.
18. Laing 31.
19. Heikamp, *Bandinelli*, no. 79/80, 532–5.
20. For Vesalius as inspiration, I. M. Veldman, 'Maarten van Heemskerck and St Luke's Medical Books', *Simiolus* 7.2 (1974), 91–100.
21. J. Hall, *The Self-Portrait*, London 2014, 35.
22. D. Bernini, *The Life of Gian Lorenzo Bernini*, trans. F. Mormando, University Park, PA 2011, 103. Caravaggio is the first artist to depict himself holding an artificial light, in *The Taking of Christ* (1602).
23. B. Cellini, *Discorso sopra l'arte del disegno*, in P. Barocchi, *Scritti d'arte del Cinquecento*, Milan 1971–6, 2.1931–2. F. Jacobs, 'Vasari's Vision of the History of Painting', *Art Bulletin* 66 (1984), 405.
24. Vasari 2.1022. D. Biow, *Vasari's Words*, Cambridge 2018, 109–24.
25. H. Chapman and M. Faietti, *Fra Angelico to Leonardo: Italian Renaissance Drawings*, London 2010, 120–1.
26. He resembles Archimedes. E. Gowers, 'Augustus and "Syracuse"', *Journal of Roman Studies* (2010), 79.
27. Vasari 2.740.
28. Thornton 45.
29. Laing 36.

30. Pliny 35.138, 96.
31. Jacobs 399–416.
32. N. Sabatini, *Pratica di fabricar scene e machine ne' teatri*, Ravenna 1638, 61–4; T. Crow, *Painters and Public Life in Eighteenth-Century Paris*, New Haven 1987, 138.
33. Illustration in *L'Encyclopédie Diderot et D'Alembert: Dessin et peinture*, Tours 1994, 5 (1, b), Planche 1, b.
34. F. Härb, '"Dal vivo" or "Da se": Nature versus Art in Vasari's Figure Drawings', *Master Drawings* (2005), 326–38.
35. C. Goldstein, *Teaching Art*, Cambridge 1996, 30–3.
36. S. Hale, *Titian: His Life*, London 2012, 146–9.
37. Giulio Mancini in F. Haskell, *History and Its Images*, New Haven 1993, 124.
38. Brooklyn Museum, 11.504e; Frans Hals Museum.
39. A. E. P. Sanchez and E. A. Sayre, *Goya and the Spirit of Enlightenment*, Boston, MA 1989, 41–2, n. 18.
40. J. Richardson, *A Life of Picasso*, London 1992, 2: 17, 20, 34; 17–18 for life models; 442, n. 20 for possible use of photographs.
41. Laing 24.
42. P. Cabanne, *Dialogues with Marcel Duchamp*, trans. R. Padgett, London 1971, 27.
43. Kandinsky, *Complete Writings on Art*, ed. K. C. Lindsay and P. Vergo, London 1982, 369–70.
44. *Lucian Freud: The Studio*, ed. C. Debray, Munich 2010, 44.

Chapter 10

1. C. Piccolpasso, *Three Books of the Potter's Art*, ed. R. Lightbown and A. Caiger-Smith, 2 vols, London 1980.
2. B. Palissy, *The Admirable Discourses of Bernard Palissy*, trans. A. La Rocque, Urbana, IL 1957.
3. L. N. Amico, *Bernard Palissy*, Paris 1996. For François Boucher's natural history collection, J.-H. Costa de Beauregard, *Journal de Voyage*, ed. P. Michel, Villeneuve 2013, 98–100.
4. Palissy 208, 358–9.
5. H. R. Shell, 'Casting Life, Recasting Experience', *Configurations* 12:1 (2004), 11–12.
6. V. Avery, 'The House of Alessandro Vittoria Reconstructed', *The Sculpture Journal* 5 (2001), 7–32. See also P. Findlen, *Possessing Nature*, Berkeley 1994, 273–7.
7. L. de Girolami Cheney, *The Homes of Giorgio Vasari*, New York 2006
8. Piccolpasso I: xxi.
9. Piccolpasso I: xix–xx.
10. J. Connors, 'Ars tornandi', *JWCI* 53 (1990), 217–36. W. Koeppe et al., *Making Marvels*, New York 2021
11. *Three Copernican Treatises*, trans. E. Rosen, Mineola, NY 2004, 148. C. Koslofsky, *Evening's Empire*, Cambridge 2011, 3.
12. W. S. Melion, 'Jesus, Mary and Joseph as Artisans of the Heart and Soul', in *Quid est Secretum?*, ed. R. Dekoninck et al., Leiden 2020, 122–6. Quote from Gracián.
13. R. Borghini, *Il Riposo*, Florence 1584, 14–15.
14. V. Frascarolo, in A. Tacke (ed.), *Künstlerhäuser/Artists' Homes*, Petersberg 2018, 204, 208 nn. 17 and 18.
15. Borghini 19–22.
16. *Abraham Bosse: savant graveur*, ed. S. Join-Lambert and M. Préaud, Paris 2004, no. 199; C. David, 'Prints as Sources: Ridolfo Sitigatti's Marble Venus', *Fontes* 59 (2011), 1–25.
17. It recalls sculpture by the Bernini-inspired Jacques Sarazin.
18. S. Bailey, 'Metamorphoses of the Grimani Vitellius', *J. Paul Getty Museum Journal* 5 (1977), 105–22.
19. E. Panofsky, *Galileo as a Critic of the Arts*, The Hague 1954, 18–19.
20. Malvasia, *Felsina pittrice*, Bologna 1678, i, pt 3.
21. G. Feigenbaum (ed.), *Display of Art in the Roman Palace 1550–1750*, Los Angeles 2014.
22. C. Goldstein, *Teaching Art*, Cambridge 1996, 33–6.
23. F. de Hollanda, *On Antique Painting*, trans. A. Sedgwick Wohl, University Park, PA 2013, 214.
24. M. P. Merrifield, *Original Treatises*, London 1849, 2.798–800.
25. S. Lipton, 'The Sweet Lean of His Head', *Speculum* 80 (2005), 1172–1208.
26. C. Ridolfi, *Le Meraviglie dell'Arte*, Venice 1648, 2: 203.
27. G. P. Lomazzo, *Scritti sulle arti*, ed. R. Ciardi, Florence 1974, 2: 381 (bk 6, ch. 51).
28. B. Uppenkamp, 'Rubens's palazzetto in Antwerp', in *Künstlerhäuser*, 218–32. For earlier artists' houses in Antwerp see 115–24 (P. Maclot), 194–201 (N. Peeters). H. P. Schwarz, *Das Künstlerhäus*, Braunschweig 1990, 217–23.
29. J. M. Montias, *Artists and Artisans in Delft*, Princeton 1982, 48.
30. J. R. Martin, *Baroque*, Harmondsworth 1977, 271.
31. M. Rooses and C. Ruelens, *Correspondence de Rubens*, Paris 1898, 2: 156.
32. J. M. Muller, in *A House of Art: Rubens as Collector*, ed. K. L. Belkin et al., Antwerp 2004, 65.
33. Uppenkamp 219, fig. 2; 221, fig. 4. The niche on the right has been enclosed by a metal grille. It would have stored relics. Scholars mistake it for a window.
34. K. H. Di Dio, 'Leone Leoni's Collection in the Casa Degli Omenoni, Milan.', *Burlington Magazine*, 145:1205, (2003), 572–8.
35. Chantelou 147.
36. N. Büttner, 'The Hands of Rubens', *Appreciating the Traces of an Artist's Hand*, ed. T. Nakamura, Kyoto 2017, 41–54.
37. E. G. Holt, *A Documentary History of Art*, New York 1958, 2: 190–6.
38. Suetonius, *The Twelve Caesars*, trans. R. Graves, London 2007, 85.
39. Roger de Piles in *Lives of Rubens*, ed. J. Wood, London 2005, 68.
40. P. Cavazzini in Faigenbaum, 98–102.
41. Holt 190.
42. P. M. Lukehart, 'The Accademia di San Luca between Reforms', in *The Italian Academies*, ed. J. E. Everson et al., Cambridge 2016, 174.
43. T. Crow, *Painters and Public Life in Eighteenth-Century Paris*, New Haven 1985, 25.
44. P. Cavazzini in Faigenbaum, 104–10.
45. Chantelou 125–6.
46. J. A. Rouquet, *The Present State of the Arts in England*, London 1755, 42–3; *Souvenirs of Madame Vigée Le Brun*, New York 1880, 346.
47. S. Sloman, 'Artists' Picture Rooms in Eighteenth-Century Bath', *Bath History* 6 (1996), 132–54.
48. *The Letters of Peter Paul Rubens*, ed. and trans. R. S. Magurn, Cambridge, MA 1955, 393, no. 235.
49. Merrifield 2.798–800.
50. Merrifield 2.766–7, 812–3, ch. 9.

Chapter 11

1. *Abraham Bosse: savant graveur*, ed. S. Join-Lambert and M. Préaud, Paris 2004, no. 164. G. Child, *World Mirrors*, London 1990. D. Wootton, *The Invention of Science*, London 2015, 214 ff.
2. P. Thornton, *Authentic Decor*, London 2000, 53–4.
3. Samuel van Hoogstraten, *Introduction to the Academy of Painting*, trans. J. Jacobs, Los Angeles 2021, 157, bk 3.8.

4. G. Lairesse, *Le Grand livre des peintres*, Paris 1787, 116, bk 2.3.
5. M. Zell, 'The Mirror as Rival', *Ut pictura amor*, ed. W. S. Melion et al., Leiden 2017, 370–410. See also Charles Lebrun, *Everhard Jabach and his Family*, c. 1660, New York, Met.
6. A. Bowett, *English Furniture 1660–1714*, Woodbridge 2002, 130.
7. J. M. Montias, *Vermeer and His Milieu*, Princeton 1989, 342, no. 4.
8. See https://jhna.org/articles/introduction/, a series of articles on Lairesse.
9. Lairesse (Paris) 2.139–40, bk 7.2.
10. M.-H. Huet, *Monstrous Imagination*, Cambridge, MA 1993, 1–55.
11. *Souvenirs of Madame Vigée Le Brun*, New York 1880, 36.
12. G. de Lairesse, *The Art of Painting*, London 1738, 349–50, bk 7.2.
13. British Museum 1868, 0822.7579.
14. *Conseils pour la peinture du portrait*, https://books.openedition.org/inha/3706?lang=en.
15. Bowett 134–5.
16. Montias 78–80, 138. For Spanish glass-making, Child 30–1.
17. J. Brown, *Velázquez*, New Haven 1986, 111, 194, 245–6, fig. 314.
18. M. Kemp, *The Science of Art*, New Haven 1990, 104–5.
19. Brown 45.
20. K. Wedd, *Creative Quarters*, London 2001, 23–31, 32–5.
21. M. K. Talley, *Portrait Painting in England*, London 1981, 350.
22. H. Walpole, *Anecdotes of Painting*, ed. R. N. Wornum, London 1876, 2:202.
23. Talley 349. For Kneller's first studio, J. Douglas Stewart, *Sir Godfrey Kneller and the English Baroque Portrait*, Oxford 1983, 184–5.
24. Celia Fiennes, quoted C. Saumarez Smith, *The Rise of Design*, London 2000, 23.
25. T. Barker, http://www.artandthecountryhouse.com/essays/essays-index/the-petworth-beauties.
26. D. Solkin, *Painting for Money*, New Haven 1993, 32–6.
27. Chantelou.
28. George Vertue in Talley 331.
29. I. Bignamini and M. Postle, *The Artist's Model*, Nottingham 1991, no. 9.
30. Van Hoogstraten, 270–1, bk 6.10. E. van der Wetering, *Rembrandt: The Painter at Work*, Berkeley 1997, 81–7. G. P. Bellori, *Vite*, Rome 1672, 73, for a similar contest and outcome.
31. Stewart 9.
32. J. Richardson, *Essay on the Theory of Painting*, London 1725, 23.
33. Chantelou 115–16, 190.
34. Wootton 347. Descartes and Locke compared the process of painting to the development of the mind: J. Hall, *The World as Sculpture*, London 1999, 44, 71–3. S. Alpers, *The Art of Describing*, Chicago 1983.
35. P. Fara, 'Newton Shows the Light', *Philosophical Transactions of the Royal Society* (2015), A.37320140213.
36. Talley 350.
37. Van der Wetering 24–5.
38. Bowett 130.
39. *Thomas Lawrence*, ed. A. Cassandra Albinson, New Haven 2010, 179–81.
40. Diary of James Beattie. See J. Northcote, *The Life of Sir Joshua Reynolds*, London 1818, 1.299–300. *Reynolds*, London 1986, ed. N. Penny, 257–9, no. 87 (D. Mannings).
41. C. Avison, *An Essay on Musical Expression...*, London 1753, 119–20.
42. E. Malone, *The Works of Sir Joshua Reynolds*, London 1809, I: cvi–cvii.
43. Chantelou 19.
44. Kemp 199.
45. Northcote 2.58.
46. W. Hazlitt, *Conversations of James Northcote*, London 1830, 30–1. See also E. R. and J. Pennell, *The Life of James McNeill Whistler*, London 1903, 410.
47. B. R. Haydon in G. Darley, *John Soane: An Accidental Romantic*, New Haven 1999, 276.
48. J. Soane and Mrs B. Hofland, *Description of the House and Museum*, London 1832, 2.
49. It was preceded in 1821 by Benjamin West's short-lived memorial picture gallery, which closed in 1829. H. Effra and A. Staley, *The Paintings of Benjamin West*, New Haven 1986, 142 ff.; G. Walkley, *Artists' Houses in London*, Aldershot 1994, 14–15 and 28.
50. J. Bialostocki, *Dürer and his Critics*, Baden-Baden 1986, ch. v.
51. Darley 275.
52. L. Vinge, *The Narcissus Theme*, Lund 1967, 277 ff.
53. Goethe, *Elective Affinities*, trans. R. J. Hollingdale, Harmondsworth 1971, 170. See also D. Buren, 'The Function of the Studio (1971)', *October* 10 (1979), 51–8: 'In the studio the artwork is closest to its own reality.'

Chapter 12

1. Gerard de Lairesse, *The Art of Painting*, London 1738, 1: 29, 131.
2. W. S. Melion, 'Jesus, Mary and Joseph as Artisans of the Heart and Soul', in *Quid est secretum?*, ed. R. Dekoninck, Leiden 2020, 37–144.
3. R. E. Spear and P. Sohm, *Painting for Profit*, New Haven 2010.
4. *Abraham Bosse: savant graveur*, ed. S. Join-Lambert and M. Préaud, Paris 2004, nos 71, 77, 158, 161.
5. W. Gibson, *Women in Seventeenth-Century France*, Basingstoke 1989, 105, 128–9.
6. J. C. Brown, 'A Woman's Place Was in the Home', *Rewriting the Renaissance*, ed. M. W. Ferguson et al., Chicago 1986, 215; J.-J. Rousseau, *Emile, or Education*, trans. B. Foxley, London 1921, 163.
7. J. Woods-Marsden, *Renaissance Self-Portraiture*, New Haven 1999, 218; P. Cavazzini in K. Christiansen and J. W. Mann, *Orazio and Artemisia Gentileschi*, New York 2001, 286.
8. E. Welch, *Shopping in the Renaissance*, New Haven 2005, 218.
9. H. Draper, '"Her Painting of Apricots": The Invisibility of Mary Beale', *Forum for Modern Language Studies* 48.4 (2012), 396.
10. H. Maddicott, 'Qualis vita, finis ita: The Life and Death of Margaret Lemon, Mistress of Van Dyck', *Burlington Magazine* 160 (2018), 93–100.
11. *Abraham Bosse*, no. 74.
12. C. C. Gillispie, *A Diderot Pictorial Encyclopedia*, New York 1959, 2: 326.
13. *Van Dyck and Britain*, ed. K. Hearn, London 2009, 16.
14. N. Birnfeld, *Der Künstler und seine Frau*, Weimar 2009; J. Woodall, 'Love Is in the Air', *Art History* 19 (June 1996), 208–46.
15. *Widowhood in Early Modern Europe*, ed. S. Cavallo and L. Warner, Harlow 1999. S. McPhee, *Bernini's Beloved*, New Haven 2012, for Costanza Scoltore.
16. M. E. Wiesner, 'Spinsters and Seamstresses', in *Rewriting the Renaissance*, ed. M. W. Ferguson et al., Chicago 1986, 191–205; Gibson 106–12.
17. A. Grafton and L. Jardine, *From Humanism to the Humanities: Education and the Liberal Arts*, London 1986, 32.
18. See http://resources.huygens.knaw.nl/vrouwenlexicon/lemmata/data/Rozee.
19. H. Wine, *The Eighteenth-Century French Paintings*, New Haven 2018, 187–99.
20. Samuel van Hoogstraten, *Introduction to the Academy of*

Painting, trans. J. Jacobs, Los Angeles 2021, 216.
21. M. Warner, *Monuments and Maidens*, Berkeley 1980.
22. M. D. Garrard, 'Artemisia Gentileschi's Self-Portrait as the Allegory of Painting', *The Art Bulletin* 62:1 (1980), 97–112.
23. Christiansen and Mann 420.
24. C. P. Murphy, *Lavinia Fontana*, New Haven 2003, 195–6.
25. Chantelou 285.
26. B. Bohn, 'Collecting Women's Art in Early Modern Bologna', in *Reframing Seventeenth-Century Bolognese Art*, Amsterdam 2019, 73–94; *By Her Hand: Artemisia Gentileschi and Women Artists in Italy, 1500–1800*, ed. E. Straussman-Pflanzer and O. Tostmann, New Haven 2021.
27. Malvasia, *Felsina pittrice*, Bologna 1678, 2.453–87.
28. W. Kloek, *Jan Steen (1626–1679)*, Amsterdam 2005, 52–3, no. 45.
29. See also Constance Mayer, *Self-Portrait with Father*, 1801, Wadsworth Atheneum.
30. B. Bohn, 'Patronizing pittrici in Early Modern Bologna', in *Bologna: Cultural Crossroads*, Bologna 2013, 113–26.
31. Malvasia 2.478.
32. *Ibid.* 473–4.
33. *Ibid.* 468.
34. Felsina is Bologna's Etruscan name.
35. Malvasia, *Felsina pittrice*, vol. 9 (1): *Life of Guido Reni*, ed. and trans. L. Pericolo, London 2019, 152–5, 164–5.
36. M. Garrard, *Artemisia Gentileschi*, Princeton 1991, 141–71.
37. F. Baldinucci, *The Life of Bernini*, trans C. Engass, University Park, PA 1966, 76.
38. Chantelou 118–19.
39. Chantelou 220–1. C. Lougee, *Le Paradis des femmes*, Princeton 1976; F. Beasley, *Salons, History, and the Creation of Seventeenth-Century France*, Aldershot 2006.
40. Gibson 44.
41. *Ibid.* 18.
42. Chantelou 220, 208–9, 229, 273–4, 302, 138.
43. Gibson 18.
44. C. Bischoff, 'Women Collectors and the Rise of the Porcelain Cabinet', in *Chinese and Japanese Porcelain for the Dutch Golden Age*, ed. J. van Campen and T. Eliëens, Zwolle 2014, 171–89.
45. Chantelou 141 and n. 165; 150, 164, 171. For gendered styles, Vitruvius, *On Architecture*, 1.2.5; 4.1.7; Persians were considered feminine.
46. Hoogstraten 150. Lairesse 2.337. Paul Taylor's suggestion.
47. P. Steadman, *Vermeer's Camera*, Oxford 2001, 98–9.
48. G. du Maurier, *Trilby*, London 1894. J. Milner, *The Studios of Paris*, New Haven 1988, 17 and passim.
49. Lairesse 1.65.
50. Lairesse 1.131.
51. See also *The Artist and His Model*, engraving, c. 1630.
52. S. Alpers, *Rembrandt's Enterprise*, London 1988, 46–7.
53. G. P. Bellori, *Lives of the Modern Painters...*, trans. A. S. Wohl, Cambridge 2005, 367; Malvasia (Pericolo), 71. Malvasia gives more emphasis to female models, 179.
54. Malvasia (Pericolo), 181, 406, n. 567.
55. George Vertue's notebooks. I. Bignamini and M. Postle, *The Artist's Model*, Nottingham 1991, 11.
56. J. R. Hale, 'Art and Audience: The *Medici Venus*, c. 1750–1850', *Italian Studies* 31 (1976), 37–58; C. Avery, *Bernini: Genius of the Baroque*, London 1997, 54; F. Haskell and N. Penny, *Taste and the Antique*, New Haven 1981, no. 66, 274–9. Late variants include Degas's *Henri Michel-Lévy* (1878), with Niobid mannequin, and Rodin's *Mask of Camille Claudel with the Hand of Pierre de Wissant* (c. 1895).
57. Chantelou 300.
58. *The Artist's Model* 14.
59. J. Newman in *Reynolds*, ed. N. Penny, London 1984, 344–54.
60. See https://www.royalacademy.org.uk/article/from-life-history-of-life-drawing-annette-wickham.
61. *Ibid.*
62. *The Artist's Model* 17–18 (Postle).
63. A. Rauser, *The Age of Undress*, New Haven 2020, 33–63.
64. Quoted in *ibid.* 40.
65. I. Jenkins and K. Sloan, *Vases and Volcanoes*, London 1996, no. 192.

Chapter 13

1. M. Praz, *An Illustrated History of Interior Decoration*, London 1964, 371. *Makart: Painter of the Senses*, ed. A. Husslein-Arco and A. Klee, London 2011, 219.
2. E. de Goncourt, *La Maison d'un Artiste*, Paris 1880, Preface; A. Rodin, *The Cathedrals of France*, trans. E. C. Geissbuhler, Redding Ridge 1965, 14–15.
3. R. Penrose, *Picasso: His Life and Work*, Harmondsworth 1971, 412–13.
4. Praz 52–3; W. Rybczynski, *Home: A Short History of an Idea*, London 1987, 31.
5. W. Hofmann, *Caspar David Friedrich*, London 2000, 101.
6. *Ibid.* 101. A second version, with Friedrich standing behind the chair, was painted in 1819. S. Rewald, *Rooms with a View*, New Haven 2011, 74–6, no. 24.
7. *Art in Theory 1815–1900*, ed. C. Harrison et al., Oxford 1998, 49.
8. *Ibid.* 50.
9. *Art in Theory 1648–1815*, ed. C. Harrison et al., Oxford 2001, 964.
10. W. Vaughan, *Caspar David Friedrich*, London 2004, 18–25, 72–4.
11. This was preceded by Emperor Joseph II of Austria's Edict on Idle Institutions (1780), which closed contemplative monastic orders.
12. J. H. Rubin, 'New Documents on the Méditateurs', *Burlington Magazine* 117:873 (1975), 785–91.
13. G. Levitine, *The Dawn of Bohemianism*, London 1978, 73–86.
14. *Ibid.* 78.
15. A. Bonnet, *Artistes en groupe*, Rennes 2007.
16. Levitine 113–17.
17. J. Milner, *The Studios of Paris*, New Haven 1988, 11–14.
18. J. Britton, *Union of Architecture, Sculpture and Painting*, London 1828, 42, 6.
19. *Art in Theory 1815–1900*, 51–2.
20. J. Morley, *Furniture: The Western Tradition*, London 1999, 223–4.
21. *Art in Theory 1815–1900*, 50.
22. Rewald 108–9, no. 39.
23. Hofmann 101, 77.
24. R. Darnton, *The Business of Enlightenment*, Cambridge, MA 1979, 33–7.
25. L. Jaucourt in Diderot and d'Alembert, *Encyclopédie...*, Paris 1765, 12: 476; https://artflsrv03.uchicago.edu/philologic4/encyclopedie1117/navigate/12/1879/.
26. For the cult of Socrates, R. Trousson, *Socrate devant Voltaire, Diderot et Rousseau*, Paris 1967.
27. P. N. Firbank, *Diderot: A Critical Biography*, London 1992, 39–40. R. Sennett, *The Craftsman*, London 2008, 88–104. For similar workshop visits, Thomas Sheraton, *The Cabinet Maker's and Upholsterer's Drawing Book*, London 1791–4, 352–3.
28. Diderot and d'Alembert, Paris 1751, 1.713–17.

29. J.-J. Rousseau, *Emile*, trans. B. Foxley, London 1921, 57.
30. Rousseau 150–64.
31. C. Tomkins, *The Bride and the Bachelors*, New York 1968, 24. Carpentry's *Las Meninas* is *Christ in the Carpenter's Shop* (1849–50) by the Pre-Raphaelite painter John Everett Millais. Joseph is making a new door in an unadorned workshop. The setting derived from careful study of a carpenter's shop in London's Oxford Street.
32. Madame de Genlis, *Adelaide and Theodore; or, Letters on Education*, London 1788, 3: 112–13; 2: 144 (visit to cabinet-maker).
33. Vaughan 196.
34. Hofmann 101; cf. the makeover of Diderot's *cabinet* by Madame Geoffrin. https://iainbamforth.com/2017/03/12/my-old-dressing-gown/. P. Saint-Amand and J. Curtiss Gage, 'Diderot's Dressing Gown', *Diderot Studies* 31 (2009), 71–81.
35. H. Murger, *Bohemians of the Latin Quarter*, London 1887, 16.
36. *Ibid.* 40–3.
37. M. Myrone, *Making the Modern Artist*, New Haven 2020, 179–85.
38. E. Texier, *Tableau de Paris*, Paris 1852, 1: 81.
39. E. and J. Pennell, *The Life of James McNeill Whistler*, London 1908, 1.123–5; D. M. Bendix, *Diabolical Designs: Paintings, Interiors and Exhibitions of James McNeill Whistler*, Washington DC 1995, 51–2.
40. See vangoghletters.org, no. 194, 29 December 1881 (and no. 196, 3 January).
41. O. Batschmann, *The Artist in the Modern World*, New Haven 1997, 87. See also A. Frasca-Rath, 'Via della Fontanella 4: John Gibson's Workshop in Rome', in *Tate Papers* 29 (Spring 2018).
42. Baudelaire, *Art in Paris*, trans. J. Mayne, London 1965, 205.
43. *Letters of Courbet*, ed. and trans P. Chu, Chicago 1992, 130, nos 54–7.
44. A. Elsen, *In Rodin's Studio*, London 1980, nos 32–3.
45. *Letters of Rainer Maria Rilke 1892–1910*, trans. J. B. Greene and M. D. H. Norton, New York 1945, 79, 81.
46. R. Butler, *Rodin: The Shape of Genius*, New Haven 1993, 151–2.
47. P. Gsell, *Art*, Boston 1912, 25.
48. Butler 24–38.
49. H. Spurling, *The Unknown Matisse*, London 1998, 1.337, 407.
50. Butler 461.
51. R. Descharnes and J.-F. Chabrun, *Auguste Rodin*, trans. E. Lausanne, Secaucus, NJ 1967, 118.
52. J. Hall, *The Sinister Side*, Oxford 2008, 342–50; R. Irwin, 'Afterword', in J.-K. Huysmans, *Là-Bas*, trans. B. King, Sawtree 2001, 327.
53. J. Richardson, *A Life of Picasso*, London 1991, 1.314.
54. S. Miller, *Constantin Brancusi*, London 2010, 76–101.
55. A. Dannat et al., *Impasse Ronsin*, New York 2016.
56. I. Vermeulen, in *Piet Mondrian: The Studios*, ed. C. W. de Jong, London 2015, 96.
57. Man Ray, *Self-Portrait*, New York 1963, 208–9.
58. J. Hall, *The Self-Portrait*, London 2014, 216–29.
59. Paul Gauguin, *Noa Noa*, trans. O. F. Theis, San Francisco 1994, 76.
60. Man Ray 208–9.
61. John Ruskin, *The Stones of Venice*, London 1851–3, 2: 6: §14, §8.
62. *Piet Mondrian: The Studios*, 11, 33.
63. *Mondrian and His Studios*, ed. F. Manacorda and M. White, London 2014, 34–7.
64. *Piet Mondrian: The Studios*, 75, 78.
65. *The New Art – The New Life: the Collected Writings of Piet Mondrian*, ed. and trans. H. Holtzman and M. S. James, London 1987, 64–9, 91.
66. Vermeulen in *Piet Mondrian: The Studios*, 104.
67. Manacorda and White 76.
68. Manacorda and White 65–6 (M. Wieczorek).
69. P. Thornton, *Authentic Decor*, London 1993, figs 437, 442, 450, 452.
70. Thornton 313.
71. C. Gere, *The House Beautiful*, London 2000, 15, 25–30.
72. R. Ellmann, *Oscar Wilde*, London 1988, 43–4.
73. Manacorda and White 104.
74. B. O'Doherty, *Inside the White Cube*, Berkeley 1976.
75. Le Corbusier, *The Decorative Art of Today*, trans. J. Dunnett, Cambridge, MA 1987, 188, 192.
76. B. Bosker, https://www.nytimes.com/2017/04/03/t-magazine/hiroshi-sugimoto-photograph-architect-enoura-observatory.html.

Chapter 14

1. M. Droste, *Bauhaus 1919–33*, Berlin 2020, 30, for Wilhelm Worringer.
2. P. Rössler and A. Blümm, 'Soft Skills and Hard Facts', in *Bauhaus Bodies*, ed. E. Otto and P Rössler, New York 2019, 3–24. *Anni Albers*, ed. A. Coxon et al., London 2018, 52–5.
3. A. Dorner in *Bauhaus: 1919–28*, New York (MoMA) 1938, 14; Droste 38.
4. *Des Cennino Cennini Handbüchlein der Kunst*, Strasbourg 1916. A French translation with preface by Renoir was published in 1911.
5. Droste 19.
6. *A Diderot Pictorial Encyclopedia*, ed. C. C. Gillispie, New York 1959, 2: 408, 412.
7. B. Bergdoll and L. Dickerman, *Bauhaus 1919–33*, New York 2009, nos 109, 110.
8. Gropius quoted in *the dessau bauhaus building 1926–1999*, ed. M. Kentgens-Craig et al., Basel 1998, 17.
9. Kentgens-Craig 116.
10. *Art into Life: Russian Constructivism, 1914–1932*, Seattle 1990, 67.
11. Droste 262.
12. G. Walkley, *Artists' Houses in London*, London 1994, 61–4. C. Dakers, *The Holland Park Circle*, New Haven 1999, 158–70.
13. Walkley 178–87.
14. Droste 258; Kentgens-Craig 23.
15. Theatre was also central to Dadaism and Constructivism.
16. J. Hall, *The World as Sculpture*, London 1999, 186–95.
17. See Moholy-Nagy, 'From Wine Jugs to Lighting Fixtures', in *Bauhaus: 1919–28*, 136–8.
18. Bergdoll and Dickerman, nos 305 and 308.
19. Gropius 73. M. Ridler, 'The Bauhaus Wall Painting Workshop: Mural Painting to Wallpapering, Art to Product' (2016), *CUNY Academic Works*.
20. Droste 386. W. Gropius, *Bauhausbauten Dessau*, Munich 1930, 79.
21. Droste 334–5.
22. Droste 485–505.
23. J. House, *Monet: Nature into Art*, New Haven 1986, 147–51; C. Joyes, *Monet at Giverny*, London 1975, 118; J. Milner, *The Studios of Paris*, New Haven 1988, 189–90.
24. Paul Tucker et al., *Monet in the Twentieth Century*, New Haven 1998.
25. D. Pérez-Tibi, *Dufy*, New York 1989, 250–75. R. Golan, *Muralnomad: The Paradox of Wall Painting, Europe 1927–1957*, New Haven 2009.
26. P. Adam, *Art of the Third Reich*, London 1992, 195.

27. A. W. Lee, *Painting on the Left*, Berkeley 1999, 88–114.
28. *Ibid.* 93.
29. Quoted in C. A. Jones, *Machine in the Studio*, Chicago 1996, 102.
30. M. Stevens and A. Swan, *De Kooning*, New York 2016, 119, 79–80. T. Hess, *Willem de Kooning*, New York 1968.
31. M. Peppiatt and A. Bellony-Rewald, *Imagination's Chamber*, London 1983, 78.
32. R. Harbison, *The Built, the Unbuilt and the Unbuildable*, London 1991, 123–4.
33. Jones 189 ff.; V. Bockris, *Warhol*, London 1989, 188 ff.; B. Gopnik, *Warhol*, London 2020, 353 ff.
34. T. Kiedrowski, *Andy Warhol's New York*, New York 2011, 70.
35. Bockris 188–9.
36. Gopnik 350–1.
37. Bockris 191–2.
38. *OED*, 'Salon'.
39. R. Wrigley, 'Between the Street and the Salon...', *Oxford Art Journal*, 21:1 (1998), 53, n. 36. For hairdressers as sculptors, W. Barker, *A Treatise on the Principles of Hair-Dressing*, London c. 1785, 52–3.
40. Bockris 379.
41. T. Hess, 'De Kooning Paints a Picture', *Reading Abstract Expressionism*, ed. R. Pipes, New Haven 1991, 172–80.
42. See https://www.metmuseum.org/art/collection/search/206984.
43. Gopnik 589.

Chapter 15

1. P. Chu, 'Showing Making in Courbet's *The Painter's Atelier*', in *Hiding Making – Showing Creation: The Studio from Turner to Tacita Dean*, ed. R. Esner et al., Amsterdam 2013, 62–72.
2. *Letters of Courbet*, ed. and trans P. Chu, Chicago 1992, 42–3, no. 42–4; 44–5, no. 44–1; 49, 44–4.
3. *Letters of Courbet* 98–9, no. 50–4.
4. S. Adams, *The Barbizon School and the Origins of Impressionism*, London 1994, 178.
5. Adams 8.
6. J. J. Rousseau, *Confessions*, in *Oeuvres Complètes*, Paris 1964, 1.404.
7. *Letters of Courbet* 86–7, no. 49–7.
8. *Letters of Courbet* no. 50–1.
9. P. Thornton, *Authentic Decor*, London 1993, 233, no. 296.
10. G. S. Davidson et al., *House Proud*, New York 2008, 47, 155. H. Honour, *Chinoiserie*, London 1961, 204–6.
11. Honour 205.
12. M. Praz, *An Illustrated History of Interior Decoration*, London 1964, 352–5.
13. Chu, 'Showing Making', 68.
14. Two hours was in fact standard. Adams 32. Pomarede in P. Conisbee et al., *In the Light of Nature: Corot and Early Open Air Painting*, Washington, DC 1996, 85, 98–102 (for painting from memory).
15. P. Galassi, *Corot in Italy*, New Haven 1991, 12–14.
16. M. Kemp, *The Science of Art*, New Haven 1992, 189, 200. M. P. Salé, *Dessiner en Plein Air*, Paris 2017.
17. *Art in Theory 1648–1815*, ed. C. Harrison et al., Oxford 2000, 961.
18. I. Pears, *The Discovery of Painting*, New Haven 1988, 182–7.
19. E. Malone, *The Works of Sir Joshua Reynolds*, London 1809, 1. cvi–cvii, xcix. See also William Hazlitt's essay 'On the Pleasure of Painting' (1821).
20. Adams 52.
21. Adams 76.
22. J. Milner, *The Studios of Paris*, New Haven 1988, 40.
23. V. Sueur-Hermel, in Salé 71–91.
24. *Reminiscences of Rosa Bonheur*, ed. T. Stanton, London 1910, 17–20, with plan of Paris studio; 29–30, 382–3; 41. For Meissonier's stable, J. Milner, *The Studios of Paris*, New Haven 1988, 175–7. For Landseer's cage and stables, G. Walkley, *Artists' Houses in London*, London 1994, 119–20.
25. See Thomas Couture's *The Realist*, 1865.
26. H. Toussaint, *Gustave Courbet 1819–1877*, London 1977, 241–77; *Gustave Courbet*, New York 2008, no. 74 (L. des Cars); J. Hall, *The Self-Portrait*, London 2014, 202–5; I. Pludermacher, 'Le Réel et l'allégorie', in *La Correspondance de Courbet*, ed. Y. Sarfati et al., Paris 2018, 265–92.
27. Chu, 'Showing Making', 65–6.
28. *The Journal of Eugene Delacroix*, ed. H. Wellington, London 1951, 309 (3 August).
29. Chinese villas feature in Léon Isabey, *Villas...*, Paris 1867.
30. *Letters of Courbet* 143, no. 55–6.
31. *Letters of Courbet* 131–3, no. 54–8.
32. T. J. Clark, *Image of the People: Gustave Courbet and the 1848 Revolution*, London 1973, 21.
33. *Gustave Courbet*, New York 2008, no. 42: *The Peasants of Flagey Returning from the Fair.*
34. M. Fried, *Courbet's Realism*, Chicago 1990, 159–61.
35. *Letters of Courbet*, no. 110.
36. A. Callen, *The Work of Art: Plein-air Painting and Artistic Identity*, London 2015. See also Mrs L. Birch, *Stanhope A. Forbes, ARA, and Elizabeth Stanhope Forbes, ARWS*, London 1906, 25–9; B. D. Barrett, *North Sea Artists' Colonies 1880–1920*, PhD thesis, University of Groningen, 2008, 80.
37. See vangoghletters.org, 119, 811.
38. *Ibid.* 583, 585, 599, 609, 623, 660.
39. *Ibid.* 515.
40. D. B. Brown, *Oil Sketches from Nature*, London 1991, 9.
41. S. Rewald, *Rooms with a View*, New Haven 2011.
42. E. and J. Pennell, *The Life of James McNeill Whistler*, London 1908, 1. 218.
43. See vangoghletters.org, 599. For Corot's rentals, Conisbee 100.
44. Praz 275, fig. 254.
45. M. Rosenthal and A. Lyles, *Turner and Constable: Sketching from Nature*, London 2013, 37–8.
46. See https://www.tate.org.uk/art/artworks/turner-snow-storm-steam-boat-off-a-harbours-mouth-n00530.
47. G. Levitine, 'Vernet Tied to a Mast in a Storm', *Art Bulletin* 49:2 (1967), 93–100. C. J. Lindström, *The French Artist*, 1840, Stockholm, National Museum, NMH 71/1876.
48. N. M. Athanassoglou-Kallmyer, 'Imago Belli: Horace Vernet's L'Atelier', *Art Bulletin* 68:2 (1986), 268–80.
49. 'Mr. Fenton's Crimean Photographs', *Illustrated London News* 769 (10 November 1855), 557.
50. Salé 93–119.
51. Adams 190.
52. He later dropped a 't', calling it *Botin.*
53. Degas called Zola a giant striving to create a *Bottin*. G. Moore, *Impressions and Opinions*, London 1891, 319.
54. See J. House, *Monet: Nature into Art*, New Haven 1986, 140.
55. *Ibid.* 140.
56. *Ibid.* 135–41.
57. *The Journal of Eugène Delacroix*, ed. W. Pach, New York 1937, 525.
58. House 140, 146–56.
59. *Ibid.* 12–13.
60. *Ibid.* 145.
61. H. Aurisch and T. Paul, *Monet and the Seine: Impressions of a River*, New Haven 2014.
62. House 222–4.

63. First published 1884. Trans. W. Fowlie, A. Rimbaud, *Complete Works, Selected Letters*, Chicago 2005.
64. See the grey studio pictures by Whistler, *The Artist's Studio*, and Hammershøi's *Interior with an Easel, Bredgade 25*.
65. See http://tomchance.org/wp-content/uploads/2018/03/Glazing_the_Crystal_Palace.pdf.
66. Walkley 40–1; 139–59, 'Mass-produced Studios'.
67. S. Waller, 'Realist Quandaries: Posing Professional and Proprietary Models in the 1860s', *Art Bulletin* 89:2 (2007), 256. House 137, for Manet's ironic subtitle: 'Monet? his studio in his boat'.
68. Waller 239–65.
69. Horace Lecoq de Boisbaudran, *L'Education de la Mémoire Pittoresque et la Formation de l'Artiste*, Paris (n.d.), 54.
70. B. Alsdorf, *Fellow Men*, Princeton 2013, 146.
71. B. C. Morden, *Laura Knight: A Life*, London 2013.
72. C. A. Jones, *Machine in the Studio*, Chicago 1996, 60 ff.
73. E. G. Landau, *Jackson Pollock*, London 1989, 156.
74. Jones 47.
75. Jackson Pollock, 'My Painting,' *Possibilities* I (Winter 1947–8), 78–83.
76. J. Hall, *The World as Sculpture*, London 1999, 203–5.
77. S. Risalti and F. C. Comparini, *Jackson Pollock: La figura della furia*, Florence 2014; *Lee Krasner: Living Colour*, ed. E. Nairne, London 2019, 57–68, studies from the nude.
78. A. Kaprow, *Essays on the Blurring of Art and Life*, ed. J. Kelley, Berkeley 1993, 7–8.
79. See https://www.theguardian.com/artanddesign/2015/jun/18/marina-abramovic-the-planet-is-dying-we-have-to-be-warriors.
80. Jones, 268 ff. *The Fall of the Studio*, ed. W. Davidts and K. Paice, Amsterdam 2009.
81. R. Smithson, *The Collected Writings*, Berkeley 1996, 107.
82. D. Cohn, *Anselm Kiefer Studios*, London 2013.
83. *Ibid.* 38.
84. *Ibid.* 46.

Select Bibliography

General: Studios

Munro, J., *Silent Partners: Artist and Mannequin from Function to Fetish*. New Haven, 2014

Peppiatt, M. and A. Bellony-Rewald, *Imagination's Chamber: Artists and Their Studios*. London, 1983

Schwartz, H.-P., *Das Künstlerhaus*. Braunschweig, 1990.

Tacke, A. (ed.), *Künstlerhäuser/Artists' Homes*. Petersberg, 2018

Waterfield, G. (ed.), *The Artist's Studio*. London, 2009

General: Contextual

Hall, J., *The Self-Portrait*. London, 2014

O'Dea, W. T., *The Social History of Lighting*. London, 1958

Pevsner, N., *Academies of Art*. Cambridge, 2014

Praz, M., *An Illustrated History of Interior Decoration*. London, 1964

Ramazzini, B., *Diseases of Workers*, trans. W. Wright. Birmingham, AL, 1983

Sennett, R., *The Craftsman*. London, 2008

Thornton, D., *The Scholar in His Study*. New Haven, 1997

Thornton, P., *Authentic Décor*. London, 2000

Wittkower, R. and M., *Born under Saturn*, New York, 1963

Antiquity to the Middle Ages

Alexander, J. G., *Medieval Illuminators and their Methods of Work*. New Haven, 1992

Burford, A., *Craftsmen in Greek and Roman Society*. London, 1972

Coldstream, N., *Medieval Craftsmen: Masons and Sculptors*. London, 1991

Egbert, V. W., *The Medieval Artist at Work*. Princeton, 1967

Gullick, M. (ed.), *Pen in Hand: Medieval Scribal Portraits*. Walkern, 2006

Martindale, A., *The Rise of the Artist*. London, 1972

Ruggles, D. F., *Islamic Art and Visual Culture*. Oxford, 2011

Stewart, A. F., *Greek Sculpture: An Exploration*. New Haven, 1990

Renaissance to 1800

Alpers, S., *Rembrandt's Enterprise*. London, 1988

Ames-Lewis, F., *The Intellectual Life of the Early Renaissance Artist*. New Haven, 2000

Amman, J., and H. Sachs, *The Book of Trades*. New York, 1973

Birnfeld, N., *Der Künstler und seine Frau*. Weimar, 2009

Cassanelli, R. (ed.), *La bottega dell'artista tra Medioevo e Rinascimento*. Milan, 1998

Chantelou, P. F. de, *Diary of the Cavaliere Bernini's Visit to France*, ed. A. Blunt et al. Princeton, 1985

Cole, M., and M. Pardo (eds), *Inventions of the Studio*. Chapel Hill, 2005

Farr, J. R., *Artisans in Europe 1300–1914*. Cambridge, 2000

Feigenbaum, G. (ed.), *Display of Art in the Roman Palace 1550–1750*. Los Angeles, 2014

Gillispie, C. C. (ed.), *A Diderot Pictorial Encyclopedia*. New York, 1959

Nash, S., *Northern Renaissance Art*. Oxford, 2008

Spear, R. E. and P. Sohm, *Painting for Profit: The Economic Lives of Seventeenth-Century Italian Painters*. New Haven, 2010

Thomas, A., *The Painter's Practice in Renaissance Tuscany*. Cambridge, 1995

Welch, E., *Shopping in the Renaissance*. New Haven, 2005

Wetering, E. van der, *Rembrandt: The Painter at Work*. Berkeley, 2009

After 1800

Alsdorf, B., *Fellow Men: Fantin-Latour and the Problem of the Group*. Princeton, 2013

Batschmann, O., *The Artist in the Modern World*. New Haven, 1997

Bignamini, I., and M. Postle, *The Artist's Model*. Nottingham, 1991

Blazwick, I. (ed.), *A Century of the Artist's Studio 1920–2020*, London, 2022

Davidts, W., and K. Paice (eds), *The Fall of the Studio*. Amsterdam, 2009

Esner, R., et al., *Hiding Making – Showing Creation: The Studio from Turner to Tacita Dean*. Amsterdam, 2013

Hoffmann, J. (ed.), *The Studio*. London, 2012

Jacobs, M. J., and M. Grabner (eds), *The Studio Reader: On the Space of Artists*. Chicago, 2010

Jones, C. A., *Machine in the Studio*. Chicago, 1996

Liebermann, A., *The Artist in His Studio*. New York, 1988

Milner, J., *The Studios of Paris*. New Haven, 1988

O'Doherty, B., *Studio and Cube*. New York, 2007

Rewald, S., *Rooms with a View*. New Haven, 2011

Robertson, B., J. Russell and Lord Snowdon, *Private View*. London, 1965

Walkley, G., *Artists' Houses in London*. Aldershot, 1994

Wedd, K., *Creative Quarters: The Art World in London, 1700–2000*. London, 2001

Picture Credits

Listed by page number.
Dimensions are given in cm followed by inches, height before width before depth.

Frontispiece Wilhelm Redemann, *Kurt Schwitters, Merzbau in Hanover*. Sprengel Museum, Hanover. Photo Scala, Florence/ bpk, Bildagentur für Kunst, Kultur und Geschichte, Berlin. **6** Perry Ogden, *Francis Bacon's Studio at 7 Reece Mews, London*. Dublin City Gallery The Hugh Lane. © The Estate of Francis Bacon. All rights reserved, DACS/Artimage 2022. Photo Perry Ogden. **8** Eugène Delacroix, *Corner of the Studio*, 51 × 43 (20⅛ × 17). Musée du Louvre, Paris. **12** Tosa Mitsunobu, *The Picture Contest* from *The Tale of Genji*, 24.3 × 18.1 (9½ × 7⅛). Harvard Art Museums/Arthur M. Sackler Museum, Bequest of the Hofer Collection of the Arts of Asia. **16** Foundry Painter, *Hephaestus and Thetis*, interior of a terracotta drinking cup, Vulci, Italy. Antikensammlung, Berlin. **18–19** Attributed to the Amasis Painter, *Textile Workers*, terracotta lekythos (oil flask), Greek. The Metropolitan Museum of Art, New York. Fletcher Fund, 1931. **23** Pierre Subleyras, *The Artist's Studio*, 125 × 99 (49¼ × 39). Akademie der Bildenden Künste, Vienna. Photo De Agostini/Getty Images. **25** Attributed to a painter of the Leagros Group, *A Pottery Workshop* (detail), Greek. Staatliche Antikensammlungen, Munich. **26, 27** Foundry Painter, *A Bronze Workshop*, exterior of a painted clay kylix (drinking cup). Antikensammlung, Berlin. Photo Scala, Florence/bpk, Bildagentur für Kunst, Kultur und Geschichte, Berlin. **32** Plousios Painter, *A Shoemaker's Workshop*, exterior of an amphora. Museum of Fine Arts, Boston. Photo Museum of Fine Arts, Boston. All rights reserved/Henry Lillie Pierce Fund/Bridgeman Images. **36** Jean Raoux, *Pygmalion and Galatea*, 134 × 100 (52⅞ × 39⅜). Musée Fabre, Montpellier. **37** Anonymous, *The Cupid Frieze: Goldsmiths' Workshop*, wall painting from the triclinium (dining room), House of the Vettii, Pompeii. Photo Prisma Archivo/Alamy. **40** *Scribe and Illuminator at Echternach Abbey*. Miniature from the Echternach Pericope Book. Staats- und Universitätsbibliothek, Bremen. **41** *Eadwine at Work*, psalter, Christ Church, Canterbury. Trinity College, Cambridge. **42** Mohammed Daulat, colophon portrait from the *Khamsa* of Nizami, The British Library, London. **44** *Hildebertus and Everwinus*, marginal illustration in Saint Augustine, *City of God*. The Library of the Metropolitan Chapter, Prague. **45** *Plan of an Ideal Monastery with 52 Buildings* (detail), Saint Gall. Stiftsbibliothek St. Gallen. **46** Simon Bening, *Self-Portrait*, 8.5 × 5.7 (3⅜ × 2¼). The Metropolitan Museum of Art, New York. Robert Lehman Collection, 1975. **50, 51, 69 (detail)** Bezalel and Aholiab in the Paduan Bible Picture Book. The British Library, London. Photo Bridgeman Images. **55** Étienne Delaune, *Goldsmiths' Workshop*, 8.3 × 12 (3⅜ × 4¾). Petit Palais, Musée des Beaux-Arts de la Ville de Paris. **58, 59 (detail)** *The Conversion of Lisbius* from a *Life of Saint Denis*. Bibliothèque Nationale de France, Paris. Photo World History Archive/Alamy. **60** Master of the Madonna della Misericordia, *Saint Eligius in His Goldsmith's Workshop*, 35 × 39 (13⅞ × 15⅜). Museo del Prado, Madrid. **63** Petrus Christus, *A Goldsmith in his Shop*, 100.1 × 85.8 (39⅜ × 33¾). The Metropolitan Museum of Art, New York. Robert Lehman Collection, 1975. **66, 72 (detail)** Reliquary diptych, Umbria or the Marches, Italy, 17.3 × 22.3 × 4.6 (6¾ × 8¾ × 1¾). The Metropolitan Museum of Art, New York. Gift of J. Pierpont Morgan, 1917. **70** *Eirene in her* Studietto, illumination from Giovanni Boccaccio, *On Famous Women*. Bibliothèque Nationale de France, Paris. Photo BnF, Dist. RMN-Grand Palais / image BnF. **76** Pan Gongshou, *Wang Yuyan Sketching Orchids* (detail), 111.5 × 41.6 (44 × 16½). The Palace Museum, Beijing. **79** Attributed to Andrea Pisano, *Painting*, 83 × 69 (32¾ × 27¼). Museo dell'Opera del Duomo, Florence. **82, 84 (detail)** Johann von Troppau, *The Legend of St Luke*, Gospel Book. Österreichische Nationalbibliothek, Vienna. **86, 87 (detail)** Rogier van der Weyden, *Saint Luke Drawing the Virgin*, 137.5 × 110.8 (54⅛ × 43⅝). Museum of Fine Arts, Boston. Photo Museum of Fine Arts, Boston. All rights reserved/Gift of Mr and Mrs Henry Lee Higginson/Bridgeman Images. **89** Workshop of Maso Finiguerra, *Youth Drawing*, 19 × 11.3 (7½ × 4½). British Museum, London. Photo British Museum Images. **93** Marco Zoppo, *Virgin and Child with Angels*, 89.2 × 72.5 (35⅛ × 28⅝). Musée du Louvre, Paris. **95** Albrecht Dürer, *Draughtsman Making a Perspective Drawing of a Reclining Woman*, The Metropolitan Museum of Art, New York. Gift of Henry Walters, 1917. **96** Leonardo da Vinci, *Design for a Hydraulic Pump and a Draftsman Drawing an Armillary Sphere with a Perspectograph*. Atlantic Codex. Biblioteca Ambrosiana, Milan. Photo Album/Alamy. **98** Antonio Pollaiuolo, *Male Nude Seen from Front, Side and Back*, 26.5 × 35.7 (10½ × 14⅛). Musée du Louvre, Paris. Photo Josse/Bridgeman Images. **102** Casa del Mantegna (Mantegna's House), Mantua, Italy. Photo Matz Sjöberg/agefotostock. **108–9** Conjectural re-creation of Leonardo da Vinci's studio. Château du Clos Lucé, Amboise. Photo © Leonardo da Vinci's workshops, Château du Clos Lucé – Parc Leonardo da Vinci in Amboise. Photographer Léonard de Serres. **111** Lavinia Fontana, *Self-Portrait*, 16 cm (6¼) diameter. Galleria degli Uffizi, Florence. Photo Nicolò Orsi Battaglini/Bridgeman Images. **112** Michelangelo, *Sonnet with Self-Portrait*, 28.3 × 20 (11⅛ × 7⅞). Casa Buonaroti, Florence. The Picture Art Collection/Alamy. **115** Unknown Florentine artist, *A Sculptor at Work*, from Cristoforo Landino's edition of Dante's *Divine Comedy*. Biblioteca Vallicelliana, Rome. **116** *Sphera de Ariete* (detail), illustration from Sigismondo Fanti's *Triompho di Fortuna*. The Metropolitan Museum of Art, New York. Gift of Paul Sachs, 1925. **118** Flemish School, *Portrait of Giambologna*, 89 × 66 (35⅛ × 26). National Gallery of Scotland, Edinburgh. Photo Picture Art Collection/Alamy. **121 (above), 124 (detail)** Agostino Veneziano after Baccio Bandinelli, *The Academy of Baccio Bandinelli*, 27.4 × 30 (11⅛ × 12⅛). The Metropolitan Museum of Art, New York. The Elisha Whittelsey Collection, The Elisha Whittelsey Fund, 1949. **121 (below)** Ambrogio Brambilla, *Aerial View of the Vatican Belvedere*, 33 × 47.5 (13 × 18¾). The Metropolitan Museum of Art, New York. Harris Brisbane Dick Fund, 1941. **125, 127 (left)** Enea Vico after Baccio Bandinelli, *Bandinelli's Night Class*, 30.6 × 43.8 (12 × 17¼). The Metropolitan Museum of Art, New York. Purchase, Joseph Pulitzer Bequest, 1917. **127 (right)** *Secunda musculorum tabula*, from Andreas Vesalius, *De humani corporis fabrica*, Basel. Wellcome Collection, London. **128** Carlo Urbino, *Of Fire. Third Demonstration of Shadow*. Codex Huygens f. 90. The Morgan Library & Museum, New York. **130** Giorgio Vasari, the fireplace wall of the reception room (detail), Casa Vasari, Florence. Photo Kunsthistorisches Institut in Florenz, Max-Planck-Institut. **131** Giorgio Vasari, *The Greek Painter's Studio*, reception room, Casa Vasari, Florence. **134** David Dawson, *Lucian Freud Photographed in His Night Studio with Model Ria Kirby*. Private collection. © David Dawson. All rights reserved 2022/Bridgeman Images. **136** Cipriano Piccolpasso, *Li tre libri dell'arte del vasaio*, Umbria. Victoria and Albert Museum, London. Photo V&A Images. **137** Bernard Palissy, rustic basin, 7.8 × 52.5 × 40.5 (3⅛ × 20¾ × 16). Musée du Louvre, Paris. Photo Musée du Louvre, Dist. RMN-Grand Palais / Martine Beck-Coppola. **138** Frontispiece to Ferrante Imperato's *Dell'historia naturale*. Naples. The Getty Research Institute, LA. **139** Lathe with oblique cam, from Jacques Besson, *Theatrum instrumentorum et machinarum*, Paris. Scholarly Editions, Smithsonian Libraries. **141** Abraham Bosse, *The Sculptor's Studio*, 25 × 31.7 (9¾ × 12½). The Metropolitan Museum of Art, New York. The Elisha Whittelsey Collection, The Elisha Whittelsey Fund, 1951. **143** Palma il Giovane, *Portrait of an Artist*, 111.8 × 103 (44⅛ ×

40⅝). Birmingham Museum & Art Gallery. Photo Bridgeman Images. **146 (above)** Jacobus Harrewijn after Jacques van Croes, *View of Rubens's House*, 28.7 × 35.7 (11¼ × 14). The Metropolitan Museum of Art, New York. The Elisha Whittelsey Collection, The Elisha Whittelsey Fund, 1951. **146 (below), 149 (details)** Jacobus Harrewijn after Jacques van Croes, *View of Rubens's House in Antwerp*, 34 × 43.3 (13½ × 17⅛). Rijksmuseum, Amsterdam. **147** Peter Paul Rubens, *Rubens and Helena Fourment in their Garden*, 98 × 130 (38⅝ × 51¼). Neue Pinakothek, Munich. Photo akg-images/Erich Lessing. **152–3** Willem van Haecht, *Apelles Painting Campaspe*, 104.9 × 148.7 (41⅜ × 58⅝). The Mauritshuis, The Hague. **157** Abraham Bosse, *Five Senses: Sight*, 26.7 × 33.8 (10½ × 13¼). The Metropolitan Museum of Art, New York. Harris Brisbane Dick Fund, 1926. **158** Johannes Gump, *Self-Portrait with Mirror and Easel*, 128 × 98 (50½ × 38⅝). Private collection. Photo Picture Art Collection/Alamy. **160** Diego Velázquez, *Las Meninas*, 320.5 × 281.5 (126¼ × 110⅞). Museo del Prado, Madrid. **163** Godfrey Kneller, *Self-Portrait*, 107 × 114 (42¼ × 45). Private collection. Photo Sotheby's/akg-images. **166** Godfrey Kneller, *Isaac Newton*, 75 × 62.5 (29⅝ × 24⅝). Earl of Portsmouth. **168** Joshua Reynolds, *Self-Portrait at Easel*, 63.5 × 74.3 (25 × 29¼). National Portrait Gallery, London. **170** John Soane, breakfast room/study at 13 Lincoln's Inn Fields, Sir John Soane's Museum, London. Photo Richard Bryant/Arcaid Images. **173 (above)** Marcus Gheeraerts the Elder, *The Unfortunate Painter and His Family*, 24 × 37.6 (9½ × 14⅞). Bibliothèque Nationale de France, Paris. Photo BnF, Dist. RMN-Grand Palais/image BnF. **173 (below)** Abraham Bosse, *The Shoemaker's Shop*, 25.7 × 33.6 (10⅛ × 13¼). Published by Melchior Tavernier. The Metropolitan Museum of Art, New York. The Elisha Whittelsey Collection, The Elisha Whittelsey Fund, 1951. **176** Pieter Jalhea Furnius after Johannes Stradanus, *Cornelia, Mother of the Gracchi*, 22.3 × 29.7 (8⅞ × 11¾). Rijksmuseum, Amsterdam. **177** François-Hubert Drouais, *Madame de Pompadour at Her Tambour Frame*, 217 × 156.8 (85½ × 61¾). The National Gallery, London. **180** Artemisia Gentileschi, *Allegory of Painting*, 98.6 × 75.2 (38⅞ × 29⅝). Royal Collection Trust, London. **181** Elisabetta Sirani, *Self-Portrait Painting Her Father*, 96 × 78 (37⅞ × 30¾). The State Hermitage Museum, St Petersburg. **183** Adélaïde Labille-Guiard, *Self-Portrait with Two Pupils, Marie Gabrielle Capet and Marie Marguerite Carreaux de Rosemond*, 210.8 × 151.1 (83 × 59½). The Metropolitan Museum of Art, New York. Gift of Julia A. Berwind, 1953. **185** Matteo Borboni, *Catafalque of Elisabetta Sirani*, 29.9 × 16.3 (11⅞ × 6½). Cooper Hewitt, Smithsonian Design Museum, New York. Museum purchase through gift of various donors and from Eleanor G. Hewitt Fund. **188** Johannes Vermeer, *The Art of Painting*, 120 × 100 (47¼ × 39⅜), Kunsthistorisches Museum, Vienna. **191** Constantijn Daniel van Renesse, *Rembrandt and His Pupils Drawing from a Nude Model*, 18 × 26.6 (7⅛ × 10½). Hessisches Landesmuseum, Darmstadt. **192** Godfrey Kneller, *Grinling Gibbons*, 125.5 × 101 (49½ × 39⅞). The State Hermitage Museum, St Petersburg. Photo Fine Art Images/Heritage Images/Getty Images. **194–5** Johann Zoffany, *The Academicians of the Royal Academy*, 101.1 × 147.5 (39⅞ × 58⅛). Royal Collection Trust, London. **196** Thomas Rowlandson, *Lady H******* Attitudes*, 23.7 × 17 (9⅜ × 6¾). Private Collection. Photo Bridgeman Images. **200** Rudolf von Alt, *The Studio of Hans Makart in Gusshausstrasse, Vienna*. Wien Museum, Vienna. Photo De Agostini/Agefotostock. **201** Georg Kersting, *Caspar David Friedrich in His Studio*, 54 × 42 (21⅜ × 16⅝). Hamburger Kunsthalle, Hamburg. Photo Bridgeman Images. **202** Georg Kersting, *Gerhard von Kügelgen in His Studio*, 53.5 × 42 (21⅛ × 16⅝). Staatliche Kunsthalle, Karlsruhe. **205** Jean Broc, *School of Apelles*, 375 × 480 (147¾ × 189). Musée du Louvre, Paris.

208 Diderot and d'Alembert, *Encyclopedia, or a Systematic Dictionary of the Sciences, Arts and Trades*, vol. 2, plate 1, 'Silk Stocking Frame'. Photo Alfredo Dagli Orti/Shutterstock. **210** François-Étienne Calla, *Carpenter's Workshop*, scale model. Musée des Arts et Métiers-Cnam. Photo Musée des Arts et Métiers-Cnam/Sylvain Pelly. **212** Bertall, 'Cinq étages du monde parisien' (Five levels of Parisian life), in Edmond Texier, *Tableau de Paris*, vol. 1, Paris. **214** Ditlev Martens, *Pope Leo XII Visits Thorvaldsen's Studio near the Piazza Barberini, Rome, on Saint Luke's Day, 18 October 1826*, 100 × 138 (39⅜ × 54⅜). Thorvaldsen Museum, Copenhagen. **216** Eugène Druet, *Rodin in his Pavilion Studio*. Musée Rodin, Paris. **221** Edward Steichen, *Brancusi in His Studio, Paris, 1925*. © Sucession Brancusi – All rights reserved. ADAGP, Paris and DACS, London 2022. © The Estate of Edward Steichen / ARS, NY and DACS, London 2022. **222** Frans Postma, *Reconstruction of Mondrian's Studio Based on Paul Delbo's 1926 Photograph*. © 2022 STAM, Research and Production, Frans Postma Delf-NL. **225** Yasutomo Ebisu, *Hiroshi Sugimoto in His Tokyo Home Studio*. © Yasutomo Ebisu. **227** Metal workshop, Bauhaus, Weimar. Original photograph, Bauhaus-Universität Weimar. **229** Cover for the *Bauhaus magazine*, no. 1. Photograph (centre left) Lucia Moholy © DACS 2022; floor plans (below, left and right) Walter Gropius © DACS 2022. **231** Marianne Brandt, *Metal Workshop, Bauhaus, Dessau*. Harvard Art Museums/Busch-Reisinger Museum, Gift of Walter Gropius. Marianne Brandt © DACS 2022. **233 (above)** Fritz Kuhr, *Wall-Painting Scheme for the Atelier of Paul Klee's Master House*, 24 × 34 (9½ × 13½). Bauhaus Archive, Berlin. © Hermann Famulla, Berlin. **233 (below)** Lucia Moholy, *Paul Klee in His Atelier*, Dessau. Lucia Moholy © DACS 2022. **234** Marianne Brandt, *Self-Portrait in Atelier*. Bauhaus Archive, Berlin. Marianne Brandt © DACS 2022. **236** Henri Manuel, *Monet in His Studio in Front of 'Morning'*. Musée Marmottan Monet, Paris. **237** 'In the World's Largest Atelier', *Berliner Illustrirte Zeitung*, no. 51. Drawing of Josef Thorak's studio by Hans Liska. Josef Thorak © DACS 2022. Hans Liska © DACS 2022. **238** Diego Rivera, *The Making of a Fresco Showing the Building of a City*. San Francisco Art Institute. © Banco de México Diego Rivera Frida Kahlo Museums Trust, Mexico, D.F./DACS 2022. **242–3** Bob Adelman, *Andy Warhol on the Red Couch at The Factory*, New York City, 1964. Bob Adelman Archive. © Bob Adelman Estate. **246** Gustave Courbet, *Self-Portrait with Black Dog*, 46.3 × 55.5 (18¼ × 21⅞). Petit Palais, Musée des Beaux-Arts de la ville de Paris. **249** Carl Jacob Lindström, *The German Painter*, 19.2 × 25.8 (7⅝ × 10¼). Nationalmuseum, Stockholm. Photo Erik Cornelius/Nationalmuseum. **250** *The Studio of Rosa Bonheur*, engraving from *L'Illustration*, no. 479, vol. XIX (1 May 1852). Photo De Agostini/agefotostock. **251** Gustave Courbet, *The Painter's Studio*, 361 × 598 (142¼ × 235½). Musée d'Orsay, Paris. **254** Vincent van Gogh, *The Painter on the Road to Tarascon*, 48 × 44 (19 × 17⅜). Formerly in Kaiser-Friedrich Museum, Magdeburg. **256** Horace Vernet, *Joseph Vernet Tied to a Mast in a Storm* (detail), 275 × 336 (108⅜ × 132⅜). Musée Calvet, Avignon. **257** Roger Fenton, *Photographic Van, with Marcus Sparling*, 17.4 × 15.9 (6⅞ × 6⅜). Royal Collection Trust, London. **258** Charles-François Daubigny, *The Boat Studio*, from the series *The Boat Trip*, 13 × 17.8 (5⅛ × 7). The Metropolitan Museum of Art, New York. Gift of Theodore De Witt, 1923. **261** Claude Monet, *The Studio Boat*, 72.7 × 60 (28⅝ × 23⅝). Barnes Foundation, Philadelphia. **263** Frédéric Bazille, *Bazille's Studio*, 98 × 128 (38⅝ × 50½). Musée d'Orsay, Paris. **265** Hans Namuth, *Jackson Pollock and Lee Krasner*. © The Pollock-Krasner Foundation ARS, NY and DACS, London 2022. © 1991 Hans Namuth Estate, Courtesy Center for Creative Photography, University of Arizona. **269** Anselm Kiefer's studio in Barjac, France. Photo Charles Duprat. © Anselm Kiefer.

Index

Page numbers in **bold** refer to illustrations.

Abramović, Marina 14, 267
Achilles 15, 24–6
Adelman, Bob, *Andy Warhol on the Red Couch at The Factory* (1964) 241, **242–3**
Aiguillon, Madame d' 187
Alberti, Leon Battista 53, 71, 78, 88, 92, 95, 101, 104, 161
Alembert, Jean le Rond d' *see* Diderot, Denis; and d'Alembert
Alexander the Great 17, 18, 35
Alt, Rudolf von, *The Studio of Hans Makart in Gusshausstrasse, Vienna* (1885) 199, **200**
Amasis Painter (attr.), *Textile Workers* (c. 550–530 BCE) 17, **18–19**
amateur artists 138–40, 248–9
anatomical study 97–101, 106, 117, 126, 135
Angelis, Peter 192
Anguissola, Sofonisba 179
Anne of Austria 186, 189
Anonymous, *A Sculptor at Work* (c. 1503–10) 115, **115**
Anonymous, *The Cupid Frieze: Goldsmiths' Workshop* (before 79 CE) **37**, 38
Anthony of Padua, Saint 67
anti-studio sentiment 14, 113, 259, 267
Apelles 18, 35
Apollodorus 20
apprentices 44, 64, 74, 90, 131–2, 145; training 67, 72, 73, 88, 91, 101; *see also* assistants
Arellius 37
arks 56
Arnheim, Rudolf 230
art academies 14, 31, 91, 99, 120–2, 135, 176, 190
art schools 88–94, 182, 190, 193
artisans/applied arts 10, 11, 15–17, 29–30, 207–10; patron saints for 52, 60; secular 43–5, 47, 49; standing 20, 53, 54; status of 20–1, 39, 48, 49, 81; *see also* workshops; *specific types*
artist interviews 13, 217
assistants 53, 79, 80, 91–2, 100, 106, 119, 132, 150, 240; *see also* apprentices
atelier, use of term 10
Augustine, Saint, *City of God*, manuscript (c. 1150) 43–4, **44**
Augustus, Emperor 77, 148, 151
automata 15, 22, 25, 30, 37, 119, 209–10

Bacon, Francis 7, 113, 199; Reece Mews Studio, London **6**, 7
Bandinelli, Baccio 120–2, 126, 129; Academy of 120–8, **121**, **124**, **125**, **127**
Barzizza, Gasparino 73, 78, 91
basements/cellars 54, 169–70
Bauhaus 226–35, 262; magazine 229, **229**; metal workshop **227**, 228, **231**, 231–2, 235
Bazille, Frédéric, *Bazille's Studio* (1870) 262–4, **263**
Beattie, Dr James 167–8
Bening, Simon 133; *Self-Portrait* (1558) **46**, 47
Berliner Illustrierte Zeitung, 'In the World's Largest Atelier' (1938) 236, **237**
Bernini, Gian Lorenzo 9, 14, 99, 127, 149, 154, 164–5, 169, 179–81, 186–7, 189, 193
Bertall, 'Cinq étages du monde parisien' (1852) **212**, 213
Besson, Jacques, *Theatrum instrumentorum et machinarum* (1582) **139**, 140
Beuret, Rose 217–18
Bible 47–52, 83; Genesis 22, 80
boat studios 14, 255–61
Boccaccio, Giovanni: *Decameron* 64; *On Famous Women* 64, 68–70, **70**
Boisbaudron, Horace Lecoq de 263
Bonheur, Rosa, studio in *L'Illustration* (1852) 250, **250**
Borboni, Matteo, *Catafalque of Elisabetta Sirani* (1665) 184–6, **185**
Borghini, Raffaele, *Il Riposo* 138
Bosse, Abraham: *Five Senses: Sight* (1635–8) 156, **157**; *The Sculptor's Studio* (1642) 141, **141**, 193; *The Shoemaker's Shop* (c. 1632–3) **173**, 174, 175
bottega 92, 101, 122, 140
Botticelli, Sandro 61
Boullan, Abbé 218
Bourdon, David 241
Bourgeois, Louise 266
Bramante, Donato 122
Brambilla, Ambrogio, *Aerial View of the Vatican Belvedere* (1579) **121**
Brancusi, Constantin 110, 219–22, **221**; *Princess X – Portrait of Princess Marie Bonaparte* (1915–16) 220
Brandt, Marianne 231; *Metal Workshop, Bauhaus, Dessau* (c. 1928) **231**, 232; *Self-Portrait in Atelier* (1928–9) 234, **234**
Brant, Isabella 145
Breton, Jules 249
Breuer, Marcel 232
bridges 57–9, 61
Broc, Jean, *School of Apelles* (1800) 204–5, **205**
Bruyère, Jean de la 187
Buffalmacco 123

cabinets (studio type) 10, 150, 188, 189
Calla, François-Étienne, *Carpenter's Workshop* (1783) **210**
Campaspe 35, 151, 187, 205
candles 45, 122–5, 128–9, 131, 133
Canova, Antonio 214
car studios 264
Carleton, Sir Dudley 150, 154
carpenters 207, 209–10, 220, 225, 235; importance of wood 228, 248; Saint Joseph 140, 172, 207
Carracci family 142
Castiglione, Baldassare, *The Courtier* 123
caves 19
Cellini, Benvenuto 20, 100, 128
Cennini, Cennino 72–3, 77–9, 98, 99, 110; *The Book of Art* 64, 65–74, 228; *studietto* in Padua 13, 68–73, 75, 78, 81
ceramicists 15, 25, 29–30, 135–7, 140; kilns 29, 135
Cézanne, Paul 78, 220
Chantelou, P. F. de 186, 189
chapels 81, 119, 218, 245, 250, 252; *see also* churches
Charles I, King 175
Charles II, King 165–6
Charles V, Holy Roman Emperor 126
Charlotte, Queen 133
Château, Guillaume 179
Chernetsov brothers 255
Chevalier, Adèle 218
Christina, Queen of Sweden 186
Christus, Petrus, *A Goldsmith in his Shop* (1449) 61–2, **63**
churches 52, 71, 74, 125, 145, 203; converted 14, 145, 203–6, 217, 245; *see also* chapels; monasteries
cleanliness 160, 172, 209, 210, 224–5
Cleiton 33
clocks 74–5, 119
closets (studio type) 10, 164
Clothar, King of the Franks 62
clothing: aprons 27, 79, 228; costumes 104, 107, 191–2;

fine 62, 105, 117, 119, 189, 244; fur-lined 78, 85, 122; headwear 47, 129, 133, 258; jerkins 47; monkish 204, 206, 227; none 25, 27, 28; togas 79; velvet 78, 85, 117, 119; warm 9, 122, 259; women's 175; workwear/overalls 113, 116, 219, 231
cold conditions 9, 43, 53, 54, 68, 85, 97, 129, 241, 264; heating 17, 99, 232, 245; *see also* seasonal work cycles
colonies, artists' 60, 204–6, 218, 249, 253
comfort 199–200, 263; massage and yoga 68, 227–8
Condivi, Ascanio 113, 117
Copernicus 140
Cornelia (mother of the Gracchi) 176, **176**, 187
Corot, Camille 77
Courbet, Gustave 14, 99, 215, 245–6, 262; *The Painter's Studio: A Real Allegory Summing up a Seven-Year Phase of My Artistic Life* (1854–5) 250–3, **251**; *Self-Portrait with Black Dog* (1842) 245, **246**; studios in Ornans 245–8
courtyards 31, 103–4, 115, 145
Cowper, William, *The Task* 244
Cranach, Lucas 81

Dante Alighieri 70; *Divine Comedy* 21, 114–16, **115**
Daubigny, Charles-François, *The Boat Studio* (1862) 256, **258**, 258–9
Daulat, Mohammed, portrait in Nizami's *Khamsa* (1595–6) 41–3, **42**
David, Jacques-Louis 14, 203–4
Dawson, David, *Lucian Freud Photographed in His Night Studio with Model Ria Kirby* (2007) 134, **134**
de Kooning, Willem 239, 244
Delacroix, Eugène 112–13, 251; *Corner of the Studio* (c. 1830) **8**
Delaune, Étienne, *Goldsmiths' Workshop* (1576) **55**
Della Robbia, Luca 129
Denis, Saint: *Life of St Denis* (1317) 57, **58**, **59**
Diderot, Denis 10, 209; and d'Alembert, *Encyclopédie* (*Encyclopedia*) 207–10, **208**, 228
Diogenes 211
Donatello 33, 92
Dondi dall'Orologio family 74
Dongen, Kees van 223
drawing implements: cases 122; erasers 47; ink 13, 43, 119, 122; penknives 41, 43; pens 39, 128; *porte-crayon* (case for charcoal or chalk) 111, 119; quills 39–41, 43, 128; styli 39, 64, 87; *see also* paper
Drouais, François-Hubert, *Madame de Pompadour at Her Tambour Frame* (1763–4) **177**, 178
Druet, Eugène, *Rodin in his Pavilion Studio* (c. 1902) 215, **216**
Du Maurier, George, *Trilby* 190–1
Duchamp, Marcel 209; *Etant donnés* (1946–66) 78; New York studio 133–4
Dufy, Raoul, *The Electricity Fairy* 236
Dumont, François 20
Dunstan, Saint 52
Duprat, Charles, *Anselm Kiefer's studio in Barjac, France* (2011) **269**
Dürer, Albrecht 77, 78, 97, 99–100, 120, 123, 170, 185; *Draughtsman Making a Perspective Drawing of a Reclining Woman* (1525/c. 1600) 94–5, **95**
Duris of Samos 34
Duval, Jeanne 252
Dyck, van Anthony 150, 163, 174

Eadwine at Work, Christ Church, Canterbury, psalter (c. 1140) 41, **41**
Ebisu, Yasutomo, *Hiroshi Sugimoto in His Tokyo Home Studio* (2019) 225, **225**
Echternach Abbey **40**
Eirene 68–70, **70**
Eligius, Saint 52, 57, 60–1, 62, 81
Elizabeth I, Queen of England 107
embroidery 176–8, 184
Emin, Tracey 59
entertainment 17, 105, 106–7, 148
Erasmus, *On Christian Marriage* 176
Este, Isabella d' 107
Everwinus 44, **44**
Eyck, Jan van 99, 107; Rolin *Madonna* (c. 1435) 85
eyesight 43, 62, 127, 171; spectacles 47, 169

factory studios 14, 178, 235, 239–40; Warhol's Factory 240–4, **242–3**; *see also* industrial spaces
Famulus 79
Fanti, Sigismondo, *Triompho di Fortuna* **116**, 116–17
Feliciano, Felice 91, 104
feminine studios 14, 187–9, 220, 223, 244, 263
Fenton, Roger, *Photographic Van, with Marcus Sparling* (1855) 256–7, **257**
Fialetti, Odoardo, drawing manual 142
Finiguerra, Maso (workshop), *Youth Drawing* (1450s) **89**, 90–1
fire 20, 55, 57, 129–31
fireplaces 126, 130, 148
Flemish School, *Portrait of Giambologna* (1570s) **118**, 119
Fontana, Lavinia 110, 179; *Self-Portrait* (1579) 111, **111**
Foundry Painter: *A Bronze Workshop* (c. 510 BCE) **26**, 26–8, **27**; *Hephaestus and Thetis* (c. 510 BCE) **16**, 26
Francis I, King of France 106
Freud, Lucian, night studio 134, **134**
Friedrich, Caspar David 200, **201**, 203, 206–7, 210; *Cross in the Mountains* (1808) 203, 207; *Winter Landscape* (c. 1811) 206
furniture 200; book wheels 83; built-in 68, 234; chairs and stools 31, 43, 54, 83, 119, 126, 234; cushions 27, 43; design of 207, 220, 225, 232; desks 43, 45, 47, 68–70, 207, 244; easels 79, 84, 223–4, 232, 265; elaborate 83, 85, 203; footstools 54; industrial 228; lecterns 43; minimal 71, 200–2, 207–14, 252; none 14, 35, 211–13; shelving 83, 92, 94, 111, 119, 142; sofas and armchairs 241–4, 263–4; storage 83–4, 125, 137, 140; upholstery 26, 200, 252, 263–4; *see also* tables
Furnius, Pieter Jalhea, after Johannes Stradanus, *Cornelia, Mother of the Gracchi, with Female Companions Engaged in Needlework* (c. 1580) 176, **176**

Gainsborough, Thomas 133, 154, 165
gallery studios 14, 148–9, 151–4; display of artists' own work 28, 106, 113, 119, 151–4, 232, 251; picture rooms 154
gardens 14, 122, 145–8, 151, 260, 262; outlooks to 47, 162
Garlande, Jean de, *Dictionarius* 57, 61, 62
garrets 14, 211–13
Gauguin, Paul 220
Gautier, Théophile, 'Chinoiserie' 247
Genlis, Madame de 210
Gentileschi, Artemisia 174, 178;

Allegory of Painting (c. 1638–9) 179, **180**
Gheeraerts, Marcus the Elder 174; *The Unfortunate Painter and His Family* (1577) 172, **173**
Giambologna **118**, 119, 138
Giocondo, Lisa del (Mona Lisa) 77, 106, 107
Giotto 64, 72, 80
Giovio, Paolo 113, 117
glass 230, 231, 266; engraving (*verre églomisé*) 67–8, 71–3, 78; manufacturing advances 48, 156, 262; plate 157, 161, 219; *see also* mirrors; windows
Goethe, Johann Wolfgang von 226, 227; *Elective Affinities* 171
Gogh, Vincent van 213, 253–5; *The Painter on the Road to Tarascon* (1888) 253, **254**; Yellow House 253
goldsmiths 49, 52–62, 81, 175–6, 228; workshops 13, 38, 49, 54–5, 60
Goncourt, Edmond de 199
Gonzaga family 101–3, 145
Goya, Francisco 133
Grand Pont, Paris 57–9, 61
Gropius, Ilse 234
Gropius, Walter 226, 228–30, 232, 234
Gsell, Paul 217
Gump, Johannes, *Self-Portrait with Mirror and Easel* (1646) **158**, 159
Gutai group 266
Guzon, Francesco 88, 90, 97

Haecht, Willem van, *Apelles Painting Campaspe* (c. 1630) 151, **152–3**, 187–8
hairdressing salons 10, 241
Hamilton, Emma (Hart) 197–8, 204–5
Harrewijn, Jacobus, views of Rubens's house **146**, **149**
hazards 19–20, 28; damp 157, 245; draughts 53, 68, 71, 85, 119; dust 110, 119, 157; flooding 57, 219; fumes 20, 131; heat 9, 257; noise 119, 123; poisoning 20; smells 49, 106, 129–30, 219, 239; vermin 9, 44; *see also* cold conditions
heating 17, 99, 232, 245; fireplaces 126, 130, 148; *horigotatsu* (foot-warming pit) 54
Henri IV, King 187
Henrietta Maria, Queen 175, 179
Hephaestus (fire god) 13, 15–17, 19, 21–2, 24, 37, 103
Herford, Laura 197
Hesiod, *Works and Days* 22
Hess, Thomas 240, 244
Hildebertus 43, **44**
Hilliard, Nicholas 107
Hogarth, William 13, 193
Homer: *Iliad* 13, 15, 19–20, 21–2, 24–5, 26; *Odyssey* 21, 24
Homer, Winslow 255
Homeric *Hymns* 29
Hoogstraten, Samuel van 156, 165, 178, 179, 189
Hooke, Robert, *Micrographica* 166
Horace, *The Art of Poetry* 73
hotel studios 217–19, 225, 260
Hugh of Saint Victor, *On the Mystical Ark of Noah* 56–7
Hugo, Master 44–5
Huysmans, Joris-Karl, *Là-Bas* 218

Ibsen, Henrik, *When We Dead Wake* 220
imagination (*fantasia*) 65, 73, 83, 128, 179
Imperato, Ferrante, *Dell'historia naturale* 137, **138**
industrial designers 228, 232, 235
industrial spaces 226, 235, 239, 246–7, 268; Bauhaus 226–35; huge hangar-like 235–6; *see also* factory studios
Isidore of Seville, Saint 39, 43
Itten, Johannes 227–8

James I, King 150
Johann von Troppau, *The Legend of Saint Luke* (1368) **82**, 83, **84**
John, Gwen 218
Joseph, Saint 140, 172, 207
Julien, Guillaume 59

Kandinsky, Wassily 134, 230, 232, 234, 235
Kaufmann, Angelica 193, 196
Kersting, Georg 203, 207; *Caspar David Friedrich in His Studio* (1811) **201**, 202; *Gerhard von Kügelgen in His Studio* (1811) **202**, 202–3
Kiefer, Anselm 19; studio in Barjac, France 267–8, **269**
Klee, Paul 228, 232, **233**, 234
Klein, Yves 266
Kneller, Godfrey 163–7; *Grinling Gibbons* (1680s) **192**, 193; *Hampton Court Beauties* (1690s) 164; *Isaac Newton* (1689) **166**, 167; *Self-Portrait* (c. 1670) **163**, 165
Knight, Laura 264
Krasner, Lee 264, **265**, 266
Kügelgen, Gerhard von 200, **202**, 202–3, 207
Kuhr, Fritz, *Wall-Painting Scheme for the Atelier of Paul Klee's Master House* (1926) 232, **233**

Labille-Guiard, Adélaïde, *Self-Portrait with Two Pupils, Marie Gabrielle Capet and Marie Marguerite Carreaux de Rosemond* (1785) 182, **183**
Lairesse, Gerard de 156–7, 159–60, 172, 191; *The Great Book on Painting* 159–61, 163
Langtry, Lillie 224
Le Corbusier 224
Leagros Group painter, *A Pottery Workshop* (520–510 BCE) 25, **25**
Lebrun, Pierre, *Collection of Essays on the Wonders of Painting* 143, 154–5, 187
Lely, Peter 163, 164, 165
Lemon, Margaret 174
Leonardo da Vinci 13–14, 54, 77, 84, 95, 97, 99, 104, 105, 113, 122, 123, 131, 161; Château Clos Lucé, Amboise 106–10, **108–9**; *Design for a Hydraulic Pump and a Draftsman Drawing an Armillary Sphere with a Perspectograph* (1478–82) 95–7, **96**; *The Last Supper* (1495–8) 77, 110, 113; *Mona Lisa* (1503–6) 77, 106, 107
Leoni, Leone 149
life drawing 13, 81, 90, 97–101, 104, 132–3, 227, 266; *see also* models
lighting: artificial 45, 120–4, 128, 133, 169; candelabras 169, 228; candles 122–5, 128–9, 131, 133; chandeliers 125, 131, 169, 185, 193, 197; electric 230–2, 236; fireplaces/hearths 17, 126, 130, 148; gaslight 133–4; natural 17, 45, 52, 53, 61, 71, 162, 230; oil lamps 45, 126–7, 131, 133; studio effects 215, 220; studio versus piazza 113; toplighting 14, 148–50; *see also* night working; outside working; windows
Lindström, Carl Jacob, *The German Painters* (1840) 248, **249**
living areas 61, 106, 234; sleeping 53, 68, 129, 150, 260
Locke, John, *Some Thoughts Concerning Education* 248
loft studios 239–40, 267
Lomazzo, Giovanni Paolo 144
Lotto, Lorenzo 100
Louis XIV, King of France 9, 14, 164–5, 175, 189

Lucas, Sarah 59
Luke, Saint 81–7; brotherhood of 205–6
Lysippos 18, 35

Makart, Hans, Vienna studio of 199, **200**
Malanga, Gerard 240
Malvasia, Carlo Cesare 182, 184–6
Man Ray 219, 220
Manet, Édouard 262
Mantegna, Andrea 88, 94, 101; antique sculpture collection 103–4; house in Mantua 101–4, **102**; *Santa Maria della Vittoria* 102; *The Triumphs of Caesar* (1484–92) 103
manual labour, virtues of 48–9, 114, 231, 248
Manuel, Henri, *Monet in His Studio in Front of 'Morning'* (c. 1924–5) **236**, 241
Mariana of Austria 161
Marinetti, Filippo Tommaso 133
Martens, Ditlev, *Pope Leo XII Visits Thorvaldsen's Studio near the Piazza Barberini, Rome, on Saint Luke's Day, 18 October 1826* (1830) **214**, 214–15
masculine studios 189, 223
Master of the Madonna della Misericordia, *Saint Eligius in His Goldsmith's Workshop* (c. 1370) 60, **60**, 61, 62
Matisse, Henri 14, 217
Mawlana Ali, Sultan 43
Maximilian I, Emperor 140
Medici, Cosimo I de' 130
Medici, Francesco I de' 140
Medici, Lorenzo de' 103, 115
Medici, Marie de' 150, 186, 187
Medici family 119, 132
Melzi, Francesco 106
metalworkers 15, 19–20, 26–8, 44, 48, 49, 52, 53, 57, 60; breastplate makers 31, 33–4; furnaces 18, 20, 55, 62; *see also* goldsmiths
Meyer, Hannes 234–5
Michelangelo Buonarroti 13–14, 33, 57, 99, 101, 113–19, **116**, 120, 124, 129–30, 131, 140, 142–3, 266; *Bacchus* (1496–7) 115; *David* (1501–4) 114–16; *Sonnet with Self-Portrait* (1511–12) **112**, 113, 117
Mies van der Rohe, Ludwig 235
Milton, John, *Paradise Lost* 22
Mirror of Princes, frontispiece 161
mirrors 14, 47, 62, 156–62, 166–71; Claude glass 169, 252; convex 47, 62, 156, 169, 171; polished metal or glass 45–7, 164; swing 167, 252; use in portraiture 156–68; using mercury/silver backing 157; Venetian-made 156, 161, 164
Mitsunobu, Tosa, *The Picture Contest* from *The Tale of Genji* (1509–10) 11, **12**
models 33, 90, 91, 97, 104, 132–3, 141, 162, 247; bathers 99–100; decency 100–101; female 35–7, 95, 99–100, 132, 151, 186, 189–98, 217–18, 220, 252, 263; male 97–101, 104, 128, 132, 181, 192, 197, 206; Parisian market 190–1; *see also* life drawing; sexual activity
Modigliani, Amedeo, Paris studio 7–8
Moholy, Lucia 230; *Paul Klee in His Atelier* (1926) 232, **233**
Moholy-Nagy, László 231
monasteries 39, 49, 52–3, 140, 145; *Plan of an Ideal Monastery with 52 Buildings* (c. 819) 44–5, **45**; *see also* churches; monks' cells
Mondrian, Piet **222**, 222–4
Monet, Claude 14, 241, 259–60; Giverny 235–6, **236**, 260; *The Studio Boat* (1876) 260–2, **261**
monks' cells 10, 14, 71, 203, 206, 210, 217, 234
Motherwell, Robert 239–40
Munro, Alexander 110
Murger, Henry, *Scènes de la vie de bohème* (1851) 211–13
musicians 17, 105, 106–7
mythical and divine artists 13, 15–16, 21, 25; creation myths 11, 129; God 11, 48, 56; patron saints 83, 84; votive pictures 28, 29; *see also* Hephaestus; Pygmalion

Namuth, Hans, *Jackson Pollock and Lee Krasner* (1950) 264, **265**, 266
Nash, John 247
Nauman, Bruce, *Mapping the Studio* (2001) 9
Nazarenes (group) 206
Newton, Isaac **166**, 167
night work 47, 120–6, 129–34, 144, 185
Nodier, Charles, *Meditations from the Cloister* 204
Nollekens, Joseph 197
Northcote, James 169, 197
nudes *see* life drawing; models

office studios 138, 150, 244
Ogden, Perry, *Francis Bacon's Studio at 7 Reece Mews, London* (1998) **6**, 7
Oldenburg, Claes, The Store 59
outside working 77, 83, 245–69; bridges 57–9, 61; courtyards 31, 103–4, 115, 145; portable equipment 248, 257, 258; verandahs 43; *see also* gardens; temporary studios
Ovetari Chapel, Padua 103–4
Ovid 37, 162

Paduan Bible Picture Book (c. 1400) 48, 49, **50–1**, 65–7, 68, **69**, 77
painting equipment: brush holders 13, 84; brushes 13, 84, 110, 111; easels 79, 84, 223–4, 232, 265; oil paints 77, 248; palette knives 247–8; palettes 13, 70; pigments 47, 74, 81, 83–4, 122, 172–4
painting rooms 10, 80, 148, 150, 159, 198
Palissy, Bernard 135–6, 140, 172; rustic basin (c. 1565) 137, **137**
Palma il Giovane, *Portrait of an Artist* (c. 1590–1600) **143**, 143–4
Pan Gongshou, *Wang Yuyan Sketching Orchids* (1790) **76**, 77
paper 90, 94, 111, 129; *cartellini* 94, 135; making 49; papyrus 43
parchment 39–41, 47
Parrhasius 33
parties 132, 223, 250–1
Pélerin, Jean, *De artificiali perspectiva* 94
performance, art-making as 230–1, 266–7
Pericles 18, 31
perspective 88, 94–7, 127–9
Petrarch 64, 70–1, 75
Phidias 17–19
Philip II, King of Spain 145
Philip IV, King of France 57
Philip IV, King of Spain 161
Philip the Good, Duke of Burgundy 62
photographs of studios 215, 220–2, 232
photography studios 230; vans 14, 256
Phryne 35–7
Picasso, Pablo 133, 199, 218, 265–6; Bateau-Lavoir studio 218; *Demoiselles d'Avignon* (1907) 133
Piccolpasso, Cipriano, *Li tre libri dell'arte del vasaio* (1557) 135, **136**, 139–40
Pisano, Andrea (attr.), *Painting* (c. 1337) **79**, 80
Pistias 33–4
Plato: *Apology* 30; *The Republic* 31; *Symposium* 37–8

Pliny the Elder, *Natural History* 34–7, 74, 79, 84, 130, 138, 142, 145
Plousios Painter, *A Shoemaker's Workshop* (c. 500–490 BCE) 31, **32**
Poe, Edgar Allan 267
Pollaiuolo, Antonio, *Male Nude Seen from Front, Side and Back* (early 1470s) 91, 97–9, **98**
Pollock, Jackson, Long Island barn 264–6, **265**
Polygnotos 18
Polykleitos, *Canon* 34
Pompadour, Madame de **177**, 178, 189, 241–4
portrait sittings 78, 104, 159–68; entertainment during 107; use of mirrors 156–68
Postma, Frans, *Reconstruction of Mondrian's Studio Based on Paul Delbo's 1926 Photograph* 222, **222**
Poussin, Nicolas 113
Praxiteles 18, 35–7
Prometheus 103, 124, 127
props 119, 120, 189
Prudentius, *Psychomachia* 39
Pygmalion 13, 22, 37, 99

Quintilian 75

al-Rahim, Abd 41–3, **42**
Ramazzini, Bernardino, *Diseases of Workers* 19–20, 106
Raoux, Jean, *Pygmalion and Galatea* (1717) **36**, 37
readers 106–7, 148
Redemann, Wilhelm, *Kurt Schwitters, Merzbau in Hanover* (1933) **frontispiece**
reliquaries 67–8, 71, 78, 83, 94; diptych with Nativity and Crucifixion (late 14th c.) **66**, **72**, 73
Rembrandt van Rijn 156, 160, **191**, 191–2; *The Night Watch* (1642) 8
Renesse, Constantijn Daniel van, *Rembrandt and His Pupils Drawing from a Nude Model* (c. 1650) 191, **191**
Reni, Guido 186, 192
Reynolds, Joshua 154, 167–9, 197, 198, 248; *Self-Portrait at Easel* (c. 1749) 168, **168**
Richard of Saint Victor 56–7
Richardson, Jonathan 165
Rilke, Rainer Maria 215–17
Rimbaud, Arthur, 'Le Bateau ivre' 261–2
Ripa, Cesare, *Iconologia* 179
Rivera, Diego, *The Making of a Fresco Showing the Building of a City* (1931) **238**, 239
Rodin, Auguste 199, 215–19, 263; Dépôt des Marbres, Paris 217, 218; Villa des Brillants, Meudon 215–16, **216**, 218, 219
Röell, W. F. A. 223, 224
rooftop studios 230, 255
Rousseau, Jean-Jacques 209, 246
Rowlandson, Thomas 197; *Lady H******* Attitudes* (c. 1791) **196**, 198
Rozee, Catharina 176–8
Rubens, Peter Paul 14, 145–7, 154, 162; *Battle of Amazons* (c. 1615) 151; *Rubens and Helena Fourment in their Garden* (1631) 147, **147**; studio block and garden 145–54, **146**, **149**, **152–3**
Ruskin, John 110, 220

Samaras, Lucas 267
Sargent, John Singer 249
Schlemmer, Oscar 230–1
Schwitters, Kurt **frontispiece**; *Cathedral of Erotic Misery* (1920–37) 199
Scott, Sir Walter, *Ivanhoe* 200
Scribe and Illuminator at Echternach Abbey, Pericope Book (mid-11th c.) 39, **40**
scribes 39–47, 56
scriptoria (writing-rooms) 13, 39, 44–5, 56
seasonal work cycles 97, 100, 104; *see also* cold conditions; winters
secrecy, culture of 100–101
secret places 13, 61, 65, 68, 71, 83, 150–1, 165–6
sedentary working 17, 248
Serlio, Sebastiano, *Third Book of Architecture* 149
Seurat, Georges 209
sexual activity 35–7, 129, 159, 218, 219–20; abstinence 175, 186, 227; exploitation/violence 100, 132, 197
Shikibu, Murasaki, *The Tale of Genji* 11, **12**, 75–7
shoemakers 30–1
shops 14, 59, 61–4, 85, 103, 174; window displays 154
Simon the Shoemaker 30–1
Sirani, Elisabetta 14, 181–6; catafalque of 184–6, **185**; *Record of the Paintings Made by Me, Elisabetta Sirani* 182–4; *Self-Portrait Painting Her Father* (c. 1665) **181**, 182
Sirigatti, Ridolfo 140–2, 144
Smithson, Robert 267
Soane, John, Lincoln's Inn Fields home and museum 169–71, **170**, 206
Socrates 13, 17, 30–4, 209
solitude 70–1, 119, 129, 240
Solon 17, 21
Sperling, Otto 148, 150
squalid/filthy studios 7, 13, 113, 130, 133, 218
Squarcione, Francesco 88–94, 101, 103, 135
standing-up working 128, 168, 224, 248–9
stanze 140–2, 184
Steichen, Edward, *Brancusi in His Studio, Paris, 1925* 220, **221**
studietti 68–73, 75, 78, 81, 142
studio, origin of term 10
studioli 68, 81, 83, 85, 103, 110, 111, 122, 138, 140, 150–1, 176
The Studio: An Illustrated Magazine of Fine and Applied Art 10
studium 92
study collections 10, 14, 90, 92, 94, 103, 137, 140, 143–4, 149, 169, 170, 191; anatomical 97–101, 106, 117, 126, 135; books 126, 129, 147, 162, 184; costumes 104, 107, 191–2; drawings 90, 91, 106, 129, 132; labelling 135–7; live animals 135, 250; natural history specimens 135, 147, 232; plaster casts 24, 65, 111, 119, 140–4, 170, 190–3, 214–16
Subleyras, Pierre, *The Artist's Studio* (1746) **23**, 23–4
Suetonius, *Twelve Caesars* 148, 151
Sugimoto, Hiroshi 225, **225**

tables 119, 142, 228, 232, 234; sunken 53–4; tabletops 67–8; trestle 114, 126, 232
temples 28, 71, 225; workshops near 15, 18
temporary studios 14; boats 14, 255–61; cars 264; hotels 217–19, 225, 260; umbrella 248–9; vans 14, 256
Texier, Edmond, *Tableau de Paris* **212**, 213
textile art 62, 78–9, 176–8; embroidery 176–8, 184; weaving 17, 61, 145, 175, 176–8, 226
theft 19, 53, 91
Theophilus, *On Diverse Arts* 43, 48–56, 64, 77
Thetis (sea nymph) 13, 15, 19, 26
Thorak, Josef, *Comradeship* 236
Thorvaldsen, Bertel, Rome studio **214**, 214–15
time/timekeeping 73–8, 79; bells 74, 80; clocks 74–5, 119; multitasking 148; procrastination 78

Timurid royal workshops 43
Tintoretto, Marietta 174
Titian 77, 80, 132
tools 17, 31, 83–4, 119, 140, 142, 190; electric power 220, 232, 236; hand 28, 60, 62–4, 114; machine 140, 207–9, 228; measuring 62–4, 206–7; tablets 43, 67, 71, 87, 90; technical processes 49; *see also* drawing implements; painting equipment
tourism 139, 249, 253
Turner, J. M. W. 255

Uccello, Paolo 129
umbrella studios 248–9
underground studios 19, 54, 169–70
Urban VIII, Pope 179–81
Urbino, Carlo, *Of Fire. Third Demonstration of Shadow* (c. 1560–70) 127, **128**

Vanni, Francesco di 60
Vasari, Giorgio 101, 106–7, 113, 114, 119, 123, 126, 140; house frescoes, Florence and Arezzo **130**, 130–2, **131**, 138, 178–9; *Lives* 129–30, 142, 179
Vaucanson, Jacques de 209–10
Vecchietto, Bernardo 138–41
Velázquez, Diego 14, 78, 162; *Las Meninas* (1656) **160**, 161–2, 167, 187; *The Toilet of Venus* (1647–51) 162
Veneziano, Agostino, after Baccio Bandinelli, *The Academy of Baccio Bandinelli* (1531) 120–2, **121**, **124**
verandahs 43
Vermeer, Johannes 84, 157, 190; *The Art of Painting* (1666–8) 14, **188**, 189–90; *The Music Lesson* (c. 1662–4) 157–9
Vernet, Horace, *Joseph Vernet Tied to a Mast in a Storm* (c. 1822) 255–6, **256**
verre églomisé see glass
Vesalius, Andreas, *De humani corporis fabrica* 126, **127**, 135
Vettii, House of the, Pompeii **37**, 38, 54
Vico, Enea, after Baccio Bandinelli, *Bandinelli's Night Class* (1545–50) **125**, **127**
Vigée-Lebrun, Elisabeth 159, 161
violence 39–41, 44
visits/visitors 13, 57, 123, 143, 210, 226, 229; etiquette 154–5; female 14, 21, 186–7; open studios 136–7; patrons 17, 106, 184, 188; popularity of 154; tourism 139, 249, 253; working in front of 154, 184; of workshops 30–5, 106
Vittoria, Alessandro 138, 144

Wackenroder, Wilhelm, *Confessions from the Heart of an Art-Loving Friar* 203
walls, collage/painting on 135, 213, 223
Walpole, Horace 164
Warhol, Andy 20, 244, 264; Factory studio 240–4, **242–3**; Union Square studio 244
weaving 17, 61, 145, 175, 176–8, 226
Westhoff, Clara 215
Weyden, Rogier van der 99; *Saint Luke Drawing the Virgin* (c. 1435–40) 85–7, **86**, **87**, 107
Whistler, James McNeill 213, 249, 255
white cube spaces 14, 216, 224–5
whitewashed walls 17, 47, 128, 217, 219, 222–4, 235, 240, 251, 253
Wilde, Oscar 224
windows: facing direction of 45, 52, 162, 240; glazed 45, 47, 52, 85, 145, 169; grilles 68, 91; none 122, 179, 240, 241; numerous 45, 52; oiled cloth and paper 68, 119; shutters 52, 61, 202, 207; size and placement of 52–4, 71, 244, 247, 262; skylights 148, 247; views from 255, 260
winters 43, 99, 123, 230, 245, 255, 259
women 172–98, 200, 205, 210, 226; artisans 15, 17, 174–6; artists 14, 77, 110, 178–82; make-up 67; portrait sitters 159; studio visitors 14, 21, 186–7; *see also* models: female
workshops: ancient 15–26, 29–34; filthy 110; large-scale commercial 79–80, 90, 92, 103, 119; medieval 39, 43, 48–64; respect for 207–10; use of term 10; visits to 30–5, 106; *see also* artisans; factory studios; industrial spaces
Wren, Christopher 189
writing-rooms *see* scriptoria

Xenophon 17, 20–1; *Memorabilia* 30–4, 114

Zeuxis 99
Zoffany, Johann, *The Academicians of the Royal Academy* (1771–2) 193–7, **194–5**
Zoppo, Marco, *Virgin Child with Angels* (1455) 92–4, **93**

Acknowledgments

I am greatly indebted to everyone at Thames & Hudson (Mohara Gill, Gary Hayes, Anna Perotti, Camilla Rockwood, Lise Seguin and Editorial Director Roger Thorpe), to my agent Caroline Dawnay and the librarians and staff at the Warburg Institute and the University of Southampton (especially Bren O'Donnell). The exhibitions of Giles Waterfield (1949–2016) were inspirational. Crucial help was given by Joseph Ackley, Rea Alexandratos, Victoria Avery, Emma Barker, Babette Bohn, Federico Botana, Beverly Brown, John Cherry, Rita Copeland, Claudia Echinger-Maurach, Barbara Furlotti, John Gash, Laura Jacobus, Andrew King, Helen Langdon, Gregory Martin, Martina Mazzotta, Liz McGrath, Charlotte Mullins, Susie Nash, Charles Robertson, Bill Sherman, Giorgio Tagliaferro, Paul Taylor, Humphrey Wine and Alison Wright. I hope all other debts are acknowledged in the notes (apologies to any missing persons).